The Origins of the Cold War

PROBLEMS IN AMERICAN CIVILIZATION

The Origins of the Cold War

Third Edition

Edited and with an introduction by

Thomas G. Paterson
University of Connecticut

Robert J. McMahon
University of Florida

D. C. HEATH AND COMPANY
Lexington, Massachusetts   Toronto

Acquisitions Editor: James Miller

Developmental Editor: Sylvia Mallory

Production Editor: Renée M. Mary

Production Coordinator: Lisa Arcese

Text Permissions Editor: Margaret Roll

Cover: Cover cartoon by Leo Abbett.

International Standard Book Number: 0-669-24445-7.

Library of Congress Catalog Card Number: 90-82002.

10 9 8 7 6 5 4 3 2 1

For Thomas Graham Paterson, Jr.,
Thomas W. McMahon, and Michael P. McMahon

The Editors

Thomas G. Paterson

Born in Oregon City, Oregon, and graduated from the University of New Hampshire (B.A., 1963) and the University of California, Berkeley (Ph.D., 1968), Thomas G. Paterson is professor of history at the University of Connecticut. He has written *Meeting the Communist Threat* (1988), *On Every Front* (1979), *Soviet-American Confrontation* (1973), and *American Foreign Policy* (3rd edition, revised, 1991, with J. Garry Clifford and Kenneth J. Hagan). Tom has edited and contributed to *Kennedy's Quest for Victory* (1989), *Major Problems in American Foreign Policy* (3rd edition, 1989), and *Cold War Critics* (1971). He is also co-author of *A People and a Nation: A History of the United States* (3rd edition, 1990). His many articles have appeared in such journals as the *American Historical Review, Journal of American History*, and *Diplomatic History*. He has sat on the editorial boards of the latter two journals. The National Endowment for the Humanities and the Institute for the Study of World Politics, among others, have assisted his research and writing. He has served as president of the Society for Historians of American Foreign Relations and has directed National Endowment for the Humanities Summer Seminars for College Teachers. Active in the profession, he has worked on committees of the Organization of American Historians and the American Historical Association. Tom has lectured widely in the United States on topics in the history of foreign relations. He has also lectured in the Soviet Union, Puerto Rico, China, Canada, and New Zealand.

Robert J. McMahon

Born in Bayside, New York, Robert J. McMahon is associate professor of history at the University of Florida. He was educated at Fairfield University (B.A., 1971) and the University of Connecticut (Ph.D., 1977). Bob has written *Colonialism and Cold War: The United States and the Struggle for Indonesian Independence, 1945–49* (1981) and edited *Major Problems in the History of the Vietnam War* (1990). He has also co-edited several volumes in the U.S. State Department's documentary series, *Foreign Relations of the United States*. His essays have appeared in numerous books and in the *Journal of American History*,

Political Science Quarterly, *Pacific Historical Review*, and *Diplomatic History*. He sits on the editorial board of *Diplomatic History* and serves as an associate editor of *American National Biography*.

Preface

Since the publication of the second edition of this book, voluminous, challenging scholarly work has appeared and changed our thinking about the origins of the Cold War. This third edition makes the recent scholarship accessible to students and instructors.

Nearly all the essays in this book are new. All perspectives are represented. The new introduction explains the evolution of interpretation from the 1940s to the present. Part I offers broad explanations for the onset of the Cold War. Part II explores specific policies, events, and issues in chronological progression and focuses primarily on Europe. Finally, Part III studies the extension of the Soviet-American confrontation to regions outside Europe (what analysts have called the Third World). The introductory notes place each selection in broad context and identify key themes. The chronological chart has been revised and expanded. The maps and the chronology include important names and dates mentioned in the essays. The extensive bibliography, organized by topic, identifies other readings in this fascinating field.

We thank the authors and publishers of the works reprinted in this volume for their cooperation. *The Origins of the Cold War* was improved by the constructive suggestions of Robert L. Messer, University of Illinois, Chicago; Donald Raleigh, University of North Carolina, Chapel Hill; Emily S. Rosenberg, Macalester College; and William Stueck, University of Georgia.

We also appreciate the help given to this project by John Lewis Gaddis, Konstantin V. Pleshakov, Vladimir Pechathov, Benedict V. Maciuika, and David Holloway. Maria Miller expertly translated the essay by Konstantin V. Pleshakov. James Miller, Sylvia Mallory, Margaret Roll, and Renée Mary of D. C. Heath applied high standards and gave enthusiasm to the project. We thank them very much.

Thomas G. Paterson

Robert J. McMahon

Contents

II. The Origins of the Cold War in Europe

III. Toward a Global Cold War

Introduction

The Second World War alliance of the United States, the Soviet Union, and Great Britain crumbled quickly in 1945 after the defeat of Germany and Japan. Soon a different kind of war—the Cold War—troubled international relations. The United States and the Soviet Union, the primary adversaries in this new contest for world power, entered a bitter, decades-long competition for spheres of influence, economic and strategic advantage, nuclear-weapons supremacy, control of international organizations, and ideological superiority.

The two competitors never sent their troops into battle directly against one another but instead engaged in an intense, expensive armaments race, armed and aided their allies and client states, intervened in civil wars by supporting different factions, built rival alliance systems, sponsored exclusionist foreign economic programs, and initiated noisy propaganda campaigns—all of which divided much of the world into rival blocs or empires (popularized too simply as "the West" and "the East"). If the Soviets came to fear "capitalist encirclement," Americans complained against an "international communist conspiracy." Each side, in mirror image, saw the other as aggressive and intransigent. The Cold War contest became the dominant feature of international relations. From the start, however, many newly independent nations in the southern half of the globe—eventually called the Third World— preferred not to choose sides. They became the objects of keen superpower attention as they created another pole of power in the already volatile international system.

In the late 1980s and early 1990s, as stunning political changes were sweeping the Soviet Union and Eastern Europe in the aftermath of Soviet Premier Mikhail S. Gorbachev's new policies of *glasnost* and *perestroika*, many people celebrated the end of the Cold War. Some claimed that the United States had actually won the near half-century conflict. Those observers, on the other hand, who believed that the Cold War had always been a struggle for power, and that ideology had been an instrument to wage the war rather than the essence of the war itself, suggested that Soviet-American competition for influence around the world still persisted. The two nations' huge military arsenals, moreover, remained stocked with enough nuclear weapons to destroy people and property in awesome numbers. Other analysts pointed to America's declining economic competitiveness, troubled and underfunded educational system, plague of drug abuse, sizable "underclass," huge budget deficit, environmental crisis, and deteriorating infrastructure to argue that the Cold War had no winners. These questions of Cold War demise and Cold War victory cannot be answered without knowing what the Cold War was and how and why it began. This book, then, presents a picture of the past essential to our grappling with the present and future.

For those contemporaries who knew their history, the escalating Soviet-American friction after the Second World War was not unexpected. Indeed, prolonged antagonism had marked the Soviet-American relationship since the Russian or Bolshevik Revolution of 1917. Virulent anticommunism had long coursed through domestic American politics, much as a deep suspicion of capitalist nations like the United States had typified Soviet leadership. The Bolshevik government that took power in 1917 espoused a Marxist anticapitalist ideology, championed world revolution, repudiated czarist debts (much owed to Americans), and confiscated American-owned property. President Woodrow Wilson's goal of a liberal, capitalist international order seemed threatened by what he called the "poison of Bolshevism." In 1918 many Americans found another reason to dislike Moscow's new regime when Soviet leaders withdrew their weary nation from the First World War by accepting a harsh peace from Germany. Wilson worked to topple or at least to contain the Soviets by refusing to recognize the new government, aiding anti-Bolshevik forces, restricting trade, sending thousands of American troops into Soviet Russia, and excluding the upstart nation from the postwar peace conference in Paris. At home, the Wilson administration further demonstrated its vigorous anticommunism by suppressing radicals in the Red Scare of 1919–1920. From the birth of the Soviet experiment, then, Soviet-American relations suffered deep fissures.

In the 1920s, Soviet-American antagonism continued, albeit less intensely, as the Republican administrations extended Wilson's nonrecognition policy. Still, in 1921–1924 the American Relief Administration shipped food and medicine to famine-stricken Russia. American businesses like General Electric and Ford Motor began to enter the Soviet marketplace. By 1928 one-quarter of all foreign investment in the Union of Soviet Socialist Republics (U.S.S.R.) was American, and

American agricultural and industrial equipment became familiar fixtures there.

When President Franklin D. Roosevelt took office in 1933, he reasoned that the nonrecognition policy had failed and that improved relations would stimulate trade (helping to pull America out of the Great Depression) and deter Japanese expansion in Asia. He subsequently struck several agreements with the Soviets, including United States recognition. The first American embassy in the Soviet Union opened in 1934. But relations remained strained. Official and public opinion in the United States registered sharp disapproval of Joseph Stalin's bloody purges, collectivization of agriculture, and brutal efforts to modernize the Soviet economy. Americans, moreover, feared that the Soviets were fomenting revolution through the Comintern.

Especially upsetting to the United States was the 1939 Nazi-Soviet pact, which stamped the Soviet Union as one of the aggressors (indeed, it soon seized part of Poland and attacked Finland) responsible for the outbreak of the Second World War. Americans rejected the Soviet argument that Great Britain and the United States, by practicing appeasement toward Adolf Hitler's Germany, had left the Soviet Union little choice but to make peace with Berlin in order to buy time to prepare for an expected German attack. Following that German attack of June 1941, Roosevelt ordered Lend-Lease aid to the beleaguered Soviets (by war's end the assistance would total $11 billion), calculating that they could hold down scores of German divisions in the east and hence ease German pressure against Britain in the west.

After the United States itself entered the Second World War in December 1941, it formed a Grand Alliance with the Soviet Union and Great Britain. Always tension-ridden, this coalition of convenience for national survival was held together by the common objective of defeating the Axis. The Allies differed frequently over the timing for the opening of a second or western front. Numerous American promises, followed by delays, angered Moscow. Roosevelt, Stalin, and Winston S. Churchill—the Big Three—met at several wartime conferences to devise military strategy and to map plans for the postwar era. At Teheran (1943) they agreed to open the second front in early 1944 (it finally came in June in France); at Bretton Woods (1944) they founded the World Bank; and at Dumbarton Oaks (1944) they planned the United Nations Organization, granting only the United States, the

Soviet Union, and three other nations veto power in the Security Council.

In February 1945, as the Red Army was fighting through Eastern Europe into Germany, the three leaders met again at the Yalta Conference. In a series of trade-offs, which included a coalition government in Soviet-dominated Poland, the division of Germany into zones, and Soviet agreement to negotiate a treaty with United States ally Jiang Jieshi (Chiang Kai-shek) in China, the Big Three seemed to have reached accord on major postwar issues. Hopes for continued Soviet-American cooperation were soon dashed, however, as the Allies jockeyed for international influence at the war's close. The Potsdam Conference of July 1945, after the defeat of Germany and just before the collapse of Japan, saw as much disagreement as agreement. Nor did the Soviets' fulfillment in August of their Yalta pledge to enter the war against Japan improve relations, because it came after the American atomic bombing of Hiroshima, a point when United States leaders no longer desired Soviet participation.

Disputes broke out with alarming frequency on a wide range of issues in the early postwar years. The American destruction of two Japanese cities by atomic bombs posed a significant diplomatic question: Would international control follow, or would the United States retain its atomic monopoly in order to gain negotiating advantage on postwar issues? How and by whom the economies of war-ravaged nations would be reconstructed also divided the victors. Eastern Europe became a diplomatic battleground as Soviet influence solidified in the region. So did Iran, where American influence had grown to challenge Soviet influence in a nation bordering the Soviet Union. Unstable politics and economic distress rocked Western Europe, where left and right faced off. The French, British, Americans, and Soviets squabbled over how to extract reparations from a hobbled Germany and over whether Germany's economy should be revived. The division of Germany became permanent as the occupying powers created separate economic and political institutions in their zones. In the new United Nations and World Bank, Americans quickly established domination, prompting the Soviets to use their veto in the first and to turn down membership in the second. In Asia, resurgent nationalist feelings, colonial conflicts that pitted European imperialists against native independence movements, a full-scale civil war in China, the American-directed occupation and ultimate restoration of Japan, and widespread economic dislocation produced further instability in world politics. Turmoil also shook the Middle East, sparked by the Arab-Israeli dispute and lingering resentments against European imperialism and fueled by American-Soviet competition for access to rich oil reserves and for strategic sites. The Truman Doctrine (1947), Rio Pact (1947), Marshall Plan (1948), and North Atlantic Treaty Organization (1949) stood as hallmarks of the American containment doctrine designed to thwart, if not roll back, Soviet power and influence. For their part, the Soviets knitted together into an empire several Eastern European states, first in the Molotov Plan (economic) and then through the Warsaw Pact (military). As well, a war of hyperbolic words echoed through diplomatic chambers. Each side characterized the other as the world's bully; each side blamed the other for the deterioration of the Grand Alliance and the beginning of the Cold War.

This book is devoted to explaining the origins of the Cold War. Do not expect a comforting unanimity of opinion or a satisfying synthesis. Even within the two major schools of thought—the traditional and the revisionist—disagreement abounds, although historians have narrowed some of their interpretive differences over time. Much of the debate still centers on one question: Whose fault was the Cold War? Scholars are moving beyond that simple query to examine shared responsibility for the Cold War, the contributing role of nations other than the United States and the Soviet Union, and the nature of the conflict-ridden international system. But the question of blame remains at the forefront of the debate.

Until the 1960s the traditional or orthodox interpretation of the origins of the Cold War prevailed. This point of view held that the Soviets, with unlimited ambitions for expansion, an uncompromising ideology, and a paranoid dictator bent on world domination and the elimination of democracy and capitalism, wrecked the postwar peace. Moscow caused the Cold War, pure and simple. This view goes on to explain that the United States, lacking self-interest and committed to democracy and high ideals, rejected a spheres-of-influence approach in favor of an open world, passed up opportunities to grab power after the war, and sought continued friendly relations with the Soviet Union. As the Cold War emerged, traditionalists have argued, negotiations with the Soviets and their communist allies elsewhere, as in China, proved useless. Forced by communist hostility and aggression to take defensive measures, the Harry S Truman administration declared the ultimately successful containment doctrine and blunted communist aggression. The Soviets acted; the Americans reacted. Moscow exploited; Washington saved. Not only did policymakers like President Truman explain events this way; until the 1960s most historians did as well.

In the early 1960s three important changes coincided to invite a very different interpretation—the revisionist—of the origins of the Cold War. First, in the late 1950s the decline of McCarthyism, a virulent version of the Cold War anticommunism, calmed the repressive atmosphere whipped up by the Wisconsin senator and by the Truman and Dwight D. Eisenhower administrations. That atmosphere had stymied discussion of alternative interpretations, for the Cold War consensus treated dissent as something close to disloyalty. Indeed, unorthodox opinion sometimes earned a scholar a trip to the intimidating hearings of the House Un-American Activities Committee. With the decline of McCarthyism came more questioning of traditional assumptions, as when William Appleman Williams published his provocative book *The Tragedy of American Diplomacy* (1959), which depicted the United States not as an innocent simply reacting to overseas events but rather as a self-conscious, expansionist nation with imperial drives.

The second source for revisionism was the Vietnam War. By the mid-1960s that tragic conflict had stimulated debate not only on the origins and conduct of the war but on the Cold War assumptions that compelled American intervention around the globe. What was the precise nature of the threat posed by communism? Who exactly was the enemy? Was the containment doctrine too vaguely defined and indiscriminately applied? How did Americans get started in their Cold War globalism? Were the foreign-policy assumptions judged by many to be wrong-headed in the 1960s also wrong-headed in the 1940s? To question the Vietnam War was to question American ideas and behavior in the early Cold War.

The third factor that inspired doubts about the Cold War consensus was the declassification and opening to scholars in the 1960s of documents from the early Cold War period—National Security Council reports, presidential memoranda, briefing papers, telegrams from embassies, diaries, and more. Historians could now test their questions in the rich documentary record; they would no longer have to rely upon the often inaccurate and self-serving memoirs of policymakers. The once-secret papers, examined at a time of questioning permitted by the decline of McCarthyism and stimulated by the Vietnam War, revealed a picture of the 1940s that did not resemble that sketched by the traditionalists.

Although revisionists, like traditionalists, have not always agreed among themselves, the basic outline of their interpretation became clear by the late 1960s and early 1970s. Revisionists have held that the traditional interpretation is too one-sided, blaming all trouble on the Soviets and ignoring the United States' own responsibility for conflict. The United States was not simply reacting to Soviet machinations; rather, it was acting on its own needs and ideas in a way that made American behavior alarm not just the Soviets but some of America's allies as well. The United States, argue the revisionists, was not an innocent defender of democracy but a self-consciously expansionist power in search of prosperity and security. Americans were determined to mold a postwar world that corresponded with their own needs. They projected their predominant power again and again, and they too often abandoned diplomacy in favor of confrontation. Nor should analysts apply a double standard, say the revisionists, because the United States was itself building spheres of influence. And if "free elections" were good for Eastern Europe, as Americans insisted, why were they not also good for Latin America, where the United States nurtured dictators like Anastasio Somoza of Nicaragua and Rafael Trujillo of the Dominican Republic?

Revisionists have written too that Americans exaggerated the Soviet/communist threat, imagining an adversary possessing more power and ambition than the postwar Soviet Union had. The Soviets actually suffered serious weaknesses in their economy and military, and they were often driven not by an unbridled thirst for empire or ideological fervor but by concern for security after suffering at least 20 million dead in the Second World War. The postwar American refusal to acknowledge Soviet security fears helped bring down the "iron curtain" in Eastern Europe. Finally, a rigid way of thinking—globalist containment—blinded Americans so much that they overlooked the indigenous sources of conflict (religious, political, and ethnic, for example) and failed to grasp the complexities of world politics.

The revisionist-orthodox debate was exciting and important because it focused on the fundamental question of what kind of people Americans were. Were they exceptional, selfless, anti-imperialist, acting on high principle in the face of ugly challenges to democracy? Or were they something else, perhaps not that much different from other great

nations through history—seeking hegemony at the expense of others?
Or were they a mix, because nothing can be so simply defined?

In the 1970s and 1980s historians, traditionalists and revisionists
alike, groped for elusive synthesis. Some scholars began to speak of
post-revisionism, a term broad in meaning and difficult to define
because it seemed to lack a core point of view recognizably different
from either of its predecessors. To critics, post-revisionism was essentially traditionalism: first, because it placed primary responsibility for the
Cold War upon the Soviets, and, second, because it interpreted United
States empire-building as defensive, a result of invitation by recipients of
American foreign aid seeking security and recovery rather than of
American design. To proponents of post-revisionism, however, the
term meant a blending of the two schools of thought—an acceptance of
the traditionalist proposition that Soviet expansion had precipitated the
Cold War and of the revisionist proposition that the United States too
had become an empire-builder.

Besides the problem of responsibility, other core questions run
through the literature on the origins of the Cold War. First, what
driving forces propelled American and Soviet foreign policy: ideology?
economic needs? security? power? Second, why did Americans come
to see the Soviet Union as such an unparalleled menace to United States
interests and survival: because of Soviet military power? Moscow's
manhandling of neighbors? communism's ideological appeal? the economic crisis in Europe and around the world? American misperception
and exaggeration? Third, did the Cold War emerge because the two
great powers simply misunderstood each other, or rather because they
actually understood one another quite well—that is, they squabbled
because their interests and their power stood starkly at odds? Finally,
why and how did the Cold War, largely originating in Europe, spread
to the Third World and become a global phenomenon?

History is seldom tidy or ordered with hard, fast formulae. The
diversity of opinion on the origins of the Cold War reflects the vast
complexity of the 1940s events themselves. That there is no soothing,
simple answer or that there is no synthesis or consensus seems
inevitable. One person's truth will always be someone else's half-truth
or misinterpretation. Oversimplification for the sake of synthesis,
moreover, is dangerous, especially when historians do not yet have
access to all of the documents, especially those in the Soviet Union,
China, and France. Major interpretive quarrels among scholars will

likely remain the norm. This condition should not be cause for alarm. Rather, it is an opportunity to be grasped: to enlarge our knowledge, to refine our definitions, to respect diversity, to understand complexity, and, yes, even to narrow our differences of opinion. In this spirit of discovery, we have selected essays for this book that reflect the most recent scholarship.

Acronyms and Abbreviations

Acronyms and abbreviations in Cold War history include:

ANZUS	Australia–New Zealand–United States alliance
ARAMCO	Arabian American Oil Company
Benelux	Belgium–The Netherlands–Luxembourg
Cominform	Communist Information Bureau
Comintern	Third Communist International
EAM	Greek National Liberation Front
ECA	Economic Cooperation Administration
ECE	Economic Commission for Europe
EDES	National Republican Greek League
ERP	European Recovery Program
FDR	Franklin D. Roosevelt
GNP	Gross National Product
GARIOA	Government and Relief in Occupied Areas
JCS	Joint Chiefs of Staff
NATO	North Atlantic Treaty Organization
NEA	Office of Near Eastern, South Asian, and African Affairs of the U.S. Department of State
NEP	New Economic Policy
NSC	National Security Council
OAS	Organization of American States
OSS	Office of Strategic Services
OEEC	Organization for European Economic Cooperation
PPS	Policy Planning Staff of the U.S. Department of State
SAC	Strategic Air Command
SEA	Southeast Asia
SWNCC	State-War-Navy Coordinating Committee
UK	United Kingdom
UN	United Nations Organization
UNRRA	United Nations Relief and Rehabilitation Administration
USSR	Union of Soviet Socialist Republics
V-E	Victory Day in Europe
V-J	Victory Day in Japan

Chronology

1944 *June*: Cross-channel invasion opening second front. *July*: Bretton Woods Conference. *August–October*: Dumbarton Oaks Conference. *October*: Churchill-Stalin sphere-of-influence agreement at Moscow; Litvinov-Snow conversation. *November*: Roosevelt elected to fourth term with Truman as vice-president. *December*: Battle of the Bulge.

1945 *January*: USSR requested loan. *February 4–11*: Yalta Conference. *February*: Cease fire in Greek civil war. *April*: Litvinov-Sulzberger interview; Roosevelt's death; Truman-Molotov argument. *May*: German surrender; cessation of Lend-Lease to Russia; Hopkins mission to Moscow. *June*: UN Charter signed at San Francisco. *July*: Byrnes became secretary of state; U.S. recognition of Communist government in Poland. *July 17–August 2*: Potsdam Conference. *August 6*: Atomic bomb on Hiroshima. *August 8*: USSR declaration of war against Japan. *August 9*: Atomic bomb on Nagasaki. *August*: USSR requested loan; independent Republic of Indonesia proclaimed. *September 11–October 2*: London Foreign Ministers meeting. *September*: independent Democratic Republic of Vietnam proclaimed. *October 27*: Truman's Navy Day speech. *November*: Communists defeated in Hungarian national elections. *December 16–26*: Moscow Foreign Ministers meeting.

1946 *January*: UN Atomic Energy Commission formed; Iran charged Soviet Union with interference in its internal affairs; Soviets charged Britain with interference in Greek affairs. *February*: Stalin election speech. *March*: U.S. found "lost" Russian loan request; Churchill's Fulton speech. *April*: Soviet troops left Iran. *April–October*: Paris Peace Conference meetings. *May*: Greek civil war began again; Clay halted German reparations to USSR. *June*: Baruch Plan; Litvinov-Hottelet interview; Bikini atomic tests began. *July*: Philippines became independent. *August*: USSR sought base from Turkey; U.S. charged Poland with failure to create democracy. *September*: Wallace speech and firing from Cabinet; Clifford report on

U.S.-USSR relations. *November*: Republicans captured Congressional elections; U.S.-China treaty. *November 4–December 12*: New York Foreign Ministers meeting. *December*: Anglo-American fusion of German zones.

1947   *January*: Marshall became secretary of state. *February*: British notes on Greece and Turkey. *March*: Communists began subversion of Hungarian government; Truman Doctrine. *March 10–April 24*: Moscow Foreign Ministers meeting. *May*: Aid to Greece-Turkey bill signed by Truman. *June*: Marshall Plan speech at Harvard. *July*: USSR rejected Marshall Plan at Paris; publication of Kennan's "X" article on containment. *August*: India and Pakistan became independent; Rio Pact in Latin America; Polish-Russian trade agreement. *October*: USSR created Cominform. *November 25–December*: London Foreign Ministers meeting. *December*: Brussels Conference on European defense; Interim Aid to Europe bill signed; Greek regime outlawed EAM and Communist Party.

1948   *February*: Brussels Treaty signed; coup in Czechoslovakia. *March*: Senate passed Marshall Plan; USSR walked out of Allied Control Council in Germany charging destruction by other three powers; House passed Marshall Plan. *April*: Truman signed European Recovery Act of $5.3 billion; Committee of European Economic Cooperation formed; OAS established; U.S. recognized new nation of Israel. *June*: Currency reform announced in western zones of Germany; Berlin blockade by USSR; Yugoslavia expelled from Cominform. *November*: Truman elected president.

1949   *January*: Truman suggested idea of Point Four program; USSR set up Council of Economic Assistance (Comecon); Acheson became secretary of state. *April*: NATO organized. *May*: West German federal constitution approved; Berlin blockade lifted. *July*: Truman signed NATO Treaty. *August*: U.S. White Paper on China; Soviets test first atomic bomb. *September*: Federal Republic of Germany established (West). *October*: People's Republic of China proclaimed; Greek civil war ended. *December*: Indonesia became independent; Jiang's government completed evacuation from mainland to Formosa; NSC 48/1 called for containment of Communism in Asia.

1950   *January*: Acheson's "defensive perimeter" speech; Truman authorized hydrogen bomb development. *January–August*: USSR boycotted UN Security Council. *February*: U.S. recognized Bao Dai regime in Vietnam; McCarthy opened attacks on alleged subversives in government; Sino-Soviet Friendship Treaty. *April*: NSC 68. *June*: Outbreak of Korean War.

From Thomas G. Paterson and Robert J. McMahon (eds.), The Origins of the Cold War (3rd ed., 1991).

I

Explanations

Walt W. Rostow

THE OFFENSIVE OF THE INTERNATIONAL COMMUNIST MOVEMENT

In his *The United States in the World Arena* (1960) Walt W. Rostow argued the case for the prevailing traditionalist or orthodox interpretation of the origins of the Cold War. He laid responsibility for the onset of the Cold War squarely on the Soviet Union, which he claimed was masterminding a plot to expand postwar communism in Asia as well as in Europe. The United States, defensive and reactive, was much the innocent in the face of this global threat. Washington rejected Soviet unilateralism in favor of international collective security. The Truman administration, Rostow wrote, was forced by communist machinations finally to launch a counteroffensive.

Rostow served in the United States Department of State in the early Cold Wars years. After an academic career at the Massachusetts Institute of Technology, where he taught economic history, Rostow reentered government service in the John F. Kennedy administration. In 1961 he became chairman of the State Department's Policy Planning Council. From 1966 to 1969 he was special assistant for national security affairs to President Lyndon B. Johnson, whom he advised to escalate America's role in the Vietnam War. Rostow later went to the University of Texas, where he continued to write in the traditionalist style. Among his many books are *The American Diplomatic Revolution* (1947), *The Stages of Economic Growth: A Non-Communist Manifesto* (1960), *The Diffusion of Power* (1972), *The Division of Europe After World War II, 1946* (1981), and *Eisenhower, Kennedy, and Foreign Aid* (1985).

The post-1945 struggle for the control of Eurasia arose from a sequence in which two emerging mature powers—Germany and Japan—were defeated in war, leaving a third—Russia—in command of much of the battlefield, while a fourth vast but transitional power—China—became caught up in a civil conflict the course of which was affected by that war and the outcome of which directly affected the interests of major powers.

The roots of the Cold War thus reach far back in modern history. At the latest, the Cold War can be linked directly to the sequence that

Excerpts from *The United States in the World Arena* by W. W. Rostow, pp. 141–45, 148, 165–71. Copyright 1960, 1988 by the Center for International Studies, M.I.T. Reprinted by permission of Harper & Row Publishers, Inc.

begins in the decades after 1840 with the opening of China and Japan to Western trade and influence, the unification of Germany, and the freeing of the Russian serfs; it embraces the pattern of industrialization between (say) 1860 and 1914, the First World War, and its aftermath, including the Russian Revolution; and the sequence flows on to the launching of Japanese aggression in the 1930's, the rise of [Adolf] Hitler, and [Joseph] Stalin's pact with Hitler on the eve of the Second World War. All that brought the new powers into the world arena and ruptured the world of 1815 is relevant to the setting of the Cold War.

Narrowly, however, the Cold War can be dated from the time that the Politburo was clear that Stalingrad would hold [against the Germans]—roughly from the beginning of 1943. From some such time Moscow returned with vigor to the territorial preoccupations which were at the center of its diplomacy in the period 1939–1941. This shift was manifest in the spirit and tactics of Soviet diplomatic behavior in many areas during the year 1943. Communist doctrines and, perhaps more important, the Bolshevik experience of gaining power in the aftermath of Russian defeat in 1917 converged to make Stalin and his men regard the postwar period as one of great opportunity for the extension of Communist power under control from Moscow. After November 1917 the internal weaknesses and problems of the new Soviet regime were too great to permit Lenin to exploit successfully the disruptive consequences of World War I; Stalin and his colleagues were determined that no trick was to be missed after World War II. But the form, technique, and extent of Moscow's extension of power could not be determined until the character of specific opportunities and the degree of Western resistance had emerged. . . .

American thought about the postwar looked primarily to the organization of a world structure for permanent peace which would avoid the failures of Wilson's effort and the interwar mistakes in general as those failures were then understood. The factor of power was not absent from American considerations, but it took the form of seeking a particular method for the settlement of major power conflicts—private negotiations of agreement among the Big Three [the United States, Soviet Union, and Great Britain].

This overriding American interest in the creation of conditions for world peace—rather than with the details of territorial power— accurately reflected both old American patterns of thought and a fatalistic conviction that American forces could not be kept in Eurasia beyond a few postwar years. Thus the nation did not define or seek systematically to achieve the power position requisite for the achievement of the grand design.

If Big Three unity were to be achieved and held as the basis of postwar organization, it could be accomplished only by making it the most attractive alternative realistically open to Moscow. This meant not merely that Moscow be treated with dignity as an ally; it meant also that Moscow be denied by Western strength and purpose and by geographical positions held by the West the realistic alternative of expanding its power by unilateral action.

This possibility was not finally lost to the West until after the end of the war, roughly during the period from Potsdam (July 1945) to the spring of 1946, when Moscow apparently decided, in the face of American demobilization and the general weakness of the West, that it could do better by pursuing a unilateral rather than a collective power policy. Nevertheless, American wartime attitudes, policies, and decisions contributed to the result.

No man can say with honesty and with confidence, even with all the benefits of hindsight, that it lay within American military and diplomatic capabilities to win the war in Europe in the course of 1944; or to face Stalin down in Poland without major war; or to have so strengthened the Nationalist government in China as to have avoided the Communist victory in the postwar years; or to persuade the American people to support an American occupation of Manchuria. And even if it were possible to establish firmly that these specific possibilities once lay within American grasp, it would be of extremely limited value and interest to do so. But it is possible and useful to examine the frames of mind and the paramount interests which determined decisions which did not maximize the possibility of these results; for frames of mind and interests persist, while the field of action and decision changes unceasingly, never exactly to recur. In this limited perspective it is worth summarizing certain American wartime attitudes and decisions which failed to maximize the possibility of protecting persistent American interests.

A serviceable American policy in Europe during the Second World War had to answer two questions. How shall the Soviet Union be prevented from dominating Western Eurasia in succession to Germany or in alliance with Germany? How shall Germany be prevented from again threatening to dominate Western Eurasia?

It was clear that, if British, American, and Russian interests in Germany converged, the Big Three commanded sufficient power to rule out a resurgence of a military threat from Germany. In this century Germany was constituted a threat only when permitted by the cross-purposes, weakness, or distraction of Britain and France, Russia, and the United States. It was evident that postwar Britain would have no interest in succeeding to the German wartime position of active dominance on the Continent; and the American interest was certainly not in that direction. How, then, should the Western Allies have proceeded to reconcile the two questions? The answer lay in establishing such a strong *de facto* position throughout Europe during the war that Moscow would have to negotiate defensively to assure its national security, ruling out in the process the possibility of seeking the dominance of Western Eurasia.

The Western conception of peace was based on a separation of issues of military security from issues of political, social, and economic orientation. Communist doctrine led directly to the contrary principle: namely, that the distinction between political orientation and military control is false, and that security for the major Communist power can lie only in the extension from Moscow of total control over societies. Under these circumstances the task of the West was to force Stalin to look at Germany and Europe as a Russian rather than as a Communist. The Kremlin had to be made to look at Germany as an area to be neutralized rather than as a pawn to be manipulated in its unilateral interest. The Western powers thus had a fundamental vested interest in bringing the war to an end at the earliest stage consistent with Western interests and with Soviet troops as far east as possible; and in establishing Western positions in the east in order to prevent Moscow from achieving total dominance and using Eastern Europe as a military staging area. These objectives would appear to have justified the use of Western military as well as diplomatic bargaining strength both during and after the war so long as their use was compatible with Hitler's defeat.

From such a base of *de facto* dominance of Western Eurasia a long-term foundation for Big Three unity in Europe might have been established. If the best terms available to Moscow were a military neutralization of Germany and Eastern Europe at the cost of the direct exercise of Soviet political and military domination there, then it is possible that Stalin would have opted for a unified policy. More than that, if the West held all of Germany, it is altogether likely that Stalin would have traded the military neutralization of Germany for such direct dominance as his advancing armies permitted him in Eastern Europe.

In the upshot, the war was so fought as to give Moscow the possibility of dominating the whole region from the Soviet border to the Elbe. Moscow lost the Ruhr to the West; but it held a continuous military and political belt running through Poland to the heart of Central Europe; and, above all, since it held in East Germany the key to German unification, it could exercise for the long run a formidable influence over the orientation of all of Germany.

This Soviet position of strength, arising from the course of the war, was not actually consolidated until the postwar years; but it is clear that American thought and policy during the war did not address themselves soberly to preventing its coming about. Wartime policy was dominated by the military requirement of defeating Germany; wartime thought about the postwar future of Europe centered on the problem of preventing the Germans from again undertaking aggression. The problem was not defined as one of forcing the Soviet Union into a position where its interests demanded that it join the Western Allies in a unified policy toward Germany and Europe—although this was the condition for Big Three unity over Germany, and only such unity could create an environment which would leave the Germans no realistic option except a policy of peace. American diplomacy by and large acted on the proposition that if Big Three unity were achieved then the details of a European settlement would fall into place. The truth was that Big Three unity hinged on a particular kind of European settlement—one in which the Soviet Union was forced to bargain away the possibilities of unilateral power to achieve a basis for long-run Russian security in collaboration with the Western powers. . . .

As the war in Europe drew to a close in the spring of 1945 and the postwar issues emerged for decision behind advancing armies, the relationship of Soviet objectives to Big Three unity could no longer be suppressed as a major problem for the West. The question came rapidly to a head around the formation of a provisional Polish government and the prompt holding of free elections in Poland. In March and April both Roosevelt and Churchill appeared to be hardened for a fundamental showdown on this issue—although the old American ambiguity about the meaning of Eastern Europe persisted to the end. But Roosevelt's death and Churchill's removal from the scene during the Potsdam conference led, essentially, to a *de facto* acceptance of a split of Europe on the Elbe which proved impossible to eliminate by normal diplomacy, so attractive was it to Moscow as opposed to any alternative compatible with minimum Western interests. The United States continued to separate the pursuit of peace from the maintenance of its strength and bargaining position vis-à-vis Moscow until the collapse of Western Eurasia was imminent in 1947. By that time, however, disintegration had proceeded so far among the Big Three that the recapture of Western strength and bargaining position could proceed only in the context of a Cold War. . . .

The Second World War ended with the balance of power in Eurasia clearly in the grasp of the United States and forces allied to, or dependent upon, the United States. The reality of American primacy was projected with great psychological force to the world by Japan's surrender in the wake of atomic attack.

In Europe the Western Allies held the Ruhr and the bulk of Germany. They had confirmed at Yalta the Soviet commitment to free elections in Eastern Europe; they had confirmed at Potsdam the Soviet commitment to a Germany to be treated as an economic unit and to be unified by democratic process. In Asia the United States held Japan, and the Nationalists in China had an apparent 3 to 1 advantage in arms over the Chinese Communists as well as the prestige of formal recognition from the Big Three, including explicit guarantees from the Soviet Union of sovereignty and territorial integrity. Underlying the existing political and territorial commitments and positions was the fact of the American monopoly in atomic weapons and the ability to deliver them from the air.

Despite this apparently favorable situation, it was possible even by the time of the surrender ceremonies aboard the *Missouri* to perceive conditions which made the Eurasian balance of power susceptible to the threat of Communist expansion; and there were plain evidences of the Soviet intentions to exploit these conditions in the period from Yalta through Potsdam (that is, January–August 1945).

Although the underlying realities were sensed both inside the government and, to a degree, outside the government as well, those responsible for American policy did not warn the American public that a further desperate struggle for the Eurasian balance of power was imminent—if not already under way. In what appeared to be a mood of national complacency there was pell-mell American demobilization. American political leaders dismantled the military and civil paraphernalia of total war, proceeding on the illusion that the goal of Big Three unity might still be achieved through the negotiation of differences with Stalin by a diplomacy in which the American military potential was not evoked.

In short, from V-J Day to the enunciation of the Truman Doctrine some nineteen months later, the United States acted as if its interests could be protected by a steady retraction of commitment in Eurasia, permitting a concentration of attention and resources on domestic affairs—a mood dramatized and heightened by the issues and the outcome of the Congressional elections of November 1946.

The reversal of American policy and the nation's mood in the two years after V-J Day took place in reaction to Communist policy. The situation created by Stalin's and Mao's efforts to expand their power in the postwar setting came gradually to be regarded as a major threat to the national interest.

To say that American policy was reactive, however, is not quite the whole story; for there was a quite complex interplay between Washington and Moscow. The behavior of each power was determined, in part, by what it judged to be the capabilities and intentions of the other. Moreover, in the immediate postwar years, each was so powerful a force on the world scene that the environment it faced was in part a product of its own past and current actions. For example, American demobilization after V-J Day and the American failure to insist upon the execution of the Yalta provisions in Poland strongly encouraged Moscow to extend its power to the limit in Europe. Thus the situation the United States faced as of, say, the spring of 1947 was in part a consequence of American policy over the two previous years.

When all this is taken into account, it is still fundamentally true that American postwar policy was systematically defensive and reactive. Before examining how that policy unfolded, it is necessary, therefore, to look briefly at the evolution of Communist policy in the immediate postwar years.

What was the policy to which the United States and the West defensively responded?

In one sense there has been a complete continuity in Communist foreign policy since the successful defense of Stalingrad. Over the entire period Moscow has actively sought to expand to the maximum the area over which it could exercise authority in Eurasia. And there has been an equal degree of basic continuity in the objectives of the Chinese Communists. Ever since the end of the Long March in 1935 they have steadily looked forward not merely to the achievement of power in China but also to hegemony in Asia and major power status on the world scene. . . .

This period [1943–May 1946] can be dated roughly from the Soviet defensive victory at Stalingrad to the breakdown of negotiations in the Control Council in Berlin over German economic unity. A fundamental Soviet decision to seize total control in Eastern Europe at the cost of Big Three unity was foreshadowed in the uncompromising tone of Stalin's electoral speech of February 9, 1946, in which he returned to the inevitable conflict between Communist and capitalist worlds as the foundation for the domestic as well as the foreign policy he outlined.

Truman's firmness in forcing the Soviet withdrawal from Iran on March 1946 may have given Stalin pause; but viewing the American performance as a whole, Stalin apparently concluded sometime in the first half of 1946 that it would be safe and profitable openly to ignore his Yalta commitment to free elections in Eastern Europe and his Potsdam commitment to move promptly toward the treatment of Germany as an economic unit. The United States, demobilizing its military strength at an extraordinary rate, was evidently not prepared to make the political disposition of Poland or the issue of German unity an issue of war or peace. Perhaps more important than the fact of demobilization, the American will to assert its interests throughout Eurasia must have seemed feeble. In China the American Marines were used indecisively; and there was evidently no American intent to use its own forces to try to shape the outcome in China. Stalin must have concluded that the United States regarded the area east of the Elbe (as well as China) as regions of secondary concern, worth the expenditure of diplomacy and even money but not military strength. In this setting, he ignored protests over Poland and Eastern Europe generally and permitted a breakdown of key negotiations in the Control Council in Berlin on the issue of German economic unity in May 1946.

The American and Western willingness to accept for the long term the split of Germany and Europe was further underlined in the negotiation of the Italian and satellite treaties in 1946, when, in effect, certain Soviet concessions on the Italian Treaty were traded against a *de facto* recognition of Soviet dominance of the Eastern European states.

With his eastern base, in effect, safely within his hands, Stalin looked to the south and west as an area of opportunity. This second, more ambitious period in Soviet policy in Western Eurasia runs approximately from mid-1946 to Stalin's sudden ending of the Berlin blockade in April 1949.

During the summer of 1946 Stalin increased Soviet pressure in Western Eurasia in many directions: against Turkey by diplomacy and threat, in Greece by supporting substantial guerrilla warfare, and in Italy and France by vigorous Communist Party efforts to gain parliamentary power. Meanwhile, the process of consolidating Germany into two organized entities proceeded. In 1947 Stalin responded to the Truman Doctrine and the Marshall Plan by accelerating the movement toward total control in the East, symbolized by the creation of the Cominform in September 1947. He succeeded in Prague (February 1948), but failed in Belgrade, where Tito's defection was announced in June 1948. The Communist effort in Greece proceeded then to collapse, the election in April 1948 saved Italy, and France found a group of center parties capable of governing, if uncertainly, and containing the domestic Communist menace. The deadlock in the Berlin Control Council, already two years old, was dramatized by the Soviet walk-out on March 20, 1948, which set the stage for the blockade which began on March 31.

This phase of Soviet consolidation in Eastern Europe ended with the effort to disengage the West from Berlin which was defeated by the air lift in the winter of 1948–1949. In the West this interacting process yielded the Brussels Pact (February 1948), NATO (March 1949), and the creation (May 1949) of a Federal Republic of Germany, including Berlin, which symbolized and confirmed the Western intent to resist further Soviet expansion.

There was a basic continuity in Communist policy in China over the decade from the launching of the popular front in China by the Communists, climaxed by the kidnapping of Chiang Kai-Shek [Jiang Jieshi] in 1936 and the Nationalist-Communist Agreement of 1937, to the end of the Marshall mission a decade later. In that period the Chinese Communists sought to expand their power within the framework of truce or limited hostilities with the Nationalists.

In the course of 1946 the negotiations for a truce in China broke down. The Communists—strengthened with Japanese arms furnished in the spring of 1946 by the Soviet Union, with some Soviet weapons, and with Soviet staff assistance—launched an all-out civil war. In 1946 Stalin probably advised against an all-out effort by the Communists to seize power; but once Mao was well started, he was backed by Stalin in 1947–1949, mainly through diversionary operations of the international Communist movement.

This stage [December 1946–June 1951] embraces the Communist victory in China, an upsurge of Communist efforts throughout Asia, and the Korean War. It ended, roughly, with Jacob A. Malik's broadcast in New York on June 23, 1951, announcing Communist willingness to see the Korean War ended by a cease-fire along the 38th Parallel.

In terms of larger strategy, the Communist struggle and victory in the Chinese civil war was the center of a general Communist effort to exploit the weakness of postwar Asia and achieve a definitive victory which would spread through the Middle East and Africa and shift the balance of the world's power radically against the United States and Western Europe.

Communist policy in Asia formally changed in the course of 1947, the new ambitious objectives being enunciated by [Andrei] Zhdanov at the founding meeting of the Cominform in September. Open guerrilla warfare began in Indochina as early as November 1946, in Burma in April 1948, in Malaya in June, and in Indonesia and the Philippines in the autumn. The Indian and Japanese Communist parties, with less scope for guerrilla action, nevertheless sharply increased their militancy in 1948. As victory was won in China in November 1949, Mao's political-military strategy was openly commended by the Cominform to the Communist parties in those areas where guerrilla operations were under way. The meeting of Stalin and Mao early in 1950 undoubtedly confirmed the ambitious Asian strategy and planned its climax in the form of the North Korean invasion of South Korea, which took place at the end of June 1950.

The American and United Nations response to the invasion of South Korea, the landings at Inchon, the march to the Yalu, the Chinese Communist entrance into the war, and the successful U.N. defense against massive Chinese assault in April–May 1951 at the 38th Parallel brought this phase of military and quasi-military Communist effort throughout Asia to a gradual end. Neither Moscow nor Peking was willing to undertake all-out war or even to accept the cost of a continued Korean offensive. And elsewhere the bright Communist hopes of 1946–1947 had dimmed. Nowhere in Asia was Mao's success repeated. Indonesia, Burma, and the Philippines largely overcame their guerrillas. At great cost to Britain, the Malayan guerrillas were contained and driven back. Only in Indochina, where French colonialism offered a seed-bed as fruitful as postwar China, was there real Communist momentum; but Ho Chi-minh was finally forced by Moscow and Peking to settle for half a victory (Geneva, 1954) in the interest of the larger policy of the Communist Bloc which had begun to shape up in Asia from the summer of 1951.

At both end of Eurasia there was, then, a period of uncertain probing in 1945–1946 which gave way to more ambitious Communist ventures. In both Europe and Asia the Communist decision to proceed was based in part on an assessment of American intentions and capabilities as revealed in the first postwar year. Stalin became convinced that the United States would not oppose with force the full consolidation of the Soviet position in Europe up to the Elbe. Stalin and Mao became convinced that the United States would not oppose with force an all-out Communist effort in China; and Mao, at least, was convinced that, despite his numerical inferiority and despite American support in arms and funds for Chiang, the Nationalists could easily be beaten. And beyond Eastern Europe and China, Stalin and Mao saw in the unsettled state of the postwar world and the weakness of American purpose potentialities for expansion which they judged worth prompt exploitation.

The two efforts were, to a degree, certainly linked. It is probable that the vigorous Communist activities in Europe over the period 1947–1949 (and perhaps even the Berlin blockade itself) were designed to divert American and Western attention and resources from China just as it is certain that this objective (rather than firm hopes for decisive victory) partially motivated the aggressive tactics of the Communist parties throughout Asia in the climactic period of the Chinese Civil War.

The whole of this sequence occurred within the setting of a technological race in weapons stemming from the scientific and engineering breakthroughs of the Second World War. The Soviet Union was initially far behind American military technology in the key areas of atomic energy and electronics; but in a purposeful effort, involving an acute concentration of talent and resources, it proceeded to catch up. From 1945 to 1949 the United States never exploited its monopolistic position in nuclear weapons except as a check on Soviet ground forces. This restraint proceeded from a convergence of two factors: the moral inhibitions of the West, built into political institutions and processes, against initiating war; and the vulnerability of America's Western European allies to occupation by Soviet ground forces in case of major war. After September 1949—the first Soviet atomic explosion—the Soviet possession of atomic weapons became a factor in the world's power policies; and as the arms race proceeded, the existence of Soviet and American capabilities for mutual destruction and their efforts to avoid a position of decisive inferiority at any point in the competitive sequence moved to the center of the stage.

The first two stages of Communist postwar policy posed the central challenges to the Truman Administration. It was Truman who conducted against Stalin the counteroffensive of 1947–1951 which blocked the Communist offensive at both ends of Eurasia, leaving a Western Europe which, in 1952, had gathered economic momentum, weathered the war fears of 1950, and built a substantial common military establishment in NATO. In Korea the negotiations for a truce went on; but, except in Indochina, the rest of non-Communist Asia, including the Nationalists on Formosa, recovered at least temporary poise while fighting and diplomacy proceeded in the northern peninsula. The Communists were thus held around the periphery which had emerged from the Second World War; and in the sense that minimum essential American interests were protected without major war, Truman succeeded where the pre-1914 and interwar statesmen of the West had failed.

Joyce and Gabriel Kolko

AMERICAN CAPITALIST EXPANSION

In his *The Politics of War* (1968) and *The Limits of Power* (1972) (the latter work coauthored with Joyce Kolko), Gabriel Kolko argues that America's postwar goal of preserving world capitalism—and expanding the American hold on it—produced conflict not only with the Soviet Union but also with the political left. In an early, radical version of the revisionist perspective that starkly contrasts with Walt W. Rostow's traditionalist viewpoint and with that of many other revisionists, Kolko claims that postwar tension grew not from external pressures on the United States but from the internal needs of American capitalism, which required overseas business expansion. Flushed with power but fearing economic depression, American leaders used foreign aid as a major tool to seek trade, the reformation of the world economy, and American prosperity. According to Kolko, American officials mistakenly saw the Left and the Soviets as intricately linked, and hence they blamed the Cold War on Moscow rather than on Washington's own drive to save capitalism.

Abridged from *The Limits of Power: The World and United States Foreign Policy, 1945– 1954*, by Joyce and Gabriel Kolko, pp. 1–3, 4–5 (introduction) and pp. 11, 20–22, 23, 710–11. Copyright © 1972 by Joyce and Gabriel Kolko. Reprinted by permission of Harper & Row Publishers, Inc. (Footnotes deleted.)

A radical scholar recognized for his sustained criticism of United States interventionism, Gabriel Kolko has also written *The Triumph of Conservatism* (1963); *The Roots of American Foreign Policy* (1969); *Anatomy of a War* (1986), a study of the Vietnam War; and *Confronting the Third World* (1988). He teaches at York University in Canada. Joyce Kolko is the author of *America and the Crisis of World Capitalism* (1974).

World War II was a prelude to the profound and irreversible crisis in world affairs and the structure of societies which is the hallmark of our times.

The war had come to an end, but no respite allowed the wounds of the long era of violence to heal completely. Two vast epics of bloodletting within thirty years' time had inflicted seemingly irreparable damage to traditional societies everywhere. From the moment World War II ended, civil war, uprisings, and the specter of them replaced the conflict between the Axis and Allies in many nations, and implacable hostility superseded tense relations between the Soviet Union and the other members of what had scarcely been more than a temporary alliance of convenience born wholly out of necessity. After global conflagration came not peace, but sustained violence in numerous areas of the world—violence that was to intensify with the inevitable, broadening process of social transformation and decolonization that became the dominant experience of the postwar epoch.

For the individual in vast regions of the world, the war's outcome left hunger, pain, and chaos. Politically, conflict and rivalry wracked nations, and civil war spread in Greece and in Asia. Outside of the Western Hemisphere, ruin and the urge toward reconstruction were the defining imperatives in all the areas that war had touched. Affecting the very fabric of world civilization, the postwar strife threatened to undermine the United States' reasons for having fought two great wars and its specific aims in the postwar world.

Surrounded by this vast upheaval, the United States found itself immeasurably enriched and, without rival, the strongest nation on the globe. It emerged from the war self-conscious of its new strength and confident of its ability to direct world reconstruction along lines compatible with its goals. And these objectives, carefully formulated during the war, were deceptively simple: Essentially, the United States' aim was to restructure the world so that American business could trade, operate, and profit without restrictions everywhere. On this there was absolute unanimity among the American leaders, and it was around this core that they elaborated their policies and programs. They could not consider or foresee all the dimensions of what was essential to the attainment of their objective, but certain assumptions were implicit, and these in turn defined the boundaries of future policy options. American business could operate only in a world composed of politically reliable and stable capitalist nations, and with free access to essential raw materials. Such a universal order precluded the Left from power and necessitated conservative, and ultimately subservient, political control throughout the globe. This essential aim also required limitations on independence and development in the Third World that might conflict with the interests of American capitalism.

The United States therefore ended the war with a comprehensive and remarkably precise vision of an ideal world economic order, but with only a hazy definition of the political prerequisites for such a system. With these objectives before it, Washington confronted the major challenges to their fulfillment. Preeminent among these were the prewar system of world capitalism and its accumulation of trade and investment restrictions and autarchic economic nationalism that World War I and the subsequent depression had created. Traditional nationalism, consequently, was an obstacle to America's attainment of its goals, and this shaped the United States' relations to Britain and its huge economic alliance, the sterling bloc. Washington's dealings with Britain throughout the war had been profoundly troubled because of London's reticence in collaborating with American plans for restructuring world trade. To the English such a program looked very much like expansion in the name of an internationalism that ill concealed the more tangible advancement of American power along quite conventional lines. This rivalry among nominal allies was to become a basic theme of the postwar experience as well, because in attempting to attain the leading role for itself in the international economy the English had to consider whether the United States might also recast Britain's once-dominant role in major areas of the earth.

It was this same effort to foster a reformed world economy that compelled the United States to turn its attention, with unprecedented energy and expense, to the future of the European continent and Germany's special position in it. The failure of Germany and Japan to collaborate economically with the world throughout the interwar period was, in Washington's opinion, the source of most of the misfortunes that had befallen mankind. And however weak Europe might be at the moment, the United States had to consider how its reemergence—with or without Germany—might potentially affect the United States' contemplated role on the Continent should Europe once again assume an independent role. Allied with Russia, or even a resurgent Germany, Western Europe could become the critical, perhaps decisive, factor in international economic and political power. And it was an unshakable premise of America's policy that world capitalism [would] become a unified system that would cease being divided into autonomous rivals.

Its desire and need for global economic reform, integration, and expansion almost immediately required the United States to confront the infinitely more complex issue of the political preconditions for establishing an ideal world order. This meant relating not only to the forces of nationalism and conservatism that had so aggressively undermined America's goals until 1945 but more especially to the ascendant movements of change we may loosely associate with the Left—forces that posed a fundamental threat to America's future in the world. The war had brought to fruition all the crises in the civil war within societies that World War I had unleashed, a conflict that interwar fascism and reaction had forcibly, but only temporarily, suppressed. The intensity of these national, social and class conflicts was to increase with time, spreading to Asia and the Third World even as the United States was now compelled to consider how best to cope with the immediate threat of the radicalized European workers. The manner in which America balanced its desire for the reformation of European capitalism against its need to preserve it immediately as a system in any form, in order to later attempt to integrate it, is a key chapter in postwar history involving all of Europe and Japan. For the sake of its own future in the world, Washington had to resolve whether it wished to aid in the restoration of the traditional ruling classes of Germany and Japan—the very elements who had conducted wars against America in the past. . . .

In much of Asia and Europe a resurgent and formidable Left was a major effect of World War II, just as the Soviet Union was the main outcome of World War I. Each war had generated vast upheavals and a period of flux, and the United States' own goals and interests had colored its responses to them. Washington neither feared nor suspected that the world was irrevocably in transition, decentralized, unpredictable, and beyond the control of any nation—and especially its own mastery. But, in the short run, American leaders had to consider whether the Left had the will and capacity to act and take power—and how to respond in the event it did. At the same time they had to confront the question of the future of the USSR, a prospect that the deepening wartime diplomatic crisis between Russia and the West had left enshrouded in dark pessimism. The Left and Russia usually appeared as synonymous in America's litany, as Washington often assigned the Kremlin powers in the world that must have surprised the quite circumspect rulers of that war-devastated country. For the USSR's very existence was a reminder of the profound weakening of European capitalism and the traditional order after World War I, and potentially a catalyst for undermining capitalism in the future. But was Russia, given America's self-assigned destiny, *the* critical problem for the United States to confront in the postwar era? To place this question in perspective, one has only to ask, given its articulation of its larger goals, what the United States' policy would have been regarding innumerable problems and areas had the Bolshevik Revolution never occurred. As it was, during the war the Russians repeatedly showed their conservatism in their inhibiting advice to the various Communist parties and their refusal to move freely into the power vacuum capitalism's weakness had created everywhere. And what were the possibilities of negotiations and conventional diplomacy in resolving the outstanding issues with the Soviet Union, such as Eastern Europe, the future of Germany, and Russia's future role in the world, especially given America's definitions of the causes of the world's problems as well as its own interests? In light of American needs and perspectives, and the nature of the postwar upheaval and the forces of our age, were expansion and conflict inevitable? Washington never dissociated the USSR from the Left, not only because bolshevism is but one twentieth-century expression of a much larger revolutionary trend but also because it was often politically convenient for America's leaders to fix the blame for capitalism's failures on the cautious men in the Kremlin. . . .

The United States' ultimate objective at the end of World War II was both to sustain and to reform world capitalism. The tension between doing both eventually prevented America from accomplishing either in a shape fully satisfactory to itself. The task confronting Washington was to dissolve the impact not merely of World War II on the structure of the world economy but of the depression of 1929 and World War I as well—to reverse, in brief, most of the consequences of twentieth-century history. "The main prize of the victory of the United Nations," the State Department summed up the United States' vision in November 1945, "is a limited and temporary power to establish the kind of world we want to live in." That was the prodigious task before it. . . .

The deeply etched memory of the decade-long depression of 1929 hung over all American plans for the postwar era. The war had ended that crisis in American society, but the question remained whether peace would restore it. The historical analyst is perpetually challenged and confounded by the danger that the effects of a policy may only rarely reveal its true motives, and specific interests and causal elements may distort its visible roots. But at the end of World War II the leadership of the United States determined on a policy intended to prevent the return of an economic and social crisis in American society—a policy that explicitly demanded that they resolve America's dilemma in the world arena.

The official and unofficial wartime debate on the postwar economic challenge was immense in scope and alone sufficient for a book. Yet the facts—and goals—were clear in the minds of nearly all commentators: the depression had damaged profoundly the United States' position in the world economy, lowering by almost half its share of a far smaller world trade, and the problem in the postwar era was to restore and then extend this share, to maintain the high wartime profits that had followed the parched 1930s, and to utilize a labor force temporarily absorbed in the military services and war plants. By June 1945 the capital assets in American manufacturing had increased 65 percent, largely from federal sources, over the 1939 level. Stated simply, for Washington's planners the question was how to use this vast plant after the end of hostilities. In the farm sector, the return of surplus gluts, largely due to the depression's impact on the world economy, seemed probable if no action were taken to prevent it. Apart from the vague measures and assumptions that Congress wrote into the Full Employment Bill of [1946], steps focused mainly on mitigating the extent and hardships of mass unemployment which the Senate's Committee on Banking anticipated would likely produce 6 or 7 millions out of work by the winter of 1945–1946, tangible proposals occurred mainly in foreign economic policy. "Our international policies and our domestic policies are inseparable," Secretary of State Byrnes informed the Senate on August 21, 1945. In extending its power throughout the globe, the United States hoped to save itself as well from a return of the misery of prewar experience.

From the 1932 low of $1.6 billion in exports, the United States attained $12.8 billion in 1943 and $14.3 billion in 1944, most of the new peak representing a favorable balance of trade. The figure of $14 billion in postwar exports—well over four times the 1939 level—

therefore became the target of most wartime planners and their calculated precondition of continued American prosperity. Assistant Secretary of State Dean Acheson, by early 1945, publicly endorsed a $10 billion minimum figure, but Commerce Department experts thought it to be too low. Even if backlogged domestic wartime savings and demand sustained business activity for two or three years after 1946, Commerce experts warned, this alone would not prevent unemployment of as great as 4.5 million men in 1948. The most optimistic estimates calculated that the United States would not import more than $6 billion a year through 1947, and probably much less, and American private business could not, at best, profitably invest more than $3 billion a year for some time—figures that later proved much too high.

At the very least, $5 billion in annual United States loans and grants would for a time be required to attain the $14 billion export target for domestic prosperity, though some estimates ran to $8 billion. For this reason, key Washington officials publicly warned before the end of the war that the United States would have to provide ". . . the necessary financing of our foreign trade during the crucial period of reconversion at home and reconstruction abroad. . . ." From the outset, Washington set the entire question of postwar American foreign economic policy and aid in the context, as Clayton phrased it as late as November 1946, that ". . . let us admit right off that our objective has as its background the needs and interests of the people of the United States." Such a formulation was also based on the premise, as Byrnes had put it one year earlier, that "[p]olitical peace and economic warfare cannot long exist together." The failure to restore world trade would not only affect American prosperity but in addition lead to a continuation of the world trade restrictions which it was a prime American goal to eliminate as part of the reformation of world capitalism. For if the nations of Europe could not finance reconstruction via American aid, they would attempt to find the resources by tight exchange and import controls—in effect, continuing the status quo in the world economy inherited from the debacle of 1929. Loans would also become the key vehicle of structural change in the capitalist world. "We cannot play Santa Claus to the world but we can make loans to governments whose credit is good, provided such governments will make changes in commercial policies which will make it possible for us to increase our trade with them," Byrnes added. Trade, the reformation of foreign capitalism, and American prosperity were all seen as part of one interlocked issue.

From this viewpoint, even before America's leaders could evaluate the specific political and economic conditions of Europe—indeed, even when they were relatively sanguine—they determined on a postwar economic policy compatible with American interests. Not only, therefore, did Washington have to confront both bolshevism and the social-economic consequences of the great upheaval in the war-torn world, but it had also to redefine the nature of world capitalism as it had evolved after 1918. No responsible American leader had any illusions regarding the nation's critical role in the postwar world economy or any grave doubts as to its ability to fulfill its self-appointed role. . . .

The question of foreign economic policy was not the containment of communism, but rather more directly the extension and expansion of American capitalism according to its new economic power and needs. Primarily, America was committed to inhibiting and redirecting other forces and pressures of change abroad in the world among non-, even anti-, Soviet states. Russia and Eastern Europe were an aspect of this problem, but the rest of the world was yet more important even in 1946. . . .

Just as we insist on making an expansive American capitalism the central theme of postwar history, so, too, must we place a distinct emphasis on its relative failures—defeats the outcome and consequences of which have led to an escalation of the American attempts to master its ever more elusive self-assigned destiny. But we must also place the significance of its mounting efforts in the context of whether the multiplying undertakings were ever sufficient for the American economy's needs and for the fulfillment of its ambitious global objectives. For despite the fact that the magnitude of America's postwar program satisfied specific agricultural and industrial interests, in the largest sense it was inadequate to attain its maximum objectives. The British loan of 1946 was followed by the Marshall Plan, which in turn required massive arms aid, Point Four, and the like. By the time the intensifying transformation of the Third World, and evolution in Europe itself, could be gauged, it was evident to all in Washington that the role of capital exporter initially assigned to American business in the postwar world was woefully utopian. The state therefore undertook that key role during the first postwar decade, and wholly assumed the obligation of furnishing the political and military protection it knew an integrated world capitalism demanded. This merger of public and private power and goals, so traditional in American history, despite its vastly greater extent also fell short of the goal's monumental requirements.   There were tactical successes and benefits, but the United States never attained the ideal world order it confidently anticipated during World War II.

America's leaders never fully realized the limits of American power in the world, and the use of foreign policy to express and solve the specific needs of American capitalism continued during the first postwar decade and thereafter, circumscribing the nature of American society and the process of social change throughout the globe.   This interaction between a nation with universal objectives but finite power and the remainder of mankind is critical in modern history and the essence of the American experience.

Arthur M. Schlesinger, Jr.

COMMUNIST IDEOLOGY, STALINIST TOTALITARIANISM, AND AMERICAN UNIVERSALISM

Arthur M. Schlesinger, Jr., in a 1967 essay designed to refute revisionism and to defend the basic tenets of the traditionalist case, discovers the root causes of the Cold War in the Soviets' adherence to an uncompromising Leninist ideology, Moscow's totalitarianism, and Joseph Stalin's madness. The United States could have done little to change the course of events. Schlesinger concedes that Soviet Russia had significant economic recovery problems and security fears and that American policy was sometimes rigid, but he argues that Moscow caused the Cold War. To emphasize his points, he contrasts the American "universalist" view of world order with the Soviet "sphere of influence" approach.

For many years at Harvard University, and now a professor of history at the City University of New York, Schlesinger has also been an active politician in the Democratic party. He has served as an adviser to President John F. Kennedy and has written two books in praise of the Kennedys: *A Thousand Days* (1965) and *Robert Kennedy and His Times* (1978). A prolific

From Arthur M. Schlesinger, Jr., "Origins of the Cold War," *Foreign Affairs* 46 (October 1967): 22–25, 26–27, 28–30, 31–32, 34–35, 42–47, 48–50, 52. Copyright © 1967 by Council on Foreign Relations, Inc., New York. Excerpted by special permission from *Foreign Affairs*, October 1967, and by permission of the author.

historian, Schlesinger has also written biographies of Andrew Jackson and Franklin D. Roosevelt, as well as *The Imperial Presidency* (1973) and *The Cycles of American History* (1986).

The Cold War in its original form was a presumably mortal antagonism, arising in the wake of the Second World War, between two rigidly hostile blocs, one led by the Soviet Union, the other by the United States. For nearly two somber and dangerous decades this antagonism dominated the fears of mankind; it may even, on occasion, have come close to blowing up the planet. In recent years, however, the once implacable struggle has lost its familiar clarity of outline. With the passing of old issues and the emergence of new conflicts and contestants, there is a natural tendency, especially on the part of the generation which grew up during the Cold War, to take a fresh look at the causes of the great contention between Russia and America.

Some exercises in reappraisal have merely elaborated the orthodoxies promulgated in Washington or Moscow during the boom years of the Cold War. But others, especially in the United States (there are no signs, alas, of this in the Soviet Union), represent what American historians call "revisionism"—that is, a readiness to challenge official explanations. No one should be surprised by this phenomenon. Every war in American history has been followed in due course by skeptical reassessments of supposedly sacred assumptions. So the War of 1812, fought at the time for the freedom of the seas, was in later years ascribed to the expansionist ambitions of congressional war hawks; so the Mexican War became a slaveholders' conspiracy. So the Civil War has been pronounced a "needless war," and Lincoln has even been accused of maneuvering the rebel attack on Fort Sumter. So too the Spanish-American War and the First and Second World Wars have, each in its turn, undergone revisionist critiques. It is not to be supposed that the Cold War would remain exempt.

In the case of the Cold War, special factors reinforce the predictable historiographical rhythm. The outburst of polycentrism in the Communist empire has made people wonder whether communism was ever so monolithic as official theories of the Cold War supposed. A generation with no vivid memories of Stalinism may see the Russia of the forties in the image of the relatively mild, seedy and irresolute Russia of the sixties. And for this same generation the American course of widening the war in Vietnam—which even nonrevisionists can easily regard as folly—has unquestionably stirred doubts about the wisdom of

American foreign policy in the sixties which younger historians may have begun to read back into the forties.

It is useful to remember that, on the whole, past exercises in revisionism have failed to stick. Few historians today believe that the war hawks caused the War of 1812 or the slaveholders the Mexican War, or that the Civil War was needless, or that the House of Morgan brought America into the First World War or that Franklin Roosevelt schemed to produce the attack on Pearl Harbor. But this does not mean that one should deplore the rise of Cold War revisionism. For revisionism is an essential part of the process by which history, through the posing of new problems and the investigation of new possibilities, enlarges its perspectives and enriches its insights.

More than this, in the present context, revisionism expresses a deep, legitimate and tragic apprehension. As the Cold War has begun to lose its purity of definition, as the moral absolutes of the fifties become the moralistic clichés of the sixties, some have begun to ask whether the appalling risks which humanity ran during the Cold War were, after all, necessary and inevitable; whether more restrained and rational policies might not have guided the energies of man from the perils of conflict into the potentialities of collaboration. The fact that such questions are in their nature unanswerable does not mean that it is not right and useful to raise them. Nor does it mean that our sons and daughters are not entitled to an accounting from the generation of Russians and Americans who produced the Cold War.

The orthodox American view, as originally set forth by the American government and as reaffirmed until recently by most American scholars, has been that the Cold War was the brave and essential response of free men to Communist aggression. Some have gone back well before the Second World War to lay open the sources of Russian expansionism. Geopoliticians traced the Cold War to imperial Russian strategic ambitions which in the nineteenth century led to the Crimean War, to Russian penetration of the Balkans and the Middle East and to Russian pressure on Britain's "lifeline" to India. Ideologists traced it to the Communist Manifesto of 1848 ("the violent overthrow of the bourgeoisie lays the foundation for the sway of the proletariat"). Thoughtful observers (a phrase meant to exclude those who speak in Dullese about the unlimited evil of godless, atheistic, militant communism) concluded that classical Russian Imperialism and Pan-Slavism, compounded after 1917 by Leninist messianism, confronted the West at the end of the Second World War with an inexorable drive for domination.

The revisionist thesis is very different. In its extreme form, it is that, after the death of Franklin Roosevelt and the end of the Second World War, the United States deliberately abandoned the wartime policy of collaboration and, exhilarated by the possession of the atomic bomb, undertook a course of aggression of its own designed to expel all Russian influence from Eastern Europe and to establish democratic-capitalist states on the very border of the Soviet Union. As the revisionists see it, this radically new American policy—or rather this resumption by Truman of the pre-Roosevelt policy of insensate anticommunism—left Moscow no alternative but to take measures in defense of its own borders. The result was the Cold War.

Peacemaking after the Second World War was not so much a tapestry as it was a hopelessly raveled and knotted mess of yarn. Yet, for purposes of clarity, it is essential to follow certain threads. One theme indispensable to an understanding of the Cold War is the contrast between two clashing views of world order: the "universalist" view, by which all nations shared a common interest in all the affairs of the world, and the "sphere-of-influence" view, by which each great power would be assured by the other great powers of an acknowledged predominance in its own area of special interest. The universalist view assumed that national security would be guaranteed by an international organization. The sphere-of-interest view assumed that national security would be guaranteed by the balance of power. While in practice these views have by no means been incompatible (indeed, our shaky peace has been based on a combination of the two), in the abstract they involved sharp contradictions.

The tradition of American thought in these matters was universalist—i.e., Wilsonian. Roosevelt had been a member of Wilson's subcabinet; in 1920, as candidate for vice-president, he had campaigned for the League of Nations. It is true that, within Roosevelt's infinitely complex mind, Wilsonianism warred with the perception of vital strategic interests he had imbibed from [Alfred Thayer] Mahan. Moreover, his temperamental inclination to settle things with fellow princes around the conference table led him to regard the Big Three—or Four—as trustees for the rest of the world. On occasion, as this narrative will show, he was beguiled into flirtation with the sphere-of-influence heresy. But in principle he believed in joint action and remained a Wilsonian. His hope for Yalta, as he told the Congress on his return, was that it would "spell the end of the system of unilateral action, the exclusive alliances, the spheres of influence, the balances of power, and all the other expedients that have been tried for centuries—and have always failed.". . .

It is true that critics, and even friends, of the United States sometimes noted a discrepancy between the American passion for universalism when it applied to territory far from American shores and the pre-eminence the United States accorded its own interests nearer home. Churchill, seeking Washington's blessing for a sphere-of-influence initiative in Eastern Europe, could not forbear reminding the Americans, "We follow the lead of the United States in South America"; nor did any universalist of record propose the abolition of the Monroe Doctrine. But a convenient myopia prevented such inconsistencies from qualifying the ardency of the universalist faith.

There seem only to have been three officials in the United States government who dissented. One was the secretary of war, Henry L. Stimson, a classical balance-of-power man, who in 1944 opposed the creation of a vacuum in Central Europe by the pastoralization of Germany and in 1945 urged "the settlement of all territorial acquisitions in the shape of defense posts which each of these four powers may deem to be necessary for their own safety" in advance of any effort to establish a peacetime United Nations. Stimson considered the claim of Russia to a preferred position in Eastern Europe as not unreasonable: As he told President Truman, "he thought the Russians perhaps were being more realistic than we were in regard to their own security." Such a position for Russia seemed to him comparable to the preferred American position in Latin America; he even spoke of "our respective orbits." Stimson was therefore skeptical of what he regarded as the prevailing tendency "to hang on to exaggerated views of the Monroe Doctrine and at the same time butt into every question that comes up in Central Europe." Acceptance of spheres of influence seemed to him the way to avoid "a head-on collision."

A second official opponent of universalism was George Kennan, an eloquent advocate from the American Embassy in Moscow of "a prompt and clear recognition of the division of Europe into spheres of influence and of a policy based on the fact of such division." Kennan argued that nothing we could do would possibly alter the course of events in Eastern Europe; that we were deceiving ourselves by supposing that these countries had any future but Russian domination; that we should therefore relinquish Eastern Europe to the Soviet Union and avoid anything which would make things easier for the Russians by giving them economic assistance or by sharing moral responsibility for their actions.

A third voice within the government against universalism was (at least after the war) Henry A. Wallace. As secretary of commerce, he stated the sphere-of-influence case with trenchancy in the famous Madison Square Garden speech of September 1946 which led to his dismissal by President Truman:

> On our part, we should recognize that we have no more business in the *political* affairs of Eastern Europe than Russia has in the *political* affairs of Latin America, Western Europe, and the United States. . . . Whether we like it or not, the Russians will try to socialize their sphere of influence just as we try to democratize our sphere of influence. . . . The Russians have no more business stirring up native Communists to political activity in Western Europe, Latin America, and the United States than we have in interfering with the politics of Eastern Europe and Russia.

Stimson, Kennan and Wallace seem to have been alone in the government, however, in taking these views. They were very much minority voices. Meanwhile universalism, rooted in the American legal and moral tradition, overwhelmingly backed by contemporary opinion, received successive enshrinements in the Atlantic Charter of 1941, in the Declaration of the United Nations in 1942 and in the Moscow Declaration of 1943.

The Kremlin, on the other hand, thought *only* of spheres of interest; above all, the Russians were determined to protect their frontiers, and especially their border to the west, crossed so often and so bloodily in the dark course of their history. These western frontiers lacked natural means of defense—no great oceans, rugged mountains, steaming swamps or impenetrable jungles. The history of Russia had been the history of invasion, the last of which was by now horribly killing up to 20 million of its people. The protocol of Russia therefore meant the enlargement of the area of Russian influence. Kennan himself wrote (in May 1944), "Behind Russia's stubborn expansion lies only the age-old sense of insecurity of a sedentary people reared on an exposed plain in the neighborhood of fierce nomadic peoples," and he called this "urge" a "permanent feature of Russian psychology. . . ."

The unconditional surrender of Italy in July 1943 created the first major test of the Western devotion to universalism. America and

Britain, having won the Italian war, handled the capitulation, keeping Moscow informed at a distance. Stalin complained:

> The United States and Great Britain made agreements but the Soviet Union received information about the results . . . just as a passive third observer I have to tell you that it is impossible to tolerate the situation any longer. I propose that the [tripartite military-political commission] be established and that Sicily be assigned . . . as its place of residence.

Roosevelt, who had no intention of sharing the control of Italy with the Russians, suavely replied with the suggestion that Stalin send an officer "to General Eisenhower's headquarters in connection with the commission." Unimpressed, Stalin continued to press for a tripartite body; but his Western allies were adamant in keeping the Soviet Union off the Control Commission for Italy, and the Russians in the end had to be satisfied with a seat, along with minor Allied states, on a meaningless Inter-Allied Advisory Council. Their acquiescence in this was doubtless not unconnected with a desire to establish precedents for Eastern Europe.

Teheran in December 1943 marked the high point of three-power collaboration. Still, when Churchill asked about Russian territorial interests, Stalin replied a little ominously, "There is no need to speak at the present time about any Soviet desires, but when the time comes we will speak." In the next weeks, there were increasing indications of a Soviet determination to deal unilaterally with Eastern Europe—so much so that in early February 1944 Hull cabled Harriman in Moscow:

> Matters are rapidly approaching the point where the Soviet government will have to choose between the development and extension of the foundation of international cooperation as the guiding principle of the postwar world as against the continuance of a unilateral and arbitrary method of dealing with its special problems even though these problems are admittedly of more direct interest to the Soviet Union than to other great powers.

As against this approach, however, Churchill, more tolerant of sphere-of-influence deviations, soon proposed that, with the impending liberation of the Balkans, Russia should run things in Rumania and Britain in Greece. Hull strongly opposed this suggestion but made the mistake of leaving Washington for a few days; and Roosevelt, momentarily free from his Wilsonian conscience, yielded to Churchill's pleas for a three-months' trial. Hull resumed the fight on his return, and Churchill postponed the matter. . . .

Meanwhile Eastern Europe presented the Alliance with still another crisis that same September. Bulgaria, which was not at war with Russia, decided to surrender to the Western Allies while it still could; and the English and Americans at Cairo began to discuss armistice terms with Bulgarian envoys. Moscow, challenged by what it plainly saw as a Western intrusion into its own zone of vital interest, promptly declared war on Bulgaria, took over the surrender negotiation and, invoking the Italian precedent, denied its Western Allies any role in the Bulgarian Control Commission. In a long and thoughtful cable, Ambassador Harriman meditated on the problems of communication with the Soviet Union. "Words," he reflected, "have a different connotation to the Soviets than they have to us. When they speak of insisting on friendly governments' in their neighboring countries, they have in mind something quite different from what we would mean." The Russians, he surmised, really believed that Washington accepted "their position that although they would keep us informed they had the right to settle their problems with their western neighbors unilaterally." But the Soviet position was still in flux: "the Soviet government is not one mind." The problem, as Harriman had earlier told Harry Hopkins, was "to strengthen the hands of those around Stalin who want to play the game along our lines." The way to do this, he now told Hull, was to

> be understanding of their sensitivity, meet them much more than half way, encourage them and support them wherever we can, and yet oppose them promptly with the greatest firmness where we see them going wrong. . . . The only way we can eventually come to an understanding with the Soviet Union on the question of noninterference in the internal affairs of other countries is for us to take a definite interest in the solution of the problems of each individual country as they arise.

As against Harriman's sophisticated universalist strategy, however, Churchill, increasingly fearful of the consequences of unrestrained competition in Eastern Europe, decided in early October to carry his sphere-of-influence proposal directly to Moscow. Roosevelt was at first content to have Churchill speak for him too and even prepared a cable to that effect. But Hopkins, a more rigorous universalist, took it upon himself to stop the cable and warn Roosevelt of its possible implications. Eventually Roosevelt sent a message to Harriman in Moscow emphasizing that he expected to "retain complete freedom of action after this conference is over." It was now that Churchill quickly proposed—and Stalin as quickly accepted—the celebrated division of southeastern Europe: ending (after further haggling between [Sir

Anthony] Eden and [V. M.] Molotov) with 90 percent Soviet predominance in Rumania, 80 percent in Bulgaria and Hungary, 50–50 in Jugoslavia, 90 percent British predominance in Greece.

Churchill in discussing this with Harriman used the phrase "spheres of influence." But he insisted that these were only "immediate wartime arrangements" and received a highly general blessing from Roosevelt. Yet, whatever Churchill intended, there is reason to believe that Stalin construed the percentages as an agreement, not a declaration; as practical arithmetic, not algebra. For Stalin, it should be understood, the sphere-of-influence idea did not mean that he would abandon all efforts to spread communism in some other nation's sphere; it did mean that, if he tried this and the other side cracked down, he could not feel he had serious cause for complaint. . . .

Yalta remains something of an historical perplexity—less, from the perspective of 1967, because of a mythical American deference to the sphere-of-influence thesis than because of the documentable Russian deference to the universalist thesis. Why should Stalin in 1945 have accepted the Declaration on Liberated Europe and an agreement on Poland pledging that "the three governments will jointly" act to assure "free elections of governments responsive to the will of the people"? There are several probable answers: that the war was not over and the Russians still wanted the Americans to intensify their military effort in the West; that one clause in the Declaration premised action on "the opinion of the three governments" and thus implied a Soviet veto, though the Polish agreement was more definite; most of all that the universalist algebra of the Declaration was plenty in Stalin's mind to be construed in terms of the practical arithmetic of his sphere-of-influence agreement with Churchill the previous October. Stalin's assurance to Churchill at Yalta that a proposed Russian amendment to the Declaration would not apply to Greece makes it clear that Roosevelt's pieties did not, in Stalin's mind, nullify Churchill's percentages. He could well have been strengthened in this supposition by the fact that *after* Yalta, Churchill himself repeatedly reasserted the terms of the October agreement as if he regarded it, despite Yalta, as controlling.

Harriman still had the feeling before Yalta that the Kremlin had "two approaches to their postwar policies" and that Stalin himself was "of two minds." One approach emphasized the internal reconstruction and development of Russia; the other its external expansion. But in the meantime the fact which dominated all political decisions—that is, the war against Germany—was moving into its final phase. In the weeks after Yalta, the military situation changed with great rapidity. As the Nazi threat declined, so too did the need for cooperation. The Soviet Union, feeling itself menaced by the American idea of self-determination and the borderlands diplomacy to which it was leading, skeptical whether the United Nations would protect its frontiers as reliably as its own domination in Eastern Europe, began to fulfill its security requirements unilaterally. . . .

The Cold War had now begun. It was the product not of a decision but of a dilemma. Each side felt compelled to adopt policies which the other could not but regard as a threat to the principles of the peace. Each then felt compelled to undertake defensive measures. Thus the Russians saw no choice but to consolidate their security in Eastern Europe. The Americans, regarding Eastern Europe as the first step toward Western Europe, responded by asserting their interest in the zone the Russians deemed vital to their security. The Russians concluded that the West was resuming its old course of capitalist encirclement; that it was purposefully laying the foundation for anti-Soviet regimes in the area defined by the blood of centuries as crucial to Russian survival. Each side believed with passion that future international stability depended on the success of its own conception of world order. Each side, in pursuing its own clearly indicated and deeply cherished principles, was only confirming the fear of the other that it was bent on aggression.

Very soon the process began to acquire a cumulative momentum. The impending collapse of Germany thus provoked new troubles: the Russians, for example, sincerely feared that the West was planning a separate surrender of the German armies in Italy in a way which would release troops for Hitler's eastern front, as they subsequently feared that the Nazis might succeed in surrendering Berlin to the West. This was the context in which the atomic bomb now appeared. Though the revisionist argument that Truman dropped the bomb less to defeat Japan than to intimidate Russia is not convincing, this thought unquestionably appealed to some in Washington as at least an advantageous side-effect of Hiroshima.

So the machinery of suspicion and countersuspicion, action and counteraction, was set in motion. But, given relations among traditional national states, there was still no reason, even with all the postwar jostling, why this should not have remained a manageable situation. What made it unmanageable, what caused the rapid escalation of the

Cold War and in another two years completed the division of Europe, was a set of considerations which this account has thus far excluded.

Up to this point, the discussion has considered the schism within the wartime coalition as if it were entirely the result of disagreements among national states. Assuming this framework, there was unquestionably a failure of communication between America and Russia, a misperception of signals and, as time went on, a mounting tendency to ascribe ominous motives to the other side. It seems hard, for example, to deny that American postwar policy created genuine difficulties for the Russians and even assumed a threatening aspect for them. All this the revisionists have rightly and usefully emphasized.

But the great omission of the revisionists—and also the fundamental explanation of the speed with which the Cold War escalated—lies precisely in the fact that the Soviet Union was *not* a traditional national state. This is where the "mirror image," invoked by some psychologists, falls down. For the Soviet Union was a phenomenon very different from America or Britain: it was a totalitarian state, endowed with an all-explanatory, all-consuming ideology, committed to the infallibility of government and party, still in a somewhat messianic mood, equating dissent with treason, and ruled by a dictator who, for all his quite extraordinary abilities, had his paranoid moments.

Marxism-Leninism gave the Russian leaders a view of the world according to which all societies were inexorably destined to proceed along appointed roads by appointed stages until they achieved the classless nirvana. Moreover, given the resistance of the capitalists to this development, the existence of any non-Communist state was *by definition* a threat to the Soviet Union. "As long as capitalism and socialism exist," Lenin wrote, "we cannot live in peace: in the end, one or the other will triumph—a funeral dirge will be sung either over the Soviet Republic or over world capitalism."

Stalin and his associates, whatever Roosevelt or Truman did or failed to do, were bound to regard the United States as the enemy, not because of this deed or that, but because of the primordial fact that America was the leading capitalist power and thus, by Leninist syllogism, unappeasably hostile, driven by the logic of its system to oppose, encircle and destroy Soviet Russia. Nothing the United States could have done in 1944–45 would have abolished this mistrust, required and sanctified as it was by Marxist gospel—nothing short of the conversion of the United States into a Stalinist despotism; and even this would not have sufficed, as the experience of Jugoslavia and China soon showed, unless it were accompanied by total subservience to Moscow. So long as the United States remained a capitalist democracy, no American policy, given Moscow's theology, could hope to win basic Soviet confidence, and every American action was poisoned from the source. So long as the Soviet Union remained a messianic state, ideology compelled a steady expansion of communist power. . . .

A temporary recession of ideology was already taking place during the Second World War when Stalin, to rally his people against the invader, had to replace the appeal of Marxism by that of nationalism. ("We are under no illusions that they are fighting for us," Stalin once said to Harriman. "They are fighting for Mother Russia.") But this was still taking place within the strictest limitations. The Soviet Union remained as much a police state as ever; the regime was as infallible as ever; foreigners and their ideas were as suspect as ever. "Never, except possibly during my later experience as ambassador in Moscow," Kennan has written, "did the insistence of the Soviet authorities on isolation of the diplomatic corps weigh more heavily on me . . . than in these first weeks following my return to Russia in the final months of the war. . . . [We were] treated as though we were the bearers of some species of the plague"—which, of course, from the Soviet viewpoint, they were: the plague of skepticism.

Paradoxically, of the forces capable of bringing about a modification of ideology, the most practical and effective was the Soviet dictatorship itself. If Stalin was an ideologist, he was also a pragmatist. If he saw everything through the lenses of Marxism-Leninism, he also, as the infallible expositor of the faith, could reinterpret Marxism-Leninism to justify anything he wanted to do at any given moment. No doubt Roosevelt's ignorance of Marxism-Leninism was inexcusable and led to grievous miscalculations. But Roosevelt's efforts to work on and through Stalin were not so hopelessly naive as it used to be fashionable to think. With the extraordinary instinct of a great political leader, Roosevelt intuitively understood that Stalin was the *only* lever available to the West against the Leninist ideology and the Soviet system. If Stalin could be reached, then alone was there a chance of getting the Russians to act contrary to the prescriptions of their faith. The best evidence is that Roosevelt retained a certain capacity to influence Stalin to the end; the nominal Soviet acquiescence in American universalism as late as Yalta was perhaps an indication of that. It is in this way that the death of Roosevelt was crucial—not in the vulgar sense that his policy was then reversed by his successor, which did not happen, but in the sense that no other American could hope to have the restraining impact on Stalin which Roosevelt might for a while have had.

Stalin alone could have made any difference. Yet Stalin, in spite of the impression of sobriety and realism he made on Westerners who saw him during the Second World War, was plainly a man of deep and morbid obsessions and compulsions. When he was still a young man, Lenin had criticized his rude and arbitrary ways. A reasonably authoritative observer (N. S. Khrushchev) later commented, "These negative characteristics of his developed steadily and during the last years acquired an absolutely insufferable character." His paranoia, probably set off by the suicide of his wife in 1932, led to the terrible purges of the mid-thirties and the wanton murder of thousands of his Bolshevik comrades. "Everywhere and in everything," Khrushchev says of this period, "he saw 'enemies,' 'double-dealers' and 'spies.' " The crisis of war evidently steadied him in some way, though Khrushchev speaks of his "nervousness and hysteria . . . even after the war began." The madness, so rigidly controlled for a time, burst out with new and shocking intensity in the postwar years. "After the war," Khrushchev testifies,

> the situation became even more complicated. Stalin became even more capricious, irritable and brutal; in particular, his suspicion grew. His persecution mania reached unbelievable dimensions. . . . He decided everything, without any consideration for anyone or anything.
>
> Stalin's willfullness showed itself . . . also in the international relations of the Soviet Union. . . . He had completely lost a sense of reality; he demonstrated his suspicion and haughtiness not only in relation to individuals in the USSR, but in relation to whole parties and nations.

A revisionist fallacy has been to treat Stalin as just another Realpolitik statesman, as Second World War revisionists see Hitler as just another [Gustav] Stresemann or [Otto von] Bismarck. But the record makes it clear that in the end nothing could satisfy Stalin's paranoia. His own associates failed. Why does anyone suppose that any conceivable American policy would have succeeded?

An analysis of the origins of the Cold War which leaves out these factors—the intransigence of Leninist ideology, the sinister dynamics of a totalitarian society and the madness of Stalin—is obviously incomplete. It was these factors which made it hard for the West to accept the thesis that Russia was moved only by a desire to protect its security and would be satisfied by the control of Eastern Europe; it was these factors which charged the debate between universalism and spheres of influence with apocalyptic potentiality.

Leninism and totalitarianism created a structure of thought and behavior which made postwar collaboration between Russia and America—in any normal sense of civilized intercourse between national states—inherently impossible. The Soviet dictatorship of 1945 simply could not have survived such a collaboration. Indeed, nearly a quarter-century later, the Soviet regime, though it has meanwhile moved a good distance, could still hardly survive it without risking the release inside Russia of energies profoundly opposed to Communist despotism. As for Stalin, he may have represented the only force in 1945 capable of overcoming Stalinism, but the very traits which enabled him to win absolute power expressed terrifying instabilities of mind and temperament and hardly offered a solid foundation for a peaceful world.

Daniel Yergin

AMERICAN IDEOLOGY: THE RIGA AND YALTA AXIOMS

In his *Shattered Peace: The Origins of the Cold War and the National Security State* (1977), Daniel Yergin, like Arthur M. Schlesinger, Jr., before him, explores the long-standing debate over whether Soviet foreign policy is driven by messianic Marxist-Leninist ideology, brutal totalitarianism, or Soviet Russia's security interests. Was the Soviet Union a world revolutionary nation with which compromise was impossible? Or was it a traditional nation-state with which negotiations were possible? Yergin identifies two sets of American assumptions that clashed in the early Cold War period. The Riga axioms, named for the Latvian city where many American diplomats had studied Soviet affairs before 1933, emphasized the intractability of the ideologically bound, authoritarian Soviets. The Yalta axioms, named for the Black Sea resort where Franklin D. Roosevelt, Winston Churchill, and Joseph Stalin met in 1945, posited that Soviet-American cooperation in the postwar era could be realized through agreements that respected each side's interests. After Roosevelt's death, advisers who endorsed the Riga axioms gained influence with the new president, Harry S Truman, who in early 1946 repudiated the Yalta axioms.

From Daniel Yergin *Shattered Peace*, pp. 10–11, 18–20, 29–30, 32, 35–36, 37–38, 38–39, 41–43, 55–56, 61–65, 65–66, 82–83 (no footnotes). Copyright © 1977, 1990 by Daniel Yergin. Reprinted by permission of Helen Brann Agency, Inc.

Daniel Yergin is president of Cambridge Energy Research Associates in Massachusetts.   He has edited *Energy Future* (1979), *The Dependence Dilemma: Gasoline Consumption and America's Security* (1980), and *Global Insecurity* (1982).

. . . Underlying the debate [within the American elite over how to evaluate Soviet intentions and capabilities] were two related questions that have always confronted those in the West who have to shape policies toward the Soviet Union.   They are the same two questions we face today.

The first was raised by the October 1917 Revolution itself.   What is the connection between Marxist-Leninist ideology and Soviet foreign policy?   The ideology proclaims that communism will inevitably inherit the entire world from capitalism, and calls upon Marxist-Leninists to be the conscious agents of the revolution.   But the men who have ruled the Soviet Union were not and are not merely ideologues with many idle hours to dream about tomorrow's utopia.   For the most part, they must concern themselves with today, with governing a powerful state that has pressing interests to protect, dangers to avoid, tasks to accomplish, and problems to solve.   "There is no revolutionary movement in the West," said Stalin during the debates over the Brest-Litovsk treaty in 1918.   "There are no facts; there is only a possibility, and with possibilities we cannot reckon."

The second question was brutally posed by the horrors of Stalinism, in particular by collectivization and the Great Terror of the 1930s.   Does a totalitarian practice at home necessarily produce a foreign policy that is totalitarian in intent, committed to overturning the international system and to endless expansion in pursuit of world dominance?   The policies of Adolf Hitler seemed to confirm that a powerful relationship did exist between such domestic practice and international behavior.

The changes wrought by the Second World War gave urgent and highest priority to these questions.   What was the American response to be?   Within the ensuing debate, there were two sets of generalizations, two interpretations that competed for hegemony in the American policy elite in the middle 1940s.   At the heart of the first set was an image of the Soviet Union as a world revolutionary state, denying the possibilities of coexistence, committed to unrelenting ideological warfare, powered by a messianic drive for world mastery.   The second set downplayed the role of ideology and the foreign policy consequences of authoritarian domestic practices, and instead saw the Soviet Union behaving like a traditional Great Power within the international system, rather than trying to overthrow it. The first set I call, for shorthand, the Riga axioms; the second, the Yalta axioms.

The Riga axioms triumphed in American policy circles in the postwar years and provided a foundation for the anticommunist consensus. Charles Bohlen summarized this outlook when he wrote to former Secretary of State Edward Stettinius in 1949. "I am quite convinced myself, and I think all of those who have been working specifically on the problems of relations with the Soviet Union are in agreement," said Bohlen, "that the reasons for the state of tension that exists in the world today between the Soviet Union and the non-Soviet world are to be found in the character and nature of the Soviet state, the doctrines to which it faithfully adheres, and not in such matters as the shutting off of Lend-Lease and the question of a loan."

With a view of this sort, the effort to make a diplomatic settlement became irrelevant, even dangerous, for the Cold War confrontation was thought to be almost genetically preordained in the revolutionary, messianic, predatory character of the Soviet Union. . . .

During the 1920s, a new "Soviet Service" developed in the State Department; it was anti-Bolshevik and opposed to diplomatic recognition of the USSR. Cohesive, with a strongly articulated sense of identity, this group advocated a policy of sophisticated anticommunism in an axiomatic form. Its outlook was based on personal experience, assessment, study, and pessimism. As U.S. leaders attempted, after World War II, to analyze Soviet policy and select an appropriate American course, this group's position provided one end of the spectrum of the debate. Eventually its axioms triumphed. Or, rather, they triumphed again, for they had held sway during most of the interwar years, when they had little competition, and before the problem of the Soviet Union had moved to the fore.

Initially, American officials saw the Bolshevik Revolution as a double betrayal. The revolutionaries made peace with the Germans at Brest-Litovsk early in 1918 and withdrew from the war, hurting the Allied cause. The Bolsheviks had also destroyed the hopes for the budding Russian democracy by overturning the liberal regime, which in its few months of existence had at last removed the Czarist stigma from the coalition meant to make the world safe for democracy. There was even the possibility of a third betrayal—that Lenin was a German agent.

American policymakers refused to recognize the new regime, in part because they hoped that it would be short-lived. The idea was shared by "practically all of us," recalled DeWitt Clinton Poole, who worked on Russian affairs in the State Department after World War I, "that the cure for Bolshevism was prosperity and good order and that Bolshevism would disappear under those conditions." There was, in Poole's words, a "breach between the Bolsheviks and the rest of the world." In an important memorandum addressed to his superiors in the State Department, in August 1919, Poole marshaled the arguments against giving diplomatic recognition to this "unconstitutional" regime: "Their aim is world-wide revolution . . . Their doctrines aim at the destruction of all governments as now constituted."

This outlook was widely accepted in the government and, instead of recognizing the Bolsheviks, the State Department set up a Division of Russian Affairs, with a mandate unusual for its time: to study and interpret the great mass of often contradictory information that made its way across the breach from this new Russia. It called upon the services of professors like Samuel Harper, of the University of Chicago, one of the first academic experts on Soviet Russia.

The U.S. maintained an observation post in the American mission in the Baltic port city of Riga, which was, through the interwar years, the capital of the independent republic of Latvia. Founded in 1201 by German merchants, tucked into a gulf at the very eastern end of the Baltic Sea, Riga still resembled a city of northern Germany, with narrow cobbled streets, gabled towers, and tiny squares. It was in this mission during the 1920s that much of the research on the Soviet Union was conducted, personnel trained, and fundamental attitudes formed and nurtured; and it was from the mission that there issued constant warnings against the international menace. For these reasons, I have associated place with ideas and linked Riga to the axiomatic outlook of the Soviet Service in the State department, although the ideas would receive further elaboration and gain new intensity in the latter half of the 1930s. . . .

The effects of the purges, with their great trials and sudden disappearances, on the image of the Soviet Union held by the American diplomats cannot be exaggerated. The assassination of [Sergei] Kirov inaugurated a second phase of Stalinism—the orgy of terror, now directed against the apparatus of state and party. The unprecedented and spectacular show trials—conducted not only in the major cities but in almost every *oblast*—delivered their requisite output, an endless series of perfectly outlandish confessions, which "proved" that Trotskyites and foreign agents honeycombed Soviet society with their conspiracies.

Millions suffered directly in this holocaust. In the simple words of Roy Medvedev, "Between 1936 and 1938 Stalin broke all records for political terror." Dread became a basic ingredient of Soviet life. By 1939 the purges had helped to establish firmly a highly centralized, bureaucratic, terror-driven totalitarian state, and the entire nation had become the servant of the state and of its ruler. . . .

Leninism had posed the first of the crucial questions about the Soviet Union—what was the relationship between its ideology and its behavior in the international system? Now Stalinism underlined in a stark fashion the second of the two questions—what was the connection between domestic totalitarianism and Soviet foreign policy? As with the first, there was no easy answer. Certainly, the American diplomats were correct in their judgment about the corruption of the Stalinist system. Indeed, if anything they were restrained, for they were able to see only the surface of the terror, for it has taken many years since for Westerners to begin to learn the full extent of Stalin's tyranny. Still, those diplomats concluded that the connection between the character of the state and its foreign policy was necessary and complete, that a totalitarian system at home meant a totalitarian foreign policy. If their answer was too categoric, even mistaken, one can understand—seeing what they did of collectivization, of the purges, of the daily life of terror and hypocrisy—why they came to it. . . .

By the end of the 1930s, the image of the revolutionary state and the ideas associated with it had become firmly fixed in the minds of the Soviet specialists and in those of people, like [Ambassador William] Bullitt, who had "learned" with them. "I am inclined to believe that all of us who have been in close contact with the thing itself gradually come to a common point of view," [Loy] Henderson observed in 1940. "There are a few exceptions among the chaps who are emotional and likely to become prejudiced." So codified had these beliefs become that we can now lay them out as axioms—though we must be careful not to confuse axioms with blinding dogma.

Doctrine and ideology and a spirit of innate aggressiveness shaped Soviet policy, the specialists believed. Thus, the USSR was committed to world revolution and unlimited expansion. In consequence, the United States, not just the countries around the Russian rim, was under siege and had to be continually vigilant. The "breach" of 1919 was still very real, to be bridged only by a major transformation.

Curiously, however, for all their fanatical devotion to ideology, the Soviet leaders were cool thinkers, much cooler than their Western counterparts. "They are realists, if ever there are any realists in this world," wrote Ambassador Laurence Steinhardt, [Joseph E.] Davies' successor, in 1940. The Soviet leaders always set their goals with supreme clarity. To an extent greater than that of most countries, Henderson wrote in 1936, Russian policy "has before it a series of definite objectives." Soviet officials are judged by "the progress" they can make "in the direction of those objectives." The Russians were always surefooted, and were masters of strategy and tactics.

The historian must here observe that the axiomatic notion that the Soviets worked by a foreign affairs plan, derived from ideology and with definite objectives, not only gave them more credit than they deserved, but also proved to be a central weakness in the assessments of Soviet policy after the war. For it led U.S. officials to exaggerate the policy coherence of the Kremlin—the role of ideology and conscious intentions. At the same time they understated the role played by accident, confusion, and uncertainty in Russian policy and also mistook mere reaction for planned action. A similar pattern, no doubt, would exist on the other side; what Americans would regard as their efforts to muddle through, in response to this or that problem, would be seen by the Soviets as part of a larger calculated policy. Indeed, one might even go further and hypothesize that there is a general tendency in international relations to exaggerate the policy coherence of an adversary. . . .

Confronted by such a potential adversary, the United States needed to adopt a stance of wariness and constant vigilance. Great patience and a counterassertiveness, an explicit "toughness," were required to cope with the Russian "personality." Steinhardt wrote to [Loy] Henderson in October 1940: "Approaches by Britain or the United States must be interpreted here as signs of weakness and the best policy to pursue is one of aloofness, indicating strength . . . As you know from your own experiences, the moment these people here get it into their heads that we are 'appeasing them, making up to them or need them,' they immediately stop being cooperative . . . My experience has been that they respond only to force and if force cannot be applied, then to straight oriental bartering or trading methods . . . That, in my opinion, is the only language they understand and the only language productive of results." The conclusion, therefore, was that diplomacy with the Soviet Union was not merely a questionable venture, but downright dangerous. . . .

The events that followed the 1939 pact—the Soviet role in the partition of Poland, the winter war in Finland, the annexation of the

Balkan states and Bessarabia—all of these steps involving deportations and further extension of the terror—confirmed the Riga viewpoint, and gave its advocates the confidence to speak even more categorically. The war with Finland, in general, mobilized anti-Soviet sentiment in the United States and chilled Russo-American relations. The abhorrence that had fed DeWitt Clinton Poole's strictures two decades before returned, and with greater force.

Even at the highest levels the Riga image regained acceptance. In the middle of 1940 Loy Henderson challenged his superiors: "Is the Government of the United States to apply certain standards of judgment and conduct to aggression by Germany and Japan, and not to Soviet aggression?" The answer came now: Germany and Russia were two of a kind; they were totalitarian dictatorships. Cordell Hull, on the eve of the German invasion of Russia, summarized the knowledge gleaned in the 1930s: "Basing ourselves upon our own experiences and upon observations of the experiences of other governments," U.S. policy toward the Soviet Union called for making "no approaches to the Soviet Government," treating any Soviet approaches with reserve, and rendering "no sacrifices in principle in order to improve relations."

These axioms seemed to explain satisfactorily Russia's role in world politics and to delineate an appropriate course for the United States to follow. They dominated interpretations of events until the German invasion of Russia in the night of June 21–22, 1941. With that, the Riga axioms suffered a startling loss of relevance. A new phase began in Soviet-American relations, which led to an experience radically different from that of the Soviet Service during the interwar years. A fresh image, based upon other assumptions, came to the fore. In addition, procedures were established for handling political problems that bypassed the State Department. . . .

United States policy toward the Soviet Union was now out of the hands of the State Department. In an environment sharply transformed from that of the interwar years, the Riga School was being made obsolete by the bold new span [Franklin D.] Roosevelt was constructing to bridge the breach between America and Russia in the postwar era.

One evening in March of 1943, British Foreign Secretary Anthony Eden dined privately at the White House with President Roosevelt and Harry Hopkins. The three fell into a long, ruminating conversation that continued late into the night. With an ease available only to men who number themselves among the handful of arbiters over the world's destiny, they surveyed the outstanding political questions of the entire planet, playing with borders, shifting governments like so many chess pieces, guessing at the political shadings that would color the postwar map. "A conjuror, skillfully juggling with balls of dynamite," was the way Eden remembered Roosevelt from that night. "The big question which rightly dominated Roosevelt's mind was whether it was possible to work with Russia now and after the war," he recalled.

Roosevelt asked Eden what he thought of the "Bullitt Thesis," referring to a lengthy memorandum, based upon the Riga axioms, that Bullitt had sent to the White House several weeks earlier. Bullitt, whose enthusiasms of ten years before had long since soured into fear and alarm, predicted that the Russians would succeed in communizing the Continent—unless the United States and Britain blocked "the flow of the Red amoeba into Europe."

Eden replied that a definite answer to this question was impossible. But "even if these fears were to prove correct," he continued, "we should make the position no worse by trying to work with Russia and by assuming that Stalin meant what he said." Eden agreed with Roosevelt that it would be better to proceed on a premise contrary to Bullitt's—that it would be possible to find some system of working *with*, rather than *against*, the Soviet Union. Roosevelt also did not think that a categoric answer existed. He believed Soviet goals and methods would be partly determined by Stalin's own estimate of American and British intentions and capabilities.

Certainly the most important goal of Roosevelt's wartime diplomacy was the establishment of a basis for postwar cooperation with the Soviet Union. He had a clear conception of the postwar settlement he wanted and how it might be achieved. This conception was also governed by a number of axioms, some of which had predated the war, some of which had emerged in the course of the war. Roosevelt's axioms were always more tentative than those of Riga, but at their center point, there also lay an image—derived from experience, assessment, and optimism—of Soviet Russia. . . .

As already noted, Roosevelt believed the peace had to be based upon the realities of power, which meant that it would have to be grounded in a Great Power consortium. The British easily fit into this design. The key question concerned the role of the Soviet Union. Here Roosevelt operated on a series of axioms very different from those of the Soviet specialists in the State Department.

He believed that Russia could no longer be considered an outsider, beyond the pale of morality and international politics. What that meant in the context of the war was already obvious. The President recognized that the major land war in Europe was taking place on the Eastern Front; it was there that Germany could be defeated, with a consequent reduction in American casualties. A kind of comparative advantage set in. The Russians specialized in men, dead and wounded, while the United States pushed its industrial machine to new limits. A year after the German invasion of the Soviet Union, Roosevelt declared that "Russian endurance" was "still the main strength."

The war, which promised to bequeath a great power vacuum in Europe and at the same time erased all doubts about Russia's power and capabilities, made inevitable the emergence of the Soviet Union as a paramount and indispensable factor in the postwar international system, especially in Europe. Thus, the alternative to a broad understanding would be a postwar world of hostile coalitions, an arms race—and another war.

Some such understanding was possible because the breach that had opened at the time of the Bolshevik Revolution had narrowed and could narrow further. Roosevelt thought of the Soviet Union less as a revolutionary vanguard than as a conventional imperialist power, with ambitions rather like those of the Czarist regime. In other words, Roosevelt emphasized the imperatives of statehood in Soviet policy, rather than the role of ideology. In contrast to the Riga axioms, he proceeded on the proposition that a totalitarian domestic system did *not* inevitably and necessarily give rise to a totalitarian foreign policy. As important, he assumed less coherence and purposefulness in the Kremlin's behavior in international politics than did those who operated on the Riga axioms. Since the Soviet Union was not so much a world revolutionary state, Roosevelt believed the Grand Alliance could be continued after the war in the form of "business-like relations." He also knew that the Soviet Union would be preoccupied after the war with its vast task of reconstruction, and would be desperately interested in stability, order, and peace.

Successful collaboration among the Great Powers would necessitate the allaying of many years of Soviet hostility and suspicion. Roosevelt regarded the dissipation of distrust as one of his most important challenges. The United States could prove its good faith by sticking to its agreements. Even if the West could not deliver immediately on its promised Second Front, at least it could provide the aid it had pledged—and, in that way, also do itself a considerable favor. Again and again, Roosevelt ordered that the production and delivery of lend-lease goods be speeded up, that the quantities be increased. It was a battle down the line. "Frankly," the President sharply reminded a subordinate, "if I were a Russian, I would feel that I had been given the run-around in the United States." . . .

"Roosevelt weather" was the term applied by FDR's political staff to the favorable weather that seemed to signal victory on each of those four November days that he had been elected President. The Russians adopted the same phrase to describe the unseasonably mild climate in the first two weeks of February 1945 over the Crimea, which juts down into the Black Sea from the underside of the Ukraine. At the seaside resort of Yalta, on the southern coast of the Crimea, the last Czar had maintained his summer palace. There the Big Three gathered for their final wartime conference, between February 4 and 11, under bright, clear skies that seemed a harbinger of victory, not only in the war but also over the unfamiliar terrain of postwar international politics. FDR brought his practicality to bear, in an effort to make firm the foundations of his Grand Design. The pleasant days and nights matched the climate of the conference itself—auguring victory for Roosevelt's foreign policy.

Marking the high tide of Allied unity, the Yalta Conference was a point of separation, a time of endings and beginnings. The conclusion of the war was at last in sight; the remaining days of the Third Reich were clearly numbered. Stalin, to the relief of the Joint Chiefs, gave further assurances that Russia would enter the war against Japan some three months after fighting ended in Europe, in exchange for certain territorial concessions in the Far East.

Aside from that central question, the major issues at Yalta concerned the politics of a postwar world. The decisions waited upon the energies of three tired men. "I think Uncle Joe much the most impressive" Alexander Cadogan, permanent undersecretary of the British Foreign Office, wrote to his wife. "The President flapped about and the P.M. boomed, but Joe just sat taking it all in and being rather amused. When he did chip in, he never used a superfluous word, and spoke very much to the point."

By and large, the Russians made more concessions than the West, and when they presented their own proposals, they were, in fact, sometimes simply returning proposals delivered to them at earlier dates by the Western powers.

The Russians, remembering their difficulties in the League of Nations, which culminated in their expulsion, were worried that they would find themselves isolated in a new international organization controlled by the United States and the United Kingdom through their allies, clients, dominions, and "Good Neighbors." The Russians accepted an American compromise, whereby the Great Powers retained a veto in the Security Council, and the Western leaders agreed to support the admission of two or three constituent Soviet republics. The British won assent to a modified Great Power role for France, including both a zone of occupation in Germany and participation on the German Control Commission.

Roosevelt successfully pushed for a "Declaration on Liberated Europe," an ill-defined lever for Western intervention in Eastern Europe, but which mainly interested Roosevelt as a device to satisfy public opinion at home. He took it up only after he had turned down a more binding State Department proposal for a High Commission on Liberated Areas because "he preferred a more flexible arrangement." Accord also followed on a number of less pressing points.

Two issues proved more difficult: the central question of Germany and the endless Polish imbroglio. Poland, the emblem of the early Cold War, took up more time than any other issue at the conference. The Allies did agree that the Russian-Polish border should be moved westward, to the Curzon Line, and, though not in very precise terms, further consented to compensation for Poland in the form of what had been German territory on its west.

More difficult was the nature of Poland's new government, that is, whether to install the Western-supported London exile government, bitterly anti-Soviet, or the Lublin government, little more than a Soviet puppet.

Britain went to war so "that Poland should be free and sovereign," said Churchill. Britain's only interest, he assured the other leaders, was "one of honor because we drew the sword for Poland against Hitler's brutal attack." Of course, he added, Polish independence could not be a cover for "hostile designs" against the Soviet Union.

Stalin, however, was still interested in practical arithmetic. "For Russia it is not only a question of honor but of security." As to honor—"We shall have to eliminate many things from the books." As to security—"Not only because we are on Poland's frontier but also because throughout history Poland has always been a corridor for attack on Russia." Twice in the last thirty years "our German enemy has passed through this corridor."

Churchill replied that he himself had little fondness for the London Poles, which was one element in the general weakness of the Western position on the Polish question. "Admittedly," a British diplomat commented, "Uncle Joe's masterly exposition of the Russian attitude over Poland sounded sincere, and as always was hyperrealistic."

At last, the Allies agreed to "reorganize" the Lublin government with some men from London and from the Polish underground, but details were left to Molotov and the two Allied ambassadors in Moscow to work out.

For Germany, the Russians pushed for dismemberment; in substance, their proposal was the suggestion Roosevelt had made at Tehran. The two Western governments went along, reluctantly.

The Russians also insisted on receiving reparations from Germany. Postwar planning in the U.S. had generally rejected reparations. America certainly had no need for reparations; and reparations had been in bad repute in both Britain and the United States since J. M. Keynes' *Economic Consequences of the Peace*, published shortly after the First World War. "We are against reparations," Roosevelt had bluntly said before Yalta.

At Yalta, however, the Western countries met a Soviet Union urgently determined to exact reparations. As early as September 1941, in conversations with Averell Harriman and Lord Beaverbrook, Stalin had asked flatly: "What about getting the Germans to pay for the damage?" Stalin's "second revolution" had been an industrial revolution, an upheaval that had cost much in human life and in the manner in which the survivors lived. Stalin's interest in reparations was compensatory as well as punitive; he wanted help in the huge task of reconstruction that lay ahead. By 1945, the Germans had wrought enormous destruction. Twenty million people had been killed—though it was years before the Kremlin revealed the full magnitude. Seven million horses had been lost, as were 20 out of 23 million pigs. Destroyed were 4.7 million houses, 1710 towns, and 70,000 villages. Twenty-five million people were homeless. Sixty-five thousand kilometers of railway tracks had been ruined; 15,800 locomotives and 428,000 freight cars had been either demolished or damaged.

Here, however, the Soviet concern went beyond the simple arithmetic of devastation. Reading through the minutes of meeting upon meeting during the war and after, the historian must conclude that reparations were not only a central issue, but also a highly significant symbol in Moscow's postwar vision—although always only of peripheral interest to the Americans. Perhaps the Russians could never understand the nature of American concern for Eastern Europe; similarly, the Americans could never comprehend the emotional intensity the Russians attached to reparations. Reparations may well have been as much a "test case" for the Russians as Eastern Europe was to become for the Americans.

At Yalta, Churchill adamantly opposed reparations, warning that England "would be chained to a dead body of Germany." Concerned about economic consequences and criticism at home, Roosevelt wavered until Hopkins shoved him a note: "The Russians have given in so much at this conference that I don't think we should let them down." The President finally agreed to set $20 billion, half for the Russians, as the basis for further discussions, though with the understanding that reparations were to be in goods, production, and equipment, and not in cash. . . .

Roosevelt was a realist; he knew that everything depended upon implementation of the accords, and that, in turn, would depend upon intentions and future alignments. He was gambling. He hinted at this caution in a note he scribbled to his wife the day he left Yalta: "We have wound up the conference—successfully I think."

That said, there can be no question but that Roosevelt departed the Crimea optimistic and satisfied. Basing his conclusions on conversations with Roosevelt, Admiral [William] Leahy decided that Roosevelt had "no regrets about what the Russians were to get. He thought they were valid claims." But FDR's satisfaction extended beyond the agreements themselves. He regarded the conference as a hopeful answer to the question about postwar cooperation with Russia that he had posed to Eden two years earlier, in the course of their after-dinner survey. This summit meeting in the Crimea had been a testing and, more important, a confirmation of what we might thus call Franklin Roosevelt's "Yalta axioms."

Stalin himself had gone out of his way to endorse the premise that underlay FDR's Grand Design. The dictator had pointed to "a more serious question" than an international organization. One should not worry too much about small nations. "The greatest danger was conflict between the three Great Powers." The main task was to prevent their quarreling and "secure their unity for the future."

It is true that Roosevelt, once home, delivered a speech to Congress, pure in its Wilsonianism, in which he declared that Yalta spelled the end of unilateral action, exclusive alliances, spheres of influence, power blocs, and "all other expedients that had been tried for centuries—and have always failed."

But, out of public earshot, he continued to stress the realities of power and the basic structure of a Great Power consortium. Two days after his speech to Congress, talking privately about Germany, he said, "Obviously the Russians are going to do things their own way in the areas they occupy." But he hoped that a general framework of collaboration would prevent the Soviet sphere of influence from becoming a sphere of control. . . .

[V. M.] Molotov saw the President [Truman] at five-thirty on April 23, [1945]. Struggling to follow Davies' advice in an unexpectedly tense situation, he tried to outline the Russian case, especially on the Polish question.

The President, however, was in no mood for ambiguities. Three days before, having discussed matters with Harriman and Stettinius, he had declared: "We could not, of course, expect to get 100 percent of what we wanted," but he felt that "on important matters . . . we should be able to get 85 percent." Now, bent on obtaining that chunk, Truman brushed over Molotov's statement and instead lectured the Russian in what Leahy described as "plain American language." The Russians had to stick to their agreements, as interpreted in Washington. Relations could no longer be "on the basis of a one-way street."

Molotov turned white at the dressing down. "I have never been talked to like that in my life," he said.

"Carry out your agreements and you won't get talked to like that," Truman replied curtly.

Those who had urged their views on Truman were pleased by his performance. Leahy noted in his diary that the "President's strong American stand" left the Russians only two courses of action: "either to approach closely to our expressed policy in regard to Poland" or to drop out of the new international organization. He went on to add: "The President's attitude was more than pleasing to me, and I believe it will have a beneficial effect on the Soviet attitude toward the rest of the world. They have always known we have the power, and now they should know that we have the determination to insist upon the declared right of all people to choose their own form of government." On the same day, Eden had assured Churchill that "the new President is not to be bullied by the Soviets."

Arnold A. Offner

HARRY S TRUMAN AS PAROCHIAL NATIONALIST

As chief diplomat for the United States at a time of wrenching change and critical decisions, President Harry S Truman commands our attention. Some admiring historians have claimed that he prevented a third world war through courageous, sensible, and necessary policies in the face of aggressive foreign adversaries; others have concluded that he contributed greatly to the onset of a Cold War that might have been tempered through cautious and patient diplomacy. Who was Harry S Truman, what were his assumptions, and did his style of leadership matter? More generally, what weight do we give to a powerful individual in an explanation of postwar world conflict that also includes analysis of competing national interests and ideologies and of international systemic causes? (Arthur M. Schlesinger, Jr., asks the same questions above about Joseph Stalin). Arnold A. Offner tackles such questions in a critical study of Truman as a parochial nationalist who seemed better suited to Missouri politics than to global politics.

Arnold A. Offner, professor of history at Boston University, is writing a study of Harry S Truman and the transformation of American foreign policy. Among his published works are *American Appeasement: United States Foreign Policy and Germany, 1933–1938* (1969), which won the Phi Alpha Theta Book Award for the best first book that year, and *The Origins of the Second World War: American Foreign Policy and World Politics, 1917–1941* (1975).

From the initial American-Soviet confrontations in Europe at the end of the Second World War through the bitter Korean War, President Harry S Truman directed American foreign policy in a manner that profoundly affected the nation's—and the world's—history. In recent years President Truman's public reputation has grown extremely high. During his last year in office, however, pollsters found that his "favorable" rating among the public had plummeted to a mere 25 percent, with about 55 percent rating his performance negatively. So bad was it that Democratic party leaders urged him not to seek reelection in 1952.

"The Truman Myth Revealed: From Parochial Nationalist to Cold Warrior." Revised paper first presented at the Annual Meeting of Organization of American Historians, March 1988. Copyright Arnold Offner. Reprinted with permission of the author.

Truman's low standing derived largely, or course, from the alleged "loss" of China to a communist regime in 1949; the stalemate in Korea that had cost over 50,000 American lives; Senator Joseph R. McCarthy's wild charges that communists had subverted the government; and scandals in the Internal Revenue Service and Justice Department. In sum, Truman bore the blame for the oft-proclaimed "mess in Washington."

Within a decade after he departed the White House, however, historians began to reclassify him as a "near great" president who had preserved New Deal reforms at home and the essential areas of freedom abroad. Meanwhile, Truman rose to near mythic status in American public-political life. His former White House Counsel, Clark Clifford, later celebrated Truman's "4 a.m. courage" to make brave decisions. Popular writers depicted the former President as the allegory of American life: a man nurtured on work, duty, and morality who overcame adversity from childhood through presidency. Presidents, or candidates for the job, including Gerald Ford, Jimmy Carter, Walter Mondale, and Ronald Reagan, all claimed to be latter-day Trumans. And in 1986 Britain's Roy Jenkins, a longtime Labour Party Member of Parliament and Cabinet officer turned biographer, would pen the ultimate compliment: Truman was "a backwoods politician who became a world statesman."

Despite this extraordinary bipartisan consensus, analysis of Truman's background and recently available personal and governmental records reveal a darker side to his world view and foreign policy. His parochial nationalist heritage, his perceptions about American moral-industrial-military superiority, his belief that the Soviet Union and communism were the root cause of all international problems, his quick disregard of contrary views, and his propensity to exaggerate and to oversimplify, profoundly shaped his presidential policies and contributed significantly to the onset and intensification of the Cold War.

Truman's image of his childhood in Independence, Missouri, was that of a bucolic world of family, farm, jams and pies, youthful pranks, and Baptist religiousness. It was, he recalled, "the happiest childhood that could ever be imagined." In fact, Truman imagined much of it. For example, young Harry's farsightedness and thick glasses, diphtheria and temporary paralysis cut him off from his peers and their rough-housing, and later he endured their jeers about his "sissy" piano-playing. Truman was also alienated from his father, John Truman, despite recollecting him as a man who did a day's work for a day's pay and whose guarantee of a horse in a trade was as "good as a bond." But John Truman, a feisty man-on-the-make, always favored Harry's younger, more robust brother, Vivian, and took him—not Harry—into business ventures. Harry further recalled that when he fell off a pony his father made him walk home—crying all the way—and that his father's scolding hurt more than his mother's spanking.

Young Harry's ambivalent relationship with his peers and father inspired both anguished inferiority and a sense of worship regarding powerful men. He denounced the "striped pants boys" in the State Department; the "brass hats" and "prima donnas" in the military; and political "fakirs" such as Theodore and Franklin Roosevelt. Yet Truman also idolized Tom Pendergast, his political mentor and boss of the Kansas City Democratic machine, who allegedly made decisions and always kept his word. Similarly, Truman always accorded great deference and authority over foreign policy to leading officials in his administration such as Ambassador to the Soviet Union W. Averell Harriman; Secretary of State Dean Acheson; and Secretary of State, and then Secretary of Defense, General George C. Marshall. The president also naively likened Joseph Stalin to Pendergast, and probably felt even more betrayed when the Soviet leader allegedly broke his word—or "contract"—over Poland, Iran, or Germany.

Young Harry took his nurturing from his mother, who taught him his "letters" and inspired his book and Bible reading. Later he admonished people and nations by frequent reference to the Ten Commandments and the Sermon on the Mount. But Truman derived less a system of morals or religious sense from his Biblical readings than stern belief, as he wrote in 1945, that "punishment always followed transgression," a maxim he would apply later to North Korea and to the People's Republic of China.

Truman also remembered that his mother and aunt changed churches often because they were filled with "liars and hypocrites," and that when he was fourteen years old he saw his boss in a drugstore dispense whiskey in unmarked bottles from under the counter to "amen-corner-praying-churchmen" and Anti-Saloon Leaguers who lacked courage to drink in the saloons of Independence. In sum, young Truman's world was filled with "liars and hypocrites"—terms he later thought appropriate for critics of Boss Pendergast and President Truman.

Young Harry imbibed maxims about courage and chivalry, and gained a sense of the globe, from reading history and biography—

notably Plutarch's *Lives* and C. F. Horne's 1894 didactic, four-volume *Great Men and Famous Women*. But if Truman always remembered the soldiers and statesmen—"captains of history"—he forgot the women, workers, artists, and writers. The tales of glory further heightened his defensiveness about his humble origins and later failings in farming, mining, shopkeeping, and politics.

His reading also inspired his excessively romantic and personalized sense of history; his exaggerated view that history was basically cyclical and that all current events had precise parallels or analogues in the past; and his naive belief that the "true facts" could resolve any dispute and that the "lessons of history" were the key to wise policy choices.

Truman's history provided little concept of ideology, shades of truth, or multiple perceptions. Thus in 1945 the new president was "amazed" that the Yalta accords that Roosevelt, Churchill, and Stalin had signed in February 1945 were so "hazy" and that every reading provided "new meanings." Shortly, Truman and his aides would un-critically apply inexact analogies about 1930s appeasement of Germany (especially the Munich Conference) and Japan to postwar crises with the Soviet Union.

Truman's early writings reveal his parochial nationalism. His casual language included "nigger," "coon," "Chink doctor," "dago," "Jew clerk," and "Kike town." As he wrote to his sweetheart, Elizabeth (Bess) Wallace in 1911, one man was as good as another if he was honest and decent and "not a nigger or a Chinaman." He confessed that he "hate(d) Chinese and Japs," even though this was "race prejudice." But he felt "strongly" that "negroes ought to be in Africa, yellow men in Asia, and white men in Europe and America."

Shortly afterwards he said that it was a "disgrace" that there were more "bohunks and 'Rooshans' " than white men in Montana. He regretted that the United States had not halted immigration in the 1880s so that "good Americans" could have had all the land, and he insisted that the growth of cities, factories, and teeming masses, had created a "depressed" and class-ridden society. In young Harry's eyes, for-eigners and modernization had despoiled Jeffersonian America.

Truman was ambivalent about farm and family life. He despaired at not making a dollar or personal mark as a farmer. "They say debts give a man energy—I ought to be a shining example of that quality if they do," he wrote in 1911. He was soon embittered when his mother had to buy out five siblings who contested her inheritance of the family farm, leaving Harry and his "Mamma" with a "backbreaking" $30,000 mortgage. Harry incurred more debts when he lost much of Mamma's capital in 1916–1917 in mining failures, and then in oil ventures that succeeded only after he had sold out and gone off to war. Truman concluded that ethics and rewards did not mix.

At age thirty-three Harry Truman left family, farm, and beloved fiancée to enlist in World War I. He sought to emulate "Galahad after the Grail," or to fulfill the legend of Cincinnatus, the 5th century B.C. farmer-soldier who saved Rome from foreign invaders. Lieutenant Truman ran an Army canteen successfully, shaped up the rowdy "Boys from Battery D," and saved their skins in the "Battle of Who Run" in the Vosges Mountains in Alsace in 1918 by turning a panicked retreat into a hold-the-line regrouping. He earned his promotion to captain.

But parochialism shone through Captain Harry's European experience, and not just because he may have been the only soldier in history to call the Folies Bergère "disgusting." Truman deplored France's "narrowly dirty streets and malodorous atmosphere," disliked French food, insisted that Germany smelled and that the Kaiser aimed to despoil "our great country and beautiful women." Further, "Galahad" quickly tired of fighting for principles, and did not care about the peace terms (except that the Germans deserved a "bayonet peace") or whether the Russian government was "Red" or "Purple." Truman sought only to return to "God's country," the land of "Liberty loans and green trading stamps," and never to return to Europe: "I have nearly promised old Miss Liberty that she'll have to turn around to see me again," he wrote upon reaching American shores in 1919.

In the 1920s Truman viewed the members of the newly formed American Legion as "the cream of the country," and he awaited their running it. Like many border-state politicians, he was prepared to join the Ku Klux Klan, but his initiation dues were returned because he refused to deny jobs to Catholics. Truman became a highly successful presiding judge of Jackson County, overseeing with great integrity construction of public buildings and roads. But he longed for material reward and higher office, which always seemed to go to hypocrites. "Tomorrow I'll be forty-nine," he wrote in 1933, "but for all the good I have done the forty might as well be left off." He was ready to leave office—to run a filling station and then go to "a quiet grave." Perhaps his lament at that time—"I am only a small duck in a very large puddle"—might apply to his presidency.

Luck struck the Missourian in 1934, however. After four Democrats refused their party's nomination, Truman became the

"Senator from Pendergast," as some politicos derisively referred to him. Indeed, Truman was an outsider in Washington: President Roosevelt ignored him in the 1930s, and he remained contemptuous of "professional liberals" and New Deal "crackpots." Truman also evidenced his nationalism when he praised the New Deal for redistributing wealth more peacefully than "Russia, Germany, and Italy," and insisted that opponents of Roosevelt's 1937 plan to "pack" the Supreme Court were "Tories" and "Reds" who sought the "break-down of American institutions."

Truman had long identified with Woodrow Wilson's League of Nations and emphasis on reduced trade barriers. He also backed Roosevelt's foreign policy initiatives, from his 1935 proposal that the United States join the World Court, through revision of the Neutrality Laws to allow "cash-and-carry" sale of munitions to opponents of Nazi Germany, to passage of Lend-Lease aid in 1941. "I am no appeaser," Truman proclaimed, and he was not.

But the senator's internationalism had a parochial underside. He emphasized military preparedness, and he insisted that Americans earlier had gone "hysterical on disarmament" and were still restrained by a "small and vociferous pacifist group." He called " 'outlawry' " of war "a silly phrase." Disarmament—or "sinking our navy"—was "fol-de-rol." He was too quick to blame international conflict on "outlaws," "thugs," "savages," and "totalitarians," and he was indifferent to the attack that General Francisco Franco led on Spain's Republican government during that country's tragic civil war. Truman wanted America to stay aloof from Europe's "brawls, hates, and prejudices."

During 1939 he naively tried to enlist Roosevelt in a peace initiative with a group that viewed Hitler as a bulwark against Bolshevism, and in a June 1940 radio broadcast Truman warned that Russia and Japan were at Alaska's doorway. He also urged that America put an end to "fifth column activities" and deport its "disloyal inhabitants."

After Germany attacked the Soviet Union in June 1941, Truman made his famous, hasty remark that "if we see Germany is winning we ought to help Russia and that if Russia is winning we ought to help Germany and that way let them kill as many as possible"—although he did not want Hitler to win under any circumstance. He backed Lend-Lease for the Russians—but insisted that they were as untrustworthy as "Hitler and Al Capone." And it was not long before he would begin to assail the "twin blights—atheism and communism."

Thus the evidence weighs heavily, despite Truman's strong support for a United Nations and for a Foreign Economic Commission to end "political nationalism and economic imperialism," that the man who suddenly became president in April 1945 was less an incipient internationalist and more a parochial nationalist. Above all, he was given to excessive fear that enemies from within and without, combined with renewed appeasement and lack of preparedness, would ruin America's mission (the "Lord's will") to "win the peace" on its principles.

Truman's parochialism immediately marked his choice of advisers and advice, policy and decisions. In spring 1945 Truman talked obsessively about "loyalty"; told his Cabinet officers that they had been appointed to carry out his orders; and said that he would run Cabinet meetings as had President Lincoln, whose sole "yes" vote meant that "the Ayes have it." Later Truman charged with disloyalty the senior officials with whom he had policy disputes: Secretary of State James Byrnes in 1945; Secretary of Commerce Henry Wallace in 1946; Secretary of Defense Louis Johnson in 1950; and General Douglas MacArthur in 1950–1951.

Truman also reviled public disputants: the "Crazy American Communist" who was "loyal to Stalin and not to the President," and who should be deported to Russia. He also had "no more use for Polish-Americans, Irish-Americans, Swedish-Americans or any other sort of hyphenate. . . . They all have some other loyalty than the one they should have." Similarly, Jews who lobbied over Palestine were "European conspirators," and they were never pleased, "even by Christ," while Truman dismissed representations from New York Senators Robert Wagner and James Mead: "I'm not a New Yorker. . . . I am an American."

The new president also feared that both Churchill and Stalin sought to make him "the paw of the cat" to pull their chestnuts out of the fire. Churchill was "too clever," given to "hooey" and "soft soap," and while initially Truman claimed to like Stalin ("the little son of a bitch"), the Soviet regime was "totalitarian" and based on "lies"; sustained itself at home with "clubs, pistols, and concentration camps"; intended to attack Iran and Turkey; and was as expansionist as the tsars. As for France's leader, General Charles de Gaulle, he was a "son-of-a-bitch" and "psychopath," and the French needed to be "castrated."

In July 1945 Truman met with Churchill and Stalin at Potsdam. The President was bent on fighting solely for American interests: "win, lose or draw—and we must win." "Santa Claus is dead," he said, and

Europe's starving millions had to help themselves. Never again would America "pay reparations, feed the world, and get nothing for it but a nose thumbing."

Atomic diplomacy—but *not* blackmail—was Truman's key to victory. "I have an ace in the hole *and another one showing*," he said of the atomic bomb, which inspired such new confidence that he believed he could press European negotiations to "impasse" and gain his way on German reparations, Poland, and Italy.   Further, use of the bomb would cause Japan to "fold up" before the Russians entered the Pacific war—thus he could "out maneuver" them in China and in Japan.

In September 1945 Truman backed Byrnes' "bomb in his pocket" diplomacy at the London foreign ministers' meeting with parochial advice: "stick to your guns" and "Give Em Hell." The president also sided with provincial advisers who opposed international atomic controls by conjuring misleading analogies about interwar disarmament and insisting that America's technological-industrial genius assured perpetual atomic supremacy.   Truman said similarly that America was the world's "trustee" for atomic power; that it had to preserve the bomb's "secret"; and that other nations had to catch up "on their own hook"— but America "would stay ahead" in any arms race.

Truman acceded shortly to a proposal from Dean Acheson and David Lilienthal (head of the Tennessee Valley Authority) that held the prospect of international atomic control.   But then Truman appointed as his chief atomic negotiator Bernard Baruch, whose emphasis on inspections, sanctions, and no veto minimized chances of Soviet agreement.   And as deadlock neared in July 1946, the poker-playing president told Baruch to "stand pat."   Truman also ruled out collaborating with the British.

Meanwhile, Byrnes had made progress in Moscow in December 1945 regarding drafting of European peace treaties and a credible Korean compromise, while America prevailed in China and Japan, and Russia in Bulgaria and Rumania.   But conservative critics quickly incited the president to see this Yalta-style accord as "appeasement."   Thus in his famous letter to Byrnes of January 5, 1946, the President denounced Russian "outrage[s]" in the Baltic, Germany, Poland, and Iran, and intent to invade Turkey and seize the Straits.   The Russians understood only an "iron fist" and "divisions," he insisted, and he was tired of "babying" them.   Clearly, two months before Churchill's Iron Curtain speech, the President made his personal declaration of Cold War.

Two other 1946 events reveal Truman's parochial mindset. First was his firing of Henry Wallace, the leading, and now last, New Deal cabinet official. In lengthy memoranda to Truman in March and July, Wallace had urged greater political, economic, and atomic accord with the Russians, and he also criticized American military spending, atomic tests, and search for bases. Then in a speech in September he contravened Byrnes' recent address in Stuttgart that had proposed reconstruction of western Germany, with continued American military presence. Clearly, Wallace was not long for the cabinet.

But more disturbing, Truman never gave serious thought or reply to Wallace's memoranda. Further, regardless of whether Truman had read Wallace's speech in advance "page by page" (as Wallace claimed) or barely had time to skim it (as Truman said), the president had to know that the Wallace-Byrnes jurisdictional-substantive disputes were irreconcilable, and would create public uproar. And when the time came to fire Wallace, rage replaced reason. Truman damned him as "a pacifist 100 per cent" who wanted America to disband its military and give its atomic secrets to Kremlin "adventurers." In Truman's mind, Wallace was more dangerous than German-Americans who had supported Hitler in the 1930s, and now the "Reds" and the "phonies" had become a "national danger," a "sabotage front for Uncle Joe Stalin comprised of all the Artists with a capital A, parlor pinks, and soprano-voiced men."

Significantly, at this time Truman received both the "Russian Report" of his chief White House aide, Clark Clifford, and a copy of the alleged "political testament" of Tsar Peter the Great. The Russian Report, drawn after Truman complained that he was tired of being "pushed around" by the "chiseling" Russians, was a composite of senior diplomatic and military officials' assessments of Soviet aims and policies. These officials provided highly exaggerated, or "worst-case," analyses. In their view, the Soviets sought unlimited expansion from Europe to Asia; maintained a permanent warfare state; could mobilize better than democratic America (despite the World War II "miracle of production"); and had inspired the recent industrial strikes in America and the desegregation and demobilization conflicts in the armed forces.

Tsar Peter's "will"—equal to any worst-case scenario—revealed the Russian ruler's alleged eighteenth-century exhortation to his people to insinuate into Baltic, German, and Polish state affairs; to vanquish Persia and Turkey and press on to India; and then to use their Baltic and Black Sea bases—and "Asiatic hordes"—to conquer Europe.

Astonishingly, while Truman held that the Russian Report was too "hot" to be circulated, he did not ask even one question about the Report's hypothesis-conclusion that Soviet policy was solely an aggressive amalgam of Russian imperialism and communist commitment to world revolution. Truman also took Peter's will at face value, although it was a very old forgery drawn up by anti-Russian French officials and Polish emigrés. Further, Truman soon wrote that the governments of the tsars, Soviets, and Hitler were the same; and in 1948 he replied to a critic of his foreign policy that Russian leaders had "fixed ideas . . . set down by Peter the Great in his will—I suggest that you read it." Soon told of the forgery, Truman denied that the will had influenced his policy.

By early 1947, however, Truman had already brought a near end to diplomacy with the Soviets. In his epoch-making speech on March 14, 1947, the president called for $400 million in aid—mostly military—to Greece and to Turkey to help "free peoples" resist "totalitarianism." The Truman Doctrine clearly overstated the global-ideological aspects of Soviet-American conflict, but as presidential aide Clark Clifford said, the speech was intended to be "the opening gun" in a campaign to make the American people realize that "the war isn't over by any means."

Indeed, Truman told his cabinet that he faced the "greatest selling job ever" because this was "only the beginning" of the "U.S. going into European politics." Hence in the spring of 1947 he repeatedly stated that he saw no difference between "totalitarian or police states, call them what you will, Nazi, Fascist, Communist," and that the time had come "to state our case to the world." The Soviets had broken every agreement from Potsdam to the present, he claimed, and now it was necessary to use "other methods. They understand one language, and that is the language they are going to get from me from this point." Or as Dean Acheson declared: it was impossible to negotiate with the Soviets: "You cannot sit down with them."

The president also dismissed Truman Doctrine critics as "the American Crackpots Association" represented by Wallace, Senator Claude Pepper (Florida), and "all the actors and artists in immoral Greenwich Village." Resistant congressmen were "ignorant demagogues." And in March 1947 Truman also signed Executive Order 9835, which made the basis for dismissal from employment in federal executive departments and agencies "reasonable grounds" for belief that a person was "disloyal" to the government.

The president's executive order was partly a reaction to Congress's pressure over atomic spying. But Truman's own concern about "loyalty"—political and personal—revealed his parochial outlook, and his administration now introduced an unprecedented program that confused the separate issues of loyalty and security, jettisoned basic legal procedural safeguards for the accused, and included a virtual presumption of guilt. The program was a civil liberties travesty, as well as a harbinger of the coming McCarthyism and purges of State Department experts on Asia, scene of America's later great tragedy. Clearly the events of March 1947, as Britain's ambassador in Washington wrote his government, provided "striking evidence" of how far American fear of communism at home and abroad had progressed.

The Truman administration's greatest disaster, of course, came in autumn 1950. Then, following its intervention in the Korean War in June 1950, it sought to reunify Korea by force, i.e., to destroy the North Korean state. Here Truman hoped to have punishment follow transgression, or to turn containment into liberation. But the People's Republic of China (PRC) entered the war in late November, forcing America's bitter retreat and throwing Truman's foreign and domestic policies into disarray, despite his having the United Nations brand the PRC an aggressor, and his insistence that the PRC was a Russian satellite intent on conquering Southeast Asia.

Beneath the facade of calm crisis management, moreover, Truman fantasized in 1952 about giving Russia and China ten days to quit Korea, or face "all out war" in which he would destroy every major Soviet and Chinese city from "St. Petersburg" to Vladivostok, and from Peking [Beijing] to Shanghai. "This is the final chance for the Soviet Government to decide whether it wants to survive or not," he wrote privately.

It would be unfair to close with a final image of Harry Truman as a man of apocalyptic vision. (He once wrote that two world wars were enough for him.) But the conclusion seems inescapable that Truman was a man of narrow vision, frequently unable to see beyond the immediate decision, or to visualize alternative courses of action. As Wallace and others noted, Truman was often eager to decide before thinking, and was untroubled that his mind traveled in "different directions . . . almost simultaneously." Or, as a British diplomat once observed, the president often had a "staggering disregard" for the implications of what he was saying. And scholars have documented his penchant for simplis tic historical analogizing that obstructed patient diplomacy and exacerbated Cold War tensions.

Further, Truman assumed that the United States' moral-industrial-military superiority assured his ability to order the postwar world on American terms. He quickly disregarded contrary views, impugned his critics' loyalty, and judged that Stalin had violated every agreement from Teheran in 1943 to Potsdam in 1945 and beyond. Truman failed to consider how American policies might have contributed to the Cold War. And the outgoing president remained convinced, as he wrote in his undelivered farewell address, that "Russia was at the root" of all the problems in France, Italy, Greece, Turkey, Iran, and China. But he exulted—defensively—that "Trumanism" had saved these countries from Soviet invasion and that he had "knocked the socks off the communists" in Korea and elsewhere.

The scholar must conclude that the president who spoke proudly of his knowledge of the past had little insight into the history unfolding around him. He was not only a local man thrust onto the national-international scene, but a parochial nationalist in a cosmopolitan world of atomic power, superpower rivalry, and revolutionary upheaval. Harry S Truman lacked the presidential vision and leadership needed to resolve, or at least ameliorate, postwar crises. Instead, he heightened the conflicts that gave rise to the Cold War.

Konstantin V. Pleshakov

JOSEPH STALIN'S WORLD VIEW

Until Mikhail Gorbachev launched *glasnost* (liberalization of the political system) in the Soviet Union in the late 1980s, Soviet historians largely followed the politically safe practice of not criticizing past Soviet diplomatic behavior and of blaming the Cold War on the United States. The Soviets, in short, had their "traditionalists" too. More balanced and more searching Soviet scholarship is now emerging. Although Soviet criticisms of Joseph Stalin as a leader became familiar after Premier Nikita Khrushchev denounced him in 1956, ardent defenses of the Soviet record in world affairs continued. In the following *glasnost*-era essay, Soviet scholar Konstantin V. Pleshakov explores the roots of Stalin's world view and

"Stalin i Amerika," by K. V. Pleshakov, in the journal *USA: Economy, Ideology, Policy* No. 12, 1989, pp. 52–61. Translated by Maria Miller.

emphasizes the Soviet leader's commitment to "revolutionism" and "great-powerism." Pleshakov criticizes Stalin for misinterpreting the "West," and he chides Americans for their misconceptions about the Soviet Union. Neither side would meet the other halfway. Pleshakov also appreciates how Americans might have become alarmed by Stalin's calls for world revolution and "a peaceful division of the world." And the Soviet scholar regrets that Stalin created a set of tenacious yet mistaken stereotypes about the United States and international relations that persisted in Soviet thinking until the 1980s.

Konstantin V. Pleshakov is a historian at the Institute of the USA and Canada, Academy of Sciences of the USSR, Moscow. He has written other essays on how the United States and the Soviet Union have perceived each other in the Cold War.

One of the buttresses of our [Soviet] world view is our attitude toward America, our conception of an optimal model of interaction with that country. [Joseph] Stalin undoubtedly laid down many of the principles of our foreign policy, including those pertaining to the United States. Echoes of his world view resound a third of a century after the death of "the leader of nations." Looking back therefore on the path we have traveled, and striving to understand how we have served the cause of peace—and conversely, how we have hindered it—we cannot avoid the topic of Stalin and America. In considering the origins of the Cold War, we must discover for ourselves not only George Kennan's "Long Telegram" but also postwar Stalin himself.

Stalin's foreign-policy ideas may be likened to an iceberg whose main part is hidden under water. Inasmuch as the visible tip of the iceberg seemed respectable enough, we have until recently allowed ourselves to scrutinize every aspect of Stalin except the theory and practice of his foreign policy. Only today do we seem to agree that the USSR's foreign policy was not always "consistent" and "Leninist peace-loving." But to separate the wheat from the chaff, we must first understand the sources of Stalin's world view, and this is not an easy task.

Stalin's foreign policy views cannot be reconstructed solely on the basis of his speeches, interviews, and articles. It is essential to make scholarly use of material published in the West, including memoirs, diplomatic dispatches, journalists' impressions, and—it is high time we turned to it—the [Leon] Trotsky archive at Harvard University. We must also do research in our country's own archives: party archives and the archives of the Ministry of Defense and the KGB. True, eyewitnesses testify that "compromising documents" of the Stalin era were destroyed, both at the time and later, under [Nikita] Khrushchev and [Leonid] Brezhnev. Perhaps the archives of other socialist countries will prove more promising. Or were documents destroyed simultaneously there and in Moscow?

In any case, today [1989] we must resort to "paleontologists' methods" [i.e., deduce conclusions from tiny bits of evidence] in interpreting Stalin's known pronouncements in the light of realpolitik and the international situation of those years.

Stalin's foreign-policy ideas revolved around two suns—revolutionism (which some also call revolutionary romanticism) and Russian "great-powerism." Like a complex planetary orbit, his thoughts about foreign policy at times inclined closer to one sun or the other; sometimes one of the suns was completely hidden behind the horizon or eclipsed by the other. But each sun was always there, revealing itself by an invisible but powerful field of gravity. Today [1989], when demands are heard to censure the USSR's treaties with fascist Germany and Stalin's territorial expansion in 1939–1945, it seems inappropriate to talk of Stalin's revolutionism. What kind of revolutionism can a monster have? But even monsters can have ideologies and not just pathological complexes; the most striking examples—Ivan the Terrible and [Adolf] Hitler—were fanatics about their ideas.

It would be foolish to separate Stalin from the Marxist ideological mainstream: he was created by Marxism, and from the 1930s to the 1950s he shaped Marxism as much as he could. Marxism's foreign-policy philosophy was precisely revolutionary romanticism. The latter had its roots in the eighteenth century—in the French Revolution, which proclaimed France the "natural ally" of all free nations and conceived the idea of abolishing diplomatic relations in general, replacing them with a revolutionary war to liberate Europe. When [Karl] Marx and [Friedrich] Engels began the *Communist Manifesto* with the statement, "A specter is haunting Europe, the specter of communism" and ended it with the slogan "Workers of all countries, unite!" they were standing on more than half a century's tradition of revolutionary solidarity. The struggle for freedom in one European country became the common cause of the radical European intelligentsia. Moreover, by Marx and Engels's time, professional revolutionaries had emerged who fearlessly threw themselves into any revolutionary conflagration, be it in Poland, France, Italy, Greece, or Germany.

"The workers," proclaimed the *Manifesto*, "have no fatherland." In the nineteenth century, that seemed indeed to be the case. Even on the eve of World War I, it was unthinkable to the national social democratic parties of the various countries that war would divide them by trenches, forcing German social democrats to fire on French, Belgian, and Russian social democrats. Analogously, twenty-five years later, it seemed inconceivable to our people that German workers would fire on their "class brothers."

World revolution—that was the foreign policy desired by the Soviet Communist party in its years of revolutionary ferment. Therefore the Treaty of Brest-Litovsk [1918] was a personal tragedy not only for left-wing communists but also for victorious [V. I.] Lenin; in signing that treaty, the Bolsheviks allowed the imperialists to tear the European revolutionary movement to pieces. From the beginning, the Communist International [the Comintern] was conceived as the fighting headquarters of world revolution, and such it remained until the mid-1930s, when Stalin began playing his big "great power" game.

The poem "Grenada" by [the Russian poet] Mikhail Svetlov, reflecting the world view of a Red Army cavalryman, dates not from 1936 [during the Spanish Civil War], when the fascists were approaching Madrid, but from 1926, when people had not yet forgotten the romantic fever of the Russian Civil War [1918–1921]. Before dying in battle, the Red Army commander F. K. Mironov wrote to [Mikhail] Kalinin, Lenin, and Trotsky on March 30, 1921, "I want to believe that I will lead Red regiments to victory in Budapest, Bucharest. . . ."

Of course, every politician digests ideas, just as a silkworm feeds on a mulberry leaf, spinning a cocoon that will protect him from the outside world. For Stalin, world revolution was not quite what it was for Leon Trotsky, [Bulgarian communist leader] Georgi Dimitrov, or the poet Mikhail Svetlov. Stalin envisaged world revolution not as self-sacrificing aid to free the workers of other countries from exploitation, but rather as a boundless extension of the Russian Revolution and eventually as the creation of a revolutionary empire.

Need we speak of how this revolutionary romanticism frightened America, which as early as 1793 expelled Citizen Genêt, the emissary of the Convention [of the French Revolution]? Genêt essentially wanted to draw the USA into a new round of the revolutionary movement. Therefore, in establishing diplomatic relations with the USSR, Franklin Roosevelt insisted that [Soviet foreign minister] Maxim Litvinov's message [of agreement] include the following convoluted passage: the Soviet government pledges not to permit the formation or residence on its territory of any organization or group—and to prevent the activity on its territory of any organization or group, or of representatives or officials of any organization or group—which has as an aim the overthrow or the preparation for the overthrow of, or the bringing about by force of a change in, the political or social order of the whole or any part of the United States, its territories or possessions.

In the mid-1930s, attempting to escape diplomatic isolation, Stalin dissociated himself from world revolution in meetings with Western representatives, but he encountered considerable mistrust. On March 1, 1936, in his meeting with the American newspaper publisher Roy Howard, this dialogue occurred. . . . I have added my own parenthetical comments on the exchanges:

Stalin (reasonably): If you think that the Soviet people want to change by force the face of the surrounding nations, you are completely mistaken. The Soviet people of course want to see the face of surrounding nations change, but that is the affair of those nations. . . .

Howard (mistrustfully): Do you mean to say that the Soviet Union has given up its plans and intentions to carry out world revolution?

Stalin (without a trace of embarrassment): We never had such plans and intentions. (Let us recall that in 1925 Stalin announced at the Fourteenth Communist Party Congress: ". . . our country is the base of world revolution," and a year earlier he said, "Soviet power in Russia is the base, the bulwark, the refuge of the revolutionary movement of the entire world."

Howard (beginning to understand with whom he is dealing): It seems to me, Mr. Stalin, that the whole world has had a different impression for a long time.

Stalin (cheerfully): I consider that the result of misunderstanding.

Howard (trying to understand): A tragic misunderstanding?

Stalin (flippantly): No, a comic—(catching himself) rather, a tragicomic misunderstanding. (Later in the interview, Stalin announces:) You see, we Marxists believe that the revolution will occur in other countries as well. But it will occur only when the revolutionaries of those countries find it possible or necessary. The export of revolution—that's nonsense.

Howard (beginning to get angry, refers to Litvinov's written guarantees, cited above, and asks): Please, Mr. Stalin, explain to me why Mr. Litvinov signed this letter if fulfilling the obligations on this point is incompatible with the wishes of the Soviet Union or beyond its power. (Howard did not get an intelligible reply.)

Stalin's "profession of faith" deserves a commentary. What export of revolution is "nonsense" for Stalin? The export of revolution on the saddles of [Red Army officer Semyon] Budenny's calvary at that moment (1936)—that was certainly nonsense. But what is the distinction between the export of revolution and holding heated arguments over the way revolution should develop in a particular country, training cadres for such revolutions, sending recommendations and advisers to organize armed struggle, and regulating the policies of the communist parties of other countries? "Export of revolution" was indeed a dirty word, and Stalin shunned it, just as people did before and after him. Nevertheless, the Comintern was the true headquarters of world revolution, and the USSR was its base in plan and self-perception. Especially noteworthy is Stalin's phrase that the revolution will occur when "the revolutionaries of these countries find it possible or necessary." It never occurred to Stalin to speak of "the opinion of the workers"—or indeed of "the proletariat"—of those countries.

In 1939 Stalin made a tragic mistake. He calculated that the USSR's main enemy was the Western democracies, which wanted to incite Germany and Japan to attack the Soviet Union. To him, not Germany and Japan, but rather England, France, and the USA, were "warmongers accustomed to using others to pull their chestnuts out of the fire." Such a false world view may be explained by several factors.

First, Stalin hated the Entente as the main organizer of the Intervention [of 1918–1921]. There is a paradox here. He could not forget the presence of small detachments of American forces in Archangel and Vladivostok, whereas it was Germany that had occupied the Ukraine, Belorussia, and the Baltic coast, and Japan that had tried to conquer the [Russian] Far East. (The paradox may be explained by the Entente's support of counterrevolutionaries within Russia.)

Second, by imperial logic, Stalin evidently inherited the Romanovs' Germanophilism. It was strengthened by the successful partnership between the USSR and the Weimar Republic, by the two nations' solidarity in the face of the Versailles agreements, and to some extent by Trotsky's actions at Brest-Litovsk (where Stalin's sworn enemy had displayed a highly negative stance toward Germany as a negotiating partner).

Third, Stalin was much more hostile toward the "heresies" of social democracy, and toward democracy in general, than toward fascism.

At the Eighteenth Communist Party Congress [March 1939], D. Z. Manuilsky, the Soviet Union's representative in the Comintern, included in his speech a highly ambiguous point: "The biggest capitalist state in the world, the USA, defending its interests in Latin America against Germany, Italy, and Japan, which have been rapidly penetrating the area—as well as protecting its positions in the Philippines, in China, and in the Pacific against Japan—is *knocking together* with the Latin American countries a bloc of resistance to fascist expansion." This is both a negative assessment of efforts to resist expansion and a perception of the impending conflict as a war between two equally warlike coalitions.

Stalin himself declared at the Eighteenth Congress that the "suspicious racket" stirred up by the Anglo-French and North American press to the effect that Germany wanted to annex the Soviet Ukraine to the Carpatho-Ukraine [part of Czechoslovakia until 1938, when the territory was seized by Hungary] "aims to arouse the Soviet Union's fury against Germany, to poison the atmosphere, and to provoke a conflict with Germany *without apparent grounds*." Perhaps the Anglo-French and North American press did indeed have such grounds since, three years after Stalin's statement, the Soviet Ukraine was annexed to the Reich.

Stalin did not regard the USA as his number-one enemy. England held that spot. But neither did Stalin regard the United States as an ally against aggression. He could not foresee that the United States would become his primary foreign-policy concern: first as his chief hope, and then as his chief enemy.

Stalin's image of America was influenced by views that he had formed in the 1920s and 1930s.

Beginning in the 1920s, Stalin understood that the center of economic development had shifted from the Old World to the New. He expressed this idea at the Fourteenth Party Congress [1925], using the vulgar Marxist jargon of that time: "The center of financial might in the capitalist world, the center of financial exploitation of the entire world, has shifted from Europe to America. . . . This country is growing in all ways: in the sense of production, of trade, and of accumulation."

It was precisely with America that he meant to compete. At the Eighteenth Congress, M. G. Pervukhin, the People's Commissar of Power Plants and the Electrical Industry, spoke of the need to adopt American methods. V. A. Malyshev, the People's Commissar of Heavy Machine Building, added that "we lag behind America in our increase of output of machinery." The Congress also heard calls to overtake the USA in labor productivity and so forth.

In Soviet society at that time, a fairly positive image of America was taking shape. Of course, this was "the land of the yellow devil," but it was also the Mecca of the age of electricity and steel. The poet [Vladimir] Mayakovsky, who cannot be suspected of great liking for the West, also fell under the spell of the New World's material civilization. His "Brooklyn Bridge" is a paean to American industrial genius:

I too will spare no words

> about good things.

Blush

> at my praise,

>> go red as our flag,

however

> united-states

>> -of

-america you may be. . . .

In 1931 Stalin himself conceded that the USA had a certain dynamism (though he had reservations: "We have no special regard for all things American"; "we never forget that the USA is a capitalist country"):

> We have a high regard for American enterprise in all things—in industry, in technology, in literature, in life. . . . Among Americans there are many wholesome people in a spiritual and physical sense, wholesome in their approach to work, to business. We are sympathetic to this enterprise, to this simplicity. Despite the fact that America is a highly developed capitalist country, its industrial ethos and production skills have a democratic quality that is missing in the old European capitalist countries, where the spirit of the lordly feudal aristocracy lives on.

Stalin even perceived a similarity in the spiritual values of "his" society and that of America: "The philosophy of *weltschmerz* [sentimental pessimism] is not our philosophy. Let the waning and moribund grieve. Our philosophy is fairly accurately conveyed by the American [Walt] Whitman: 'We live, our crimson blood surges with the fire of our inexhaustible strength.'"

Moreover, Stalin was personally drawn to [Franklin D.] Roosevelt. Roosevelt was "a decisive and courageous politician. There is a philosophical system, solipsism, which maintains that man does not believe in the existence of an external world, but only in the self . . . but Roosevelt is obviously not an adherent of this strange theory. He is a realist and knows that reality is what he sees."

In his [1947] conversation with Harold Stassen, Stalin delivered an envious panegyric to the United States:

> America is protected by two oceans. On the north it is bounded by a weak country, Canada; on the south, by a weak country, Mexico. The United States has nothing to fear from them. After the American War for Independence, the USA saw no fighting for sixty years, enjoying peace. All this prompted the rapid development of the USA. More-over, the USA's population consists of people who long ago freed themselves from the oppression of kings and landed aristocracy. This circumstance also facilitated the rapid development of the USA.

And later in the interview Stalin continued: ". . . two of the USA's competitors on the world market—Japan and Germany—have been eliminated. As a result, the demand for American goods grows, and this creates favorable conditions for the development of the USA. Such markets as Europe, China, and Japan are open to the USA. This will help the USA. Such conditions have never before existed." Stalin supposed that now 20 percent of American production would be slated for export and was greatly astonished when Stassen told him that the figure was not more than 15 percent.

During the war it was precisely America and England that became Stalin's allies. Moreover, they unexpectedly acknowledged him as one of the arbiters of the fate of the postwar world. By his own logic they should have left him to his fate, allowing Hitler to destroy the workers' and peasants' state. This did not occur, however: the USA and England understood that they would not win the war without the USSR.

Having stood on the periphery of world politics, unable to influence it except by infiltrating "his" parties into foreign political life, Stalin unexpectedly became an equal among equals. At the pinnacle of power, three men—Stalin, Roosevelt, and [Winston S.] Churchill—decided the postwar structure of the world. But if Stalin's fate was to pursue great-power politics, how should he contrive not to lose out or miscalculate? Which was better: to pursue the phantom of world revolution, or to redivide spheres of influence, as was being done at Moscow, Tehran, Potsdam, and especially at Yalta? At the same time, he became convinced that the Western democracies were weak, that he was not obliged to play fair with them, that they respected only power, and that victors of course were not judged.

When Stalin hit upon the idea of prolonging the division of spheres of influence by the leaders' club, the Big Three, he of course counted on America as his main partner. At a meeting with his "constituents" [voters of the district Stalin represented in the Supreme Soviet] on February 9, 1946, Stalin enunciated his proposal for putting the postwar global structure on a nonconfrontational basis. "It might be possible to avoid military catastrophes if there were a way of periodically reapportioning raw materials and markets among countries in accordance with their economic importance, through agreements and peaceful decisions." This sentence captures the quintessence of Stalin's postwar view of the world.

In his talk with Stassen, Stalin made several suggestions that he thought would facilitate such cooperation. He accepted peaceful coexistence without reservation, and he affirmed "Lenin's view that it was both possible and desirable for two economic systems to cooperate." Stalin acknowledged that world capitalism had entered a period of relative stability and was developing far more rapidly than earlier; that is, he admitted the viability of capitalism. Stalin recognized the legitimacy of the American system, saying that it was "sanctioned by the people." He called for an end to the propaganda war—for ceasing to call the Soviet system "totalitarian" and "dictatorial" and for dropping references to the American system as "monopoly capitalism." He announced that he was not a propagandist but a "businesslike man," evidently trying to please American public opinion.

Stalin never suspected how close he came to getting [Harry S] Truman to like him. Even in 1949, when the Cold War was at its worst, Truman told his friend [Jonathan W.] Daniels, "I like Stalin. Stalin is as near like Tom Pendergast as any man I know" (the leader of the Democratic party organization in Missouri in the 1920s, known as an energetic and charming man but later removed in disgrace because of a scandal and accusations of corruption). A year earlier, in June 1948, Truman has said, "I like Old Joe. He's a decent fellow, but he's a prisoner of the politburo."

Stalin's plan for a peaceful division of the world did not materialize. Let us set aside the question of why the United States did not meet Stalin halfway. (We should merely note that the West harbored many false conceptions about Stalin and the USSR. To this day, Stalin's speech of February 9, 1946, is still regarded in the West as a declaration of the Cold War.) But despite his clear desire to achieve a repetition of the Congress of Vienna and to see himself in the role of Alexander I (with Churchill as [Clemens von] Metternich), why did Stalin not try more vigorously to meet the West halfway?

We may suppose the following. In the depths of his heart, Stalin did not believe that the capitalist system would endure. His blindness was caused by his revolutionism; he was convinced of the justice of the mid–nineteenth-century [Marxist] conclusion that capitalism was heading for collapse. In his conversation with Stassen, Stalin hopefully asked whether the USA was expecting an economic crisis. Stassen diplomatically answered that under regulated capitalism, a crisis could be avoided. Stalin retorted: "For that, a strong, highly resolute government is essential."

Stalin did not understand the nature of political power in the West. Stassen attempted to inform him of changes on the political scene in the USA, explaining that "the *New York Herald Tribune* is the leading Republican organ, becoming even more important now that the Republicans have won a majority in Congress." Stalin calmly noted: "That doesn't matter, since we don't see any difference between Republicans and Democrats." The shift in balance between the executive and legislative branches in the USA was incomprehensible to him.

Conversations between Stalin and Churchill shed light on Stalin's conception of Western democracy. First, he was convinced that the multiparty system was "a misunderstanding." When Churchill tried to explain the party system in Great Britain, Stalin "with deep conviction" (noted Churchill) said, "One party is much better." Second, he believed that people everywhere valued one thing, power. At Potsdam on July 18, 1945, Churchill recorded the Generalissimo's flattering remark: "About the British election, he [Stalin] said that all his information from Communist and other sources confirmed his belief that I should be [reelected]. . . . He said that the Army preferred a strong Government and would therefore vote for Conservatives."

Stalin's posthumous existence in Soviet society demonstrated the tenacity of the stereotypes he had created. Most of our current views of America (even of the West) originated in the revolutionist consciousness of the 1920s, but they took final shape in the years 1948–1952, when Stalin pursued a policy of teetering on the brink of war. Let us enumerate these stereotypes.

America is the land of the yellow devil. Evidently Stalin truly thought that America was ruled by a secret club of rich men: such a mighty nation could not be ruled by the worthless institutions of bourgeois democracy! The worship of the golden calf propels America toward war: ". . . the aggressive forces longing for a new war . . . are the billionaires and millionaires who regard war as a lucrative thing yielding colossal profits. These aggressive forces *hold in their hands* and direct the reactionary governments (author's italics)."

America is the organizer of World War III. All countries supporting America are enemies of the Soviet Union. In 1951 Stalin identified even the United Nations as an instrument for unleashing world war: "The core of aggressors in the UN are the ten members of the aggressive North Atlantic Pact . . . and twenty Latin American countries." Enumerating his enemies and their friends, Stalin did not notice how ludicrous it was to include Luxembourg and Costa Rica among the core of aggressors.

America stands at the head of its world; the USSR, at the head of its world; and these worlds are not contiguous. In his ideological testament *Economic Problems of Socialism in the USSR*, Stalin declared that "the disintegration of a single, all-inclusive world market must be considered the most important economic outcome of World War II and its economic consequences."

America is decaying. In 1952 Stalin, trying to give this stereotype more life, embarked on self-criticism and criticism of Lenin by announcing that after World War II two theses lost their force: Stalin's own thesis about "the relative stability of markets during the general crisis of imperialism" and Lenin's thesis that "despite the decay of capitalism, on the whole it is growing immeasurably faster than before."

America does not like its government. With respect to the Korean War, Stalin declared that ". . . the most experienced generals and officers can suffer defeat if the soldiers regard the war as highly unjust, and if because of this they only go through the motions of their duties at the front, without believing in the rightness of their mission, without fervor."

America will perish in the flames of world revolution. At the Nineteenth Party Congress [1952], Stalin's entire speech was devoted to world revolution; he concluded that "we have every reason to count on the success and victory of the fraternal parties in the countries where capital rules."

Finally, America is the cause of our internal troubles. The repressions of the 1930s, as is well known, were carried out under the slogan of cleansing society of foreign spies, which, it was asserted, had penetrated into the governing bodies of the USSR. After the war, America above all was accused of such interference.

All these stereotypes led to the creation of the notorious "enemy image."

Of course, not everything from the dictator's "theoretical legacy" survived him. Thus Stalin had hoped that wars would break out again in the imperialist world, that England and France would form one bloc opposing America, and Germany and Japan a second one. He ominously hinted at the error of "certain comrades," who "think that the conflicts between the socialist and capitalist camps are stronger than the conflicts between capitalist countries, and who consider that the United States of America has subordinated other capitalist countries to prevent their warring among and weakening each other." With a sense of "historic optimism" he wrote that ". . . the inevitability of war between the capitalist countries remains in force," letting it be known that such conflicts could be nuclear ones. In general he believed that war was not the worst evil. In his ideological testament he complained that "the present peace movement is different from the World War I movement to turn the imperialist war into a civil war"; however, "it is possible that under certain circumstances the struggle for peace will develop into a struggle for socialism."

His great-power aspirations sometimes took grotesque forms: "It is characteristic of the present way of doing things in the UN," he declared indignantly, "that the small Dominican Republic in [Latin] America, with a population of barely two million, has the same weight in the UN as India and carries more weight than the People's Republic of China, which has been deprived of a vote in the UN."

At the Soviet-American historians' conference in Athens, Ohio, in 1988, the well-known American Sovietologist and biographer of Stalin, Robert Tucker, an expert on Moscow affairs in the years from 1945 to 1953, said with certainty that the Cold War ended on March 5, 1953 [the day of Stalin's death].

To some extent this is true, since the Twentieth Party Congress [1956] gave reason to believe that Stalin's foreign-policy thought was becoming a thing of the past. Nevertheless, it reappeared more than once: stripped of its absurd, discredited features, it acquired a new vitality and led logically to the sending of troops to Hungary in 1956, to the Caribbean crisis of 1962, to the paranoid enmity toward the People's Republic of China, to the dispatch of troops to Czechoslovakia in

1968, and finally to our national tragedy, the sending of troops into Afghanistan [in 1979].

A new political thinking, a kind of cleansing, became necessary in order to dissolve the Stalinist world view swiftly. The new approaches have manifested themselves in healthier Soviet-American relations, in the Soviet Union's position of noninterference in East European countries, and in the withdrawal of our troops from Afghanistan. The iceberg of Stalin's foreign-policy thought is melting.

Melvyn P. Leffler

AMERICA'S NATIONAL SECURITY POLICY: A SOURCE OF COLD WAR TENSIONS

Melvyn P. Leffler challenges the once popular view that American leaders were largely reactive as they devised postwar foreign policy. On the contrary, he asserts, American diplomatic, military, and intelligence officials— including President Harry S Truman himself—had formulated a concept of national security that propelled America abroad. American leaders became especially concerned about the geopolitical balance of power in Europe and Asia, where it seemed communists might make gains during a time of economic crisis and political unrest. American officials became more interventionist abroad not so much in reaction to Soviet military capabilities or diplomatic demands, argues Leffler, but because of their fears for the survival of United States overseas interests. If the economic and political turmoil in Eurasia persisted and American power faltered, American analysts prophesied, the Soviet Union might come to control vast resources and threaten American political and economic principles. Leffler concludes that American officials exaggerated the benefits that would accrue to the Soviet Union and that America's global pursuit of security made Moscow apprehensive.

Melvyn P. Leffler teaches history at the University of Virginia. This essay is based upon his forthcoming book on American postwar national security policy. He has also written *The Elusive Quest: America's Pursuit of European Stability and French Security, 1919–1933* (1979).

"The American Conception of National Security and the Beginnings of the Cold War, 1945–48," *American Historical Review*, vol. LXXXIX, no. 2, pp. 346–81, April 1984. Reprinted by permission of the *American Historical Review* and Melvyn P. Leffler.

In an interview with Henry Kissinger in 1978 on "The Lessons of the Past," Walter Laqueur observed that during World War II "few if any people thought . . . of the structure of peace that would follow the war except perhaps in the most general terms of friendship, mutual trust, and the other noble sentiments mentioned in wartime programmatic speeches about the United Nations and related topics." Kissinger concurred, noting that no statesman, except perhaps Winston Churchill, "gave any attention to what would happen after the war." Americans, Kissinger stressed, "were determined that we were going to base the postwar period on good faith and getting along with everybody."

That two such astute and knowledgeable observers of international policies were so uninformed about American planning at the end of the Second World War is testimony to the enduring mythology of American idealism and innocence in the world of Realpolitik. It also reflects the state of scholarship on the interrelated areas of strategy, economy, and diplomacy. Despite the publication of several excellent overviews of the origins of the Cold War, despite the outpouring of incisive monographs on American foreign policy in many areas of the world, and despite some first-rate studies on the evolution of strategic thinking and the defense establishment, no comprehensive account yet exists of how American defense officials defined national security interests in the aftermath of World War II. Until recently, the absence of such a study was understandable, for scholars had limited access to records pertaining to national security, strategic thinking, and war planning. But in recent years documents relating to the early years of the Cold War have been declassified in massive numbers.

This documentation now makes it possible to analyze in greater depth the perceptions, apprehensions, and objectives of those defense officials most concerned with defining and defending the nation's security and strategic interests. This essay seeks neither to explain the process of decision making on any particular issue nor to dissect the domestic political considerations and fiscal constraints that narrowed the options available to policy makers. Furthermore, it does not pretend to discern the motivations and objectives of the Soviet Union. Rather, the goal here is to elucidate the fundamental strategic and economic considerations that shaped the definition of American national security interests in the postwar world. Several of these considerations—especially as they related to overseas bases, air transit rights, and a strategic sphere of influence in Latin America—initially were the logical result of technological developments and geostrategic experiences rather than directly related to postwar Soviet behavior. But American defense officials also considered the preservation of a favorable balance of power in Eurasia as fundamental to U.S. national security. This objective impelled defense analysts and intelligence officers to appraise and reappraise the intentions and capabilities of the Soviet Union. Rather modest estimates of the Soviets' ability to wage war against the United States generated the widespread assumption that the Soviets would refrain from military aggression and seek to avoid war. Nevertheless, American defense officials remained greatly preoccupied with the geopolitical balance of power in Europe and Asia, because that balance seemed endangered by communist exploitation of postwar economic dislocation and social and political unrest. Indeed, American assessments of the Soviet threat were less a consequence of expanding Soviet military capabilities and of Soviet diplomatic demands than a result of growing apprehension about the vulnerability of American strategic and economic interests in a world of unprecedented turmoil and upheaval. Viewed from this perspective, the Cold War assumed many of its most enduring characteristics during 1947–48, when American officials sought to cope with an array of challenges by implementing their own concepts of national security.

American officials first began to think seriously about the nation's postwar security during 1943–44. Military planners devised elaborate plans for an overseas base system. Many of these plans explicitly contemplated the breakdown of the wartime coalition. But, even when strategic planners postulated good postwar relations among the Allies, their plans called for an extensive system of bases. These bases were defined as the nation's strategic frontier. Beyond this frontier the United States would be able to use force to counter any threats or frustrate any overt acts of aggression. Within the strategic frontier, American military predominance had to remain inviolate. Although plans for an overseas base system went through many revisions, they always presupposed American hegemony over the Atlantic and Pacific oceans. These plans received President Franklin D. Roosevelt's endorsement in early 1944. After his death, army and navy planners presented their views to President Harry S Truman, and Army Chief of Staff George C. Marshall discussed them extensively with Secretary of State James F. Byrnes.

Two strategic considerations influenced the development of an overseas base system. The first was the need for defense in depth. Since attacks against the United States could only emanate from Europe and

Asia, the Joint Chiefs of Staff concluded as early as November 1943 that the United States must encircle the Western Hemisphere with a defensive ring of outlying bases. In the Pacific this ring had to include the Aleutians, the Philippines, Okinawa, and the former Japanese mandates. Recognizing the magnitude of this strategic frontier, Admiral William E. Leahy, chief of staff to the president, explained to Truman that the joint chiefs were not thinking of the immediate future when, admittedly, no prospective naval power could challenge American predominance in the Pacific. Instead, they were contemplating the long term, when the United States might require wartime access to the resources of southeast Asia as well as "a firm line of communications from the West Coast to the Asiatic mainland, plus denial of this line in time of war to any potential enemy." In the Atlantic, strategic planners maintained that their minimum requirements included a West African zone, with primary bases in the Azores or Canary Islands. Leahy went even further, insisting on primary bases in West Africa itself—for example, at Dakar or Casablanca. The object of these defensive bases was to enable the United States to possess complete control of the Atlantic and Pacific oceans and keep hostile powers far from American territory.

Defense in depth was especially important in light of the Pearl Harbor experience, the advance of technology, and the development of the atomic bomb. According to the Joint Chiefs of Staff, "Experience in the recent war demonstrated conclusively that the defense of a nation, if it is to be effective, must begin beyond its frontiers. The advent of the atomic bomb reemphasizes this requirement. The farther away from our own vital areas we can hold our enemy through the possession of advanced bases. . . , the greater are our chances of surviving successfully an attack by atomic weapons and of destroying the enemy which employs them against us." Believing that atomic weapons would increase the incentive to aggression by enhancing the advantage of surprise, military planners never ceased to extol the utility of forward bases from which American aircraft could seek to intercept attacks against the United States.

The second strategic consideration that influenced the plan for a comprehensive overseas base system was the need to project American power quickly and effectively against any potential adversary. In conducting an overall examination of requirements for base rights in September 1945, the Joint War Plans Committee stressed that World War II demonstrated the futility of a strategy of static defense. The United States had to be able to take "timely" offensive action against the adversary's capacity and will to wage war. New weapons demanded that advance bases be established in "areas well removed from the United States, so as to project our operations, with new weapons or otherwise, nearer the enemy." Scientists, like Vannevar Bush, argued that, "regardless of the potentialities of these new weapons [atomic energy and guided missiles], they should not influence the number, location, or extent of strategic bases now considered essential." The basic strategic concept underlying all American war plans called for an air offensive against a prospective enemy from overseas bases. Delays in the development of the B-36, the first intercontinental bomber, only accentuated the need for these bases.

In October 1945 the civilian leaders of the War and Navy departments carefully reviewed the emerging strategic concepts and base requirements of the military planners. Secretary of the Navy James Forrestal and Secretary of War Robert P. Patterson discussed them with Admiral Leahy, the Joint Chiefs of Staff, and Secretary of State Byrnes. The civilian secretaries fully endorsed the concept of a far-flung system of bases in the Atlantic and Pacific oceans that would enhance the offensive capabilities of the United States. Having expended so much blood and effort capturing Japanese-held islands, defense officials, like Forrestal, naturally wished to devise a base system in the Pacific to facilitate the projection of American influence and power. The Philippines were the key to southeast Asia, Okinawa to the Yellow Sea, the Sea of Japan, and the industrial heartland of northeast Asia. From these bases on America's "strategic frontier," the United States could preserve its access to vital raw materials in Asia, deny these resources to a prospective enemy, help preserve peace and stability in troubled areas, safeguard critical sea lanes, and, if necessary, conduct an air offensive against the industrial infrastructure of any Asiatic power, including the Soviet Union. . . .

In the immediate postwar years American ambitions for an elaborate base system encountered many problems. Budgetary constraints compelled military planners to drop plans for many secondary and subsidiary bases, particularly in the South Pacific and Caribbean. These sacrifices merely increased the importance of those bases that lay closer to a potential adversary. By early 1948, the joint chiefs were willing to forego base rights in such places as Surinam, Curacoa-Aruba, Cayenne, Nounea, and Vivi-Levu if "joint" or "participating" rights could be acquired or preserved in Karachi, Tripoli, Algiers, Casablanca, Dharan, and Monrovia. Budgetary constraints, then, limited the depth of the base system but not the breadth of American ambitions. Furthermore, the governments of Panama, Iceland, Denmark, Portugal, France, and Saudi Arabia often rejected or abolished the exclusive rights the United States wanted and sometimes limited the number of American personnel on such bases. Washington, therefore, negotiated a variety of arrangements to meet the objections of host governments. By early 1948, for example, the base in Iceland was operated by a civilian company under contract to the United States Air Force; in the Azores, the base was manned by a detachment of Portuguese military personnel operating under the Portuguese flag, but an air force detachment serviced the American aircraft using the base. In Port Lyautey, the base was under the command of the French navy, but under a secret agreement an American naval team took care of American aircraft on the base. In Saudi Arabia, the Dharan air strip was cared for by 300 U.S. personnel and was capable of handling B-29s. Because these arrangements were not altogether satisfactory, in mid-1948 Secretary of Defense Forrestal and Secretary of the Army Kenneth Royall advocated using American economic and military assistance as levers to acquire more permanent and comprehensive base rights; particularly in Greenland and North Africa.

Less well known than the American effort to establish a base system, but integral to the policymakers' conception of national security, was the attempt to secure military air transit and landing rights. Military planners wanted such rights at critical locations not only in the Western Hemisphere but also in North Africa, the Middle East, India, and southeast Asia. To this end they delineated a route from Casablanca through Algiers, Tripoli, Cairo, Dharan, Karachi, Delhi, Calcutta, Rangoon, Bangkok, and Saigon to Manila. In closing out the African–Middle East theater at the conclusion of the war, General H. W. Aurand, under explicit instructions from the secretary of war, made preparations for permanent rights at seven airfields in North Africa and Saudi Arabia. According to a study by the Joint Chiefs of Staff, "Military air transit rights for the United States along the North African–Indian route were most desirable in order to provide access to and familiarity with bases from which offensive and defensive action might be conducted in the event of a major war, and to provide an alternate route to China and to United States Far Eastern bases." In other words, such rights would permit the rapid augmentation of American bases in wartime as well as the rapid movement of American air units from the eastern to the western flank of the U.S. base system.

In order to maintain these airfields in a state of readiness, the United States would have to rely on private airlines, which had to be persuaded to locate their operations in areas designated essential to military air transit rights. In this way, airports "in being" outside the formal American base system would be available for military operations in times of crisis and war. Assistant Secretary [of War John] McCloy informed the State Department at the beginning of 1945 that a "strong United States air transport system, international in scope and readily adapted to military use, is vital to our air power and future national security." Even earlier, the joint chiefs had agreed not to include South American air bases in their strategic plans so long as it was understood that commercial fields in that region would be developed with a view to subsequent military use. . . .

From the closing days of World War II, American defense officials believed that they could not allow any prospective adversary to control the Eurasian land mass. This was the lesson taught by two world wars. Strategic thinkers and military analysts insisted that any power or powers attempting to dominate Eurasia must be regarded as potentially hostile to the United States. Their acute awareness of the importance of Eurasia made Marshall, Thomas Handy, George A. Lincoln, and other officers wary of the expansion of Soviet influence there. Cognizant of the growth in Soviet strength, General John Deane, head of the United States military mission in Moscow, urged a tougher stand against Soviet demands even before World War II had ended. While acknowledging that the increase in Soviet power stemmed primarily from the defeat of Germany and Japan, postwar assessments of the Joint Chiefs of Staff emphasized the importance of deterring further Soviet aggrandizement in Eurasia. Concern over the consequences of Russian domination of Eurasia helps explain why in July 1945 the joint chiefs decided to oppose a Soviet request for bases in the Dardanelles; why during March and April 1946 they supported a firm stand against Russia in Iran, Turkey, and Tripolitania; and why in the summer of 1946 Clark Clifford and George Elsey, two White House aides, argued that Soviet incorporation of any parts of Western Europe, the Middle East, China, or Japan into a communist orbit was incompatible with American national security. . . .

Studies by the Joint Chiefs of Staff stressed that, if Eurasia came under Soviet domination, either through military conquest or political and economic "assimilation," America's only potential adversary would fall heir to enormous natural resources, industrial potential, and manpower. By the autumn of 1945, military planners already were worrying that Soviet control over much of Eastern Europe and its raw materials would abet Russia's economic recovery, enhance its warmaking capacity, and deny important foodstuffs, oil, and minerals to Western Europe. By the early months of 1946, Secretary Patterson and his subordinates in the War Department believed that Soviet control of the Ruhr-Rhineland industrial complex would constitute an extreme threat. Even more dangerous was the prospect of Soviet predominance over the rest of Western Europe, especially France. Strategically, this would undermine the impact of any prospective American naval blockade and would allow Soviet military planners to achieve defense in depth. The latter possibility had enormous military significance, because American war plans relied so heavily on air power and strategic bombing, the efficacy of which might be reduced substantially if the Soviets acquired outlying bases in Western Europe and the Middle East or if they "neutralized" bases in Great Britain.

Economic considerations also made defense officials determined to retain American access to Eurasia as well as to deny Soviet predominance over it.   [Secretary of War Henry L.] Stimson, Patterson, McCloy, and Assistant Secretary Howard C. Peterson agreed with Forrestal that long-term American prosperity required open markets, unhindered access to raw materials, and the rehabilitation of much—if not all—of Eurasia along liberal capitalist lines. In late 1944 and 1945, Stimson protested the prospective industrial emasculation of Germany, lest it undermine American economic well-being, set back recovery throughout Europe, and unleash forces of anarchy and revolution. Stimson and his subordinates in the Operations Division of the army also worried that the spread of Soviet power in northeast Asia would constrain the functioning of the free enterprise system and jeopardize American economic interests. A report prepared by the staff of the Moscow embassy and revised in mid-1946 by Ambassador (and former General) Walter Bedell Smith emphasized that "Soviet power is by nature so jealous that it has already operated to segregate from world economy almost all of the areas in which it has been established." While Forrestal and the navy sought to contain Soviet influence in the Near East and to retain American access to Middle East oil, Patterson and the War Department focused on preventing famine in occupied areas, forestalling communist revolution, circumscribing Soviet influence, resuscitating trade, and preserving traditional American markets especially in Western Europe. But American economic interests in

Eurasia were not limited to Western Europe, Germany, and the Middle East. Military planners and intelligence officers in both the army and navy expressed considerable interest in the raw materials of southeast Asia, and, as already shown, one of the purposes of the bases they wanted was to maintain access to those resources and deny them to a prospective enemy.

While civilian officials and military strategists feared the loss of Eurasia, they did not expect the Soviet Union to attempt its military conquest. In the early Cold War years, there was nearly universal agreement that the Soviets, while eager to expand their influence, desired to avoid a military engagement. In October 1945, for example, the Joint Intelligence Staff predicted that the Soviet Union would seek to avoid war for five to ten years. . . . In March 1947, while the Truman Doctrine was being discussed in Congress, the director of army intelligence maintained that the factors operating to discourage Soviet aggression continued to be decisive. In September 1947, the CIA concluded that the Soviets would not seek to conquer Western Europe for several reasons: they would recognize their inability to control hostile populations; they would fear triggering a war with the United States that could not be won; and they would prefer to gain hegemony by political and economic means. In October 1947, the Joint Intelligence Staff maintained that for three years at least the Soviet Union would take no action that would precipitate a military conflict.

Even the ominous developments during the first half of 1948 did not alter these assessments. Despite his alarmist cable of March 5, designed to galvanize congressional support for increased defense expenditures, General Lucius Clay, the American military governor in Germany, did not believe war imminent. A few days later, the CIA concluded that the communist takeover in Czechoslovakia would not increase Soviet capabilities significantly and reflected no alteration in Soviet tactics. On March 16, the CIA reported to the president, "The weight of logic, as well as evidence, also leads to the conclusion that the Soviets will not resort to military force within the next sixty days." While this assessment was far from reassuring, army and navy intelligence experts concurred that the Soviets still wanted to avoid war, the question was whether war would erupt as a result of "miscalculation" by either the United States or Russia. After talking to Foreign Minister V. M. Molotov in June, Ambassador Smith concluded that Soviet leaders would not resort to active hostilities. During the Berlin blockade, army intelligence reported few signs of Soviet preparations for war;

naval intelligence maintained that the Soviets desired to avoid war yet consolidate their position in East Germany. In October 1948, the Military Intelligence Division of the army endorsed a British appraisal that "all the evidence available indicates that the Soviet Union is not preparing to go to war in the near future." In December Acting Secretary of State Robert Lovett summed up the longstanding American perspective when he emphasized that he saw "no evidence that Soviet intentions run toward launching a sudden military attack on the western nations at this time. It would not be in character with the tradition or mentality of the Soviet leaders to resort to such a measure unless they felt themselves either politically extremely weak, or militarily extremely strong."

Although American defense officials recognized that the Soviets had substantial military assets, they remained confident that the Soviet Union did not feel extremely strong. Military analysts studying Russian capabilities noted that the Soviets were rapidly mechanizing infantry units and enhancing their firepower and mobility. It was estimated during the winter of 1946–47 that the Soviets could mobilize six million troops in thirty days and twelve million in six months, providing sufficient manpower to overrun all important parts of Eurasia. The Soviets were also believed to be utilizing German scientists and German technological know-how to improve their submarine force, develop rockets and missiles, and acquire knowledge about the atomic bomb. During 1947 and 1948, it was reported as well that the Soviets were making rapid progress in the development of high performance jet fighters and already possessed several hundred intermediate range bombers comparable to the American B-29.

Even so, American military analysts were most impressed with Soviet weaknesses and vulnerabilities. The Soviets had no long-range strategic air force, no atomic bomb, and meager air defenses. Moreover, the Soviet navy was considered ineffective except for its submarine forces. The Joint Logistic Plans Committee and the Military Intelligence Division of the War Department estimated that the Soviet Union would require approximately fifteen years to overcome wartime losses in manpower and industry, ten years to redress the shortage of technicians, five to ten years to develop a strategic air force, fifteen to twenty-five years to construct a modern navy, ten years to refurbish military transport, ten years (or less) to quell resistance in occupied areas, fifteen to twenty years to establish a military infrastructure in the Far East, three to ten years to acquire the atomic bomb, and an unspecified number of years to remove the vulnerability of the Soviet rail-net and petroleum industry to long-range bombing. For several years at least, the Soviet capability for sustained attack against North America would be very limited. In January 1946 the Joint Intelligence Staff concluded that "the offensive capabilities of the United States are manifestly superior to those of the U.S.S.R. and any war between the U.S. and the USSR would be far more costly to the Soviet Union than to the United States." . . .

If American defense officials did not expect a Soviet military attack, why, then, were they so fearful of losing control of Eurasia? The answer rests less in American assessments of Soviet military capabilities and short-term military intentions than in appraisals of economic and political conditions throughout Europe and Asia. Army officials in particular, because of their occupation roles in Germany, Japan, Austria, and Korea, were aware of the postwar plight of these areas. Key military men—Generals Clay, Douglas MacArthur, John Hilldring, and Oliver P. Echols and Colonel Charles H. Bonesteel—became alarmed by the prospects of famine, disease, anarchy, and revolution. They recognized that communist parties could exploit the distress and that the Russians could capitalize upon it to spread Soviet influence. As early as June 1945, Rear Admiral Ellery Stone, the American commissioner in Italy, wrote that wartime devastation had created fertile soil for the growth of communism in Italy and the enlargement of the Soviet sphere. MacArthur also feared that, if the Japanese economy remained emasculated and reforms were not undertaken, communism would spread. Clay, too, was acutely aware that German communists were depicting themselves and their beliefs as their country's only hope of salvation. In the spring of 1946 military planners, working on contingency plans for the emergency withdrawal of American troops from Germany, should war with Russia unexpectedly occur, also took note of the economic turmoil and political instability in neighboring countries, especially France. Sensitivity to the geopolitical dimensions of the socioeconomic crisis of the postwar era impelled Chief of Staff Eisenhower to give high priority in the army budget to assistance for occupied areas. . . .

In brief, during 1946 and 1947, defense officials witnessed a dramatic unraveling of the geopolitical foundations and socioeconomic structure of international affairs. Britain's economic weakness and withdrawal from the eastern Mediterranean, India's independence movement, civil war in China, nationalist insurgencies in Indo-China and the Dutch East Indies, Zionist claims to Palestine and Arab resentment, German and Japanese economic paralysis, communist inroads in France and Italy—all were ominous developments. Defense officials recognized that the Soviet Union had not created these circumstances but believed that Soviet leaders would exploit them. Should communists take power, even without direct Russian intervention, the Soviet Union, it was assumed, would gain predominant control of the resources of these areas because of the postulated subservience of communist parties everywhere to the Kremlin. Should nationalist uprisings persist, communists seize power in underdeveloped countries, and Arabs revolt against American support of a Jewish state, the petroleum and raw materials of critical areas might be denied the West. The imminent possibility existed that, even without Soviet military aggression, the resources of Eurasia could fall under Russian control. With these resources, the Soviet Union would be able to overcome its chronic economic weaknesses, achieve defense in depth, and challenge American power—perhaps even by military force.

In this frightening postwar environment American assessments of Soviet long-term intentions were transformed. When World War II ended, military planners initially looked upon Soviet aims in foreign affairs as arising from the Kremlin's view of power politics, Soviet strategic imperatives, historical Russian ambitions, and Soviet reactions to moves by the United States and Great Britain. American intelligence analysts and strategic planners most frequently discussed Soviet actions in Eastern Europe, the Balkans, the Near East, and Manchuria as efforts to establish an effective security system. Despite enormous Soviet gains during the war, many assessments noted that, in fact, the Soviets had not yet achieved a safe security zone, especially on their southern periphery. While Forrestal, Deane, and most of the planners in the army's Operations Division possessed a skeptical, perhaps even sinister, view of Soviet intentions, the still prevailing outlook at the end of 1945 was to dismiss the role of ideology in Soviet foreign policy yet emphasize Soviet distrust of foreigners; to stress Soviet expansionism but acknowledge the possibility of accommodation; to abhor Soviet domination of Eastern Europe but discuss Soviet policies elsewhere in terms of power and influence; and to dwell upon the Soviet preoccupation with security yet acknowledge doubt about ultimate Soviet intentions.

This orientation changed rapidly during 1946. In January, the Joint War Plans Committee observed that "the long-term objective [of the Soviet Union] is deemed to be establishment of predominant influence over the Eurasian land mass and the strategic approaches thereto." Reports of the new military attaché in Moscow went further, claiming that "the ultimate aim of Soviet foreign policy seems to be the dominance of Soviet influence throughout the world" and "the final aim . . . is the destruction of the capitalist system." Soon thereafter, [George F.] Kennan's "long telegram" was widely distributed among defense officials, on whom it had considerable impact. Particularly suggestive was his view that Soviet leaders needed the theme of capitalist encirclement to justify their autocratic rule. Also influential were Kennan's convictions that the Soviet leaders aimed to shatter the international authority of the United States and were beyond reason and conciliation. . . .

Yet these assessments did not seriously grapple with contradictory evidence. While emphasizing Soviet military capabilities, strategic ambitions, and diplomatic intransigence, reports like the Clifford-Elsey memorandum of September 1946 and the Joint Chiefs of Staff report 1696 (upon which the Clifford-Elsey memorandum heavily relied) disregarded numerous signs of Soviet weakness, moderation, and circumspection. During 1946 and 1947 intelligence analysts described the withdrawal of Russian troops from northern Norway, Manchuria, Bornholm, and Iran (from the latter under pressure, of course). Numerous intelligence sources reported the reduction of Russian troops in Eastern Europe and the extensive demobilization going on within the Soviet Union. In October 1947 the Joint Intelligence Committee forecast a Soviet army troop strength during 1948 and 1949 of less than two million men. Soviet military expenditures appeared to moderate. Other reports dealt with the inadequacies of Soviet transportation and bridging equipment for the conduct of offensive operations in Eastern Europe. And, as already noted, assessments of the Soviet economy revealed persistent problems likely to restrict Soviet adventurism.

Experience suggested that the Soviet Union was by no means uniformly hostile or unwilling to negotiate with the United States. In April 1946, a few days after a State-War-Navy subcommittee issued an alarming political estimate of Soviet policy (for use in American military estimates), Ambassador Smith reminded the State Department that the Soviet press was not unalterably critical of the United States, that the Russians had withdrawn from Bornholm, that Stalin had given a moderate speech on the United Nations, and that Soviet demobilization continued apace. The next month General Lincoln, who had accompanied Byrnes to Paris for the meeting of the council of foreign ministers, acknowledged that the Soviets had been willing to make numerous concessions regarding Tripolitania, the Dodecanese, and Italian reparations. In the spring of 1946, General Echols, General Clay, and Secretary Patterson again maintained that the French constituted the major impediment to an agreement on united control of Germany. At the same time the Soviets ceased pressing for territorial adjustments with Turkey. After the diplomatic exchanges over the Dardanelles in the late summer of 1946 the Soviets did not again ask for either a revision of the Montreux Convention or the acquisition of bases in the Dardanelles. In early 1947 central intelligence delineated more than a half-dozen instances of Soviet moderation or concessions. In April the Military Intelligence Division noted that the Soviets had limited their involvement in the Middle East, diminished their ideological rhetoric, and given only moderate support to Chinese communists. In the months preceding the Truman Doctrine, Soviet behavior—as noted by American military officials and intelligence analysts—hardly justified the inflammatory rhetoric [Dean] Acheson and Truman used to secure congressional support for aid to Greece and Turkey. Perhaps this is why General Marshall, as secretary of state, refrained from such language himself and preferred to focus on the socioeconomic aspects of the unfolding crisis.

In their overall assessments of Soviet long-term intentions, however, military planners dismissed all evidence of Soviet moderation, circumspection, and restraint. In fact, as 1946 progressed, these planners seemed to spend less time analyzing Soviet intentions and more time estimating Soviet capabilities. Having accepted the notion that the two powers were locked in an ideological struggle of indefinite duration and conscious of the rapid demobilization of American forces and the constraints on American defense expenditures, they no longer explored ways of accommodating a potential adversary's legitimate strategic requirements or pondered how American initiatives might influence the Soviet Union's definition of its objectives. Information not confirming prevailing assumptions either was ignored in overall assessments of Soviet intentions or was used to illustrate that the Soviets were shifting tactics but not altering objectives. Reflective of the emerging mentality was a report from the Joint Chiefs of Staff to the president in July 1946 that deleted sections from previous studies that had outlined Soviet weaknesses. A memorandum sent by Secretary Patterson to the president at the same time was designed by General Lauris Norstad, director of the War Department's Plans and Operations Division, to answer questions about relations with the Soviet Union "without ambiguity." Truman, Clark Clifford observed many years later, liked things in black and white.

During 1946 and early 1947, the conjunction of Soviet ideological fervor and socioeconomic turmoil throughout Eurasia contributed to the growth of a myopic view of Soviet long-term policy objectives and to enormous apprehension lest the Soviet Union gain control of all the resources of Eurasia, thereby endangering the national security of the United States. American assessments of Soviet short-term military intentions had not altered; Soviet military capabilities had not significantly increased, and Soviet foreign policy positions had not greatly shifted. But defense officials were acutely aware of America's own rapidly diminishing capabilities, of Britain's declining military strength, of the appeal of communist doctrine to most of the underdeveloped world, and of the opportunities open to communist parties throughout most of Eurasia as a result of prevailing socioeconomic conditions. War Department papers, studies of the joint chiefs, and intelligence analyses repeatedly described the restiveness of colonial peoples that had sapped British and French strength, the opportunities for communist parties in France, Italy, and even Spain to capitalize upon indigenous conditions, and the ability of the Chinese communists to defeat the nationalists and make the resources and manpower of Manchuria and North China available to the Soviet Union. In this turbulent international arena, the survival of liberal ideals and capitalist institutions was anything but assured. "We could point to the economic benefits of Capitalism," commented one important War Department paper in April 1946, "but these benefits are concentrated rather than widespread, and, at present, are genuinely suspect throughout Europe and in many other parts of the world." . . .

During late 1946 and early 1947, the Truman administration assumed the initiative by creating German Bizonia, providing military assistance to Greece and Turkey, allocating massive economic aid to Western Europe, and reassessing economic policy toward Japan. These initiatives were aimed primarily at tackling the internal sources of unrest upon which communist parties capitalized and at rehabilitating the industrial heartlands of Eurasia. . . .

Yet if war should unexpectedly occur, the United States had to have the capability to inflict incalculable damage upon the Soviet Union. Accordingly, Truman shelved (after some serious consideration) proposals for international control of atomic energy. The Baruch

Plan, as it evolved in the spring and summer of 1946, was heavily influenced by defense officials and service officers who wished to avoid any significant compromise with the Soviet Union. They sought to perpetuate America's nuclear monopoly as long as possible in order to counterbalance Soviet conventional strength, deter Soviet adventurism, and bolster American negotiating leverage. When negotiations at the United Nations for international control of atomic energy languished for lack of agreement on its implementation, the way was clear for the Truman administration gradually to adopt a strategy based on air power and atomic weapons. This strategy was initially designed to destroy the adversary's will and capability to wage war by annihilating Russian industrial, petroleum, and urban centers. After completing their study of the 1946 Bikini atomic tests, the Joint Chiefs of Staff in July 1947 called for an enlargement of the nuclear arsenal. While Truman and Forrestal insisted on limiting military expenditures, government officials moved vigorously to solve problems in the production of plutonium, to improve nuclear cores and assembly devices, and to increase the number of aircraft capable of delivering atomic bombs. After much initial postwar disorganization, the General Advisory Committee to the Atomic Energy Commission could finally report to the president at the end of 1947 that "great progress" had been made in the atomic program. From June 30, 1947, to June 30, 1948, the number of bombs in the stockpile increased from thirteen to fifty. Although at the time of the Berlin crisis the United States was not prepared to launch a strategic air offensive against the Soviet Union, substantial progress had been made in the development of the nation's air-atomic capabilities. By the end of 1948, the United States had at least eighteen nuclear-capable B-50s, four B-36s, and almost three times as many nuclear-capable B-29s as had been available at the end of 1947.

During late 1947 and early 1948, the administration also responded to pleas of the Joint Chiefs of Staff to augment the overseas base system and to acquire bases in closer proximity to the Soviet Union. Negotiations were conducted with the British to gain access to bases in the Middle East and an agreement was concluded for the acquisition of air facilities in Libya. Admiral [Richard L.] Conolly made a secret deal with the French to secure air and communication rights and to stockpile oil, aviation gas, and ammunition in North Africa. Plans also were discussed for postoccupation bases in Japan, and considerable progress was made in refurbishing and constructing airfields in Turkey. During 1948 the Turks also received one hundred eighty F-47 fighter-bombers, thirty B-26 bombers, and eighty-one C-47 cargo planes. The F-47s and B-26s, capable of reaching the vital Ploesti and Baku oil fields, were more likely to be used to slow down a Soviet advance through Turkey or Iran, thereby affording time to activate a strategic air offensive from prospective bases in the Cairo-Suez area.

Despite these developments, the joint chiefs and military planners grew increasingly uneasy with the budgetary constraints under which they operated. They realized that American initiatives, however necessary, placed the Soviet Union on the defensive, created an incendiary situation, and made war more likely—though still improbable. In July 1947, intelligence analysts in the War Department maintained that the Truman Doctrine and the Marshall Plan had resulted in a more aggressive Soviet attitude toward the United States and had intensified tensions. "These tensions have caused a sharper line of demarcation between West and East tending to magnify the significance of conflicting points of view, and reducing the possibility of agreement on any point." Intelligence officers understood that the Soviets would perceive American efforts to build strategic highways, construct airfields, and transfer fighter bombers to Turkey as a threat to Soviet security and to the oilfields in the Caucasus. The latter, noted the director of naval intelligence, "lie within easy air striking range of countries on her southern flank, and the Soviet leaders will be particularly sensitive to any political threat from this area, however remote." Intelligence analysts also recognized that the Soviets would view the Marshall Plan as a threat to Soviet control in Eastern Europe as well as a death-knell to communist attempts to capture power peacefully in Western Europe. And defense officials were well aware that the Soviets would react angrily to plans for currency reform in German Trizonia and to preparations for a West German republic. "The whole Berlin crisis," army planners informed Eisenhower, "has arisen as a result of . . . actions on the part of the Western Powers." In sum, the Soviet clampdown in Eastern Europe and the attempt to blockade Berlin did not come as shocks to defense officials, who anticipated hostile and defensive Soviet reactions to American initiatives.

The real consternation of the Joint Chiefs of Staff and other high-ranking civilian and military officials in the defense agencies stemmed from their growing conviction that the United States was undertaking actions and assuming commitments that now required greater military capabilities. Recognizing that American initiatives, aimed at safeguarding Eurasia from further communist inroads, might be perceived as endangering Soviet interests, it was all the more important to be ready for any eventuality. Indeed, to the extent that anxieties about the prospects of war escalated in March and April 1948, these fears did not stem from estimates that the Soviets were planning further aggressive action after the communist seizure of power in Czechoslovakia but from apprehensions that ongoing American initiatives might provoke an attack. . . .

Having conceived of American national security in terms of Western control and of American access to the resources of Eurasia outside the Soviet sphere, American defense officials now considered it imperative to develop American military capabilities to meet a host of contingencies that might emanate from further Soviet encroachments or from indigenous communist unrest. Such contingencies were sure to arise because American strategy depended so heavily on the rebuilding of Germany and Japan, Russia's traditional enemies, as well as on air power, atomic weapons, and bases on the Soviet periphery. Such contingencies also were predictable because American strategy depended so heavily on the restoration of stability in Eurasia, a situation increasingly unlikely in an era of nationalist turmoil, social unrest, and rising economic expectations. Although the desire of the national military establishment for large increments in defense expenditures did not prevail in the tight budgetary environment and presidential election year of 1948, the mode of thinking about national security that subsequently accelerated the arms race and precipitated military interventionism in Asia was already widespread among defense officials.

Indeed, the dynamics of the Cold War after 1948 are easier to comprehend when one grasps the breadth of the American conception of national security that had emerged between 1945 and 1948. This conception included a strategic sphere of influence within the Western Hemisphere, domination of the Atlantic and Pacific oceans, an extensive system of outlying bases to enlarge the strategic frontier and project American power, an even more extensive system of transit rights to facilitate conversion of commercial air bases to military use, access to the resources and markets of most of Eurasia, denial of those resources to a prospective enemy, and the maintenance of nuclear superiority. Not every one of these ingredients, it must be emphasized, was considered vital. Hence, American officials could acquiesce, however grudgingly, to a Soviet sphere in Eastern Europe and could avoid direct intervention in China. But cumulative challenges to these concepts of national security were certain to provoke a firm American response. This occurred initially in 1947–48 when decisions were made in favor of the Truman Doctrine, Marshall Plan, military assistance, Atlantic alliance, and German and Japanese rehabilitation. Soon thereafter, the "loss" of China, the Soviet detonation of an atomic bomb, and the North Korean attack on South Korea intensified the perception of threat to prevailing concepts of national security. The Truman administration responded with military assistance to southeast Asia, a decision to build the hydrogen bomb, direct military intervention in Korea, a commitment to station troops permanently in Europe, expansion of the American alliance system, and a massive rearmament program in the United States. Postulating a long-term Soviet intention to gain world domination, the American conception of national security, based on geopolitical and economic imperatives, could not allow for additional losses in Eurasia, could not risk a challenge to its nuclear supremacy, and could not permit any infringement on its ability to defend in depth or to project American force from areas in close proximity to the Soviet homeland.

To say this is neither to exculpate the Soviet government for its inhumane treatment of its own citizens nor to suggest that Soviet foreign policy was idle or benign. Indeed, Soviet behavior in Eastern Europe was often deplorable; the Soviets sought opportunities in the Dardanelles, northern Iran, and Manchuria, the Soviets hoped to orient Germany and Austria toward the East; and the Soviets sometimes endeavored to use communist parties to expand Soviet influence in areas beyond the periphery of Russian military power. But, then again, the Soviet Union had lost twenty million dead during the war, had experienced the destruction of seventeen hundred towns, thirty-one thousand factories, and one hundred thousand collective farms, and had witnessed the devastation of the rural economy with the Nazi slaughter of twenty million hogs and seventeen million head of cattle. What is remarkable is that after 1946 these monumental losses received so little attention when American defense analysts studied the motives and intentions of Soviet policy; indeed, defense officials did little to analyze the threat perceived by the Soviets. Yet these same officials had absolutely no doubt that the wartime experiences and sacrifices of the United States, though much less devastating than those of Soviet Russia, demonstrated the need for and entitled the United States to oversee the resuscitation of the industrial heartlands of Germany and Japan, establish a viable balance of power in Eurasia, and militarily dominate the Eurasian rimlands, thereby safeguarding American access to raw materials and control over all sea and air approaches to North America.

To suggest a double standard is important only insofar as it raises fundamental questions about the conceptualization and implementation of American national security policy.   If Soviet policy was aggressive, bellicose, and ideological, perhaps America's reliance on overseas bases, air power, atomic weapons, military alliances, and the rehabilitation of Germany and Japan was the best course to follow, even if the effect may have been to exacerbate Soviet anxieties and suspicions.   But even when one attributes the worst intentions to the Soviet Union, one might still ask whether American presuppositions and apprehensions about the benefits that would accrue to the Soviet Union as a result of communist (and even revolutionary nationalist) gains anywhere in Eurasia tended to simplify international realities, magnify the breadth of American interests, engender commitments beyond American capabilities, and dissipate the nation's strength and credibility.   And, perhaps even more importantly, if Soviet foreign policies tended to be opportunist, reactive, nationalistic, and contradictory, as some recent writers have claimed and as some contemporary analysts suggested, then one might also wonder whether America's own conception of national security tended, perhaps unintentionally, to engender anxieties and to provoke countermeasures from a proud, suspicious, insecure, and cruel government that was at the same time legitimately apprehensive about the long-term implications arising from the rehabilitation of traditional enemies and the development of foreign bases on the periphery of the Soviet homeland.

Thomas G. Paterson

INEVITABLE CONFLICT: THE UNSTABLE INTERNATIONAL SYSTEM

The debate between traditionalist and revisionist historians tended to bypass questions about the system or structure of international relations. In his book *On Every Front: The Making of the Cold War* (1979), Thomas G. Paterson argues that an unstable international system contributed signifi-

Reprinted from *On Every Front: The Making of the Cold War*, pp. x, 1–4, 8–15, 19–32, by Thomas G. Paterson, with the permission of W. W. Norton & Company, Inc. Copyright©1979 by W. W. Norton & Company, Inc.

cantly to Cold War tensions. While any international system is conflict-ridden by nature, the unprecedented physical destruction of the Second World War, with its attendant economic dislocations, social turmoil, and political chaos, intensified conflict. The complex process of creating a new structure of international relations out of the ashes of the old thus made some form of Soviet-American confrontation inevitable. Although he does not ascribe exclusive weight to this factor, Paterson contends that the characteristics of the volatile international system cannot be ignored in explanations of the origins of the Cold War.

A professor of history at the University of Connecticut, Paterson has written numerous works in the field of foreign relations and has served as president of the Society for Historians of American Foreign Relations. His books include *Soviet-American Confrontation* (1973), *American Foreign Policy: A History* (1988), *Meeting the Communist Threat* (1988), and *Kennedy's Quest for Victory: American Foreign Policy, 1961–1963* (1989).

The Cold War derived from three closely intertwined sources: the conflict-ridden *international system*, the divergent *fundamental needs and ideas* of the major antagonists, America and Russia, and the diplomatic conduct or *tactics* of American and Soviet leaders. To reduce the conflict inherent in the postwar structure, to satisfy their strategic and economic needs and ideologies, and to conduct diplomacy true to their individual personalities and domestic political environments, officials in Washington and Moscow abandoned any quest for a community of nations and instead built competing spheres of influence. They thereby expanded and protected what they respectively perceived to be their interests, divided the world, and stimulated more conflict, which took the form of a "prolonged armed truce," to use the words of Soviet diplomat Maxim Litvinov. . . .

Winston S. Churchill wore his usual bulldog visage. The ever-present cigar and hunched gait, other familiar trademarks of the British prime minister, also drew the crowd's attention on that very hot day of July 16, 1945. He was surveying the dusty remains of the Nazi capital—"that rubble heap near Potsdam," murmured one Berliner. This time a preoccupied Churchill evinced little interest in his curious onlookers. What captured Churchill's regard was the grisly aftermath in Berlin of heavy Allied bombing and artillery fire and stout German resistance. He and the passengers in his motorcade grew sick, utterly stunned by the stark display of carnage in the German city.

"There is nothing to do here," sighed a dispirited Berliner. Old men, women, and children trudged along, aimlessly pushing wheelbarrows. Over a million people lived in cellars, ruins, and makeshift suburban shacks, trading what they could for precious scraps of food to support their meager diet. Sixty-five to 75 percent of the city was levelled or damaged. The once-prized chariot of victory on the Brandenberg Gate had been reduced to a gnarled mass of molten metal. The Reichstag was a hollow shell. Some *"Nicht fur juden"* signs were still posted, ugly reminders of the German extermination of European Jews. Industrial equipment which survived the bombings had been torn from its foundations by the Russians as war booty, leaving stripped, hull-like factories. Partially buried corpses lay rotting in the sun. Visitors and citizens alike recoiled from the stench of death that hung everywhere. Lord Moran, who accompanied Churchill in Berlin, "felt a sense of nausea." Worse, "it was like the first time I saw a surgeon open a belly and the intestines gushed out."

The curious prime minister entered what was left of Adolf Hitler's Chancellery. The Führer's marble-topped desk lay in a thousand pieces. Iron Crosses, military ribbons, and papers littered the floor. Uncharacteristically, Churchill said little as the descent into Hitler's damp hideaway apparently induced quiet reflection. Members of the prime minister's party picked up souvenirs; one pocketed a fragment of Hitler's world map. Depressed by what he saw, General H. L. Ismay hurried away to his villa to take a hot bath and a strong drink. That night Churchill finally talked about his visit to the Chancellery. "It was from there that Hitler planned to govern the world," he mused. "A good many have tried that; all failed." Savoring the Allied victory, the prime minister smiled contentedly and went to bed.

The president of the United States, Harry S Truman, surveyed Berlin that same day. After reviewing the American 2nd Armored Division, the president led his entourage down the Wilhelmstrasse to the Chancellery of the Third Reich, all the while growing more awestruck by the destruction of the city. "That's what happens," he remarked, "when a man overreaches himself." For two hours Truman rode through Berlin's streets. "I was thankful," he noted later, "that the United States had been spared the unbelievable devastation of this war." Berlin had actually appeared worse a month earlier, before Berliners, under the stern guidance of Russian and other Allied soldiers, began to stack bricks and shovel ashes. American diplomat Robert Murphy found that "the odor of death was everywhere." Indeed, "the canals were choked with bodies and refuse." General Lucius Clay, who would soon become the military governor of the American zone, was also stunned. "The streets were piled high with debris which left in many places only a narrow one-way passage between mounds of rubble, and frequent detours had to be made where bridges and viaducts were destroyed. . . . It was like a city of the dead."

From urban center to rural village, Germany looked charred and ravaged. Bomb-gutted Cologne and Nuremberg were hardly recognizable. Ninety-three percent of the houses in Düsseldorf were totally destroyed. Hamburg, Stuttgart, and Dresden had been laid waste by firebombs and firestorms. In Dresden mounds of bodies had to be bulldozed into mass graves or burned on huge makeshift grills, so great was the toll and the fear of epidemic disease. An American Army Air Corpsman flying low over the country at the end of the war could not spot streets or homes in Mannheim—only tossed dirt. "Aachen," he observed, "lay bleaching in the sun like bones on a desert." A disbelieving companion gazed at the pulverized land below and asked, "Where do the people live?"

Hospitals, schools, and churches throughout Germany felt the war's fury. Fourteen of the nation's twenty-three universities were severely damaged. Transportation and communication systems were disrupted. Untreated sewage flowed into waterways, spreading disease. Water traffic on the Rhine River, which before the war had been greater than that of the Suez or Panama Canals, was now negligible; demolished bridges and sunken vessels blocked the artery. Industrial plants, once the marvel of Europe, lay prostrate. The Ruhr, which had produced 400,000 tons of coal a day, could manage only a paltry 25,000 in 1945. "If we had then realized the confusion and chaos which existed," General Clay wrote five years after the war, "we would indeed have thought ours a hopeless task." . . .

Europe lost more than 30 million people in the Second World War. The grisly statistical gallery ranked Russia an uncontested first [with 15 to 20 million dead]. Then came Poland with 5.8 million dead; Germany, with 4.5 million; Yugoslavia, 1.5 million; France, 600,000; Romania, 460,000; Hungary, 430,000; Czechoslovakia, 415,000; Italy, 410,000; Britain, 400,000; and the Netherlands, 210,000. C. Day Lewis's "War Poem" read:

> They lie in the Sunday Street
> Like effigies thrown down after a fête
> Among the bare-faced houses frankly yawning revulsion,
> Fag ends of fires, litter of rubble, stale
> Confetti sprinkle of blood. . . .

As for the living, they had to endure food shortages, closed factories, idle fields, cold stoves, currency inflation, festering wounds. In West Germany alone, two million cripples hobbled about. Thirty-four percent of the Germans born in 1924 were badly mutilated in some way by 1945. The sad photographs of ill-clad, skeletal bodies struggling for life in Germany's concentration camps provided evidence enough of the human depredation. Displaced persons (DPs) provided another picture. "The wind will tell you what has come to us; /It rolls our brittle bones from pole to pole," went "The Refugees' Testament." Many dazed refugees wandered helplessly through Europe, searching for relatives, for friends, for a livelihood, for a ride home. The words of British writer Richard Mayne have poignantly depicted the lives of Europe's survivors:

> To many of the troops who first encountered them, the people in parts of Europe seemed a population of cripples, of women and children and the very old. Some were starving; some were sick with typhus or dysentery. . . . The survivors, gray-faced ghosts in parodies of clothing, trundled their salvaged belongings in homemade handcarts—rugs, threadbare overcoats, a kettle, an alarm clock, a battered toy. They waited at stand-pipes for a dribble of brown water; they queued for bread and potatoes; they rummaged for sticks and scraps. For them, this waste land of rubble, rags, and hunger was a prison without privacy or dignity; and like all prisons, it smelled. It smelled of dust, oil, gunpowder, and greasy metal; of drains and vermin; of decay and burning and the unburied dead.

So it was in parts of Asia as well, where Japanese forces had been beaten back to their small imperial islands and finally battered with firebombs and two monumental atomic blasts. The lush vegetation of the Philippines and numerous Pacific islands was singed and burned, whole jungles disappearing. A British official who stopped at Okinawa remarked that it looked like the Somme after World War I. China had known population pressure, famine, and epidemics before the war. But Japanese plunder, the destruction of cities, disruption of vital agricultural production, and the displacement of its people increased the burdens that the Chinese had to bear in the postwar period. Hunan and Kwangsi were devastated. Along with Kwangtung, these provinces were visited by famine; millions suffered malnutrition and outright starvation. Cholera, plague, tuberculosis, smallpox, and malaria struck a population which had only 12,000 physicians—one for every 40,000 people. In 1938 the key dikes along the Yellow River—"China's

Sorrow"—were blown up, killing thousands and flooding three million acres of fertile land. China's rivers now rampaged in the Spring and Summer through vulnerable villages. Manchuria's industrial plants were destroyed or dismantled, and China's small railroad network was a shambles. Some 1.32 million Chinese soldiers died; incalculable civilian losses were greater. Kiang Ling's "The Chinese Refugee" captured the times:

> Weeping I left my loved hills;
> Now by this flat long river
> Wandering, homeless, fleeing, fearing . . .
> Wandering till what time?
> Fleeing to what clime?
> Today's riches are ashes tomorrow;
> In a moment joy turns into sorrow.
> How call this yours or mine,
> How rich and poor define?
> In the eyes of death and flame
> Rich and poor are all the same.

For defeated Japan, the bitter results of imperial dreams could be measured in the loss of 2 million lives. Tokyo's population was reduced from 6.5 million to 3 million by war's end, and 700,000 of the city's buildings were destroyed. American planes had dropped napalm-filled bombs, engulfing the city in chemically induced firestorms which generated temperatures of up to 1,800°F. The odor of burning flesh drifted upwards, sickening the pilots who delivered the horrible punishment. In one savage attack alone, on May 23, 1945, 83,000 people died in what observers described as a mass burning. The fifteen-mile stretch between Yokohama and Tokyo, said an American officer who accompanied American general Douglas MacArthur to Japan, had become a "wilderness of rubble." A light dust hung in the air, staining visitors' clothing. Wood-and-paper houses had been reduced to powdered ashes, factories to twisted metal. A shanty town of rusted, corrugated sheets and other junk ringed the capital city, its inhabitants reminding some observers of the Okies who trekked to California during the Great Depression—except that the Japanese scene was more emotionally debilitating. Only the downtown commercial district was free from the mounds of debris. One of the first American naval officers to arrive in the humbled Japanese city wrote to a friend that "I feel like a tramp who has become used to sleeping in a graveyard." A British visitor, Lord Alanbrooke, also visited Tokyo: "Everywhere the same desolation; it must be seen to be believed."

Hiroshima and Nagasaki were special cases, sharing and suffering a special fate. Hiroshima had been Japan's eighth largest city. A residential, commercial center of 250,000 people, it was singled out by American officials because it also housed regional military headquarters. Until August 6, 1945, a cloudless, warm day, Hiroshima had not had to endure large-scale American bombing raids. But at 8:15 A. M. the crew of the *Enola Gay*, a specially outfitted B-29, unleashed "Little Boy," an atomic device packing the power of 20,000 tons of TNT. The bomb fell for fifty seconds and exploded about 2,000 feet above ground. A blinding streak of light raced across the sky; a tremendous boom punctuated the air. A huge, purplish cloud of dust, smoke, and debris shot 40,000 feet into the atmosphere. At ground level the heat became suffocating, the winds violent. Buildings instantly disintegrated. Shadows were etched in stone. Trees were stripped of their leaves. Fires erupted everywhere, and the sky grew dark. Survivors staggered toward water to quench their intense thirst. Skin peeled from burned bodies. A maimed resident, Dr. Michihiko Hachiya, noted that "no one talked, and the ominous silence was relieved only by a subdued rustle among so many people, restless, in pain, anxious, and afraid, waiting for something else to happen." The toll: seventy to eighty thousand dead, an equal number wounded, and 81 percent of the city's buildings destroyed. Three days later the nightmare was repeated in Nagasaki, where at least 35,000 died. Upon hearing of the success of the world's first nuclear destruction of a city, President Truman remarked, "this is the greatest thing in history."

Whether this historical judgment was accurate or not, the tragedy at Hiroshima was but one chapter in the story of massive, war-induced destruction. This story, with all its horrid details, must be catalogued not for its shock value but for its illustration of how large were the problems of the postwar world, how shaky the scaffolding of the international order. Hitler once said about his warmongering pursuits that "we may be destroyed, but if we are, we shall drag a world with us—a world in flames." He partially succeeded, and World War II, like any war of substantial duration, served as an agent of conspicuous change, of revolution. The conflagration of 1939–45 was so wrenching, so total, so profound, that a world was overturned—not simply a material world of crops, buildings, and rails, not simply a human world of healthy and productive laborers, farmers, businessmen, and intellectuals, not simply a secure world of close-knit families and communities, not simply a military world of Nazi stormtroopers and Japanese kamikazis, but all that and more. The war also unhinged the world of stable politics, inherited wisdom, traditions, institutions, alliances, loyalties, commerce, and classes. When Acting Secretary of State Dean Acheson surveyed the problems facing American foreign policy in the postwar era, he saw as uppermost "social *disintegration*, political *disintegration*, the loss of faith by people in leaders who have led them in the past, and a great deal of economic *disintegration*."

Leaders of all political persuasions, as they witnessed the immensity of the destruction, spoke of a new age without knowing its dimensions. The normal way of doing things now seemed inappropriate, although as creatures of the past, the survivors remained attached to ideas and institutions which seemed to provide security through familiarity. They sensed the seriousness and the enormity of the tasks of cleaning up the rubble, of putting the broken world back together again, of shaping an orderly international system. Yet it was evident, too, that few nations or individuals had the material resources, talent, and desire—the sheer energy, guts, and money—to mold a brave new world out of the discredited and crumbled old. If the reconstruction tasks seemed herculean, however, the opportunities appeared boundless for the ambitious, the hearty, and the caring. One vigorous, optimistic, well-intentioned, competitive voice sounded above the rubble that constituted London, Berlin, Warsaw, Minsk, and Tokyo. That voice echoed with power from the United States, the wartime "arsenal of democracy."

At war's end President Truman declared a two-day national holiday. Horns, bells, and makeshift noisemakers sounded across the nation. Paraders in Los Angeles played leapfrog on Hollywood Boulevard; farther north, jubilant sailors broke windows along San Francisco's Market Street. In New York City tons of litter were tossed from the windows of skyscrapers on cheering crowds below. Stock market prices shot up. A five-year-old boy recorded the August 1945 moment: "This is the best year. The war is over. Two wars are over. Everyone is happy. Tin cans are rolling. Everything is confused. And little pieces of paper." It was truly a happy time. Not only was the dying over, but the United States had emerged from the global conflict in the unique position of an unscathed belligerent. No bombs fell on American cities. No armies ravaged the countryside. No American boundaries were redrawn. Factories stood in place, producing goods at an impressive rate. In August, at the General Motors plant in Moraine, Ohio, shiny new Frigidaire refrigerators and airplane propeller blades moved along parallel assembly lines. Farms were rich in crops, and full employment during the war years had buoyed family savings. "The American people," remarked the director of the Office of War Mobilization and Reconversion, "are in the pleasant predicament of having to learn to live 50 percent better than they have ever lived before."

Whereas much of Europe and Asia faced the massive task of "reconstruction," the United States faced "reconversion"—adjusting the huge war machine to peacetime purposes. Automobile plants had to convert production from tanks to cars, a delightful prospect for auto manufacturers, who knew that Americans were eager to spend their wartime earnings on consumer goods once again. With great pride Americans applauded their good fortune. They were different. They had no rubble to clear. The Russians knew, said Joseph Stalin in a grand understatement, that "things are not bad in the United States." . . .

In the rubble-strewn postwar world, international relations changed markedly from prewar interactions. Any historical period, such as the Cold War, is identified by a particular structure of relationships among the world's leading nations—by, in short, the international "system." Thus, the Napoleonic era of the late eighteenth and early nineteenth centuries was characterized by bipolarism, wherein France and Britain vied for world mastery, established alliances with lesser powers, frequently clashed in war, and managed far-flung empires. The period between the Congress of Vienna in 1815 and the outbreak of World War I in 1914, often called the era of Pax Britannica, was multipolar, with a number of leading actors on the international stage who preferred diplomatic negotiations to military combat and who deliberately set about to create a balance of power for the maintenance of a conservative, imperial, antirevolutionary world.

Any international system is conflict-ridden. "Peace," after all, is a very abstract term, difficult to employ as a description of any era. "Anarchy" probably more aptly approximates historical reality. The attempts nations make to reduce the anarchy constitute our diplomatic history. Conflict is inherent in any international system simply because countries seldom share common goals, interests, or ideologies. Some nations are more powerful or influential than others and flaunt their superiority. Others may resist. Some countries are dependent upon others. Some have what others want—territory, food, water, minerals, labor, and a multitude of things over which peoples have squabbled for centuries. Great nations are always looking for friends who will join them in formal or informal alliances to check the growth of those states they consider unfriendly or potentially so. Small nations have to be wary of the major actors, who may cast longing eyes on them and exploit their vulnerability. Nations which may wish to remain "neutral" or unaligned are wooed or cajoled.

The leading powers, whether aligned or at loggerheads, watch one another suspiciously, on the assumption that in international politics, as in business, one can supposedly trust friends seldom, enemies never. Slight shifts in the distribution of power—of resources—arouse concern. What one government considers "defense," another labels "offense." The construction of a military base, the testing of a new weapon, a request to alter a boundary, the signing of a treaty—all can be defined as both defensive or offensive, depending upon one's point of view. A rifle is a defensive weapon if seen from the butt, but it is a weapon of attack if one is staring into the muzzle. Suspicion and fear, those ancient diseases, undermine trust and prompt countermeasures. Leaders may assume evil intentions on the part of other nations and plan for the worst. Governments feel compelled to match the decisions of those whom they assume to be adversaries. Failure to develop a new weapon, for example, might entail extreme risk, for an enemy might gain advantage by producing it. Hence, leaders often escalate the level of conflict and chances for war through exaggerated perceptions of danger. In short, there is always an expanding nation, and there are countries reacting to that expansion. Differences in goals among the several parties of the international system feed instability. The degree of conflict may vary, but there is always conflict. "This is a lawless world," University of Chicago Professor Herman Finer told a radio audience in 1947, "because it is a world without a common morality or a common superior. Nationalisms and moralities collide."

Higher degrees of conflict are reached when the international system undergoes significant change, when it metamorphoses into a new or revised system. Such was the case after World War II. Change, by definition, is destabilizing. Some postwar leaders, even though immersed in day-to-day decisionmaking, pondered the general characteristics of the international system. They knew that significant changes had altered the configuration of power. As participants in and shapers of a new age, they were "present at the creation." But the outline of the new system was only vaguely evident. With the historian's advantage of hindsight, however, we can delineate the peculiar properties of the postwar world and suggest that the process of creating a new system out of the ashes of the discredited prewar system intensified the conflict inherent in any international structure.

Yet this view of systemic conflict cannot serve as a comprehensive explanation for the origins of the Cold War. For if the Soviet-American confrontation was simply the inevitable product of the conflict-ridden international system, there would be little purpose in studying the leaders, ideas, policies, or needs of individual nations, because events would be largely beyond their control. Under this interpretation the system would dictate antagonistic relations. It would not matter whether different personalities or different national policies existed. Few scholars, however, subscribe to this restricted analysis of history. We know that leaders made choices, even if they only dimly understood their consequences. Harry S Truman, Winston Churchill, and Josef Stalin helped to create the international system to which they had to react. A complete history of the beginnings of the Cold War, then, must include not only the traits of the international system but also the dynamics of particular nations and individuals. . . . [A] macroanalytic view will enable us to identify the opportunities and constraints which faced the major actors. Or, as Professor Bruce M. Russett has suggested, this level of analysis outlines the "menu" of world affairs—the choices available, as well as the limits of choice. It sketches the "big picture," so that the disparate components of the postwar system can be examined in proper relationship. It helps us to determine which nations held real or potential power and why, ultimately, they moved toward restrictive spheres of influence and away from a community of interest and international cooperation.

Conflict in the postwar years was accentuated by wrenching changes in the international system—a redistribution of power and a departure from a Europe-centered world. Two nations emerged from the rubble of World War II to claim first rank. The competitive interaction between the United States and the Soviet Union—"like two big dogs chewing on a bone," said Senator J. William Fulbright—contributed to the bipolarism of the immediate postwar years. "Not since Rome and Carthage," Dean Acheson observed, "had there been such a polarization of power on this earth." This new bipolar structure replaced the multipolar system of the 1930s, wherein at least six nations were active, influential participants. By the late 1940s, decisions made in Washington, D. C., and Moscow often determined whether people in other nations voted, where they lived, and how much they ate. The nations which had tried to wield such authority in the 1930s had fallen from their elevated status. Japan, Italy, and Germany were defeated and occupied; England, nearly bankrupt, dependent, and unable to police its empire, was reduced to a resentful second-rate power; France, much of whose territory had been held by the Germans during the war, was still suffering from unstable politics and no longer mustered international respect.

The abrupt removal of Germany and Japan from positions of high authority in international relations created power vacuums in Europe and Asia. The United States and Soviet Russia, eager to fulfill their visions of the postwar world and to seize opportunities for extending their respective influence, were attracted to these vacuums. With the old barriers to American and Soviet expansion gone, Russia and America clashed over occupation policies in Germany, Italy, Japan, Austria, and Korea. They squabbled over which political groups should replace the Nazi regimes in Eastern Europe. The filling of gaps or vacuums in any system is a natural process. In the postwar period the gaps were huge and worldwide, inviting a high degree of competition and conflict.

Another change wrought by World War II was the destruction of the economic world. The war cut an ugly scar across Europe and Asia, but bypassed one major nation, the United States. "If Hitler succeeds in nothing else," mused OSS officer Allen Dulles, "like Samson, he may pull down the pillars of the temple and leave a long and hard road of reconstruction." The postwar task was forbidding. Not only did cities have to be rebuilt, factories opened, people put back to work, rails repaired, rivers and roads made passable, and crop yields increased, but the flow of international commerce and finance had to be reestablished if nations were to raise through exports the revenue needed to buy the imports required for recovery. Many old commercial and financial patterns had been broken and, given the obstacle of economic wreckage, new exchanges were difficult to establish. Where would Germany's vital coal and steel go? Would industrial Western Europe and agricultural Eastern Europe recreate old commercial ties? Would the restrictive trade practices of the 1930s, especially the tariff barriers, continue into the 1940s? Would subservient colonies continue to serve as sources of rich raw materials? Could international agreements and organizations curb economic nationalism? Would trade be conducted on a multilateral, "open door" basis, as the United States preferred, or by bilateral or preferential methods, as many others, such as Britain and Russia, practiced? The answers helped to define the international system of the

post-1945 era. These issues held more importance than simple economics, for leaders recognized that the economic disorders of the 1930s
and the far-reaching impact of the Great Depression contributed to
political chaos, aggression, and war. The new international system, it
was hoped, would create stable economic conditions which would facilitate the development of pacific international relations. Yet the very
efforts to realize these hopes engendered conflict.

World War II also bequeathed domestic political turmoil to its
survivors. The regimes of the 1930s, now discredited, vied with insur-
gent groups for the governing power in many states. Socialists, Communists, and other varieties of the political left, many of whom had
fought in the underground resistance movements and had thus earned
some popular respect, challenged the more entrenched, conservative
elites, many of whom had escaped into exile when the German armies
rolled into their countries. In Poland, the Communist, Soviet-endorsed
Lublin Poles challenged the political standing of the Poles who had fled
to London. The conservative Dutch government-in-exile watched warily as leftist resistance groups gradually built a popular following.
Political confusion in the Netherlands was heightened by the wartime
loss of voting lists. In Greece a coalition of leftists in the National Lib-
eration Front (EAM) vigorously resisted the return to power of a
British-created government and the unpopular Greek monarchy of King
George. In France Charles de Gaulle vied for power with the Commu-
nists. In China the civil war, which had raged for years between the
Communists of Mao Tse-tung [Mao Zedong] and the Nationalists of
Chiang Kai-shek [Jiang Jieshi], flared up again at the close of the war.
Yugoslavia was the scene of political battle between Josip Broz Tito's
Partisans and a group headed by Dr. Ivan Subasic of the London emi-
gré government, which in turn suffered strained ties with King Peter.
Moreover, in the occupied nations of Germany, Austria, and Korea, the
victors created competitive zones, postponing the creation of central
governments. In the defeated countries of Japan and Italy, American
officials decided who would rule, whereas in parts of Eastern Europe,
Soviet officials placed Communists in positions of authority.

The major powers, in short, intervened abroad to exploit the
political opportunities created by the destructive scythe of World War
II. The stakes seemed high. A change in a nation's political orientation
might presage a change in its international alignment. The great powers
tended to ignore local conditions which might mitigate against alignment with an outside power. Americans feared that a leftist or Com-

munist Greece would look to the East and permit menacing Soviet bases on Greek territory or open the door to a Soviet naval presence in the Mediterranean. The Russians dreaded a conservative anti-Soviet Polish government led by the London faction, for it might prove so weak and so hostile to Moscow as to permit a revived Germany to send stormtroopers once again through the Polish corridor into the heart of Russia. A Communist China, thought Americans, might align with Russia; a Nationalist China would remain in the American camp. All in all, the rearranging of political structures *within* nations drew the major powers into competition, accentuating the conflict inherent in the postwar international system.

If the war threw politics into chaos, it also hastened the disintegration of colonial and informal empires. The Japanese movement into French Indochina and their drive for Dutch East Indies oil had led to Pearl Harbor in 1941. The initially successful Japanese expansion had the effect of demonstrating to many Asian nationalists that their white imperial masters could be defeated. Some nationalists collaborated during the war with their Asian brethren from Tokyo, and the Japanese, in need of administrators to manage occupied areas, trained and armed some native leaders. Japan granted Burma considerable autonomy in 1942, for example, and after the war the Burmese were determined not to return to a position of subservience to Great Britain. At the end of the war, the European powers, exhausted and financially hobbled, had to struggle to reestablish mastery over rebellious colonies. The appeal of the principle of self-determination, still echoing from the days of Woodrow Wilson and given new emphasis by the Atlantic Charter of 1941, was far-reaching.

No empire seemed immune to disintegration. The United States granted the Philippines independence in 1946. The British, worn low by the war and by the challenges of nationalist groups demanding independence, retreated from India (and Pakistan) in 1947 and from Burma and Ceylon in 1948. Israel, carved out of British-governed Palestine, became a new independent state in 1948. The British also found it difficult to maintain their sphere of influence in Iran, Greece, and Egypt and began retreats from those politically unsteady states. The French attempted to hold on to Indochina, where nationalist forces led by Ho Chi Minh had declared an independent Vietnam. Bloody battle ensued, leading ultimately to French withdrawal in 1954. The Dutch also decided to fight, but after four debilitating years of combat, they pulled out of Indonesia in 1949. The defeated Japanese were forced to give up their claims to Formosa and Korea, as well as Pacific island groups. Italy departed from Ethiopia and lost its African colonies of Tripolitania (Libya) and Eritrea. Lebanon, Syria, and Jordan, areas once managed by Europeans, gained independence in 1943, 1944, and 1946, respectively.

The world map, as after World War I, was redrawn. The emergence of so many new states, and the instability associated with the transfer of authority, shook the very foundations of the international system. Power was being redistributed. In varying degrees, Russia and America competed for the allegiance of the new governments, meddled in colonial rebellions, and generally sought to exploit opportunities for an extension of their influence. Again, the stakes seemed high. The new nations could serve as strategic bases, markets for exports, sources of vital raw materials, sites for investments, and votes in international organizations. States such as India, which chose nonalignment in the developing Cold War, were wooed with foreign aid and ideological appeals. In the case of Indochina, the powers supported different sides: Washington backed the ruling French, and Moscow endorsed Ho and his insurgents.

As one United States government study noted, the disintegration of empires, especially the withdrawal of the British from their once vast domain, created an "over-all situation of near chaos" in the international system. In some areas, such as Southeast Asia, it meant a "new balance of power." The upheaval was fundamental: "Old values are being changed and new ones sought. New friendships are being formed." The international system creaked and swayed under this unsettled burden.

Conflict also sprang from efforts to launch a new international organization to replace the defunct League of Nations. At the Dumbarton Oaks Conference in 1944, the Allies initiated plans for a United Nations Organization. The United States, Britain, and Russia were its chief architects, and the institution they created at the San Francisco Conference from April to June of 1945 reflected their insistence on big-power domination. They agreed upon a veto power for the five "permanent members" of the Security Council (Britain, Russia, United States, France, and China) and assigned the General Assembly, the forum for smaller nations, a subordinate status. Nevertheless, because each of the Allies recognized that the new international body was potentially an instrument, through bloc voting, of one nation's foreign policy, they argued. Churchill crudely complained that China, hardly a "great" power, would be a "faggot vote on the side of the United States," and Russia protested that France would simply represent a British vote. "China was a joke," remarked State Department veteran John Hickerson, "a[n] FDR joke." Because Britain could marshall the votes of several of its Commonwealth countries and the United States could count on most of the Latin American nations in the General Assembly, the conferees at the Yalta Conference of early 1945 granted Russia three votes, in order to alter somewhat the glaring imbalance.

Such compromise, however, broke down at the San Francisco Conference. Membership applications from Argentina and Poland produced heated differences. Against vehement Soviet objections Argentina, which had declared war against Germany at the last minute and which some critics considered a "fascist" nation, gained membership after the United States backed its application and the nations of the Western Hemisphere voted "yes" as a bloc. Yet when Lublin-led Poland, not yet reorganized according to the American interpretation of the Yalta accords, applied for entry, the United States voted "no," and the conference denied Poland a seat. Moscow railed at this, charging a double standard. The United Nations Organization, which held its first session in January of 1946, thus began amidst controversy. Rather than serving as a stabilizing force in the postwar international system, the United Nations early became a source of conflict, a verbal battleground for the allegiance of world opinion, a vehicle for condemnatory resolutions, a largely United States–dominated institution, and a graveyard for idealistic hopes—in short, part of a "masquerade peace."

The postwar international system suffered, too, from the destabilizing effect of the new atomic bomb. The "most terrible weapon ever known in human history," Secretary of War Henry L. Stimson quietly told the President, unsettled the world community, for it was an agent of massive human destruction, and "in a world atmosphere already extremely sensitive to power, the introduction of this weapon has profoundly affected political considerations in all sections of the globe." Nations which possessed "the bomb" seemed to hold an advantage in international politics, for it could serve as a deterrent against an adversary as well as a means to annihilate an enemy. When combined with air power and a long-range delivery capability, it also hurdled geographical boundaries, rendering them useless as protective elements in a nation's security shield. With the perfecting of air war in World War II, "the roof blew off the territorial state." As General Douglas MacArthur remarked after the atomic explosions: "Well, this changes warfare!"

The prospect of nuclear annihilation bothered everybody, but the United States was especially concerned about nuclear proliferation, which meant the loss of its atomic monopoly.

A question dogged the peacemakers: How were they to control the development, spread, and use of atomic energy? There had been arms races before, and ineffective disarmament conferences in the 1920s and 1930s, but the postwar nuclear race was conducted at a far different and more dangerous level. The atomic bomb was the "absolute weapon," not only more violent but also capable of speedy delivery, rapid retaliation, and immediate cataclysm. Challenging the American monopoly, the Soviet Union successfully produced its own bomb in 1949. As the two bickering major powers groped for ways in which to deal with "the bomb" and undertook their atomic development programs, others held their breath. One observer suggested that a Soviet-American war "might not end with *one* Rome but with *two* Carthages." The atomic bomb, uncontrolled, envied, copied, and brandished, became a major obstacle to a peaceful, orderly postwar international system.

The shrinkage of the world and the growth of a global outlook must be included in any estimation of the impact of World War II on the international system. Geography had not changed, but ways of moving across it and of thinking about it had. Improvements in transportation, especially in aviation, brought nations closer to one another. The world seemed more compact and accessible. People had to think now not only in traditional land miles but also in flying hours. In a popularization for school children, N. L. Englehardt, Jr., urged his young readers to think "air thoughts" and titled one of his chapters "How the World Has Shrunk." Because the Atlantic Ocean could be traversed easily and quickly, that once-prominent barrier between the Old and New Worlds disappeared. As America was brought closer to Europe and the world, American strategic thinking expanded as well. In the world contracted by science, events in Greece or Iran or China held greater significance than ever before for American security. The Japanese attack upon Pearl Harbor, accomplished after crossing 3,500 miles of the Pacific Ocean, had proved that great distances no longer served as protectors of security. "If you imagine two or three hundred Pearl Harbors occurring all over the United States," prophesied Assistant Secretary of State A. A. Berle, "you will have a rough picture of what the next war might look like. . . ." Observers began to speak not only of an "atomic age," but of an "air age" and a "global age." The global war of 1939–45 had helped spawn a postwar globalism—an international interdependence. "The entire relations of the United States with the world," declared Dean Acheson, "are a seamless web. . . ." Geographical isolation was gone with the past. Stimson perceived that the United States could never again "be an island to herself. No private program and no public policy, in any sector of our national life can now escape from the compelling fact that if it is not framed with reference to the world, it is framed with perfect futility."

United States Chief of Staff General George C. Marshall typified strategic reconsiderations. "For probably the last time in the history of warfare those ocean distances were a vital factor in our defense. We may elect again to depend on others and the whim and error of potential enemies, but if we do we will be carrying the treasure and freedom of this great Nation in a paper bag." Because frontiers had been extended, because nations were brought nearer one another, and because the world had shrunk, the major powers coveted bases far from home, much as the United States had sought and acquired bases in the Caribbean in the early twentieth century to protect the Panama Canal. "We are now concerned with the peace of the entire world," said Marshall. Two years later President Truman described a "much smaller earth—an earth whose broad oceans have shrunk and whose national protections have been taken away by new weapons of destruction." In a similar vein, a Joint Chiefs of Staff report of late 1947 looked ten years into the future and predicted a "continuing shrinkage of the world from the accelerated pace of technological progress." In short, a new aspect of the postwar international system was the interdependence or intertwining of events in all parts of the world, thereby drawing great powers into confrontations as never before. Globalism insured conflict.

Such was the postwar international system—with its opportunities and constraints, with its characteristics insuring conflict. The makers of the peace sought to reduce the conflict, but their decisions exacerbated it.

Geir Lundestad

AMERICAN EMPIRE BY INVITATION

Norwegian scholar Geir Lundestad, a self-professed post-revisionist, accepts the view that the United States was the predominant power in the early postwar years and that, as such, it built an empire. Yet, he argues, this empire developed not from American design but rather by invitation. That is, many foreign governments, especially in Western Europe, looked to the United States for economic assistance and security, pressed Washington to become more active in world affairs, and invited American economic and military support. Like Melvyn P. Leffler, Lundestad seems to acknowledge that United States officials had their own drives and plans in extending and protecting America's worldwide interests. But he leaves unanswered the question of whether the United States, given its interests, would have had to force its will on other peoples if it had not been for the "invitations" from abroad.

Geir Lundestad has taught history at the University of Tromsö and now administers the Nobel Peace Prize in Norway. He has written three books: *The American Non-Policy Towards Eastern Europe (1943–1947)* (1975), *America, Scandinavia and the Cold War 1945–1949* (1980), and *East, West, North, South* (1986).

"Traditionalist" historians have generally stressed the expansion of the Soviet Union after the Second World War. The Soviet Union did expand. It insisted on exercising near absolute control over Eastern Europe, it dominated North Korea, and it strengthened its position in Mongolia and later in Vietnam. The communists did win a momentous victory in China, but that was a victory won with little assistance from Moscow. As Mao Tse-tung [Mao Zedong] himself said in 1958, with only slight exaggeration, "The Chinese revolution won victory by acting contrary to Stalin's will." The communist victory was also to prove a rather temporary blessing for the Soviets.

Thus, there was Soviet expansion after the war. But this article puts forward two suppositions. First, it will support the "revisionist" argument that the American expansion was really more striking than the Soviet one. Only the United States became a global power in the years we are dealing with here. While America's influence could be felt in

"Empire by Invitation? The United States and Western Europe, 1945–1952," by Geir Lundestad in *Journal of Peace Research*, vol. XXIII, No. 3, 1986, pp. 263–70. Reprinted by permission of the Journal of Peace Research and of the author.

most corners of the world, with only a few exceptions the Soviet Union counted for little outside its border areas, however vast these border areas. The American expansion went so deep and affected so many different parts of the world that it can be said to have resulted in an American empire.

Second, and here I differ from the revisionists, if we choose to call this an empire, it was to a large extent an empire by invitation. Unlike the Soviet Union, which frequently had to rely on force, the United States was generally encouraged to take a more active interest in the outside world. The American influence often went deeper than the Soviet exactly because Washington's forms of control were more in accordance with the will of the local populations than were Moscow's. Not only that, but under this American empire many of the countries that welcomed American influence were also able to do considerably better, at least in long-term material terms, than was the United States itself.

The United States came out of the Second World War by far the strongest power on earth. In constant 1958 prices the American gross national product had grown from $209.4 billion in 1939 to $355.2 billion in 1945. That constituted approximately half of the world's goods and services. Steel production jumped from 53 million tons in 1939 to 80 million in 1945. Production in agriculture increased at a similar pace. With 6% of the world's population, the United States had 46% of the world's electric power, 48% of its radios, 54% of its telephones, and its businesses owned or controlled 59% of the world's total oil reserves. American automobile production was eight times that of France, Britain, and Germany combined. "Only" 400,000 Americans had lost their lives because of the war.

The population of the Soviet Union is estimated to have been around 194 million in 1940. At the end of the war it numbered around 170 million. In 1945 the Soviet Union produced 10.6 million tons of steel, only half of what it produced in 1941. The Soviet Union built 65,000 cars compared to seven million in the United States. In 1945 agricultural production was only half of what it had been in 1940, which was not a very good year, if there ever are good years in Soviet agriculture.

On the military side, only the United States had the atomic bomb. In 1944—at its highest—aircraft production reached 95,000. The US had a vast lead not only on the Soviet Union, but American production even surpassed that of Germany and Japan combined. The American navy was by far the biggest and most efficient in the world. In one field only could the Soviet Union compare with the United States. They both had roughly 12 million men under arms.

Britain was about to lose its Great Power status, to some extent because of the costs of victory. War damage amounted to roughly £3 billion. Overseas assets of more than another £1 billion had been sold or lost and the income from foreign investment halved. In 1945 Britain was spending abroad more than £2000 million and was earning only about £350 million. The balance had to be acquired primarily from one source, the United States. Britain had a brilliant war record, but little else.

Thus, in 1945 the United States had completed a triumphant war. Its technological revolution had really taken off, its rivals were exhausted economically, and it seemed that the US would more or less control world markets.

As [the historian] Paul Kennedy has argued, a similar description would also fit Britain after the triumphs of the Napoleonic wars. Yet, in some ways, the Pax Americana after 1945 was more pronounced than the Pax Britannica of the 19th century. In 1950 no country had a GNP even one-third the size of that of the United States. In 1830 both Russia and France in fact had GNP's larger than that of Britain. While Britain had pulled away from the European Congress system of the post-Napoleonic period, the United States was generally able to set up a world order of its own. . . .

In geographic terms the postwar expansion was not really that noticeable in Latin America, because this had traditionally been Washington's back yard. The American position even in the Pacific had been strong before the war, but now it was considerably expanded. The Japanese Mandated Islands were put under American control, with only the thinnest of concession to the suzerainty of the United Nations. Japan itself was to be ruled by American authorities. American influence in South Korea remained strong despite the US forces being pulled back in 1948; in the Philippines independence did not really affect this country's ties with the United States that much.

The Second World War had indicated that both Australia and New Zealand would now look to the United States. In 1951 this understanding was formalized through the ANZUS pact. Britain was excluded from taking part, rather pointedly demonstrating the decline of Britain also in this part of the world.

The American role was increasing in other parts of the Pacific and Asia as well, although the expansion was generally less striking here. As to China, Truman remarked to his Cabinet in August 1946 that "For the first time we now have a voice in China and for the first time we will be in a position to carry out the [Open Door] policy of 1898." America gave far more assistance to its side in the Chinese civil war than the Soviet Union did to its. It is another matter that not even three billion dollars could keep Chiang Kai-shek [Jiang Jieshi] afloat.

After some years of vacillation, in 1948 the United States intervened rather decisively on the side of Indonesia against Holland. From 1950 Washington came to meet the costs of a war in Indo-China which a declining France could no longer afford. Even in India, where the United States on the whole showed great deference to Britain, America's attitude had to be taken into account.

In the Middle East American oil companies had been operating before the war in Iraq, Bahrain, Kuwait, and, most important, in Saudi Arabia. Now, as [the historian] Aaron Daniel Miller has argued, "although the Americans had no desire to destroy British influence on the peninsula or in the gulf in Saudi Arabia they sought nothing less than a reversal of traditional roles. No longer would the United States be content to remain Britain's junior partner, but it would now demand primacy in the economic sphere and at least an equal voice in political matters which might affect the fate of the [ARAMCO] concession." In Iran the United States quite rapidly took over the British role in opposing Soviet expansion. The American stand there in 1945–46 was to signal what would follow later in other parts of the world. When the British abandoned Palestine in 1948, the Americans again moved in to take over the British role, first in Israel and later in the moderate Arab countries as well.

In North Africa, as elsewhere, American interests expanded after the war. The United States continued to operate its base in Morocco and nationalist leader Habib Bourguiba in Tunisia came to look to America for support, although he would be disappointed after the expectations Franklin D. Roosevelt had created during the war.

South of the Sahara, Liberia had long been under considerable American influence, but in this part of the world the United States played a more limited role than almost anywhere else.

Western Europe, however, was what really counted. Latin America would be bitterly disappointed by Washington's lack of interest.

In North Africa, in India, in Indo-China, Washington would soft-pedal its skepticism to colonial rule, not to disturb relations with the European big powers. With regard to China the Republicans were right in accusing the Truman Administration of not being willing to do there what it did in Europe. But the fact of the matter was that not even the Republican right wing was willing to do in China what it favored in Europe.

In Eastern Europe, Washington tried to play an active role. Yet, again and again the Americans were to run up against the fact that the Western half of Europe counted for more than the Eastern. The Truman Doctrine did not apply even to all of Europe. In the spring of 1947 the Nagy government in Budapest, which had resulted from free elections in the fall of 1945, was still struggling to survive against Soviet pressure. With quite limited support from the United States, Nagy would soon fall. Repeatedly Washington entered into agreements or undertook actions which actually strengthened the Soviet hold on Eastern Europe. Thus, when the last of the countries in Eastern Europe, Czechoslovakia, "fell" in February 1948, this was an event which many policy makers in Washington had predicted. The Prague coup was in part the result of the Marshall Plan. But, again, nothing could be done about it. Western Europe was simply too important for that.

The American influence in Western Europe was rapidly growing in the years after 1945, militarily, politically, economically, and culturally. In many ways the last aspect was the most important, although it will not be dealt with here.

Militarily, the events of the two world wars had shown that the United States would intervene to prevent Western Europe from falling under the control of a hostile power. The same could happen again, alliance or no alliance. The American monopoly on the atomic bomb also gave the Western Europeans some protection before the creation of NATO.

The American forces in Germany would provide the trip-wire in this context. Before NATO the United States had military bases on Greenland, the Azores, in Britain, and a civilian facility in Iceland.

Still NATO of course greatly strengthened the American role. The outbreak of the Korean war provided an equally important stimulus. Military assistance skyrocketed, the American troop commitment was increased and a joint military apparatus and joint defense plans established under American leadership.

Politically and economically, the American influence varied from country to country, as had Britain's influence on its dominions and colonies. Washington's role was the strongest in the US zone in Germany. There General Lucius Clay and the army leadership, with support from Washington, first modified local plans for socialization in Hesse, and then maneuvered to prevent British and local schemes for the socialization of the coal mines in North Rhine-Westphalia in the Bizone. In a similar way Clay was able to limit labor-management codetermination in the American zone and in the Bizone.

In Greece the Americans dominated the administration to such an extent that Americans actually wrote both the Greek application for aid and the thank-you notes in connection with the Truman Doctrine. Under the Marshall Plan the national bureaucracies in Greece and Turkey broke down to such an extent that Americans were closely involved in running the two countries.

In semi-occupied Italy the State Department and Ambassador James Dunn in particular actively encouraged the non-communists to break with the communists and undoubtedly contributed to the latter being thrown out of the government in May 1947. In more normal France the American role was more restrained when the Ramadier government threw out its communists at about the same time. After the communists were out, Washington worked actively, through overt as well as covert activities, to isolate them as well as leftist socialists. On the other side of the coin, the Americans tried to strengthen the political center, including social democratic forces in the political parties and in the labor unions.

US economic assistance was normally given with several strings attached. The French had to agree to promote trade with the rest of the world and to discourage the setting up of regional trading blocs. The loan agreement with Britain of December 1945 contained even stronger clauses meant to promote freer trade. The Attlee government had to make the pound convertible with the dollar and in principle to agree to remove restrictions that discriminated against imports from the United States.

The strings attached to the Marshall Plan further limited Europe's freedom of action. Trade within Western Europe had to be liberalized; trade with Eastern Europe curtailed; American investments encouraged. The establishment of the counterpart funds represented an instrument with great potential for intervention, since the various countries could only draw upon these funds with the consent of the United States.

Equally important were the indirect effects of the Marshall Plan. Policies had to be conducted with an eye on what might be the reaction in Washington. Thus, even the British cabinet feared that "increased investment in the social service might influence Congress in their appropriations for Marshall Aid."

Many motives can be found for the American expansion after the Second World War. Most traditionalists have referred to America's and Western Europe's needs for security and protection of democracy; most revisionists have instead pointed to America's capitalism with its requirements for exports, imports, and investments. Post-revisionists have been more eclectic in their approaches and have thrown in an assortment of additional factors ranging from bureaucratic politics in the US to the seemingly natural fact that the US, as any other Great Power in history, was bound to expand more or less regardless of its political or economic system. The debate on this point very much resembles the debate on the origins of British imperialism in the 19th century.

I count myself among the post-revisionists and in this context I just take it for granted that the United States had important strategic, political and economic motives of its own for taking on such a comprehensive world role. This article, however, focuses on the reactions of local governments and populations to the American expansion.

The revisionist view of the United States thrusting itself into the affairs of other countries can undoubtedly be supported by examples from several parts of the world. Vietnam was to prove the prime illustration of massive intervention with a rather limited local popular basis. Yet, the basic pattern in the early post-war years, particularly in Western Europe, was a different one. The rule was that the United States was invited in.

Even outside of Europe, leaders in Iran, in Saudi Arabia, in Egypt, in India, in Australia and New Zealand were all looking to the United States. Their motives might vary: the need for economic assistance; a desire to employ America as a counterweight to the Soviet Union, to Britain, or to some other power; or admiration for what the United States stood for.

In this article, the focus is on Western Europe. The Europeans even more strongly than most others attempted to influence the Americans in the direction of taking greater, not lesser, interest in their affairs.

Britain offers the best example in this respect. Although London underestimated Britain's fall from Great Power status, the Attlee, as the Churchill, government clearly favored both financial assistance from

America and a strong US military presence in Europe. In line with this, Whitehall expressed disappointment when Lend-Lease was abruptly curtailed; hoped for a credit substantially larger than the $3.75 billion it received; wished to continue wartime cooperation in atomic energy and the existence of at least some of the combined Anglo-American boards, particularly the Combined Chiefs of Staff; wanted the United States to carry a larger share of the expenses in the German Bizone. . . .

With regard to the desire for economic assistance, the situation was much the same in most European countries. There was a desperate need for economic assistance, and there was really only one major source, the United States. In the period from July 1945 through June 1947 Western Europe in fact on a yearly average received a larger amount of assistance than it did through the Marshall Plan. And then the more than $3 billion which the Western Europeans received in humanitarian aid from the United States is not taken into account. Britain's share alone was $4.4 billion. France received $1.9 billion, Italy $330 million and the Be-Ne-Lux countries $430 million. In this period Eastern Europe only got $546 million. The Eastern Europeans tried to get much more, but their main stumbling block was Washington's unwillingness to grant such assistance to countries dominated by the Soviet Union.

The Europeans also played an important role in shaping the Marshall Plan. The crucial person here was British Foreign Secretary Ernest Bevin. Although Washington was skeptical of working through the Economic Commission for Europe (ECE) and of having the Soviets participate, Washington left much of the initiative for the follow-up to Marshall's Harvard speech on June 5, 1947, to the British and the French. In the ensuing British-French-Soviet conference in Paris, Bevin dominated the scene. The Russian attempt to substitute a bilateral approach for the multilateral one favored by Washington was rejected. The ECE was to be bypassed. The Russians were to be left out. After less than a week the meeting broke down in disagreement. The British Foreign Secretary received unexpectedly firm support from his French counterpart Georges Bidault, considering the complicated domestic scene in Paris.

Under the Marshall Plan the Europeans first requested $28 billion from the United States. This was far more than Washington was willing to give. The Truman Administration cut this down to $17 billion and Congress in turn appropriated approximately $14 billion. Only Moscow's opposition prevented Finland, Czechoslovakia, Poland and even other Eastern European countries from taking part. Washington's own attitude blocked Spanish participation. So, at least on the economic side, there can be no doubt that the Europeans were most interested in involving the United States closely in Europe's affairs.

The same was true in most European countries even on the military side. After the ending of the London meeting of the Council of Foreign Ministers in December 1947, Bevin presented his thoughts on military cooperation to Secretary of State Marshall. The British wanted to set up an arrangement for regional military cooperation in Western Europe. It was also obvious that they wanted to commit the Americans as closely as possible to this arrangement.

Bevin and the British were not the only ones who tried to involve the United States quite closely in the defense problems of Western Europe. At this early stage, Belgian Prime and Foreign Minister Paul-Henri Spaak even went so far as to argue that any defense arrangements which did not include the United States were without practical value. The Dutch favored the same line. . . .

The European pressure on the United States was building up. This perspective of Europe pulling upon the United States, instead of the other way around, should not be taken too far. Washington could not be, and was not, forced into anything against its will. Important groups in the American capital, for many different reasons, favored a strong military role in Western Europe. The point here is that at least the Europeans clearly speeded up the clarification process on the American side. [In 1949 the North Atlantic Treaty Organization was created, and the United States became a prominent member.] . . .

Thus, American expansion was one of the most striking phenomena of the post-war period; this expansion can be said to have created an American empire equal in scope to any the world had seen before. Yet, this was to a large extent an empire by invitation and it turned out that many of those who issued the invitations prospered more in material terms under the new order than did the United States itself.

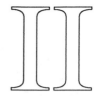

The Origins of the Cold War in Europe

Barton J. Bernstein

SAVING AMERICAN LIVES AND PRESSING THE SOVIETS: THE ATOMIC BOMB DECISION AND THE COLD WAR

President Truman's explanation for his decision in August 1945 to annihilate the Japanese cities of Hiroshima and Nagasaki with atomic bombs was characteristically brief and pointed: to end the Second World War as quickly as possible in order to save American lives. The following essay does not dispute Truman's point but does build beyond it by arguing that both Roosevelt and Truman also assumed that the atomic bomb would serve as a bargaining lever—a diplomatic bonus—in dealing with the Soviet Union. The atomic bomb, Barton J. Bernstein concludes, was one of many causes of the Cold War. The bomb gave American leaders a sense of power and thus reduced incentives to compromise. American foreign policy might have been less demanding and more cautious if the atomic bomb had not rested so conspicuously in the United States arsenal.

Barton J. Bernstein is a professor of history at Stanford University. He is the editor of *Politics and Policies of the Truman Administration* (1970) and *The Atomic Bomb* (1975).

Ever since the publication in 1965 of Gar Alperovitz's *Atomic Diplomacy*, scholars and laymen have developed a new interest in the relationship of the atomic bomb to wartime and postwar diplomacy and to the origins of the Cold War. This bold book revived and sometimes recast old themes and thereby sparked renewed interest in questions that once seemed settled: Why was the atomic bomb dropped on Japan? Why weren't other alternatives vigorously pursued? How did the bomb influence American policy before and after Hiroshima? Did the dropping of the bomb and postwar American atomic policies contribute to the Cold War?

Unfortunately many studies of these questions have focused exclusively on the Truman period and thereby neglected the Roosevelt

From Barton J. Bernstein, "Roosevelt, Truman and the Atomic Bomb, 1941–1945: A Reinterpretation," Political Sscience Quarterly, XC (Spring 1975), pp. 23–24, 30, 31, 34–35, 35–37, 39–43, 44–45, 46, 47–50, 59–64, 67–69.   Footnotes deleted. Reprinted by permission of The Academy of Political Science.

administration, which bequeathed to Truman a legacy of assumptions, options, and fears. Acting on the assumption that the bomb was a legitimate weapon, Roosevelt initially defined the relationship of American diplomacy and the atomic bomb. He decided to build the bomb, to establish a partnership on atomic energy with Britain, to bar the Soviet Union from knowledge of the project, and to block any effort at international control of atomic energy. These policies constituted Truman's inheritance—one he neither wished to abandon nor could easily escape. He was restricted politically, psychologically, and institutionally from critically reassessing this legacy.

Like Roosevelt, Truman assumed that the bomb was a legitimate weapon and also understood that it could serve as a bargaining lever, a military counterweight, a threat, or a combat weapon in dealing with the Soviet Union in the postwar world. In addition to speeding the end of the war, the combat use of the bomb, the Truman administration understood, offered the United States great advantages in the postwar world. Policy makers assumed that use of the bomb would help shape the world in a desirable mold: The bomb would impress the Soviets and make them more tractable. Contrary to some contentions, this consideration about the postwar world was not the controlling reason why the United States used the bomb. Rather, it was an additional reason reinforcing an earlier analysis. Ending the war speedily was the primary purpose; impressing the Soviet Union was secondary. This secondary aim did constitute a subtle deterrent to reconsidering combat use of the bomb and to searching for alternative means of ending the war. Had the use of the bomb threatened to impair, rather than advance, American aims for the postwar peace, policy makers would have been likely to reassess their assumptions and perhaps to choose other alternatives. . . .

Running through the tangled skein of America's wartime policy on atomic energy is the persistent evidence of concern about the Soviet Union. Roosevelt knew that the Soviets were gathering information about the bomb project, and on September 9, 1943, Henry L. Stimson, the secretary of war, informed the president that spies "are already getting information about vital secrets and sending them to Russia." In late December 1944, at two sessions, they again discussed these issues. On December 31, Roosevelt told Stimson that he, too, was worried about how much the Soviets might know about the project, and they briefly discussed trading information for substantial Soviet concessions. As Stimson later summarized the conversation in his diary:

> I told him . . . that I knew they [Russia] were spying on our work but that they had not yet gotten any real knowledge of it and that, while I was troubled by the possible effect of keeping from them even now that work, I believed that it was essential not to take them into our confidence until we were sure to get a real quid pro quo from our frankness. I said I had no illusions as to the possibility of keeping permanently such a secret but that I did think that it was not yet time to share it with Russia. He said he thought he agreed with me.

They did not discuss the specific nature of the concessions, and perhaps Stimson and the president would not have agreed on how to use the bomb as a bargaining lever and what to demand from the Soviet Union. Whatever their unexplored differences on these issues, they did agree to continue for a period the same policy: exclusion of the Soviets. "It was quite clear," recorded General Leslie Groves, commanding general of the Manhattan Project, "that no one present was interested in bringing Russia into the picture, at least at this time." It is less clear why Roosevelt and Stimson, faced with the realization that the Soviet Union knew about the American research, still did not want formally to notify the Soviets about the bomb project. There is no direct evidence on this subject, but probably they feared that formal disclosure would lead to explicit Soviet inquiries and then to demands for participation that American leaders were not prepared to handle. As long as the United States technically kept the project secret, the Soviets could never raise issues about the bomb without admitting their espionage. . . .

Had Roosevelt lived, perhaps he would ultimately have reversed the policy of secrecy and decided to move toward international control in return for a *quid pro quo*—perhaps on Eastern Europe which he had "ceded" at Yalta to the Soviet Union. Any consideration of what "might have happened" is, of course, a matter of speculation, since the evidence is skimpy and oblique on what Roosevelt might have done. What is clear is that he had maintained the strategy of excluding the Soviets from knowledge of the bomb and of reserving the options of using it in the future as a bargaining lever, threat, military counterweight, or even a weapon against the Soviets.

It was not that he lacked opportunities to reverse his policy. He did not want to change policy—at least not up to April. At Yalta, in February, for example, Roosevelt might have approached Stalin on the bomb, but the president neither discussed this subject nor the loan that the Soviets wanted, and thereby he simply kept open the options for the future of using economic leverage and the bomb to secure concessions.

His position, then, made possible the future strategy of "atomic diplomacy"—of using the bomb as an implied or explicit threat to influence negotiations and to compel concessions from the Soviets. Would he have practiced "atomic diplomacy"? Probably. But that answer is speculative and rests principally upon the theory that he would not have wasted the options he was jealously guarding.

Roosevelt and his advisers had more clearly defined another issue: the combat use of the bomb. From the inception of the project, when it was directed primarily against Germany, they usually assumed, and most policy makers never questioned, that the bomb was a legitimate weapon to be used in combat. This assumption was phrased as policy on a number of occasions. In October 1942, for example, Stimson had directed Groves that the mission is "to produce [the bomb] at the earliest possible date so as to bring the war to a conclusion." Any time "that a single day could be saved," the general should save that day. In 1944, policy makers were also talking comfortably about "*after* S–1 [the bomb] is used." "At no time," Stimson later wrote, "did I ever hear it suggested by the President, or by any other responsible member of the government, that atomic energy should not be used in war." . . .

When Harry S Truman became president on April 12, 1945, he was only dimly aware of the existence of the Manhattan Project and unaware that it was an atomic-bomb project. Left uninformed of foreign affairs and generally ignored by Roosevelt in the three months since the inaugural, the new president inherited a set of policies and a group of advisers from his predecessor. While Truman was legally free to reverse Roosevelt's foreign policies and to choose new advisers on foreign policy, in fact he was quite restricted for personal and political reasons. Because Truman was following a very prestigious president whom he, like a great many Americans, loved and admired, the new president was not free psychologically or politically to strike out on a clearly new course. Only a bolder man, with more self-confidence, might have tried critically to assess the legacy and to act independently. But Truman lacked the confidence and the incentive. When, in fact, he did modify policy—for example, on Eastern Europe—he still believed sincerely, as some advisers told him, that he was adhering to his predecessor's agreements and wishes. When seeking counsel on foreign affairs, he usually did not choose new advisers but simply drew more heavily upon those members of Roosevelt's staff who were more anti-Soviet and relied less upon those who were more friendly to the Soviet Union. Even in this strategy, he believed that he was adhering to the policies of his predecessor, who, in his last weeks, Truman stressed, had become more suspicious of Stalin, more distressed by Soviet action in Eastern Europe, and more committed to resisting Soviet encroachments.

In the case of the international-diplomatic policy on the bomb, Truman was even more restricted by Roosevelt's decisions, for the new president inherited a set of reasonably clear wartime policies. Because Roosevelt had already decided to exclude the Soviets from a partnership on the bomb, his successor could not *comfortably* reverse this policy during the war—unless the late president's advisers pleaded for such a reversal or claimed that he had been about to change his policy. They did neither. Consider, then, the massive personal and political deterrents that blocked Truman from even reassessing this legacy. What price might he have paid at home if Americans learned later that he had reversed Roosevelt's policy and had launched a bold new departure of sharing with the Soviets a great weapon that cost the United States $2 billion? . . .

During his first weeks in office, Truman learned about the project from Stimson and from James F. Byrnes, Roosevelt's former director of the Office of War Mobilization and Reconversion who was to become Truman's secretary of state. Byrnes, despite his recent suspicions that the project might be a scientific boondoggle, told Truman, in the president's words, that "the bomb might well put us in a position to dictate our own terms at the end of the war." On April 25, Stimson discussed issues about the bomb more fully with Truman, especially the "political aspects of the S–1 [atomic bomb's] performance." The bomb, the secretary of war explained in a substantial memorandum, would probably be ready in four months and "would be the most terrible weapon ever known in human history [for it] . . . could destroy a whole city." In the future, he warned, other nations would be able to make atomic bombs, thereby endangering the peace and threatening the world. The bomb could be either a threat to or a guarantor of peace. "[I]n the light of our present position with reference to this weapon, the question of sharing it with other nations and, if so shared, upon what terms, becomes a primary question of our foreign relations," Stimson lectured the president. If "the problem of the proper use of this weapon can be solved, we would have the opportunity to bring the world into a pattern in which the peace of the world and our civilization can be saved."

The entire discussion, judging from Stimson's diary record and Groves's memorandum, assumed that the bomb was a legitimate weapon and that it would be used against Japan. The questions they discussed were not *whether* to use the bomb, but its relationship to the Soviet Union and the need to establish postwar atomic policies. Neither Stimson nor Truman sought then to resolve these outstanding issues, and Truman agreed to his secretary's proposal for the establishment of a high-level committee to recommend "action to the executive and legislative branches of our government when secrecy is no longer in full effect." At no time did they conclude that the committee would also consider the issue of whether to use the bomb as a combat weapon. For policy makers, that was not a question; it was an operating assumption.

Nor did Stimson, in his own charge to the Interim Committee, ever *raise* this issue. Throughout the committee's meetings, as various members later noted, all operated on the assumption that the bomb would be used against Japan. . . .

Though the Interim Committee and high administration officials found no reason not to use the bomb against Japan, many were concerned about the bomb's impact, and its later value, in Soviet-American relations. "[I]t was already apparent," Stimson later wrote, "that the critical questions in American policy toward atomic energy would be directly connected with Soviet Russia." At a few meetings of the Interim Committee, for example, members discussed informing the Soviets of the bomb before its use against Japan. When the issue first arose, [Vannevar] Bush and [James B.] Conant estimated that the Soviet Union could develop the bomb in about four years and argued for informing the Soviets before combat use as a preliminary to moving toward international control and thereby avoiding a postwar nuclear arms race. Conant and Bush had been promoting this strategy since the preceding September. Even though Roosevelt had cast them to the side in 1943, when he cemented the Anglo-American alliance, the two scientist-administrators had not abandoned hope for their notions. They even circulated to the Interim Committee one of their memoranda on the subject. But at the meetings of May 18 and 31 they again met defeat. General Groves, assuming that America was far more advanced technologically and scientifically and also that the Soviet Union lacked uranium, argued that the Soviets could not build a bomb for about twenty years. He contributed to the appealing "myth" of the atomic secret—that there was a secret and it would long remain America's monopoly. James Byrnes, with special authority as secretary of state—designate and Truman's representative on the committee, accepted

Groves's analysis and argued for maintaining the policy of secrecy—which the committee endorsed. Byrnes was apparently very pleased, and Stimson agreed, as he told Truman on June 6, "There should be no revelation to Russia or anyone else of our work on S–1 [the atomic bomb] until the first bomb has been laid successfully on Japan."

At a later meeting on June 21, the Interim Committee, including Byrnes, reversed itself. Yielding to the pleas of Bush and Conant, who were strengthened by the scientific panel's recommendations, the Interim Committee advised Truman to inform the Soviets about the bomb before using it in combat. Like the Franck Committee [a group of atomic scientists in Chicago headed by Jerome Franck], the Interim Committee concluded (as the minutes record):

> In the hope of securing effective future control and in view of the fact that general information concerning the project would be made public shortly after the [Potsdam] conference, the Committee *agreed* that there would be considerable advantage, if suitable opportunity arose, in having the President advise the Russians that we were working on this weapon with every prospect of success and that we expected to use it against Japan.
>
> The President might say further that he hoped this matter might be discussed some time in the future in terms of insuring that the weapon would become an aid to peace.

Because of this recommendation, and perhaps also because of the continuing prodding of Bush and Conant, Stimson reversed his own position. He concluded that if the United States dropped the bomb on Japan without first informing the Soviet Union, that act might gravely strain Soviet-American relations. Explaining the committee's position to Truman, Stimson proposed that if the president "thought that Stalin was on good terms with him" at the forthcoming Potsdam conference, he would inform Stalin that the United States had developed the bomb, planned to use it against Japan, knew the Soviets were working on the bomb, and looked forward to discussing international control later. This approach left open the option of "atomic diplomacy."

The issues of the bomb and the Soviet Union had already intruded in other ways upon policy and planning. Awaiting the bomb, Truman had postponed the Potsdam conference, delayed negotiations with Russia, and hoped that atomic energy would pry some concessions from Russia. Truman explained in late May to Joseph Davies, an advocate of Soviet-American friendship, and in early June to Stimson that he was delaying the forthcoming Potsdam conference until the Alamogordo test, when he would know whether the United States had a workable atomic bomb—what Stimson repeatedly called the "master card." Truman also told some associates that he was delaying because he wanted to work out budget matters, but it is unlikely that the budget was the controlling reason. Certainly, there was no reason that he should have told Davies, who, unlike Stimson, was not counseling delay of the conference, that he was waiting for the bomb. Stimson's counsel of caution, offered on May 15, had apparently triumphed: it would be "a terrible thing to gamble with such high stakes in diplomacy without having your master card in your hand. . . . Over [the] tangled wave of problems the S–1 secret would be dominant." This was not the counsel for a "delayed showdown," as some have wrongly argued, but for no showdown and for delaying some negotiations until the bomb test so that policy makers could determine whether they would have to make concessions to the Soviet Union.

For the administration, the atomic bomb, if it worked, had great potential value. It could reduce the importance of early Soviet entry into the war and make American concessions unnecessary. It could also be a lever for extracting concessions from the Soviet Union. On June 6, for example, Stimson discussed with Truman "quid pro quos which should be established for our taking them [Russia] into [a nuclear] partnership. He [Truman] said that he had been thinking of the same things that I was thinking of, namely the settlement of the Polish, Rumanian, Yugoslavian, and Manchurian problems." There is no evidence that they were planning explicitly to threaten the Soviets to gain these concessions, but, obviously, they realized that the Soviets would regard an American nuclear monopoly as threatening and would yield on some issues in order to terminate that monopoly and thereby reduce, or eliminate, the threat. Neither Stimson nor Truman discussed brandishing the bomb or using it explicitly as a threat to compel concessions. "Atomic diplomacy," as a conception, advanced no further than the notion of possibly trading in the future an atomic partnership, which was still undefined, for Soviet concessions.

For policy makers, the atomic weapons scheduled for combat use against Japan were intimately connected with the problem of Russia. In recent years some historians have focused on this relationship and raised troubling questions: Did the bomb, for policy makers, constitute an alternative to Soviet intervention in the Pacific war? Did they delay or even try to prevent Soviet entry because the bomb made it unnecessary? If so, did they do this in order to use the bomb? Was the bomb dropped on Japan primarily to influence Russia? Did the bomb influence American policy at Potsdam?

At Yalta, Roosevelt had granted the Soviet Union concessions in China in order to secure Soviet entry into the Pacific war, which Stalin promised, within two to three months after V-E Day (May 8). Stalin made it clear that Soviet entry would await a Sino-Soviet pact ratifying these concessions. At the time of Yalta, American military planners were counting on a Soviet attack in Manchuria to pin down the Kwantung army there and hence stop Japan from shifting these forces to her homeland to meet an American invasion.

But by April, war conditions changed and military planners revised their analysis: Japan no longer controlled the seas and therefore could not shift her army, so Soviet entry was not essential. In May, the State Department asked Stimson whether Soviet participation "at the earliest possible moment" was so necessary that the United States should abide by the Far East section of the Yalta agreement. Stimson concluded that the Soviets would enter the war for their own reasons, at their schedule, and with little regard to any American action, that the Yalta concessions would be largely within the grasp of Soviet military power, and that Soviet assistance would be useful, but not essential, if an American invasion was necessary. If there is an invasion, "Russian entry," he wrote, "will have a profound military effect in that almost certainly it will materially shorten the war and thus save American lives." But if the bomb worked, he implied in other discussions, then an invasion would probably not be necessary and Soviet help would be less important. As a result, he urged a delay in settling matters with Russia on the Far East until after the Alamogordo test, and the president apparently followed this counsel. . . .

Truman claimed that he went to Potsdam to secure Soviet entry and that he never changed his position. The first part of that claim is correct, but the second part is dubious, for Truman did nothing substantive at Potsdam to encourage Soviet intervention and much to delay or prevent it. The successful test at Alamogordo emphasized to policy makers that prompt Soviet entry was no longer necessary and that the United States might even be able to end the war without Soviet entry. After the unexpectedly glowing report of the test, Truman wanted to know whether [General George C.] Marshall considered Soviet entry necessary. "Marshall felt," Stimson recorded, "that now with our new weapon we would not need the assistance of the Russians to conquer Japan." "The bomb as a merely probable weapon had seemed a weak reed on which to rely, but the bomb as a colossal reality was very differ-ent," Stimson later explained.   From Potsdam on July 23, Churchill cabled London: "It is quite clear that the United States do not at the present time desire Russian participation in the war against Japan." The bomb had eliminated the importance of Russia's prompt entry, since the planned American invasion no longer seemed necessary.   Invasion and the bomb were the likely alternatives.   As a result, Truman had no rea-son to offer concessions to secure early Soviet entry. . . .

Byrnes purposely impeded Sino-Soviet negotiations in order to *prevent* the Soviets from entering the war.   Did Truman support Byrnes for the *same* reasons?—as Byrnes claimed later and as Truman obliquely denied.   Perhaps.   But, more likely, Truman supported his secretary's strategy for a different reason: the early entry of the Soviets was no longer important and, therefore, Truman did not want Chiang [Kai-shek] to make the required concessions, which could later weaken Chiang's government.   In addition, Truman *may* have concluded that Russia's delayed entry would weaken her possible claims for a role in the postwar occupation government in Japan. . . .

At Potsdam, on July 24, Truman told Stalin casually that the United States had developed "a new weapon of unusual destructive force" for use against Japan but did not specify an atomic weapon. Why didn't Truman explicitly inform Stalin about the atomic bomb? Was Truman, as some have suggested, afraid that the news would prompt Stalin to hasten Soviet intervention and therefore end the war and make combat use of the bomb impossible?   Did Truman simply want to delay Soviet entry and did he, like Byrnes, fear that his news would have the opposite effect?   Did Truman think that the destruction wrought by the bomb would not impress the Soviets as forcefully if they were informed in advance?   Why did Truman reject the counsel of the Interim Committee, of Stimson, and even of Churchill, who, after the [g]lowing news of the Alamogordo test, "was not worried about giving the Russians information on the matter but was rather inclined to use it as an argument in our favor in the negotiations"?

Many of these questions cannot be definitively answered on the basis of the presently available evidence, but there is enough evidence to refute one popular interpretation: that Truman's tactic was part of an elaborate strategy to prevent or retard Soviet entry *in order* to delay Japan's surrender and *thereby* make combat use of the bomb possible. That interpretation claims too much.   Only the first part can be sup-ported by some, albeit indirect, evidence: that he was probably seeking to delay or prevent Soviet entry. Byrnes later said that he feared that Stalin would order an immediate Soviet declaration of war if he realized the importance of this "new weapon"—advice Truman dubiously claimed he never received. Truman was not trying to postpone Japan's surrender *in order* to use the bomb. In addition to the reasonable theory that he was seeking to prevent or retard Soviet entry, there are two other plausible, complementary interpretations of Truman's behavior. First, he believed, as had some of his advisers earlier, that a combat demonstration would be more impressive to Russia without an advance warning and therefore he concealed the news. Second, he was also ill-prepared to discuss atomic energy with Stalin, for the president had not made a decision about postwar atomic policy and how to exploit the bomb, and probably did not want to be pressed by Stalin about sharing nuclear secrets. Perhaps all three theories collectively explain Truman's evasive tactics.

Even without explicit disclosure, the bomb strengthened American policy at Potsdam. The Alamogordo test stiffened Truman's resolve, as Churchill told Stimson after the meeting of the Big Three on July 22: "Truman was evidently much fortified . . . and . . . he stood up to the Russians in a most emphatic and decisive manner, telling them as to certain demands that they absolutely could not have." Probably, also, the bomb explains why Truman pushed more forcefully at Potsdam for the Soviets to open up Eastern Europe. It is less clear whether the bomb changed the substance of American policy at Potsdam. Probably Byrnes endorsed a reparations policy allowing the division of Germany because the bomb replaced Germany as a potential counterweight to possible Soviet expansion.

Not only did the bomb strengthen American resolve in dealing with the Soviets, but Stimson and Truman linked the bomb and the Soviet Union in another way: the selection of targets for atomic attacks. Kyoto, a city of religious shrines, was originally on the list, but Stimson removed it, with Truman's approval. Truman "was particularly emphatic in agreeing with my suggestion," Stimson wrote, because

the bitterness . . . caused by such a wanton act might make it impossible during the long post war period to reconcile the Japanese to us in that area rather than to the Russians. It might thus, I pointed out, be the means of preventing what our policy demanded, namely, a sympathetic Japan to the United States in case there should be any aggression by Russia in Manchuria.

Scholars and laymen have criticized the combat use of the atomic bomb. They have contended, among other points, that the bombs were not necessary to end the war, that the administration knew or should have known this, that the administration knew that Japan was on the verge of defeat and *therefore* close to surrender, and that the administration was either short-sighted or had other controlling international-political motives (besides ending the war) for using the bomb. These varying contentions usually focus on the alleged failure of the United States to pursue five alternatives, individually or in combination, in order to achieve Japanese surrender before using the bomb: (1) awaiting Soviet entry, a declaration of war, or a public statement of intent . . .; (2) providing a warning and/or a noncombat demonstration . . .; (3) redefining unconditional surrender to guarantee the Imperial institution; (4) pursuing Japan's "peace feelers"; or (5) relying upon conventional warfare for a longer period. These contentions assume that policy makers were trying, or should have tried, to avoid using atomic bombs—precisely what they were not trying to do. . . .

Truman inherited the assumption that the bomb was a legitimate weapon to use to end the war. No policy maker ever effectively challenged this conception. If the combat use of the bomb deeply troubled policy makers morally or politically, they might have been likely to reconsider their assumption and to search ardently for other alternatives. But they were generally inured to the mass killing of civilians and much preferred to sacrifice the lives of Japanese civilians to those of American soldiers. As a result, they were committed to using the bomb *as soon as possible* to end the war. "The dominant objective was victory," Stimson later explained. "If victory could be speeded by using the bomb, it should be used; if victory must be delayed in order to use the bomb; it should *not* be used. So far as. . . [I] knew, this general view was fully shared by the President and his associates." The morality of war confirmed the dictates of policy and reinforced the legacy that Truman had inherited. Bureaucratic momentum added weight to that legacy, and the relatively closed structure of decision making served also to inhibit dissent and to ratify the dominant assumption.

Had policy makers concluded that the use of the bomb would impair Soviet-American relations and make the Soviets intransigent, they might have reconsidered their assumption. But their analysis indicated that the use of the bomb would aid, not injure, their efforts to secure concessions from the Soviets. The bomb offered a bonus. The promise of these likely advantages probably constituted a subtle deterrent to any reconsideration of the use of the atomic bomb. Policy makers rejected the competing analysis advanced by the Franck Committee:

> Russia, and even allied countries which bear less mistrust of our ways and intentions, as well as neutral countries, will be deeply shocked. It will be very difficult to persuade the world that a nation which was capable of secretly preparing and suddenly releasing . . . [the bomb] is to be trusted in its proclaimed desire of having such weapons abolished by international agreement.

Instead, policy makers had come to assume that a combat demonstration would advance, not impair, the interests of peace—a position shared by Conant, [J. Robert] Oppenheimer, Arthur H. Compton, Nobel laureate and director of the Chicago Metallurgical Laboratory, and Edward Teller, the physicist and future father of the hydrogen bomb. In explaining the thinking of the scientific advisory panel in recommending combat use of the bomb, Oppenheimer later said that one of the two "overriding considerations. . . [was] the effect of our actions on the stability . . . of the postwar world." Stimson's assistant, Harvey H. Bundy, wrote in 1946, that some thought "that unless the bomb were used it would be impossible to persuade the world that the saving of civilization in the future would depend on a proper international control of atomic energy." The bomb, in short, would impress the Soviets.

In addition, there was another possible advantage to using the bomb: retribution against Japan. A few days after Nagasaki, Truman hinted at this theme in a private letter justifying the combat use of the bombs:

> Nobody is more disturbed over the use of Atomic bombs than I am but I was greatly disturbed over the unwarranted attack by the Japanese on Pearl Harbor. The only language they seem to understand is the one that we have been using to bombard them. When you have to deal with a beast you have to treat him as a beast. It is most regrettable but nevertheless true.

In this letter, one can detect strains of the quest for retribution (the reference to Pearl Harbor), and some might even find subtle strains of racism (Japan was "a beast"). The enemy was a beast and deserved to be destroyed. War, as some critics would stress, dehumanized victors and vanquished, and justified inhumanity in the name of nationalism, of justice, and even of humanity.

In assessing the administration's failure to challenge the assumption that the bomb was a legitimate weapon to be used against Japan, we may conclude that Truman found no reason to reconsider, that it would have been difficult for him to challenge the assumption, and that there were also various likely benefits deterring a reassessment. For the administration, in short, there was no reason to avoid using the bomb and many reasons making it feasible and even attractive. The bomb was used primarily to end the war *promptly* and thereby to save American lives. There were other ways to end the war, but none of them seemed as effective. They would not produce victory as promptly and seemed to have greater risks. Even if Russia had not existed, the bombs would have been used in the same way. How could Truman, in the absence of overriding contrary reasons, justify not using the bombs, or even delaying their use, and thereby prolonging the war and sacrificing American lives?

Some who have searched for the causes of Truman's decision to use atomic weapons have made the error of assuming that the question was ever open, that the administration ever carefully faced the problem of *whether* to use the bombs. It was not a carefully weighed decision but the implementation of an assumption. The administration devoted thought to how, not whether, to use them. As Churchill later wrote, "the decision whether or not to use the atomic bomb to compel the surrender of Japan was never even an issue."

In examining American policy for the few months after Hiroshima, scholars have disagreed on whether the United States practiced "atomic diplomacy." Simply defined, this term means the use of nuclear weapons as threats or as bargaining levers to secure advantages from the Soviet Union. Since there were no *explicit* threats, some scholars have dubiously disposed of the problem by comfortably declaring that there was no "atomic diplomacy"—which they define too narrowly by excluding *implicit* threats. That is too simple and avoids important issues. A full investigation of the complex problem of atomic diplomacy requires detailed attention to a number of questions: Did the United States threaten, or seem to threaten, the Soviet Union? Did observers think so? How did the Soviets react and how did observers interpret their reactions? The following analysis discusses some of the available evidence and briefly indicates answers to these important questions. Because of limitations of space, this section does not prove, but only sketches, an analysis.

On August 9, the day that Nagasaki was bombed, the president delivered a national address on the Potsdam meeting. The United States, he declared, "would maintain military bases necessary for the complete protection of our interests and of world peace." The secret of the bomb, he promised, would be retained until the world ceased being "lawless." "We must constitute ourselves trustees of this new force—to prevent its misuse, and to turn it into the channels of service to mankind." He also emphasized that the Balkan nations "are not to be the spheres of influence of any one power"—a direct warning to the Soviet Union. Here was the first, albeit muted, statement of atomic diplomacy: the implicit threat that the bomb could roll back Soviet influence from Eastern Europe.

"In many quarters," Stimson lamented in late August and early September, the bomb is "interpreted as a substantial offset to the growth of Russian influence on the continent." He complained that Byrnes was wearing the bomb ostentatiously on his hip and hoping to use the weapon to secure his program at the September Conference of Foreign Ministers in London. "His mind is full of his problems," Stimson wrote in his diary. Byrnes "looks to having the presence of the bomb in his pocket, so to speak, as a great weapon to get through the thing. . . ." Assistant Secretary of War John J. McCloy concluded, after a long discussion with Byrnes, that he "wished to have the implied threat of the bomb in his pocket during the conference. . . [in London]." This evidence is unambiguous as to Byrnes's intent, and it cannot be ignored or interpreted as misleading. Byrnes had no reason to seek to deceive Stimson and McCloy about his hopes and tactics. Byrnes had no incentive to posture with them or to appear militant, since they opposed his vigorous tactics and instead counseled moderation and international control of atomic energy.

How could the United States employ the bomb in dealing with the Soviet Union? Apparently Byrnes had not decided precisely how to exploit the weapon to strengthen his position. He did not explicitly threaten the Soviets but apparently assumed that the weapon itself would be a sufficient, though implicit, threat. Even before Hiroshima, Byrnes and others, including Stimson, had assumed that the bomb would impress the Soviet Union with the need for concessions. The bomb, itself, even without any explicit statements, as Conant told Bush, constituted a "threat" to the Soviet Union. Because Byrnes wanted the bomb's power in negotiations and distrusted the Soviets, he opposed Stimson's plea in September for approaching the Soviets promptly and directly on international control of atomic energy. At the same time, he was urging America's scientists to continue their work to build even more powerful nuclear bombs.

At the London Conference, an uneasy Vyacheslav Molotov, the Soviet foreign minister, twitted Byrnes about America's nuclear monopoly and tried uneasily to minimize its importance. Molotov's humor betrayed Soviet fears. On September 13, three days into the conference, "Molotov asks JFB if he has an atomic bomb in his side pocket. 'You don't know Southerners,' Byrnes replied. 'We carry our artillery in our hip pocket. If you don't cut out all this stalling and let us get down to work I am going to pull an atomic bomb out of my hip pocket and let you have it.'" In response to this veiled threat, according to the informal notes, "Molotov laughed as did the interpreter." Byrnes's barb emphasized American power. A few nights later, after a stormy session during the day, Molotov commented once more, with strained jocularity, that Byrnes had two advantages that the Soviet minister could not match—eloquence and the atomic bomb. . . .

Did the bomb make a critical difference in shaping the early Cold War? Roosevelt's repeated decisions to bar the Soviets from the nuclear project and Truman's decision to use the bomb in combat without explicitly informing the Soviet Union and inviting her to join in postwar control of atomic energy undoubtedly contributed to the Cold War and helped shape the form that it took. Yet, in view of the great strains in the fragile wartime Soviet-American alliance, historians should not regard America's *wartime* policy on the bomb as *the* cause, but only as one of the causes, of the Cold War. The wartime policy on atomic energy represented one of a number of missed opportunities at achieving limited agreements and at testing the prospects for Soviet-American cooperation on a vital matter.

The atomic bomb, first as prospect and then as reality, did influence American policy. The bomb reduced the incentives for compromise and even stiffened demands by the time of the Potsdam meeting in July 1945 because the weapon gave the United States enhanced power. Without the bomb, policy makers probably would have been more conciliatory after V-J Day in dealing with the Soviet Union, especially about Eastern Europe. The president certainly would have been unable to try to use atomic diplomacy (implied threats) to push the Soviets out of Eastern Europe. Rather, he might have speedily, though reluctantly, agreed to the dominance of Soviet power and to the closed door in that sector of the world. The bomb, as potential or actual weapon, did *not* alter the administration's conception of an ideal world, but possession of the weapon did strengthen the belief of policy makers in their capacity to move toward establishing their goal: an "open door" world with the Soviets acceding to American demands. This ideal world included free elections, an open economic door, and the reduction of Soviet influence in Eastern Europe. Without the bomb, the Truman administration would not have surrendered these ultimate aims, but policy makers would have had to rely primarily on economic power as a bargaining card to secure concessions from the Soviet Union. And economic power, taken alone, would probably have seemed insufficient—as the record of lend-lease and the Russian loan suggests.

The atomic bomb was the most important weapon in the American arsenal, but its promise proved to be disappointing for it did not make America omnipotent. It did not allow her to shape the world she desired, perhaps because in 1945–1946 neither policy makers nor most citizens were willing to use the bomb as a weapon to "liberate" Eastern Europe, a section of the world that was not then deemed worth war or the risk of war.

Without the bomb, in summary, American policy after V-J Day would have been more cautious, less demanding, less optimistic. Such restraint would not have prevented the breakdown of the Soviet-American alliance, but probably the Cold War would not have taken the form that it did, and an uneasy truce, with less fear and antagonism, might have been possible.

David Holloway

FEAR AND COMPETITION: THE SOVIET RESPONSE TO AMERICA'S ATOMIC MONOPOLY

Soviet leaders learned during the Second World War that American and British scientists, backed by their governments, were busily developing an atomic bomb. Joseph Stalin thereupon ordered a Soviet project. The American atomic bombings of Japan gave greater urgency to this work, for, argues David Holloway, the Soviets now read the atomic bomb as a threat.

From *The Soviet Union and the Arms Race*, second edition, by David Holloway, 1984, pp. 15–20, 21–24, 24–25, 27–28. Reprinted by permission of Yale University Press.

Like many other scholars, Holloway notes that Anglo-American wartime secrecy and resolve not to consult with the Soviets on the bomb's development doomed any chances, however small, for international control of the bomb and for avoiding a nuclear-arms race. He further suggests that Moscow positioned forces in Eastern Europe not only as a safeguard for Soviet interests there, but also as a counterweight to superior American air power that could punish Soviet cities with atomic bombs.

David Holloway is a specialist in Soviet foreign relations and military policies and a professor of political science at Stanford University. Besides his authorship of the book from which this essay is selected, he has edited *The Warsaw Pact* (1984) and *The Reagan Strategic Defense Initiative* (1985).

Victory over Germany brought the Soviet Union political gains that must have been inconceivable in the early months of the war. Stalin now had a say in the political arrangements of Eastern Europe, and Soviet security was thereby enhanced. Stalin's policy in Eastern Europe, however, soon brought him into conflict with his allies. Strains were evident at the Potsdam Conference in July and August 1945. This was the last meeting of the allied leaders to try to resolve their differences about the post-war settlement. It was also the first occasion on which the atomic bomb cast its shadow over relations between the Soviet Union and the Western powers.

The Americans and the British had pondered for some time what to tell Stalin about the atomic bomb. Neither Roosevelt nor Churchill had been impressed by the advice of the great Danish physicist Niels Bohr that they should inform Stalin before the bomb was tested and try to get agreement on international control. The first atomic bomb test took place on 16 July while the Potsdam Conference was in progress. On 24 July President Truman approached Stalin after the formal session had broken up and "casually mentioned" to him that "we had a new weapon of unusual destructive force." Truman wrote later that Stalin replied that "he was glad to hear of it and hoped we would make 'good use of it against the Japanese.' " Truman and Churchill (who was watching intently from nearby) were convinced that Stalin had not grasped what the President was referring to. They were mistaken, however, for Stalin knew of the Manhattan Project and had initiated Soviet work on the bomb early in 1943.

When nuclear fission was discovered in Berlin in December 1938, Soviet physicists were as quick as their counterparts in other countries to see that one of its potential applications was the creation of a bomb with unprecedented destructive force. In 1939 Igor Tamm, a leading theoretical physicist, remarked to a group of students, "Do you know what this new discovery means? It means a bomb can be built that will destroy a city out to a radius of maybe ten kilometers."

The discovery of nuclear fission at once stimulated new directions of research in the Soviet Union. Leningrad was the leading centre for this work. Here the prime mover was Igor Kurchatov, who headed the nuclear laboratory at the Leningrad Physicotechnical Institute and was later to be scientific director of the atomic project. He coordinated the research not only of his own laboratory, but also of scientists working at the Radium Institute and at the Institute of Physical Chemistry. The Radium Institute was directed by V. G. Khlopin, a radiochemist who later developed the industrial processes for producing plutonium. The director of the Institute of Physical Chemistry was N. N. Semenov, who had done important work on chain reactions for which he later received a Nobel Prize.

Nuclear physics in the 1930s was the very model of an international scientific community. The dramatic progress of research was built on discoveries by scientists in several different countries. Although they had no centre of nuclear research to compare with Paris, Cambridge or Copenhagen, Soviet physicists followed international progress avidly and made some significant contributions to it. Now their work on nuclear fission paralleled that done elsewhere. In April 1939 two of Kurchatov's junior colleagues established that each fissioned nucleus emitted between two and four neutrons, thus indicating that a chain reaction might be possible. Two physicists at Semenov's institute investigated the conditions under which a chain reaction would take place in uranium, and concluded early in 1940 that an experimental attempt to achieve a chain reaction could now be undertaken. In the same year two other physicists, working under Kurchatov's close direction, discovered the spontaneous fission of uranium (i.e., fission without bombardment by neutrons). Inspired by these results, Kurchatov and his colleagues wrote to the Presidium of the Academy of Sciences, urging an expansion of work on nuclear fission.

In June 1940 the Academy set up a Uranium Commission, with Khlopin as chairman, to direct research on the "uranium problem." This commission was a clear sign of the Academy's interest in nuclear fission. Work was now to proceed on a broad front: exploration for uranium deposits (lack of uranium was an important constraint on early Soviet work); the production of heavy water; rapid construction of cyclotrons; studies of isotope separation; measurement of the nuclear constants. But Kurchatov was disappointed with the scale of this effort. In August he and a colleague sent the Academy Presidium a plan of research, proposing that an experimental reactor be built. They drew attention to the military and economic importance of nuclear energy and urged the Academy to approach the government for additional funds in view of the exceptional significance the uranium problem had for the defence of the country.

In November, at a conference on nuclear physics in Moscow, Kurchatov received a reply to his proposal. Speaking after a paper by Kurchatov, Khlopin, the head of the Uranium Commission, declared that some young physicists, in particular Kurchatov's students, were so captivated by the uranium problem that they forgot about current needs. Nuclear energy, he said, was still a distant prospect, still a beautiful dream; it would be wrong to draw creative minds and national resources into unreal schemes. Khlopin thus made it clear that the Uranium Commission would not act on Kurchatov's proposal.

Work on nuclear fission continued, though not at the pace or on the scale that Kurchatov desired. He made a further attempt to put his case before the authorities. Semenov wrote on his behalf to the government about the possibility of creating a bomb, the destructive power of which would be incomparably greater than that of any existing explosive. This letter, written at the end of 1940 or early in 1941, elicited no response before the German invasion brought nuclear research in the Soviet Union to a halt.

Early in 1942 the possibility of an atomic bomb became a serious issue for the Soviet leadership, as a result of information obtained about British, American and German work on the bomb. In April M. G. Pervukhin, Deputy Premier and People's Commissar (i.e., Minister) of the Chemical Industry, was sent for by Molotov, who gave him a thick file containing secret reports about the foreign work. Soviet sources do not say what was in the file, but it may have contained Klaus Fuch's earliest reports on British work; it appears also that the Soviet Union had by this time received information about German interest in the bomb. Molotov told Pervukhin that he was giving him the papers on Stalin's instruction, and that he was to read them and advise what should be done. Pervukhin recommended that the papers be shown to physicists who would be able to make a precise evaluation of their significance. He himself was given responsibility for the uranium problem.

Information came also from an unexpected source. In May 1942 G. N. Flyorov, one of Kurchatov's former students, wrote to Stalin that "it is essential not to lose any time in building the uranium bomb." Flyorov, now a lieutenant in the Air Force, was serving at the front in Voronezh, where he had visited the University library to look at the physics journals. He was anxious to see if there had been any response to the discovery, which he had helped to make, of spontaneous fission. A note about this had been published in the American journal *Physical Review*. On looking through the journals, however, he found no reaction to this discovery; moreover, he saw that little of importance was being published about nuclear fission, and that the big names in the field had vanished from the journals. He concluded, rightly, that research was now secret and that the Americans must be working on an atomic bomb. Hence the letter to Stalin.

In the course of 1942 Soviet leaders held consultations with prominent scientists about the development of an atomic bomb. In one meeting Stalin made clear his anger that it was a young lieutenant at the front, and not the members of the Academy, who had drawn the possibility of such a bomb to his attention. He was worried about the cost of developing a bomb, for he was advised by two of the scientists that it would cost as much as the whole war effort. He decided, nevertheless, to initiate a small-scale project. Kurchatov, who had abandoned nuclear research on the outbreak of war, was chosen as scientific director. He finally began work in February or March 1943.

The decision to build an atomic bomb was taken when the war with Germany still hung in the balance. (The counteroffensive at Stalingrad, planned in September and October 1942, had the code name *Uran*, which though normally translated as Uranus, is also the Russian for uranium. This may indicate that the atomic bomb was preying on Stalin's mind at the time.) There were many who thought the effort a pointless waste of resources which could be used to meet more pressing needs. Stalin can hardly have thought that a Soviet bomb could be built in time to affect the outcome of the war. Soviet physicists had estimated in 1942 that the development of a uranium bomb would take between ten and twenty years. Perhaps Stalin had it in mind that after the war the Soviet Union would have to face a nuclear-armed Germany, for at this early period he may have had only minimum war aims, which did not necessarily include the destruction of the Nazi state. Perhaps he foresaw that even with the defeat of Germany the Soviet Union would come into conflict with Britain and the United States; after all, they were conducting their atomic projects in great secrecy, without informing the Soviet Union. More probably, the decision should be seen as a hedge against uncertainty. Given that Germany, Britain and the United States were interested in the atomic bomb, was it not as well to initiate a Soviet project, even though the circumstances in which the new weapon might be used could not be foreseen?

Kurchatov drew up a plan of research with three main goals: to achieve a chain reaction in an experimental reactor using natural uranium; to develop methods of isotope separation; to study the design of both the U-235 and the plutonium bombs. He built up his team slowly, drawing largely on those with whom he had worked before. By the end of 1943 he had fifty people working in his new laboratory; by the end of 1944 he had one hundred scientists. This was a tiny effort compared with the Manhattan Project. As the country was liberated, other institutes were drawn into the project, and in 1945 some German scientists and technicians were brought to the Soviet Union to take part. In the spring of 1945 Kurchatov ordered work to begin on the design of an industrial reactor for producing plutonium. By the time of the Potsdam Conference the Soviet Union had a serious atomic bomb project under way.

In spite of this, however, the American success in building the bomb came as a blow for the Soviet Union. Alexander Werth, who was in Moscow at the time, wrote that the news of Hiroshima had "an acutely depressing effect on everybody." The atomic bomb was seen as a threat to Russia, and "some Russian pessimists . . . dismally remarked that Russia's desperately hard victory over Germany was now 'as good as wasted.' " In December 1945 the British Ambassador wrote to the Foreign Secretary:

> the German invasion caught them still unready and swept them to what looked like the brink of defeat. Then came the turn of the tide and with it first the hope and then a growing belief that the immense benison of national security was at last within their reach. As the Red Army moved westwards belief became confidence and the final defeat of Germany made confidence conviction . . . Then plump came the Atomic Bomb. At a blow the balance which had now seemed set and steady was rudely shaken. Russia was balked by the west when everything seemed to be within her grasp. The three hundred divisions were shorn of much of their value.

Ambassador Harriman reported to Washington in much the same terms.

The small Soviet project laid the basis for the all-out effort that was now launched. Stalin's immediate reaction to Truman's casual remark was to tell Kurchatov to speed up his work. In the middle of August, shortly after his return from Potsdam, Stalin summoned B. L. Vannikov, the People's Commissar of Munitions, and his deputies to the Kremlin. There they were joined by Kurchatov. "A single demand of you, comrades," said Stalin. "Provide us with atomic weapons in the shortest possible time. You know that Hiroshima has shaken the whole world. The balance has been destroyed. Provide the bomb—it will remove a great danger from us." Kurchatov and his colleagues were asked how long it would take to build the atomic bomb if they received all-round support. Five years, they replied. In the event, the first Soviet test took place four years to the month after that August meeting with Stalin.

Compared with his failure to heed the warnings of a German attack in 1941, Stalin's decision about the atomic bomb in 1942 showed considerable foresight. The last thing he can have wanted to hear then was that Germany, Britain and the United States were working in great secrecy to develop a weapon of unprecedented destructive force. In spite of the critical war situation, he took the precautionary step of setting up a small-scale project. The Soviet leaders were nevertheless shaken by the American success in building a bomb. When Molotov heard what Truman had said at Potsdam, he saw it as an attempt to gain concessions from the Soviet Union. The Soviet leaders regarded the use of the bomb in Japan as part of an effort to put pressure on them, as a demonstration that the United States was willing to use nuclear weapons. Soviet security now seemed to be at risk from a new threat.

If Niels Bohr's advice had been heeded, and Stalin had been told officially about the bomb, his post-war policy might have been just the same. But Western secrecy contributed to Soviet suspicion and spurred the Soviet Union to develop its own bomb. As [the scholar] Margaret Gowing has written, "If Russia had been formally consulted about the bomb during the war . . . it might have made no difference. The fact that she was not, guaranteed that the attempts made just after the war to establish international control, which might have failed anyway, were doomed. . . ."

On 8 August 1945, two days after Hiroshima, the Politburo initiated work on a new Five Year Plan, which was formally adopted in March 1946. The Soviet leaders had to make decisions about the plan in the context of the new weapons programs. The then Minister of Finance has written in his memoirs that finding the financial resources for the plan proved more difficult than anticipated because the drop in defence spending was not as great as expected, and because "significant resources" were required for the development of military technology.

By the summer of 1946 the basic institutional framework had been created for developing nuclear weapons, long-range rockets, radar and jet propulsion. Special bodies were set up in the Party, the government, the secret police and the Armed Forces to direct these programs. In 1945 Scientific-Technical Councils were created for atomic bomb and rocket development. These consisted of scientists, engineers and industrial managers, and discussed the major technical and industrial problems connected with the programs. B. L. Vannikov headed the atomic council, with Pervukhin and Kurchatov as his deputies. The rocket council was chaired by D. F. Ustinov, the present Minister of Defence, who was then the People's Commissar of Armament. A special department of government, also headed by Vannikov, was set up to manage the nuclear program. The secret police had a department for atomic energy; half of all research for nuclear weapons development was done in prison institutes, while most of the construction and mining was done by prison labour. Overall control of the nuclear program lay in the hands of [Lavrenti P.] Beria, the chief of the secret police.

The object of these arrangements was to exercise tight central control over the new weapons programs, and to ensure that they had first claim on resources. Soon after the Potsdam Conference Kurchatov became a regular visitor to the Kremlin. One of the industrial managers remarked to him that "It's easy for you to solve problems: you meet Stalin every day." Kurchatov replied that problems were indeed solved quickly in meetings with Stalin. (The Soviet authors who recount this exchange comment that Kurchatov kept to himself the thought that dealing with Stalin almost every day was more difficult than walking a tightrope across an abyss; and it can have been no easier to deal with Beria, who is never mentioned now in Soviet accounts of their early nuclear program, but with whom Kurchatov must have had frequent contact.) Policy was developed in meetings between the Party leaders and those directly in charge of the programs. In April 1947, for example, Stalin summoned scientists, industrial managers and military men to the Kremlin for a series of meetings to decide on an overall plan for rocket development. Stalin's personal interest ensured that these programs had the highest priority; the best scientists, engineers, workers and managers were assigned to them. Each decision was backed by

Stalin's authority, and this helped to overcome obstacles in the way of executing policy.

The war provided the Soviet Union with a major infusion of foreign technology, mainly in the form of captured German scientists, technicians, equipment and production plant. Foreign technology also came through Lend-Lease, and by more fortuitous routes. The Tu-4 bomber, for example, was a copy of the American B-29, three of which made a forced landing on Soviet territory in 1944. Foreign technology was important for the post-war programs, but its contribution varied from field to field. In 1945 the Soviet atomic bomb project was better organized than the German, and while the Soviet Union acquired some scientists, technicians and equipment, most of the leading German nuclear scientists fell into Western hands. The information passed by Klaus Fuchs and other atomic spies was more important for the Soviet effort, perhaps speeding up the development of the atomic bomb by as much as a year or two. But it is certainly wrong to say that this is how the Soviet Union acquired the "secret" of the atomic bomb, for, as Niels Bohr remarked, the only secret of the atomic bomb is that it can be built.

The Soviet Union gained more from German rocket technology. In 1945 a team of Soviet rocket scientists was sent to Germany to study the German effort, and the first Soviet long-range rocket, the R-1, which was test-fired in October 1947, was a modification of the German V-2. The United States too gained from the German rocket program, for as the Red Army approached Peenemunde, the main centre of German rocketry, Wernher von Braun took his team and their most important papers to meet the American forces. Unlike the United States, however, the Soviet Union gave high priority to rocket development. In October 1946 thousands of German engineers and technicians were taken to the Soviet Union, where they worked under Soviet supervision. In spite of the purge, there was still a cadre of experienced and gifted rocket scientists who were able to build on the German technology. In 1947 a Council of Chief Designers was set up to coordinate the Soviet program. In was chaired by S. P. Korolev, who was later to design the first Soviet intercontinental ballistic missile. The other leading designers of the time, who were probably on the Council, were V. P. Glushko (whose design bureau was to develop the liquid-propellant rocket motors for most of the Soviet strategic missiles), A. M. Isaev (Chief Designer of a bureau for rocket motors since 1944), and A. N. Pilyugin (Chief Designer of Control Systems). In 1950 the Soviet

Union test-fired the R-2, a development of the R-1, but with a range of 600 km, about twice that of the earlier rocket. By this time work had begun on the SS-3, which was deployed in the mid-1950s.

On 29 August 1949 the Soviet Union tested its first atomic bomb. (This was a plutonium bomb; the first test of a U-235 bomb took place in 1951.) The United States detected the first Soviet test and made it public, to the apparent consternation of the Soviet government, which had made no announcement. News of the test caused a shock in Washington where, despite some accurate forecasts, it was generally believed that the Soviet Union would not have an atomic bomb until the early 1950s. This shock contributed to the decision announced by President Truman on 31 January 1950 to speed up work on thermonuclear weapons. Such bombs have a yield many times greater than the atomic bombs used in Japan, and the decision to develop them marked a major new stage in nuclear arms competition.
. . .

The Soviet atomic bomb test of August 1949 helped to speed up American work on thermonuclear weapons, and American policy in turn stimulated Soviet weapons research and development. Soviet work on the thermonuclear bomb began in 1948 when Kurchatov set up a theoretical group (which included Andrei Sakharov) under Igor Tamm, after reports of a superbomb had been received from the West. Soviet interest in thermonuclear weapons may have been aroused by Klaus Fuchs, who told his Soviet contact about studies of these weapons at Los Alamos. He could have told the Soviet Union that in the spring of 1946 discussion had taken place about two possible types of thermonuclear bombs: one in which a relatively small amount of thermonuclear fuel is ignited by a relatively large fission explosion (later known as a boosted fission weapon) and the other in which a relatively small fission explosion ignites a very large mass of thermonuclear fuel (the superbomb). Fuch's account of these early discussions of the superbomb would have been misleading rather than helpful to Soviet scientists in a scientific sense, because the early ideas were later shown not to work. But it is possible that Fuch's reports stimulated Soviet work on these weapons.

By the time of the first atomic bomb test, Tamm's group had concluded that thermonuclear weapons were possible, and two months after the test—that is, about 1 November 1949—Kurchatov began to work on the development of a thermonuclear bomb as a matter of priority. The first thermonuclear bomb test took place almost four years later, on 12 August 1953. Soviet writers tend to stress the role of American actions in stimulating Soviet nuclear weapons development. It is therefore interesting that they do not mention as providing any impetus to Soviet efforts Truman's announcement on 31 January 1950 of his decision to accelerate development of the superbomb. But one of Kurchatov's biographers does stress that the American test of October 1952 led to an intensification of Soviet work; after the test "Kurchatov and those taking part in the creation of the terrible new weapon increase the tempo of work. Alongside the design work, experiments are conducted to investigate different variants." This implies that besides working on the "Joe-4" bomb, Soviet scientists now worked to develop a superbomb. The American test stimulated Soviet research, and analysis of the fallout from the American test would have helped Soviet scientists to discover the mechanism behind the very high yield of the explosion. The first Soviet superbomb was tested in November 1955. . . .

From August 1945 Stalin faced a dual problem: to build a Soviet bomb as quickly as possible, and to deprive the United States of any military or political advantage from its atomic monopoly. The first part of this problem was solved by launching the new research and development programs. The second was tackled by providing a counterweight to American air power. Soviet forces in Eastern Europe were the main element in this policy. American bombers could threaten Soviet cities and industrial centres, but Soviet forces could not strike the United States. Consequently the Soviet Army was deployed in Eastern Europe not only to safeguard Soviet interests there, but also to strike Western Europe in the event of war. (Soviet forces were certainly not strong enough for Stalin to contemplate an invasion out of the blue.) Conventional weapons were modernized and air defences strengthened.

Stalin took pains to play down the significance of nuclear weapons. In September 1946, for example, he said that "I do not consider the atomic bomb as serious a force as some politicians are inclined to do. Atomic bombs are meant to frighten those with weak nerves, but they cannot decide the fate of wars since atomic bombs are quite insufficient for that." The effort the Soviet Union was making to develop the atomic bomb makes it clear that Stalin did in fact attribute great importance to nuclear weapons. Such statements were designed to weaken any American attempt to use its atomic monopoly to put pressure on the Soviet Union, and also to prevent Soviet troops, who would have to fight without nuclear weapons, from being intimidated by the threat of nuclear war.

Vojtech Mastny

THE AMERICAN FAILURE TO GET TOUGH EARLY

Some scholars critical of American behavior in the early Cold War fault the United States for vigorously wielding its power and alarming the Soviets. Vojtech Mastny takes a very different tack. He holds that the United States' failure to confront the Soviets over Eastern European issues earlier must be counted as a cause of the Cold War. Mastny draws upon the views of Maxim Litvinov, a former commissar for foreign affairs who left office in 1939 but who spoke privately to several Americans in the 1940s. Litvinov claimed that the Soviet appetite for absolute security seemed insatiable, and that as long as the British and Americans accepted Soviet demands, Stalin would ask for more. The Soviet diplomat did not explain precisely how Anglo-American toughness could have rolled back Soviet influence in Eastern Europe, where American power was minimal. But Mastny hints that Stalin was cautious; thus the Soviet leader likely would have limited his ambitions if the United States had faced him with firmness in 1945. This issue, like so many relating to the origins of the Cold War, centers on a key interpretive question: Was the United States active or reactive, hesitant or bold, expansive or restrained?

Vojtech Mastny teaches at Boston University and has written *The Czechs Under Nazi Rule* (1971), *Russia's Road to the Cold War, 1941–45* (1979), and *Helsinki, Human Rights, and European Security* (1986).

Toward the end of his long and distinguished career in the Soviet diplomatic service, Maxim Litvinov tantalized his foreign interlocutors with increasingly candid expressions of dissent from his employers' official line. There are several such incidents on record from May 1943 to February 1947—only some of which have been familiar to specialists in Soviet affairs though never adequately analyzed for what they are worth. Yet they raise altogether fundamental questions—about Litvinov and about the whole pattern of Russian behavior during the formative years of the cold war.

There is, to begin with, the obvious question of authenticity, particularly since some of the conversations took place on the premises of the Foreign Commissariat where walls were notorious for having ears.

Vojtech, Mastny, reprinted by permission of *Foreign Affairs*, January 1976, Vol. 54 by the Council on Foreign Relations, Inc.

Nevertheless, although Litvinov's views must have been well known in the Kremlin, he was allowed to remain in an official function until August 1946, only to be sent into relatively comfortable retirement afterwards. Why was he able to speak his mind for so long in a country where this was a transgression punished swiftly and routinely regardless of rank?

So anomalous does Litvinov's position seem that his own widow, when queried about it in 1974, flatly denied that he could have possibly said what the various Western accounts of his talks claim he did. To be sure, allowance must always be made for a measure of distortion in any account written down from memory—no matter how fresh—after the event rather than recorded simultaneously on the spot. Even so, the different testimonies are unequivocal, independent of one another, and revealing of a consistent train of thought on the part of the Soviet statesman.

Nor were Litvinov's indiscretions of the sort governments some-times plant in order to test each other's reactions or to influence each other's policies; they expressed truly independent opinion. Can new conclusions therefore be drawn about the extent of permissible dissent during the process of foreign policy formulation even in the heyday of Stalin's autocracy? And if there was a debate, what were the points of disagreement among the participants?

Admittedly, Litvinov after 1939 was no longer one of the inner circle responsible for the conduct of foreign affairs. But he still remained close enough to those who were to speak with authority; what he had to say about their perceptions and decisions therefore amounts to much more than a mere outsider's guess. Indeed, because of his sharp dissent from the conventional Soviet wisdom, he may be regarded as the first of the rare breed of Russian cold-war revisionists. And because of his unique position he brings into the controversy the kind of inside information about Soviet policy the absence of which has made their Western counterparts' attempts to apportion the blame for the conflict seem like so many exercises in make-believe. . . .

In the late summer of 1944, a chain reaction was set into motion once the Red Army had opened its drive into countries where it was regarded as a conqueror rather than a liberator. This was a dramatic challenge to Soviet statesmanship to which the regime, never distin-guished by generosity or tolerance toward weaker opponents, responded in conformity with its traditions. Understandably enough, its response generated misgivings about its intentions—misgivings in turn conducive to Moscow's reassessment of the alliance as a suitable vehicle of its interests.

The pattern emerged in all its melancholy logic as the Poles in August attempted to establish in Warsaw an independent government before the imminent arrival of Russian troops, and Stalin in turn proved unwilling to move fast enough to save them from annihilation by the Germans. At the same time, however, he moved only too fast into Romania and proceeded, without any advance notice to his allies, with the conquest of nonbelligerent Bulgaria in early September. This was the time Churchill saw his nightmare of "the Red Army spreading like cancer from one country to another" and Harriman began dispatching to Washington his ever more urgent warnings that the Soviet Union might become "a world bully."

Litvinov, to be sure, did not see the situation in quite the same light. In his [October 1944] interview with [Edgar] Snow, he stated emphatically that he disagreed with his "government on many things, but we are absolutely right about Poland. In fact we have been too lenient if anything." He rather castigated what he regarded as the "revival of British traditional diplomacy in Europe . . . this time fully backed up by America." In his opinion:

> Britain has never been willing to see a strong power on the continent . . . without organizing a counter-force against it. The idea of collaborating with the strong power is alien to her thinking. She is at work in France and the Lowlands doing that already. She will want to use her occupation of Germany for the same ends.

Litvinov was referring especially to the British-sponsored plan for an association of West European nations and had already predicted that "we won't be able to agree on a common program for Germany."

But, cautioning repeatedly that he was speaking merely for himself, the Soviet statesman was by no means inclined to put all the blame on others. Admitting regretfully that "we are drifting more and more in the same direction," he suggested that "diplomacy might have been able to do something to avoid it if we had made our purposes clear to the British and if we had made clear the limits of our needs, but now it is too late, suspicions are rife on both sides." And, trying to account for the conspicuous negligence by his government, he singled out startling deficiencies of some of its leading representatives.

Among the most revealing passages of Litvinov's long chat with Snow was his lament that the Foreign "Commissariat is run by only three men and none of them understand [sic] America or Britain," namely [V. M.] Molotov with his deputies [Andrei Ia.] Vyshinsky and [Vladimir G.] Dekanozov. Deploring the trio's disastrously parochial outlook, he commented that Dekanozov, the ex-Ambassador to Nazi Germany, "sat next to Ribbentrop for a year and that's all he knows about foreign countries." Although Litvinov did not mention Stalin by name, he hinted that the supreme leader, too, was prone to certain misconceptions, especially to reading too much into occasional unfriendly statements in the free Western press. And implying that the responsibility for cultivating these misconceptions rested not so much with the dictator himself as with his entourage, he concluded that "absolutely the only way . . . to improve matters" was by direct talks between Stalin and Roosevelt.

The Assistant Foreign Commissar seemed to worry lest the President, too, might not be exposed to similar prejudicial influences by his respective aides. Indicating that the gist of Harriman's recent alarming messages to Washington was no secret among Soviet officials, Litvinov implored Snow not to mention their conversation to anyone in Moscow, especially not to the American Ambassador. Snow complied. Only after his return to the United States two months later did he send the record of the interview directly to Roosevelt. The President replied graciously that he was "tremendously interested," whereupon the document was filed without further action.

But whatever the uncanny influence of his camarilla, Stalin himself did not seem to accept readily the disturbing proposition that his subjugation of East-Central Europe would necessarily lead to a clash with the West. Indeed, his November 6, 1944 speech conveyed in especially effusive terms a faith in the indestructibility of the alliance as the foundation of the postwar order. And a month later, Litvinov was given the opportunity to further develop his thoughts about the preconditions of that order. In a second "Malinin" article [written under the name "N. Malinin" in the magazine *Zvezda*], he focused on "regionalism," which, as he had hinted to Snow, was another matter about which he differed with those who stood between him and Stalin.

Litvinov advocated the creation of regional groupings within the framework of the United Nations but otherwise under the aegis of the great powers with paramount interests in the respective regions. He took pains to emphasize that he did not mean spheres of influence in which "from the point of view of peace nothing alluring can be found." It was different with "security zones" which he insisted would entail only mutually beneficial military arrangements between the great and the small powers. No matter how dubious this distinction, it was suggestive of a genuine concern lest excessive preoccupation with security lead to unrestrained competition and ultimately the partition of Europe into hostile blocs. The author pointedly warned that "by no means all states need enter one or another of the zones."

While directed primarily against the much-discussed West European bloc under British auspices, the warning applied more immediately to the Soviet Union. For Moscow, increasingly heavy-handed in manipulating the politics of the rapidly expanding area under its military control, had been carving out in East-Central Europe the very sphere of influence Litvinov loathed. At Yalta, Stalin behaved as if he believed the West had acquiesced to such practices—a misconception nourished in turn by his allies' negligence in making sufficiently clear to him what *their* purposes and the limits of *their* tolerance were. But once he went ahead and they remonstrated, the slide to hostility that Litvinov had predicted inevitably ensued.

After 1944, the Cassandra in the Foreign Commissariat never again found an outlet in print. The next time he opened his heart to a Western visitor—on April 5, 1945, to Cyrus L. Sulzberger of *The New York Times*—he sounded like "a regular Jeremiah, full of gloom." He mused that "first the Western powers make a mistake and rub us the wrong way. Then we make a mistake and rub you the wrong way." He was now thoroughly pessimistic—about the prospects of the United Nations and about the whole future course of East-West relations.

If Litvinov had so far attributed the spiraling cycle of action and reaction mainly to mutual misperception, for which he had held the West as much responsible as the East (if not more), he was soon to revise his estimate. The end of the European war, far from making the limits of Russia's goals clear (as he had wished), witnessed instead an expansion of its desiderata beyond those already on record: territory and bases in Turkey, a share in the administration of Italy's former African colonies, a role in the western Mediterranean. When Snow again came to Moscow in June 1945, he therefore heard from Litvinov a very different diagnosis of the incipient cold war.

Having asked the rhetorical question, "Why did you Americans wait till right now to begin opposing us in the Balkans and Eastern Europe?" the veteran diplomat also provided an answer: "You should have done this three years ago. Now it's too late and your complaints only arouse suspicion here." Thus Litvinov finally arrived at an interpretation which was as independent as it was eminently fair: his country's striving for power and influence too far in excess of its reasonable security requirements was the primary cause of conflict; the West's failure to resist that effort early enough was an important secondary one.

The Soviet statesman continued on the same pessimistic note in a subsequent talk with none other than Harriman, whom he had mistrusted so much only a year earlier. Having met him accidentally during a Moscow theater performance in November 1945, Litvinov deplored the recent breakdown of the London conference of foreign ministers. Now he no longer saw any hope of reversing the steady trend toward confrontation. Asked by the Ambassador what the United States could do to satisfy the Soviet Union, he replied: "Nothing." And when further questioned about what his own government could do to improve matters he gave the same curt answer, adding the enigmatic qualification: "I believe I know what should be done but I am powerless." Shortly afterwards, the foreign ministers' decision to hold their next meeting in the Soviet capital briefly elated the skeptic, but by May of the next year his gloom was deeper than ever before: "I now feel that the best that can be hoped for is a prolonged armed truce."

On June 18, 1946, Litvinov gave another lengthy confession of his heresy to CBS correspondent Richard C. Hottelet, similar to that given to Snow almost two years earlier. Some of his themes remained the same: the belief that only a great-power condominium of the world could save the peace, and the conviction that a partition of Germany was inevitable. But his other views showed vividly how his dissent had grown as his direst predictions materialized.

The disillusioned prophet of collective security now singled out as the root cause of all evil Moscow's reversion to the antiquated concept of security through the possession of a land mass. Indeed, he made the alarming suggestion that its appetite might be insatiable. Hottelet could not believe his ears as his host, chafing in the ornate Soviet foreign service uniform, gravely pronounced the damning judgment: "If the West acceded to the current Soviet demands it would be faced, after a more or less short time, with the next series of demands." Having been made privy to such a shocking affidavit, the correspondent fully expected to be arrested as soon as he set foot on the street, or else to hear within the next few days that Litvinov had suddenly died, most likely in an accident.

Nothing so drastic happened, at least not immediately, but two months later the dissenter was finally dismissed and pensioned. In retrospect, Hottelet has speculated whether Litvinov might not have received advance notice of this shortly before the conversation; for during the interview, which took place in Litvinov's office on a hot summer day, a fire was blazing in the fireplace as if the old man had been in the process of burning his papers. But it is more plausible that the talk in which he set the record of his outspokenness was also the last straw that broke the camel's back.

In September 1946, the pensioner was seen at a diplomatic reception, apparently pleased that the "anomalous situation which he had occupied for such a long time had been rectified by his release from duties." But even after that, he could not resist speaking his mind if an opportunity arose. On another social occasion in February of the next year, he told British journalist Alexander Werth that at the end of the war Moscow had had two choices: either to cash in on the goodwill it had accumulated in the West, or to embark alone on the elusive quest for absolute security. Litvinov lamented that "they"—meaning those wily men in the Kremlin who would not listen to him—had refused to believe that goodwill could possibly constitute the lasting basis of any policy. Instead they had opted for the second alternative, trying to grab "all they could while the going was good."

As Werth was listening, Vyshinsky passed by, giving the speaker an exceedingly dirty look, and that was the end, as far as we know, of Litvinov's indiscretions. A quarter of a century later, a revealing postscript to this extraordinary episode was provided by as authoritative a source as Nikita S. Khrushchev, by then himself out of grace and confiding his own unconventional views to a tape recorder for posterity's sake. He reported that when secret files had been examined and police officers questioned after Stalin's death they had revealed that "Beria's men" had devised a plan to dispose of Litvinov in a particularly dastardly way: like his fellow-Jew, actor Solomon M. Mikhaels, he was to be thrown in front of a truck and run over.

The reasons why the dissenter was spared this gruesome end and eventually allowed to die of natural causes in 1952 may have been purely accidental. But they may have also been the result of his undoubtedly unique relationship with Stalin—a relationship which alone can account for his having survived for so long in the first place. Conceivably, the dictator—himself fundamentally insecure in the depth of his mind—respected what Louis Fischer has described as Litvinov's "intestinal courage." It is even more probable that Stalin was impressed by the diplomat's definite reluctance to put any blame on him personally: according to Ilya Ehrenburg, Litvinov was always reticent in expressing an opinion about the boss. But none of these personality traits would have counted if it had been in conflict with political considerations; it is therefore on the political level that our main conclusions must be drawn.

The spectacular manifestations of Litvinov's dissent should not obscure the extent of his basic agreement with Stalin. There was no quarrel between these two devotees of power politics about the axiom that the Soviet Union could and indeed should advance its international status by whatever means it saw fit; only about the fitness of the different means did they come to disagree. Neither saw anything wrong with twisting the arms of weaker nations—except, that is, if relations with the stronger ones might suffer excessive damage as a result. Thus, no matter how appealing his features as a man, Litvinov as a politician wore no halo.

The issue which vexed the Soviet leadership toward the end of World War II was not the desirability of an empire—that was taken for granted—but rather the ways and means of its possible integration into an international order compatible with the Western notions. Litvinov regarded Anglo-American support of any settlement his government would wish to enforce in East-Central Europe as indispensable for Russia's true security. And, keenly aware as he was of the depth of Western sympathy for his country's security needs, he was also convinced that such support could be obtained if only the limits of those needs were stated sensibly and clearly enough.

Nor was Stalin—a cautious tyrant despite all his excesses—rushing headlong to set his exhausted country on a collision course with its mighty coalition partners. Though inclined by nature and experience to expect the worst, he was not so reckless as to ignore all opportunities to avert it. Eager to have the cake of Western cooperation while eating his East Europeans, too, he temporized in search for a solution. Meanwhile it was in his paramount interest not to discourage subordinates from formulating their ideas on the subject—certainly not such knowledgeable ones as Litvinov was.

This was all the more advisable since the men in the dictator's closer entourage, particularly Molotov and his assistants, had a vested interest in stressing obstacles to any long-term accommodation with the West. After all, they were the ones entrusted with the actual conduct of

policy and, consequently, vulnerable to being singled out—in conformity with Stalin's familiar habit—as scapegoats for its possible failure.
As long as their taskmaster did not make up his mind they were therefore the primary agents of that fateful drift which Litvinov deplored and
to which Stalin himself eventually succumbed.

Thus Litvinov's testimony supports the conclusion that the Soviet
leaders realized they had options and weighed them in good awareness
of long-term consequences.   Reduced to essentials, the choice was
between a policy of low tension, which would give a chance for the
alliance to continue as the bulwark of the postwar order, and a policy of
high tension, conducive to its ultimate breakdown.   Litvinov's most
original contribution to the cold-war debate is his contention that
Moscow resorted to the latter course not so much because the Anglo-
American attitude had stiffened—as the Western revisionists would
have it—but rather because it had not stiffened enough.   The choice, to
be sure, was predetermined—not by external factors however, but by
the Stalinist system and the mentality of the leaders it bred.

Fraser J. Harbutt

BRITISH INFLUENCE: WINSTON CHURCHILL AND THE IRON CURTAIN SPEECH

The early historical literature on the Cold War concentrated almost exclusively on the two principal actors: the United States and the Soviet Union.
Other nations, including Great Britain, were relegated to the role of bit
players. In recent years some historians have disputed such a bipolar focus,
asserting that other powers assumed leading parts in the Cold War drama.
Fraser J. Harbutt argues that Great Britain's role in those events was central.
Focusing especially on former prime minister Winston Churchill's catalytic
speech of March 1946, Harbutt suggests that the British succeeded in reori-
enting American policy toward a more aggressively anti-Soviet stance. He
locates the origins of the Cold War, then, in the critical early months of 1946
and attributes major responsibility for the shift in American thinking and
policy to British statesmen—and particularly to Churchill.

Selected pages from *The Iron Curtain: America and the Origins of the Cold War* by Fraser
J. Harbutt. Copyright © 1986 by Fraser J. Harbutt.   Reprinted by permission of Oxford
University Press, Inc.

Fraser J. Harbutt is the author of *The Iron Curtain: Churchill, America, and the Origins of the Cold War* (1986), from which this selection is drawn. This book was awarded the Stuart L. Bernath Memorial Book Prize by the Society for Historians of American Foreign Relations. Harbutt is a professor of history at Emory University.

. . . [T]he study of almost any aspect of [Winston] Churchill's career seems to lead one inexorably toward questions of broad significance, so closely connected was he with the profound events of our century. This is certainly true of the origins of the Cold War. Here, as we explore his thought and action, we will find both a distinctive angle of vision and a personal impact that was, in certain respects, decisive.

Surely the United States has never had a more persistent courtier than Churchill. He was active in the British effort to bring America into belligerency against Germany in World War I and again, as Prime Minister, in World War II. His initial efforts to create an Anglo-American front against the Soviet Union also go back to the first great conflagration. His reaction to the 1917 revolution was bitterly hostile. He quickly established himself as his country's leading anti-Bolshevik, defining the new regime in Russia as Britain's primary future antagonist and, even before the Armistice in November 1918, talking about the need to build up the defeated German army against this new menace. During 1919 he vigorously directed the British intervention in Russia and enthusiastically defended the use of gas against revolutionaries he seems to have regarded as subhuman. Meanwhile, he tried to draw the United States more fully into the military confrontation with the Soviets. President Woodrow Wilson, however, proved unresponsive. Churchill, deeply disappointed, did not give up. As late as 1931 we find him touring the United States and warning audiences that "the two great opposing forces of the future will be the English-speaking peoples and Communism."

Through most of the interwar period, Churchill conducted a personal campaign against the Soviet regime that included the approval of fascism as a necessary European antidote. The appearance of a renewed German menace in the mid-1930s, however, inspired second thoughts. He now accepted the Soviet state as a necessary fixture. There was then a considerable further mellowing with the responsibility of supreme leadership in Britain during the war that followed. He formed a personal bond of sorts with Joseph Stalin and even collaborated with him briefly in a plan to divide postwar Europe. But, as we will see, the old hostility remained just beneath the surface, and Churchill's postwar hopes, for the most part, centered on the notion of a dominant Anglo-American military and economic combination confronting a petitionary Soviet Union. Here again, though, except briefly in 1945, he was successively rebuffed by Presidents Franklin D. Roosevelt and Harry S Truman. Only in the crisis of early 1946, when a sudden reorientation in American policy led to the Cold War, was he finally and completely successful.

In that transformation Churchill took a leading part. The most obvious manifestation of this was his "iron curtain" speech on March 5, 1946, at Fulton, Missouri. There, for a moment, the twentieth century was reduced to the dimensions of Periclean Greece, as the famous orator brought together the two themes that had dominated his political outlook for nearly three decades—fear of Soviet Russia, belief in a countering Anglo-American mission—at precisely the moment when much of the world was poised receptively in uneasy, half-conscious transition to a new international system based on that very proposition. But Churchill's contribution to the transformation went far beyond the Fulton speech itself. Indeed, as we follow the course of events and try to understand the political relationships and perceptions involved in this crisis, we will find that he exerted considerable influence upon both the American reorientation and the Soviet response.

So far as the origins of the Cold War are concerned, this focus on Churchill offers a valuable European perspective. The historical treatment of the Cold War, we do well to remember, has been an overwhelmingly American enterprise. There is nothing surprising in this. Diplomatic historians cleave instinctively to grandeur. Thus, for many years after World War II, when the power of the United States in the world rose so visibly and dramatically, scholars in this country clustered thickly around the germinating events of the early Cold War, unquestionably a moment of high American destiny. The study of American foreign policy in earlier periods languished by comparison. Precisely the opposite trend developed in Britain, a great power now in steep decline. Historians there, always less interested in recent history than their American colleagues anyway, explored the politics of the 1930s, Churchill's wartime leadership, and the exploits of the desert generals. But they seem to have drawn a kind of line for themselves around 1945. Certainly there was little interest in recording the grim adjustment to postwar reality and second-rank status presided over by Foreign Secretary Ernest Bevin, a dynamic figure who has nevertheless had to wait nearly four decades for a full biography. The result is that, partly for lack of a British balance, partly because there were so few acceptable Soviet contributions, the study of Cold War origins rapidly acquired the excessively Americocentric cast that, despite heartening signs of change in recent years, it continues to exhibit.

One consequence of this imbalance is that we know a great deal about the indigenous impulses that lie behind the making of American foreign policy. We know much less than is commonly supposed, however, about the international environment—the crises, the points of political connection, and the sometimes frantic diplomatic maneuvering—out of which the Cold War actually developed. It is symptomatic of this that we do not even know when the Cold War began, though opinions proliferate, and that the crisis of 1946, though long acknowledged to have been the occasion of an important reorientation in American policy toward the Soviet Union, has not yet, so far as I am aware, inspired a monographic treatment or been analyzed fully from the point of view of international diplomacy. We have, perhaps, elevated unduly the "new" diplomacy of popular opinion, mass ideology, and bureaucratic factionalism at the expense of the "old" state-oriented, political diplomacy of the international chessboard. Both perspectives, the one characteristically American, the other so often associated with European political struggle, are necessary if we are to understand the process that drew these two continental structures of power together in the postwar era. We need this broadening of vision to remind us of, among other things, the stake European leaders in the mid-1940s felt they had in American diplomacy. We will then be in a position to see that the final crisis of 1946, for example, was not only the product of a calculated initiative by the Truman administration but also the culmination of a long struggle between Churchill and Stalin over the future direction of American power, the one trying desperately to attach, the other to deflect, its potentially decisive weight. . . .

The speech [at Fulton], as Churchill had intended, provoked a worldwide reaction. Communist publications everywhere heaped abuse upon its author. The first Soviet response was calm. But Western correspondents soon saw signs of public anxiety and some political agitation in Moscow. And on March 13 Stalin showed his concern in a bitter personal attack on Churchill, comparing him to the Nazis. Meanwhile, the initiative had created an immediate sensation in the United States. A fog of ambiguous official rhetoric had long obscured the rising tensions between the victorious powers. Churchill's unprecedentedly blunt talk alarmed many and drove Truman and Secretary of State James F. Byrnes to deny their actual complicity. But the deeper consequence, already evident by March 15, was the rapid polarization of American opinion into rival attitudes of hostility to and support for the Soviet Union.

It is surely a matter of historical curiosity that a speech by an individual who was neither American nor Russian, and whose leadership in his own country had recently been overwhelmingly repudiated, could so agitate the governments and peoples of the world's two most formidable powers. Much of the explanation will be found in that close examination of events in early 1946 toward which our discussion will steadily lead. But it derives also from two more deeply rooted causes—one structural, the other personal—which have a prior claim on our attention. The first is the pivotal position that Britain occupied between the United States and the Soviet Union throughout and immediately after the war, for Britain had with each of the stronger powers a much closer relationship and a wider range of historical and geopolitical connections than they had with each other. The comparative mutual detachment of the United States and the Soviet Union gave to each a sense of insulation during the immediate postwar period. But the persisting strength of Anglo-American ties, despite some attrition after the Potsdam conference, meant that when the Soviets commenced their "war of nerves" against Britain in 1945 they risked eventual confrontation with the United States. By March 1946 their campaign had reached the point where a provocative speech in the United States by any British leader would have created a diplomatic furor.

But the fact that it was Churchill greatly intensified the reaction, for Churchill personally, like Britain geopolitically, had a deeply etched association with both the United States and Russia. In each case he was the embodiment of certain central attitudes. In Soviet eyes he was still the leading European anti-Bolshevik of the postrevolutionary era. He had also been for nearly three decades the ardent and persistent promoter of a close Anglo-American combination that the Soviets could only view with suspicion. To some Americans he was the man who, above all others, stood for the preservation and perhaps expansion of the still-hated British Empire, who had somehow harnessed American power to British interests during the war and was now threatening to do so again; to others, by contrast, he was the brilliant world statesman and admired hero who had foreseen and successfully defied Hitler and whose warnings now about Stalinist Russia therefore carried the authority of a vindicated prophet's. . . .

We now approach a great divide in early postwar history. So far we have been tracing the emergence of a postwar situation that, by the beginning of 1946, clearly revolved around two fundamental facts: first, the intensifying Soviet pressure on a declining Great Britain and her anxious connections that Churchill had long foreseen and, second, an American detachment from that confrontation, obscured though it was by an impressive array of tripartite conferences and commissions, by the still considerable American military presence in Europe, and by the apparent victory of internationalism over isolationism at home. But this initial postwar order never established itself, and by the middle of 1946 the constituent elements of a different order—the United States–Cold War system we know—were already clearly visible. It is to the crucial transitional period in the first months of that year, therefore, that we must turn for some answer to the question, When did the Cold War begin?

The transition commenced with a sudden American challenge to the Soviet Union in mid-February, a challenge that evolved rapidly into a general reorientation of the Truman administration's policy from accommodation to a state described at the time as "firmness." This reorientation was in fact a unilateral American act, or rather series of acts. But, at least in its formative stages, it was carefully shaped to appear to the Soviets as the expression of an Anglo-American joint design—one that seemed to portend that coming together of American power and British worldwide connections which was believed in Washington to be the particular Soviet nightmare. In the creation of this image a crucial and doubtless congenial role was played by Winston Churchill, who now returned dramatically to the center of events by virtue of his "iron curtain" speech on March 5 at Fulton, Missouri. There, in Truman's presence, he advocated an Anglo-American "fraternal association" to resist Soviet expansion. As we will see later, this was taken in Moscow, and was intended by American leaders to be taken, as an authoritative definition of the new American militancy. . . .

The Fulton speech was born in political innocence. In August 1945 the president of Westminster College, a quiet campus at Fulton, Missouri, wrote to Churchill inviting him to speak there during his forthcoming American vacation. As an inducement President Truman, whose support had meanwhile been solicited by Missourian intermediaries in the White House, added a note saying, "This is a fine old college out in my state. If you'll come out and make them a speech I'll take you out and introduce you." Churchill accepted six weeks later, noting it would be his only public appearance on the visit. . . . Churchill wrote to Truman on January 29, "I have a message to deliver to your country and to the world and I think it likely that we shall be in agreement about it. Under your auspices anything I say will command some attention." Truman replied cordially that he knew the Englishman had "an important message to deliver." Elaborate arrangements were made for the two to meet in Florida to discuss it. When a sudden rash of strikes forced Truman to cancel his trip, Churchill flew to Cuba for a few days and then, on February 10, traveled to Washington, where he visited the President at the White House that evening.

The little direct evidence we have about this meeting comes from four sources. In a 1962 interview Truman told an inquiring historian that Churchill had wanted him to help write the speech but that he had replied, "It's your own speech, you write it." A more informative source is Admiral [William] Leahy, who recorded in his diary on February 10,

> From 8:30 until 10:00 p.m. Mr. Churchill talked with the President in the White House principally in regard to an address that Churchill will make on 5th March at Westminster College in Missouri. The subject of the address will be the necessity for full military collaboration between Great Britain and the United States in order to preserve peace in the world until the U.N. is fully able to keep the peace which will be at some time in the distant future. Mr. Churchill believes it to be necessary to our safety that the combined British-American Staff be continued in operation. I can foresee forceful objections by the Soviet to our having a bilateral military association. I returned with Mr. Churchill to the British Embassy where, together with the Ambassador, we talked until midnight on the same subject.

Leahy also recorded that during the late-night embassy discussion of Churchill's speech the three men "talked a good deal about how he [Churchill] should present it from the point of view of the Russians, which he thinks he can manage." Meanwhile, Churchill told Halifax that Truman "was quite happy, and more than happy, about his making the kind of fraternal association speech that he has in mind to deliver."

Some further clue to the Truman-Churchill meeting comes from remarks that Churchill made to the American minister in Havana, which the latter, who privately believed the British statesman was "suffering from a Messiah complex," forwarded directly to Truman on February 7 with the comment "He gave me a strong impression that he wanted these thoughts passed on to you." Churchill, in this preview of his Fulton themes, pronounced himself "apprehensive" about the United Nations. In reality everything depended "upon the political relations between the three great powers." The report continued, "Churchill's great fear, as he expressed it, is that Russia will not only master the secret of atomic warfare, but will not hesitate to employ it for her own ends in this atmosphere of postwar friction and confusion." Then the United Nations would perish with the epitaph "U.N. Orphan." The only escape, and hope, was "the development over the years of some definite working agreement between the American and British Governments." Churchill "fully understands" that a formal merger or alliance was "impracticable," the report concluded, and would be "untimely and unpopular on both sides of the Atlantic." But "the sheer pressure of events will force our two great commonwealths together in some workable manner if the peace and order of the world are to be preserved from chaos."

Churchill came away from the meeting with Truman greatly buoyed by the prospect now opening up. He began to act with his wartime zest, calling in the Canadian ambassador with a view of getting Prime Minister Mackenzie King down from Ottawa for consultations on the speech. Halifax noted on February 10, "I can see that it is the one thing on which all Winston's thought and willpower and dynamic nature are concentrated." During the next two days, while staying at the embassy, Churchill discussed the speech again with Halifax, who recorded on February 11, "He wants to speak very frankly about the importance of maintaining very close Anglo-American cooperation . . . and thinks he can do this without upsetting Uncle Joe who will, however, read, and it is hoped read to his profit, between the lines." By February 12 the ambassador was beginning to feel the strain. "He rehearsed to me a great deal of the speech that he has in mind to deliver," Halifax wrote, "with tears almost rolling down his cheeks as he thought of the great strategical concept of the future which was the cottage home of happy humble people, and quoted 'Childe Harold' to reinforce his eloquence. He really is a most astonishing creature but Dorothy and I agreed that we had never seen him so benign." Churchill then departed for Miami to resume his vacation.

Churchill's excitement is understandable, for the evidence makes it clear that Truman had licensed him to advocate publicly, in the legitimizing presidential presence, an intimate and exclusive world-girdling

Anglo-American military combination whose purpose could only be the containment, if not the eventual elimination, of Soviet power. And this was, of course, a radical departure from existing American policy and principle. Both men must have been aware of this. Had Truman been embarrassed by Churchill's proposal, he could easily have vetoed it; or he could have accepted it and maintained a careful detachment until March 5. In fact, as we will see, both Truman and Byrnes worked hard to show the Russians, if not the American people, that they supported and were directly party to Churchill's design.

Truman certainly knew what he was doing. He was well aware of the Rooseveltian dogma that good relations with the Soviet Union depended very largely on an ostentatious diplomatic detachment from Britain. He had himself, after all, rebuffed Churchill's vigorous Anglo-Americanism in the late spring of 1945 and again at Potsdam. He was not caught unawares now, as the February 7 message from Cuba shows. . . .

. . . [I]t seems clear that the real question is not the degree of Truman's foreknowledge or complicity with Churchill—for that was clearly substantial—but why he made this radical departure from American diplomatic doctrine. One way to answer this question is to suggest that, though Truman was willing to follow up the Fulton initiative with a general reorientation of policy if it proved successful, he was moved mainly by short-term considerations. He wanted to act. But, for good reason, he shrank from a dramatic personal initiative. Suddenly, here was Churchill offering to do the job for him, only a day after Stalin's "hostile" election speech, which must have stirred thoughts of a response in kind. Churchill's speech would presumably frighten Stalin, especially if given in a context that suggested American endorsement. If domestic opinion was receptive, which must have seemed possible in the increasingly anti-Soviet atmosphere, then all well and good. If not, the American involvement could be disavowed and any momentary embarrassment given the appearance of virtue by simply asserting Churchill's right to free speech. In short, it was an excellent gamble. It involved no dangerous commitment of presidential power. At the very least, it would reveal the state of public opinion.

No doubt these calculations were in Truman's mind. Yet it is a superficial and incomplete explanation, for in the course of our discussion it will become clear that the President saw his sponsorship of Churchill's proposal as the first step in a basic commitment to general and radical change. And this was logical, because, as we have already seen, Truman, like Roosevelt, Hopkins, Byrnes, and other American leaders, attached fundamental importance to the principle of "no ganging up" with Britain against the Soviet Union. He thought instinctively in tripartite terms. This first serious departure from the principle, though masked by the fiction of Churchill's individual responsibility, therefore led Truman to decide, with perfect logic, to go all the way and establish immediately a new basis for his Soviet policy, even while Churchill was still preparing his speech. The proof of this lies only partly in contemporary documents, for the conversion was managed with considerable political discretion; and it does not lie in any later acknowledgment in the memoirs, for Truman and Byrnes preferred to develop a different scenario of the origins of the Cold War. It lies instead in the simple fact that, two days after the Truman-Churchill meeting, we see the beginning of a remarkably comprehensive transformation of policy that, by the time Churchill mounted the stage at Fulton, had already changed the fundamental direction of American diplomacy. . . .

On March 5, while Churchill was giving his speech in Missouri, Byrnes sent three separate geopolitical messages to Moscow. Each can be explained in terms of its own regional configuration. But the decision to send them together on that day is consistent only with the administration's firm determination to convey an impression of complete solidarity with Churchill. The first March 5 cable was a direction to [George F.] Kennan to ask the Soviets to provide copies of all economic agreements they had made with the East European governments, as enjoined by the Yalta accords but never invoked by the United States until now. The era of ambiguity in United States–Soviet relations was coming to an end. At the same time Byrnes sent a critical aide-mémoire to the Bulgarian representative in Washington. This was immediately characterized by the *Washington Star*, which noted the simultaneous initiatives in other areas, as "obviously part of a general policy." Indeed it was, as the flurry of other American complaints about Soviet conduct in Eastern Europe that . . . erupted at the beginning of March eloquently testifies.

The second March 5 initiative, the rekindling of an old front rather than the opening of a new one, was a protest to [V. M.] Molotov against Soviet economic demands upon China. These, it was said, were not only unwarranted by the Sino-Soviet treaty but were also a threat to American commercial interests in Manchuria. In this sphere, too, Byrnes took two associated steps on the same day to dramatize the change in policy. One was his release to the press of a number of diplomatic documents on the Manchurian issue that had been collected in preceding weeks. These intended to confirm rumors, already appearing in the Western press, that the Soviets were pursuing a policy of selective looting, destruction, and confiscation of industrial materials in Manchuria. The other was a statement claiming that General MacArthur's authority as Supreme Allied Commander in Japan extended to all areas where there were Japanese forces, including Russian-controlled Manchuria.

Third, the United States sent a strong protest to the Soviet Union on the Iranian issue. Hitherto the problem had been Soviet interference with Iran's efforts to assert some jurisdiction in the Soviet-occupied north. Now the Russians were caught by the Anglo-Soviet treaty of 1942, which bound them to withdraw their troops within six months of the end of hostilities. This date fell on March 2. It had long been anticipated, correctly, that the Soviets would not withdraw. Byrnes now sent a note to Molotov asking for explanations, calling for immediate withdrawal, and, very much in the spirit of the new militancy, stressing that the Soviet Union had "created a situation with regard to which the Government of the United States . . . [could] not remain indifferent." What is significant here is that the Secretary again chose March 5 to send his protest. The purpose was clearly to link up with the other messages and especially the Fulton attack. The impressive coincidence of all these diplomatic moves did not go unnoticed. The *New York Times*, which picked up the Manchurian and Iranian protests but apparently missed the East European notes that worked to similar effect, editorialized, "One would have to go back far . . . to find two United States' protest notes to one power on two different issues on the same day."

Even this was not quite the end, for the Senate Banking and Currency Committee opened its hearings on the British loan on March 5. No doubt this was coincidental. But it drew from Truman and other senior administration and public notables warm endorsements, which can only have added to Soviet suspicion. Byrnes also sent one further significant and revealing message on this remarkable day. This was a cable to London sending word to Bevin of his intention to propose to Molotov a meeting of the Council of Foreign Ministers at Paris on April 15, somewhat in advance of the next scheduled conference. But now, by contrast with his approach to the Moscow conference, Byrnes informed Bevin before rather than after consulting Molotov, looked to the Big Five rather than to the Big Three format with which he had lured the Russians in December, and promised to drop the whole idea if Bevin demurred. Finally, perhaps to make it perfectly clear in Moscow that there was real substance behind all this diplomatic activity, Byrnes made the official announcement of the *Missouri* mission on March 6.

Much had occurred in the three weeks since the Truman-Churchill meeting on February 10. Before that, despite rising political pressure and spasmodic presidential irritation, it is hard to find a militant note. Byrnes continued to search for accommodation with the Soviets, proclaiming its virtues with enthusiasm as late as February 4. The Rumanian recognition of February 7 was perhaps its last concrete expression. After February 10 the firmer policy developed rapidly and systematically, in Eastern and later Western Europe, then into the Anglo-Russian arena along the Norther Tier, finally toward the more familiar Far East. And these geopolitical thrusts were accompanied by the first serious attempt to convert the United Nations into a more self-serving medium for American and Anglo-American diplomacy, by the revival, in modified form, of the coercive strategies of 1945, and by a final burst of clustered diplomacy to support Churchill's dramatic speech. The clear evidence of system in all this, as well as the comprehensive scope of the general reorientation, which had in the space of about three weeks touched almost all aspects of United States–Soviet relations, leaves the unavoidable impression of a commitment to fundamental change. It did not necessarily foreclose the possibility of settlement with the Soviets; and it was a change that still had to find convincing support in public opinion. But the Truman administration had now set its course.

Finally, we can identify, within this multidimensional reorientation, the two cutting edges of the new Truman-Byrnes policy. The first was the sudden and novel American political intrusion into the Anglo-Soviet eastern Mediterranean and Near East. The second was the attempt, by an assertion of the supremacy of the Charter, to convert the United Nations into an instrument not simply of American diplomacy but inevitably, given the persistent Soviet pressure on Britain and her worldwide connections, of Anglo-American interests as well. This leads us again to Churchill, who now, with the ostensible approval and support of the United States government, defined the whole reorientation in terms of the Anglo-American alliance against Russia that American leaders had always, up to this point, vigorously repudiated. . . .

The Fulton address was a brilliant exercise in political prophecy. Like some master architect, Churchill laid out, in a necessarily general but easily recognizable form, much of the future shape and character of the Cold War. He anticipated the formation of an anti-Soviet Western security system based on the Anglo-American nucleus. He outlined the role that Britain would play as a junior partner, though he missed, or refused to face, the imminent devolution of European empire that later led to new problems. He envisioned the appearance of a democratic West Germany tied to the West. He clearly foresaw the course of the arms race in atomic weapons and urged further American development to maintain the lead. He set forward many of the philosophic, geopolitical, and strategic foundations of both "containment" and "confrontation-liberation," the two leading American national security doctrines of the early Cold War. He formulated a crusading Anglo-American ideology of libertarian constitutionalism embodying the central idea of freedom and embellished it with appealing images of Christian virtue opposing amoral totalitarianism. He also predicted the appearance of a postwar economic "age of plenty," a forecast vindicated, at least for the developed world, in the 1950s and 1960s. And he bequeathed to posterity a rummage bag of striking political terms whose familiarity reflects his continuing relevance: the "iron curtain," which he popularized but did not invent; the nuclear "deterrent," and the Anglo-American "special relationship," which he seems to have coined; the United Nations as "a Tower of Babel"; and, perhaps most influential of all, an instant working credo for future Cold Warriors, the assessment of the Soviets that finally begat the $300 billion defense budget: "There is nothing they admire so much as strength, and there is nothing for which they have less respect than for military weakness."

It is a tribute to the quality of Churchill's mind that this remarkable forecast of the future was at the same time a very present-minded political demarche that also had deep roots in the past. At the farthest remove, for example, it was a chance to realize the two central elements in Churchill's political outlook that go back to the World War I era: his deep longing from some form of transcendent Anglo-American intimacy and his persistent hostility toward Soviet communism. Somewhat closer to the event, he must have seen himself facing a situation closely resembling the 1930s: a menace to peace by a wound-up European totalitarian power, an escapist British government (Bevin apart), and reigning neo-isolationist tendencies in the United States associated with the accommodationist "vision" of Yalta. In this sense the Fulton speech may be viewed as a highly compressed repetition, in response to a unique opportunity, of his great prewar anti-appeasement campaign. And, most recently, it was clearly inspired by his post-Yalta perception of the Soviet threat to world security in general and to British interests in particular, and by the concurrent decline of his remaining faith in Stalin. At Potsdam he had pressed upon Truman his case for Anglo-American unity and military collaboration; and he had told Stalin of his anxiety over Soviet expansionism. But he had not linked the two. Now, in the more combustible context of March 1946, with Britain under Soviet pressure but with the reorientation of American policy already launched and a supportive Truman beside him, Churchill advanced publicly his provocative thesis: that Soviet expansionism was a dangerous threat to peace and that a fully militarized Anglo-American "fraternal association" was needed to resist it.

Fulton was really two closely interrelated speeches: one a call to arms addressed to the American people on the basis of a Soviet threat, the other a multidimensional threat to the Soviet leadership that depended for its credibility partly on the success of the first and partly on Churchill's evident association with Truman and Byrnes. The speech was prepared with great care. It is remarkable, for example, that the two main points—the premise of a Soviet menace and the conclusion that an Anglo-American response was necessary—are never brought together with an open acknowledgment of cause and effect, though the relationship was manifest, but are developed along strictly parallel lines of thought and with the use of abstractions to make the desired connections.

In much the same cautious way Churchill felt his way to the provocative points with dense preliminary imagery. Thus, before openly calling for an Anglo-American combination, Churchill prepared the ground with a long, Bunyanesque invocation of glowing American youth and its "awe-inspiring accountability to the future," which contrasts sharply with the invariably dark images he used to depict Soviet reality. The latter, indeed, he first approached through the somewhat Victorian abstraction "Tyranny," described as a "gaunt marauder" that "threatens the cottage home and ordinary people." Not until he was two-thirds through the speech did the cottagers of Fulton hear a direct critical reference to the Soviet Union.

By that time, however, they must have grasped the point, for "Tyranny" was found:

in a considerable number of countries, some of which are very powerful. In these states, control is enforced upon the common people by various kinds of all-embracing police governments, to a degree which is overwhelming and contrary to every principle of democracy. The power of the state is exercised without restraint, either by dictators or by compact oligarchies operating through a privileged party and a political police.

This is one of several passages playing up Nazi associations. In giving thanks for the temporary Western monopoly of the atomic bomb, for example, Churchill suggested that many would have slept less soundly "had the positions been reversed and some Communist or neo-Fascist state monopolized, for the time being, these dread agencies." "The fear of them alone," he went on, "might easily have been used to enforce totalitarian systems upon the free democratic world, with consequences appalling to the human imagination." The Communists were untrustworthy and ruthless. They were also inhumane, as was shown by the mass expulsion of Germans now taking place in Eastern Europe under "the Russian-dominated Polish government," and greedy and dangerous in seeking, not war, but "the fruits of war and the indefinite expansion of their power and doctrines."

But when Churchill finally came to examine the Soviet threat in detail, it was in unmistakably concrete terms. After the introductory warning "Nobody knows what Soviet Russia and its Communist international organization intends to do in the immediate future, or what are the limits, if any, to their expansive or proselytizing tendencies," he started by drawing attention to alarming portents in Eastern Europe:

> From Stettin in the Baltic to Trieste in the Adriatic, an iron curtain has descended across the Continent. Behind that line lie all the capitals of the ancient states of central and eastern Europe. Warsaw, Berlin, Prague, Vienna, Budapest, Belgrade, Bucharest and Sofia, all these famous cities and the populations around them lie in the Soviet sphere and all are subject in one form or another, not only to Soviet influence but to a very high and increasing measure of control from Moscow. . . . The Communist parties, which were very small in all these eastern states of Europe, have been raised to preeminence and power far beyond their numbers and are seeking everywhere to obtain totalitarian control. Police governments are prevailing in nearly every case, and so far, except in Czechoslovakia, there is no true democracy.

Here was a precise bill of particulars to amplify the more generalized charges Byrnes had made on February 28. This malign power, moreover, was still on the move throughout the world. The next area Churchill singled out was the British sphere in the eastern Mediterranean and Near East, where "Turkey and Persia are both profoundly alarmed and disturbed at the claims which are made upon them." He then turned to Germany, where "an attempt is being made by the Russians in Berlin to build up a quasi-Communist party in their zone of occupied Germany by showing special favors to groups of Left-Wing German leaders." Churchill viewed this as the prelude to possible Communist domination in Germany. He then described the vulnerability of Western Europe, where "the future of Italy hangs in the balance" and where France, similarly encumbered with a powerful Communist party, was also in danger. "The outlook is also anxious in the Far East," he continued, "and especially in Manchuria."

It was not just a matter of the Red Army and formal, visible Communist parties, for, "in a great number of countries, far from the Russian frontiers and throughout the world, Communist fifth columns are established and work in complete unity and absolute obedience to the directions they receive from the Communist center." In his zeal to expose the dangers of domestic subversion, Churchill resurrected "the Communist international organization"—the Comintern—which Stalin had ostentatiously dismantled in 1943. "Except in the British Commonwealth and in this United States," he stressed, "where Communism is in its infancy, the Communist parties or fifth columns constitute a growing challenge and peril to Christian civilization."

With these charges Churchill shattered the convention, hitherto observed by virtually all Western leaders, of softening their mild public criticisms of Soviet conduct with cordial references and pious hopes of future collaboration. Even Byrnes, for all the implied menace in his February 28 speech, had emphasized common interests. This note was not wholly missing at Fulton. Churchill made a complimentary reference to Stalin, acknowledged the understandable Soviet desire for security in the west, and called for negotiations and a settlement. But he emphasized the differences between the two systems, fortifying his case with various anti-Soviet images: the mechanistic expansionism of a totalitarian Communist system also portrayed by Kennan, the primitive and greedy "Bear" of traditional Foreign Office stereotype, and the analogy with Nazi Germany suggesting a renewed threat to "Christian civilization."

The identification and dramatization of the Soviet threat was only one-half of Churchill's appeal to American opinion. Meanwhile, again moving carefully behind soft introductory images, he came to "the crux" of what he had traveled to Fulton to say:

Neither the sure prevention of war, nor the continuous rise of world organization will be gained without what I have called the fraternal association of the English-speaking peoples. This means a special relationship between the British Commonwealth and Empire and the United States. This is no time for generalities. . . . Fraternal association requires not only the growing friendship and mutual understanding between our two vast but kindred systems of society but the continuance of the intimate relationships between our military advisers, leading to common study of potential dangers, similarity of weapons and manuals of instruction and interchange of officers and cadets at colleges. It should carry with it the continuance of the present facilities for mutual security by the joint use of all naval and air-force bases in the possession of either country all over the world. This would perhaps double the mobility of the American Navy and Air Force. It would greatly expand that of the British Empire forces and it might well lead, if and as the world calms down, to important financial savings. Already we use together a large number of islands; many more will be intrusted to our joint care in the near future.

Thus, nine months after Truman and Hopkins had apparently locked it in the closet, the specter of an intimate anti-Soviet Anglo-American combination was again brought unambiguously forward by its most persistent champion. . . .

Any explanation of the speech, and the American response to it, needs to take into account the nervous atmosphere of the immediate postwar period. Truman himself sounded an apocalyptic note when he introduced Churchill at Fulton. "We are either headed for complete destruction," he said, "or we are facing the greatest age in history." A few days later the former Secretary of State Cordell Hull raised the possibility of "the suicide of the human race." And the atomic bomb, of course, lent a nightmare quality to all ordinary international anxieties. Associated with this was a widespread fear of war with the Soviet Union, as the journalism and diaries of the day amply testify. As early as the spring of 1945 the columnist Kenneth Crawford noted, "War with Russia is unthinkable, yet it is being thought about constantly. It is, in fact, America's great preoccupying fear." A year later this was no longer an exaggeration. The possibility of war was discussed across the political spectrum and at the highest level. Truman himself told Harriman in the spring of 1946, that the Iranian situation "may lead to war." In *PM* Max Lerner referred to "the conflict everyone says is irrepressible" and described the Russians as "a people preparing for a struggle." And in his diary the former Vice-President Henry Wallace kept a kind of gravedigger's record of the many statesmen and journalists who shared his similar anxieties.

In this context Churchill pursued two complementary objectives. The first was to destroy the accommodationist policies and attitudes associated with Yalta. These, he insisted, would lead directly to war, just as they had done in the 1930s. Here he was able to speak with unique authority. "Our difficulties and dangers will not be removed by closing our eyes to them," he insisted. "They will not be removed by mere waiting to see what happens; nor will they be relieved by a policy of appeasement." He concluded, "Last time I saw it all coming, and cried aloud to my fellow countrymen and to the world, but no one paid any attention."

He also carefully subverted the three pillars of the vision of Yalta: Big Three cooperation, Franklin D. Roosevelt, and the existing United Nations. His direct indictment of Soviet policy simply left no room for the first in the absence of some unmistakable retreat by Stalin. Roosevelt, the object of so many Churchillian tributes while alive, was now cast aside by conspicuous omission. He went completely unremarked in his friend's first postwar speech in the United States and, as a symbol of accommodationism, was now abandoned to the Left. For the United Nations, however, an integrative strategy was employed. This institution was, after all, the essential condition of American internationalism; and the object, as Byrnes and Bevin had shown, was not to destroy it but to convert it into a useful instrument of Western purpose. Churchill carefully linked up with Byrnes by asserting the importance of the Charter, citing it on three occasions as the only standard of acceptable international behavior. But he went further, stressing that the world is moved by power rather than by ideals, that the United Nations must therefore be "a force for action" and not merely "a frothing of words," and that "before we cast away the solid assurances of national armaments for self-preservation, we must be certain that our temple is built not upon shifting sands or quagmires, but upon the rock." The "rock" shortly reappeared as the proposed Anglo-American combination, which Churchill then attempted to legitimize as the necessary foundation of a functional United Nations. . . .

As he extirpated the Yalta heresy in this way, Churchill worked on his second objective: the Fulton thesis of peace through intimate Anglo-American combination. The British connection, he asserted, would help the United States set a limit to Soviet expansion and give "an overwhelming assurance of security." This would be possible only "if all British moral and material forces and convictions are joined with your own in fraternal association." The British "moral" contribution lay in the inherited principles of libertarian constitutionalism, which "through Magna Carta, the Bill of Rights, the habaes corpus, trial by jury and the English common law, find their most famous expression in the Declaration of Independence," and in the "constancy of mind, persistency of purpose and the grand simplicity of decision" that had guided both countries to victory in the war. The "material" forces were the various elements that made up the political and strategic logic of the anti-Soviet association: the substantial forces still under British command, Britain's worldwide connections, her global system of bases, her industrial expertise, and her contribution to scientific cooperation. . . .

We must now examine Churchill's speech in its second dimension. While on the surface Churchill appealed only to Americans, in fact he also conveyed serious threats to Stalin, and perhaps to Molotov and the shadowy Politburo figures whose influence was still a matter of anxious speculation. Both these American and Soviet audiences need to be kept in mind, for, as we will see later, their distinctive reactions to Churchill's initiative set up a dynamic that, though propelled and modified by intervening causes, did much to bring them into their first serious confrontation only three weeks later.

Can we be sure of Churchill's precise purpose here? On the one hand he twice called on Stalin for a settlement, declaring, "What is wanted is a settlement and the longer this is delayed the more difficult it will be and the greater our dangers will become," and again, talking of peace, "This can only be achieved by reaching now, in 1946, a good understanding on all points with Russia." On this view his threats might be seen simply as a necessary but incidental, perhaps even regrettable, condition of his American call to arms. On the other hand his unprecedentedly hostile critique and his pointed references to Soviet vulnerabilities suggest a desire to intimidate. And while his eventual success in this respect might depend on the receptivity of American opinion, his speech must have carried immediate conviction in Moscow as a definition of the new American militancy, which, especially in its increasingly Anglo-American manifestations, must now have been Stalin's main concern. . . .

It is not likely that the Soviets saw any of this as defensive. From their perspective Churchill was formulating a carefully calculated multidimensional offensive threat: a crusading libertarian ideology to rally mass support; a vast hostile political combination working toward them from the Anglo-American nucleus in a variety of menacing institutions, including the United Nations; and a military power with air-sea superiority and the decisive world weapon. It only remained for Churchill to suggest a concrete focus for the possible use of this power against the Soviet Union to complete his aggressive world system. And this he was careful to do, in a necessarily veiled way, by drawing attention to the two areas of greatest Soviet sensitivity: Germany and Eastern Europe....

Our survey of American opinion after March 5, and mostly before March 13, leads to a firm conclusion: that Churchill succeeded in his attempt to direct the attention of the American people to the supposed Soviet menace and that he was substantially successful in persuading most of them that it could be resisted only in some kind of close association with Britain, so long as it was not a formal alliance, a conclusion fortified rather than invalidated by the increasingly shrill hostile reactions on the left. . . .

The great question, of course, is how this Anglo-Soviet Cold War [of the winter of 1945–1946], in which the United States did not participate, was suddenly converted into a United States–Soviet Cold War in which Britain was still active but only as America's junior partner. Clearly, any satisfactory answer must come not only from the study of events and changes of sentiment in the United States but also from the identification and explanation of those sudden new tense points of American connection with the Soviet Union that appeared in early 1946, and whose absence until then had encouraged mutual hopes of accommodation.

With this structural or geopolitical precept in mind, we have traced a process that, while it defies easy analysis, seemingly involved three fundamental, interacting developments. The first was the decision of the Truman administration in February to reorient its Soviet policy from accommodation to confrontation. The second was a campaign to explain and justify this reorientation to the American people in terms of a Soviet menace. And the third was a Soviet political response that was sufficiently impolite to authenticate that campaign and consolidate the change in American policy.

Winston Churchill influenced substantially the evolution of each of these vital developments. There can be no doubt that he played a part, if only as a focus but probably more than that, in the reorientation of United States policy that we have traced to February 12, 1946. His February 10 White House meeting with President Truman was a turn ing point. Before this Truman, harassed by domestic political pressures and a rising disquiet over Soviet conduct, which he shared, had been eager to stiffen his Soviet policy but reluctant to confront a supposedly confused public opinion. After discussion he endorsed Churchill's plan to urge, in his forthcoming Fulton speech, the necessity of "full Anglo-American military collaboration" in a context that could only threaten the Soviet Union. He thus reversed the American dogma that there should be no "ganging up" with the British against Russia. The actual transformation, under the direction of a suddenly converted Byrnes, presumably inspired by Churchill's intervention with Truman, began two days later. It was much more comprehensive and systematic than has been generally understood, suddenly projecting a new anti-Soviet American diplomacy into virtually every region, including most notably the Mediterranean and Near East. The calculated impression of Anglo-American collaboration (though, in fact, the British government was not directly involved) was particularly evident in a battery of American gestures clearly intended to convey solidarity with Churchill at the time of his sensational speech. This, it was plainly hoped, would both intimidate the Russians and rally American public support for the harder line.

Churchill's "iron curtain" speech on March 5 was the centerpiece of the Truman administration's campaign to bring this new militancy from the shadows of diplomacy into the open arena of American public politics. That Truman and Byrnes saw it in this light can easily be seen from the calculated stage setting of Anglo-American solidarity with which—to impress American opinion as well as the Soviets—they vigorously surrounded it. And indeed Churchill's thesis, that Soviet expansionism represented a danger to peace and freedom requiring a countering Anglo-American "fraternal association," immediately crystallized and then polarized a hitherto unclear American opinion, at the same time clarifying the issues at stake and providing a plausible basis for the rising public indictment of Soviet conduct.

The Fulton speech had an immense practical effect on the whole crisis. Indeed, despite a somewhat disappointing immediate response and some briefly distracting public suspicion, which rapidly diminished in significance as the increasing isolation of the American Left through March and April suggests, Churchill's demarche was the pivot on which the whole transformation eventually turned. It created a context of heightened American public sensitivity to Soviet conduct and of considerable Soviet anxiety, expressed in Stalin's determination to resist the new Anglo-American front by standing firm while also trying to split it through selective appeasement. All that was lacking to bring these fundamental forces into direct confrontation was a suitably concrete issue. And this now presented itself in a form that played perfectly into the moral-legal sensibilities of American opinion, namely, the occupation of northern Iran that Moscow persisted in illegally after the March 2 deadline for withdrawal. Byrnes skillfully exploited this further opportunity, covertly urging the Iranian Prime Minister to bring his case before the United Nations Security Council, while encouraging American opinion to view the looming confrontation as a test of American principle.

Stalin fell into this trap. In this third, "Soviet" phase, too, Churchill played a major role, for Stalin, impressed by Churchill's apparent diplomatic coup in Washington, reacted throughout to the first, Fulton-oriented phase of the Truman administration's reorientation with its clear Anglo-American geopolitical emphasis and did not adjust sufficiently or in time to the second, and more dangerous, United Nations phase. He believed, understandably, that Churchill was defining the scope of an already functioning Anglo-American alliance. His decision, in consequence, was to stand firm in Iran despite the illegality. Certainly the Soviets had their own interests there. But Stalin's main concern now was not to validate Churchill's proclamation to the world that Soviet policy responded only to the threat of united Anglo-American pressure, or to encourage the intrusion of American power into this almost exclusive and traditional Anglo-Russian arena. . . .

Churchill's achievement in this transitional postwar phase can perhaps be summed up finally in two central propositions. The first is that, in a season of danger, ideological confusion, exhaustion, and doubt, he clarified for the world the distinction between Soviet totalitarianism and a Western democratic outlook that he defined in terms of "freedom" and "Peace through Strength." The second is that he played the pioneering part in invoking and in helping materially to create that geopolitical combination of American power and British connections which alone in this period offered the West the prospect of security and general democratic renewal. The most eloquent political tribute to his success in this respect came from an old adversary. In a late 1946 discussion with Ernest Bevin about British politics, Molotov remarked that he "did not wish Mr. Churchill to return to power." It seems only reasonable to account this among the Soviet official's more sincere utterances.

Europe After the Second World War

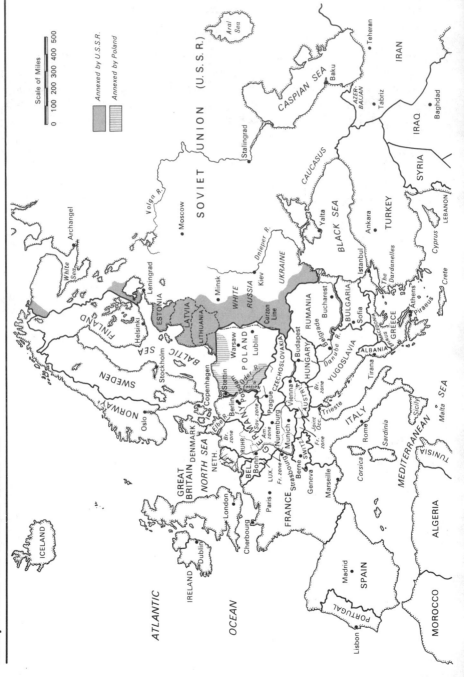

John Lewis Gaddis

ALARM OVER SOVIET UNILATERALISM

What so alarmed Americans and other peoples about Soviet actions in the early Cold War period? In an essay largely reflecting the traditionalist perspective, John Lewis Gaddis points to the unilateral nature of Soviet behavior, especially in Eastern Europe, as the major source of Cold War friction. The United States sought a balance of power through cooperation to maintain the postwar peace. When the Soviets challenged that equilibrium, President Truman necessarily but cautiously launched the containment doctrine. American leaders had little choice but to react strongly, Gaddis claims, because Stalin had become impervious to Western gestures of goodwill. Gaddis writes that the assumptions that the Soviets were driven by totalitarianism and communist ideology (what Daniel Yergin has called the Riga axioms in an earlier essay in this book) were reasonable views to be held at the time. He adds that because the Soviet Union's search for security seemed to know no bounds, Truman officials reasonably assumed the worst of Soviet intentions. Gaddis does not speculate on how or whether American actions might have alarmed the Soviets.

John Lewis Gaddis teaches the recent history of American foreign relations at Ohio University. His books are *The United States and the Origins of the Cold War, 1941–1947* **(1972);** *Strategies of Containment* **(1982);** *The Long Peace* **(1987), from which this selection is taken; and** *Russia, the Soviet Union, and the United States* **(1990).**

Wartime lack of concern over the powerful position the Soviet Union would occupy in the postwar world had been predicated upon the assumption that the Russians would continue to act in concert with their American and British allies. So long as the Grand Alliance remained intact, Western statesmen could assure each other, Moscow's emergence as the dominant Eurasian power would pose no threat. But during the final months of the war, there began to appear unsettling indications of a determination on Stalin's part to secure postwar interests without reference to the corresponding interests of his wartime associates. It was these manifestations of unilateralism that first set off alarm bells in the West about Russian intentions; the resulting uneasiness in turn stimulated deeper and more profound anxieties.

Excerpted from *The Long Peace: Inquiries into the History of the Cold War* by John Lewis Gaddis, pp. 29–47. Copyright © 1987 by John Lewis Gaddis. Reprinted by permission of Oxford University Press, Inc.

"I am becoming increasingly concerned," Secretary of State [Cordell] Hull warned Ambassador W. Averell Harriman early in 1944, "over the . . . successive moves of the Soviet Government in the field of foreign relations." Hull went on to observe in this message, drafted by Soviet specialist Charles E. Bohlen, that whatever the legitimacy of Moscow's security interests in Eastern Europe—"and as you know we have carefully avoided and shall continue to avoid any disputation with the Soviet Government on the merits of such questions"—unilateral actions to secure those interests "cannot fail to do irreparable harm to the whole cause of international collaboration." The American people would not be disposed to participate in any postwar scheme of world organization which would be seen "as a cover for another great power to pursue a course of unilateral action in the international sphere based on superior force." It was "of the utmost importance that the principle of consultation and cooperation with the Soviet Union be kept alive at all costs, but some measures of cooperation in relation to world public opinion must be forthcoming from the Soviet Government."

This document reflects as well as any other the point from which American statesmen began to develop concerns about the postwar intentions of the Soviet Union. The United States had not challenged Moscow's determination to retain the boundaries it had secured as a result of Stalin's unsavory pact with Hitler in 1939, nor had it questioned the Russians' right to a postwar sphere of influence in what remained of Eastern Europe. It was prepared to grant similar concessions in East Asia in return for eventual U.S.S.R. participation in the war against Japan. But because the Roosevelt administration had justified American entry into the war as a defense of self-determination, and because it had committed the nation to participation in a postwar world collective security organization as a means of implementing that principle, it required from the Soviet Union a measure of discretion and restraint in consolidating these areas of control. Unilateral action seemed likely to endanger the balance of power, not by allowing the Russians to dominate areas beyond their borders—that domination was assumed—but rather by weakening the American capacity for countervailing action in the postwar world by provoking, first, public disillusionment and then, as a consequence, a revival of the isolationism the President and his advisers had fought so long and so hard to overcome.

The Russians, to put it mildly, were less than sensitive to these concerns. As their armies moved into Eastern Europe in 1944 they immediately set out to undermine potential sources of opposition, not just in the former enemy countries of Rumania, Bulgaria, and Hungary, but most conspicuously of all in Poland, which had been, after all, an ally. The callousness with which the Red Army allowed the Germans to decimate the anti-communist resistance in Warsaw late that summer shocked Western statesmen; meanwhile British and American representatives on Allied Control Commissions in the Balkans found themselves denied any significant influence in shaping occupation policies there as well. Moscow had interpreted Western restraint as a sign of weakness, Harriman reported in September: "Unless we take issue with the present policy there is every indication that the Soviet Union will become a world bully wherever their interests are involved. . . . No written agreements can be of any value unless they are carried out in a spirit of give and take and recognition of the interests of other people."

Franklin Roosevelt made valiant efforts at Yalta to make Stalin aware of the need to observe the proprieties in Eastern Europe, but these proved unsuccessful almost at once when the Soviet leader interpreted agreements made to hold free elections there as in fact license to impose still tighter control on Poland and Rumania. "Averell is right," Roosevelt complained three weeks before his death. "We can't do business with Stalin. He has broken every one of the promises he made at Yalta." F.D.R. had not been prepared, on the basis of these difficulties, to write off all possibilities of postwar cooperation with the Russians. But Soviet unilateralism does appear to have convinced him, by the time of his death, that efforts to win Stalin's trust had not worked; and that future policy toward the Soviet Union would have to be based on a strict *quid pro quo* basis.

Harry S Truman emphatically agreed. Although the new Chief Executive had had no direct experience in the conduct of foreign affairs, he could hardly have believed more firmly in the importance of keeping one's word. "When I say I'm going to do something, I do it," he once wrote, "or [I] bust my insides trying to do it." It was characteristic of him that he did not believe in divorce because "when you make a contract you should keep it." Convinced that the Yalta agreements on free elections in Eastern Europe were in fact contracts, determined to demonstrate decisiveness in an awesome and unexpected position of responsibility, Truman resolved—probably more categorically than Roosevelt would have done—to hold the Russians to what they had agreed to. It was this determination that occasioned the new President's sharp rejoinder to Soviet Foreign Minister V. M. Molotov after less than two weeks in office: "Carry out your agreements and you won't get talked to like that." A month later he complained again that the Russians were not honoring their agreements: they were, he told Henry Wallace, "like people from across the tracks whose manners were very bad."

The experience of meeting Stalin personally at Potsdam seems to have modified the President's attitude somewhat. The Soviet autocrat evoked memories of the Kansas City political boss Tom Pendergast, a man with whom deals could be made because he had always kept his word. "I can deal with Stalin," Truman noted in his diary at Potsdam. "He is honest—but smart as hell." Disturbed by rumors of the dictator's ill health, the President worried about what would happen "if Joe suddenly passed out" because his potential successors lacked sincerity. For several years afterward, there persisted in Truman's mind the notion that difficulties with the Russians reflected Stalin's internal political problems—interference from a recalcitrant Politburo was the most frequent explanation—rather than any personal desire on the Soviet leader's part to violate his word.

But deals had to be honored if they were to work, and with the return of peace instances of Soviet unilateralism began to proliferate. Reasonably free elections took place in Hungary and Czechoslovakia, but only in those countries: Moscow's grip on Poland, Rumania, and Bulgaria remained as tight as ever. The Russians joined the French in resisting central economic administration of occupied Germany; they also arbitrarily transferred a substantial portion of that country's eastern territory to Poland. Attempts to reunify another divided nation, Korea, came to naught as the Russians refused to tolerate anything other than a satellite government there. The Soviet Union rejected participation in the World Bank and the International Monetary Fund, institutions American planners regarded as critical for postwar economic recovery. And Stalin was showing strong signs, as 1945 ended, of exploiting the presence of Soviet troops in northern Iran to carve out yet another sphere of influence there. He was "trying to find a basis for an understanding which would give him confidence that an agreement reached with the Russians would be lived up to," Truman told his advisers in December, 1945. He had such confidence in dealing with the British, the Dutch, and the Chinese (though not the French), "but there is no evidence yet that the Russians intend to change their habits so far as honoring contracts is concerned."

The Chief Executive's initial inclination had been to regard these difficulties simply as failures of communication; with that explanation in mind, he had authorized Secretary of State [James F.] Byrnes to make one more effort to settle them at a hastily called meeting of foreign ministers in Moscow in December. By that time, though, public and Congressional impatience with Soviet unilateralism had considerably intensified. Sensitive to these pressures, irritated by Byrnes' eagerness to reach agreements without consulting him, Truman early in 1946 proclaimed to himself—if not directly to Byrnes, as he later claimed—his intention to stop "babying" the Soviets: "Unless Russia is faced with an iron fist and strong language another war is in the making. Only one language do they understand—'how many divisions have you?' I do not think we should play at compromise any longer."

There was, in fact, no compromise when the Russians failed to meet their agreed-upon deadline for removing their troops from Iran: instead the administration confronted Moscow publicly in the United Nations Security Council and forced a humiliating withdrawal. Truman drew the appropriate conclusions: "Told him to tell Stalin I held him to be a man to keep his word," he noted in his appointment book after a meeting with the newly designated ambassador to the Soviet Union, Walter Bedell Smith, on March 23. "Troops in Iran after March 2 upset that theory." By June, he was writing to the author Pearl Buck that "the United States has performed no unfriendly act nor made a single unfriendly gesture toward the great Russian nation. . . . How has Russia met our friendly overtures?" The following month, after *New York Times* correspondent Brooks Atkinson had published a series of articles highly critical of the Russians, Truman pointedly invited him to the White House. That same day he told his advisers that he was "tired of our being pushed around," that "here a little, there a little, they are chiseling from us," and that "now is [the] time to take [a] stand on Russia."

It was in this spirit that the President authorized the first comprehensive study of Soviet-American relations to be carried out within the government. Compiled under the direction of his Special Counsel, Clark M. Clifford, and written after consultations with the Departments of State, War, Navy, the Joint Chiefs of Staff and the Director of Central Intelligence, the report acknowledged that agreements between nations were at times susceptible to differing interpretations. Nonetheless, it argued, there existed a persistent pattern on Moscow's part of either unilaterally implementing such agreements in such a way as to serve Soviet interests, or encouraging satellites to do so. "[T]here is no question," the report emphasized, "where the primary responsibility lies."

The implications could only be that the Soviet Union had no intention of cooperating with the West to maintain the existing balance of power; that it sought to expand its own influence as widely as possible without regard for the security requirements of its former allies; and that, when circumstances were right, it would be prepared to risk war to attain that objective. American policy could no longer be based upon the assumption of shared interests, therefore; priorities henceforth would have to be directed toward the accumulation of sufficient military strength to deter war if possible and to win it if necessary, while at the same time keeping open possibilities for dealing with the Russians should a change of heart in the Kremlin eventually occur. "[I]t is our hope," the report concluded, "that they will eventually change their minds and work out with us a fair and equitable settlement when they realize that we are too strong to be beaten and too determined to be frightened."

President Truman received the Clifford report on September 24, four days after he had fired Henry Wallace from the Cabinet for publicly advocating a more conciliatory policy toward the Soviet Union. There is no question that he agreed with its general conclusions: on the day before he dismissed Wallace he had complained in his diary about

> Reds, phonies and . . . parlor pinks [who] can see no wrong in Russia's four and one half million armed forces, in Russia's loot of Poland, Austria, Hungary, Rumania, Manchuria. . . . But when we help our friends in China who fought on our side it is terrible. When Russia loots the industrial plant of those same friends it is all right. When Russia occupies Persia for oil that is heavenly.

But Truman chose not to use the Clifford report, as he might have, to justify increased military appropriations; instead he ordered all copies to be locked in the White House safe, where they remained for the duration of the administration. "There is too much loose talk about the Russian situation," he had written former Vice President John Nance Garner on the day after Wallace's dismissal. "We are not going to have any shooting trouble with them but they are tough bargainers and always ask for the whole earth, expecting maybe to get an acre."

The President's cautious reaction to the manifestations of Soviet unilateralism catalogued in the Clifford report reflected a desire to avoid hasty and ill-considered action, but certainly no continuing assumption of common interests. Repeated demonstrations of Moscow's callousness to the priorities and sensibilities of its former allies had by this time virtually drained the reservoir of good will toward the Russians that had built up during the war. American leaders had been inclined, for many months, to give the Kremlin the benefit of the doubt: to assume, despite accumulating evidence to the contrary, that difficulties with Moscow had arisen out of misunderstandings rather than fundamental conflicts of interest. But such charitableness could not continue indefinitely, as Winston Churchill pointed out in the summer of 1946: "The American eagle sits on his perch, a large strong bird with formidable beak and claws. . . . Mr. Gromyko is sent every day to prod him with a sharp sickle, now on his beak, now under his wing, now in his tail feathers. All the time the eagle keeps quite still, but it would be a great mistake to suppose that nothing is going on inside the breast of the eagle."

In fact, a good deal was going on inside the breast of the eagle, all of it related in one way or another to attempting to explain the motivation for Moscow's puzzling behavior. Throughout the period of wartime cooperation there had lingered in the minds of most Americans latent but persistent suspicions about Russia, suspicions that extended back to, and even beyond, the Bolshevik Revolution. These grew out of the fact that the Soviet Union combined—as no other country in the world at that time did—two characteristics that Americans found particularly objectionable: arbitrary rule and ideological militancy. As long as the direct Axis threat remained, Americans had been willing to overlook these shortcomings, even to hope that in time they would disappear. But after 1945, with no common foe to compel unity, with ample evidence that the Russians intended to proceed on their own rather than in concert with their former allies to consolidate postwar interests, the predisposition to assume the worst about Moscow's intentions came out into the open once again. . . .

Both the "totalitarian" and the "ideological" explanations of Soviet behavior had in common the assumption that one was dealing with a compulsive internally driven process, unresponsive to gestures of restraint or goodwill from the outside. There had been yet a third interpretation of Moscow's unilateralism, popular during the war, that had seen it as growing out of a quite understandable preoccupation with security capable of being alleviated by patient Western efforts to win the Russians' trust. President Roosevelt himself had made this "insecurity" theory the basis of his policy toward the Soviet Union, and it had remained very much alive—though under increasing challenge—during the first months of the Truman administration. But theories require validation if they are to be sustained: however persuasive the "insecurity" model of Soviet behavior may be in retrospect, what struck most observers at the time was the utter imperviousness of Stalin's regime to the gestures of restraint and goodwill that emanated from the West during and immediately after the war. Moscow's perceived failure to reciprocate these initiatives made it more and more difficult to sustain an interpretation of Soviet actions based on "insecurity," as Henry Wallace found out when he attempted, during the spring and summer of 1946, to revive it within the inner councils of the government. The "totalitarian" and "ideological" models were the obvious alternatives.

It is ironic that the individual most influential in discrediting "insecurity" as an explanation of Soviet unilateralism shared many of its basic assumptions. George F. Kennan had never been inclined to interpret Soviet behavior in either strictly totalitarian or ideological terms. As a keen student of Russian history and culture, he was fully aware of the lack of self-confidence that plagued the Stalinist government, and of the extent to which its unilateralism was defensively motivated. But he emphatically did not share the view of Wallace and others that these attitudes could be modified from the outside. It was in an effort to bring official Washington to see that point that Kennan crafted the February, 1946, "long telegram," to this day the single most influential explanation of postwar Soviet behavior, and one which powerfully reinforced the growing tendency within the United States to interpret Moscow's actions in a sinister light.

The "long telegram" had the great influence that it did because it provided a way to fuse concerns about totalitarianism and communism in dealing with the Soviet Union. It portrayed that state as one in which an autocratic tradition had become incorporated within an ideological compulsion to treat the outside world as hostile. The conclusion was clear: no actions the United States or its Western allies could take would alleviate Stalin's suspicion; the best one could do was to look to one's own defenses—and to the strength and self-confidence of one's own society—and wait for the internal forces of change within the Soviet system to have their effect.

There is a definite psychological satisfaction, when confronted with a phenomenon one does not understand, in finding a simple but persuasive explanation. Whatever the actual intentions of its author, the "long telegram" performed that function within the government in 1946; a similar analysis would find a wider audience the following year in the form of the famous "X" article in *Foreign Affairs*. The "totalitarian-ideological" model of Soviet behavior provided clear, plausible, and in many ways gratifying explanation of the Russians' failure to cooperate with their former allies in building a lasting peace: it absolved the United States of responsibility for the breakdown of wartime cooperation; it made any future relaxation of tensions dependent upon changes of heart in Moscow, not Washington. Americans did not welcome the onset of the Cold War. But the rationale they worked out to account for its appearance at least had the advantage of allowing them to approach the coming contest with a reasonably clear conscience.

The Soviet Union's emergence as a potential adversary closed an obvious gap in Washington's thinking about the postwar world. A generalized sense of vulnerability, related both to historical experience and to technological change, had caused United States officials to regard preservation of a global balance of power as a vital interest even before specific challenges to that balance had manifested themselves. This situation of perceived vulnerability in the absence of apparent threat accounts for the failure of the United States to deploy forces and establish bases in the way one might have expected had the Russians been seen as the enemy from the beginning. But Soviet unilateralism, together with the conclusions about the roots of Soviet behavior that unilateralism provoked, had by 1947 created a credible source of danger, with the result that American strategy now took on a clearer and more purposeful aspect. . . .

The strategy of containment brought together the new American interest in maintaining a global balance of power with the perceived Muscovite challenge to that equilibrium in a part of the world that could hardly have been more pivotal—Western Europe. It sought to deal with that danger primarily by economic rather than military means; its goal was not so much the creation of an American hegemony as it was a re-creation of independent centers of power capable of balancing each other as well as the Russians. This is hardly the place to evaluate the success of that strategy or to trace its subsequent mutations and incarnations: these subjects have received excessively lengthy treatment elsewhere. Suffice it to say that the strategy could not have evolved without the perception of vulnerability brought about by the war, and the all-too-successful—if inadvertent—efforts of the Russians to give that abstraction an alarming reality.

Soviet historians have argued with unsurprising consistency through the years that the United States over-reacted to the "threat" posed by the U.S.S.R. in the wake of World War II. During the late

1960's and early 1970's, a number of American students of the early Cold War expressed agreement with that conclusion, though not with the methods that had been used to arrive at it. In an interesting inversion of Kennan's theory regarding Russian behavior, these accounts portrayed official Washington as having in one way or another fabricated the myth of a hostile Soviet Union in order to justify its own internally motivated drive for international hegemony. The difficulty with this argument was the impossibility of verifying it, for without access to Soviet sources there could be no definite conclusions regarding its accuracy: one cannot credibly assess responsibility when one can confirm the motives of only one side. The intervening years have brought us no nearer to a resolution of that problem, but they have witnessed the emergence of several new lines of historical interpretation that appear to call into question the thesis of American "over-reaction."

One of these involves a reconsideration of Stalin's policy by a new generation of scholars equally conversant, not only with the very limited number of Soviet and East European sources that are available, but with the overwhelming array of recently declassified American and British documents as well. The effect of this work is to confirm neither the "totalitarian" nor the "ideological" explanations of Stalin's actions that were popular during the early Cold War years, but rather to see that dictator as having followed an "imperial" model of expansion: a pattern of behavior motivated by insecurity and characterized by caution, to be sure, but one that was also incapable of defining the limits of security requirements and that sought, as a result, to fill power vacuums where this could be done without encountering resistance. The effect of this policy was twofold: to incorporate within the Soviet sphere what Vojtech Mastny has called "a cluster of sullen dependencies" that probably contributed to more than they subtracted from Moscow's nervousness; and to alarm, and ultimately alienate, the United States and its Western European allies, who saw Stalin's inability to define the full extent of his security requirements as likely to undermine their own.

It may well be, as [the scholar] William Taubman has argued, that the West gave up on the possibility of cooperation with Stalin before Stalin gave up on the possibility of cooperation with the West. But Taubman points out that any such cooperation would have been on the Kremlin leader's terms and for his purposes: it would have been designed "to foster Soviet control of Eastern Europe whether directly (in the case of Poland, Rumania, and Bulgaria) or indirectly (in Hungary and Czechoslovakia); to expand Soviet influence in Western

Europe, the Near East and Asia; to position the USSR for even greater gains when the next Western economic crisis struck; and to achieve all this while subsidized to the tune of at least six billion dollars in American credits." Western statesmen may perhaps be pardoned for not having shared this particular vision of the postwar world. . . .

History, inescapably, involves viewing distant pasts through the prism of more recent ones. The incontestable fact that the United States over-reacted more than once during the subsequent history of the Cold War to the perceived threat of Soviet and/or "communist" expansionism has, to an extent, blinded us to the equally demonstrable fact that in the immediate postwar years the behavior of the Russians alarmed not just Americans but a good portion of the rest of the world as well. How well-founded that alarm was—how accurately it reflected the realities that shaped Soviet policy—are issues upon which there are legitimate grounds for disagreement. But to deny that the alarm itself was sincere, or that Americans were not alone in perceiving it, is to distort the view through the prism more than is necessary. Fear, after all, can be genuine without being rational. And, as Sigmund Freud once pointed out, even paranoids can have real enemies.

Bruce R. Kuniholm

CONTAINING THE SOVIETS AT THE NORTHERN TIER

Most historians of postwar diplomacy view Truman's address to Congress on March 12, 1947, as a central event. The president called for financial aid to Greece and Turkey in the wake of Great Britain's imminent withdrawal from the Near East. He framed the appeal largely in ideological terms, proclaiming America's intention to support all peoples in resisting subjugation by armed minorities or external threats. He called attention to a struggle between two different ways of life: freedom versus tyranny. Historians have disagreed quite sharply in their interpretations of the origins and efficacy of the so-called Truman Doctrine. Many analysts have questioned Truman's use of alarmist language and his superficial treatment of the complex events in Greece and Turkey. But Bruce R. Kuniholm offers support for the traditionally positive appraisal of American actions along the "Northern Tier." Insisting in this essay and in his book *The Origins of the Cold War in the*

Text by Bruce Kuniholm, from *The Truman Presidency*, 1989, edited by Michael J. Lacey, pp. 299–307. Reprinted by permission of Cambridge University Press.

Near East (1980) that the Soviet Union sought to expand its influence into Greece, Turkey, and Iran by capitalizing on Britain's weakened position, he applauds Truman's response as appropriate and realistic. The president and his top advisers recognized correctly, Kuniholm concludes, that United States interests would be best served by maintaining the balance of power in the Near East.

A specialist in American relations with the contemporary Middle East, Kuniholm has written *The Origins of the Cold War in the Near East* (1980) and *The Near East Connection: Greece and Turkey in the Reconstruction and Security of Europe* (1984). He is a professor of history and public policy at Duke University.

U.S. policy in the Near East during the Truman administration was concerned primarily with the region's "Northern Tier" (Iran, Turkey, and Greece) and Palestine. Events in these two areas provided the context for several major policy decisions—the Truman Doctrine and U.S. support for the creation and establishment of Israel—that were among the best known and most controversial of the Truman years. In this essay I take a close look at these decisions, examine major questions that have been raised about the Truman administration's policies, and, in light of recent scholarship, attempt to assess them. Before such an assessment can be made, however, it is necessary to examine the geopolitical context within which the Truman administration was forced to operate.

When President Truman took office, World War II was not yet over but it already had radically altered the world power balance and shifted the loci of world power to Washington and Moscow. Within a year Stalin was exploring his options along the Soviet Union's southern borders and, it appeared, would continue to do so unless resisted. The British Empire, meanwhile, was disintegrating. By 1948, the British would be forced to withdraw their forces from Greece, Turkey, India, and Palestine. The combination of the rise of Soviet power and the demise of British influence presented the United States with new responsibilities and difficult choices.

In the nineteenth century the expanding Russian and British empires had played for high stakes. A consequence of their rivalry across an area stretching from the Balkans to India was the creation of a zone of buffer states between the two empires. The rulers of these buffer states traditionally opposed the ambitions of both empires and sought to survive by playing one off against the other. At the end of World War II this game became more difficult, and the survival of

Turkey and Iran was threatened by the relative disparity between Soviet and British power. Of the thirteen non-communist states that bordered Russia before the war, only five were independent when it was over. Finland was neutralized, and Afghanistan retained its traditional role of a buffer state. Of the remaining three—Norway, Turkey, and Iran— the latter two were in serious jeopardy of being drawn into the Soviet fold, and the United States was the only power capable of assisting them. Although almost all the states in the Middle East welcomed the decline of British influence, those on the periphery of the Soviet Union recognized the need for a countervailing force to balance Soviet influence. Invariably, they asked the United States for help.

The choices that confronted President Truman shortly after he took office in April 1945 were worrisome. Should he commit the United States to maintaining the balance of power in the region? If he did, how would the Soviets respond? If he did not, what would be the result of inaction? The president's response was articulated publicly in March 1947 in a policy statement that received wide support at the time but that subsequently became the subject of considerable scholarly debate.

The Palestine problem, meanwhile, not only complicated geopolitical categories but, it was feared, threatened to undermine U.S. attempts to maintain the balance of power in the Near East. Some observers viewed President Truman's support for the new state of Israel as entirely appropriate and in no way conflicting with other U.S. interests. Others thought that the president's actions raised profound questions about the fundamental values and priorities of public officials. What were the most appropriate guidelines for determining the national interest? Who should determine what that interest was, and should one interest be balanced against another?

Additional problems for long-term American interests were posed by the necessity of Anglo-American cooperation in effecting the policy of containment. Were British and American interests in Iran and Egypt compatible? To what extent would cooperation with the British undermine rather than facilitate the containment of Soviet influence in the region? These and other questions were constantly raised in the management of three interlocking regional issues that absorbed administration attention during the Truman years: (1) the balance of power in the Near East, (2) the Palestine problem, and (3) the emerging nationalist movements in Iran and Egypt.

In the immediate postwar years, U.S. policy toward the Near East was shaped by developments in Iran and Turkey. In Iran, the Soviets violated Allied understandings and exploited the opportunities that occupation afforded them in an effort to control the government in Teheran. Oil concessions, which the Soviets demanded, and Kurdish and Azerbaijani separatist movements, which the Soviets supported in occupied northwest Iran, were means to the same end. In Turkey the Soviets sought through a war of nerves and constant diplomatic pressure to annex Kars and Ardahan in eastern Turkey and gain control of the Turkish Straits (the Bosporus and the Dardanelles). Press and radio attacks against "hostile" governments, attempts to effect the ouster of various government leaders, and irredentist Armenian and Georgian claims, coupled with troop mobilization, all smacked of Hitler's tactics before the war.

In addition to attempting to carve out spheres of influence in Iran and Turkey, the Soviets in fact obtained one in the Balkans where they supported Bulgarian irredentism in Macedonia and Thrace. Faced in Eastern Europe with models of how *not* to deal with the Soviets, the Truman administration turned its attention to the Near East, where analogies between Stalin's and Hitler's tactics were too strong to ignore. If these analogies gave the administration pause, so did increasing evidence of Soviet designs on Iran and Turkey, particularly when supplemented by revelations concerning negotiations between Nazi Germany and the Soviet Union over the Near East in 1940. Captured German records and interviews with Hitler's interpreter, made available to the secretary of state in January 1946, underscored the continuity of Russian ambitions and suggested the desirability of a more forceful policy in opposing them.

Stalin, while acknowledging his designs on Turkey, in December 1945 had assured both Secretary of State James F. Byrnes and British Foreign Secretary Ernest Bevin that the Soviet Union had no designs, territorial or otherwise, on Iran and no intention of infringing on the sovereignty of Iran. In March 1946, however, after the date set by the Big Three for evacuation of Iran and following extremely tough discussions with the Iranian prime minister in Moscow, Stalin had moved a Soviet armed force of at least 200 tanks into northern Iran in an attempt to intimidate the government in Teheran into bending to his will. Stalin's maneuvers were thwarted only by masterful Iranian diplomacy, firm U.S. policies, and the possibility that Stalin saw further confrontation in Iran as detrimental to his designs on Turkey.

Stalin, like Hitler, the pope observed in 1946, frequently gave assurances of his peace-loving intentions. To U.S. officials, the negligible value of those assurances was illustrated by the drawn-out crisis in Iran, which also underscored the value of anticipating rather than reacting to Soviet moves. This view was reinforced by Stalin's former Foreign Minister Maxim Litvinov, who observed in June 1946 that the Soviet Union had returned to a concept of geographical security. Goodwill, Litvinov told CBS correspondent Richard Hottelet, would be ineffective in meeting the Soviets' security needs, because Soviet demands, if satisfied, would only be followed by others.

Stalin's thinking, of course, is largely unknown, although [Soviet leader Nikita] Khrushchev's memoirs [published in 1974] may give us a clue about Turkey. According to Khrushchev, Lavrenti Beria, head of Stalin's huge police network and, like Stalin, a Georgian, teased and goaded Stalin—who had negotiated the frontier between Turkey and the Soviet Union in 1921—into demanding the return of territories that had once (from 1878 to 1921) been part of Georgia. Beria's thinking was that Turkey's international status had been weakened by World War II and that the Turkish government would be unable to resist such demands. Whatever Stalin's motives, officials in the Truman administration grew increasingly skeptical of them. Faced with what they saw as a fait accompli in Eastern Europe, they eventually came to the conclusion that a similar fate should not await the countries of the Middle East's Northern Tier.

The process by which the Truman administration reached this conclusion was gradual. Declarations of idealistic principles and expressions of concern over Soviet intentions, made by U.S. representatives in the course of protracted, fruitless negotiations, had proved ineffective in moderating Soviet relations with Iran and Turkey. Direct negotiations between Iran and the Soviet Union, moreover, had failed to solve the Iranian problem in 1946 and had subjected the Iranians to heavy-handed intimidation. The exhaustive crisis in Iran, more than any other development, crystallized the Truman administration's growing understanding of Soviet tactics along the Northern Tier and conditioned its reaction to Soviet diplomatic maneuvering over Turkey in the late summer of 1946.

The Soviet Union's postwar policies toward Iran and Turkey had forced the continued mobilization of Turkey's 500,000-man army, necessitating military expenditures that consumed 38 percent of the country's budget and caused widespread discontent. In August 1946, the latest in a series of diplomatic maneuvers by the Soviets to put pressure on the Turks, in this case to agree to a joint Turco-Soviet system of defense for the Straits, precipitated what President Truman considered to be his most important decision since the bombing of Hiroshima. Soviet control over Turkey, the president concluded, would make it virtually impossible to prevent extension of that control to the Near and Middle East. Resources and communications, administration officials judged, made it imperative that the Soviet Union not gain control over Turkey, whether through force or the threat of force. Believing, ultimately, that nothing would deter Soviet aggression except the conviction that the United States was prepared to confront it, the president decided to resist any Soviet aggression against Turkey with all means at his disposal, including the force of U.S. arms. Americans might as well find out whether the Soviets were bent on world conquest now as in five or ten years, he told his advisers; he was prepared to pursue the policy "to the end."

President Truman's decision, while implemented in a restrained and nonprovocative manner, reflected a fundamental change in attitude toward the Near East. President Roosevelt had followed a traditional policy of noninvolvement in the region, which he consigned to Britain's jurisdiction as he focused on the war against Germany and Japan. Events in the Near East after Roosevelt's death, however, had schooled the Truman administration in the region's traditional balance of power politics and educated it in the fundamentals of containment, even before the containment thesis was consciously propounded. Acting on the basis of this understanding, the White House approved the formal establishment of a Mediterranean force, while Department of State guidelines underscored the importance of the independence and territorial integrity of Greece, Turkey, and Iran. These countries were seen as a bulwark against Soviet expansion and a means of protecting strategic U.S. interests in the Near and Middle East as a whole. The focal point of those interests was the Middle East's 15 billion barrels of proven oil reserves, 24 percent of which were controlled by the United States.

These developments explain the immediate U.S. reaction to Britain's February 1947 decision to withdraw support from Greece and Turkey. In the previous month, a full-scale review of U.S. policy toward Greece concluded, on the basis of considerable circumstantial evidence, that the Greek National Liberation Front (EAM) was an instrument of Soviet policy. The broad objective of the Soviets appeared to be to undermine British influence in the eastern Mediterranean and to establish their own domination of the littoral countries of that region. If, in retrospect, evidence does not bear out the conclusion that EAM was an instrument of Soviet policy, there was and still is little question that the Soviets were indirectly supporting Albania, Yugoslavia, and Bulgaria—who *were* supporting EAM. There also can be no doubt that the Soviets would have taken advantage of any situation in the Balkans that proved favorable to their interests. For this reason, Loy Henderson, director of the Office of Near Eastern and African Affairs (NEA), and Under Secretary of State Dean Acheson both believed that the United States was confronted with its most important decision since the war; they also believed that the choice was clear and there could be only one decision. It was voiced in the Truman Doctrine, which called for a $400 million appropriation to aid Greece and Turkey.

President Truman's 12 March 1947 address to a joint session of Congress expressed the necessity of choosing between alternative ways of life. One alternative, he said, was based on the will of the majority and was distinguished by free institutions. The other alternative was based on the will of a minority forcibly imposed on the majority and relied on terror and oppression. The president's declared aim was to make possible the messianic hope of everlasting freedom—through support of peoples resisting subjugation by armed minorities or by outside pressure. In retrospect, the president's high-minded definition of the national purpose was probably necessary to acquire support for the policies he was advocating. Although historians may long debate the necessity of presidential rhetoric, none doubt that the metaphoric representations President Truman used were effective in producing the consensus necessary to respond to Soviet threats along the Northern Tier.

The only way that nations can function internationally is to use the kind of metaphoric representations that the president articulated, with their attending conceptions of morality and power. It is also true, however, that the moral and power components of such imagery can only be evaluated relative to the particularities of circumstance in which they are applied. This means that they must constantly be evaluated critically, so that the imagery a nation employs can be appropriate to new circumstances. Unfortunately for the United States, this process of evaluation and reconception was overlooked in subsequent years and the view of the world presented by the Truman Doctrine, accompanied by a failure to match rhetoric with concrete policies and a defensive inclination to pursue consistently hard-line policies, hardened into myth.   The consequence was a somewhat simplistic and increasingly inflexible perception of international events that imposed itself on a world for which it was increasingly irrelevant.

At the time, however, the Truman administration's response to Soviet maneuvering along the Northern Tier was based on the realistic assumption that U.S. interests were best served by maintaining the balance of power in the Near East.   A corollary of this assumption, based on Britain's continuing role in the region even as the British withdrew from selected areas, was the necessity of a close association between U.S. and British policies in the Near East.   Exactly how this association would play itself out, however, was far from clear.   In the two years that followed the enunciation of the Truman Doctrine, although considerable assistance flowed to the region, Near East issues were superseded by others.   The administration's attention focused instead on Europe, and then on the Far East.   The objective of U.S. policy during this time was to restore the balance of power in Europe and Asia—initially through an emphasis on economic recovery (the Marshall Plan) and subsequently through a complementary emphasis on military security (the North Atlantic Treaty Organization, NATO). . . .

If the United States had not stood firm in Iran and not confronted Soviet pressures in Turkey during the early postwar years, it is likely that Stalin would have been tempted to expand the Soviet sphere of influence in the Near East as he did in Eastern Europe and the Far East.   "The fact that this did not happen when the British were driven to reduce their commitment drastically in 1947," Alan Bullock has observed, "does not prove the fears of 1945–46 to have been exaggerated or groundless."   Firmness, in short, may well have put Stalin on notice that expansion to the south could be carried out only at the risk of confrontation.

Soviet actions in Iran, following as they did Soviet expansion into Eastern Europe and the Far East, superseded the bounds of what a majority of the international community was prepared to accept.   What would be done to oppose similar Soviet actions elsewhere along the Middle East's Northern Tier or Europe was not clear.   That is why, despite its shortcomings, something like the Truman Doctrine may have been necessary when the British began to withdraw from the region. Whether Soviet pressures on Iran and Turkey can be justified by the Soviet Union's enormous losses during World War II or by its security needs depends on one's point of view.   What is striking is the extent to which, in the eyes of those whose territorial integrity was in question,

U.S. interpretations of events were seen as more accurate and U.S. concerns were seen as more legitimate than the interpretations and concerns of the Soviet Union.   U.S. involvement in the affairs of Iran and Turkey, finally, was encouraged by those countries because their governments wanted the United States to serve as a counterweight to the Soviet Union, whose influence was resented and feared.

Melvyn P. Leffler

THE TRUMAN DOCTRINE: A CRITIQUE

Melvyn P. Leffler emphatically disagrees with Kuniholm's analysis of the Truman Doctrine in particular and American policy along the Northern Tier in general.   He charges the Truman administration with a grievous distortion of regional realities in its depiction of the Greek civil war as a struggle between the forces of light and the forces of darkness.   Whereas Kuniholm characterizes United States policy in the Near East as a pragmatic, realistic, and successful response to Soviet aggression, Leffler sees Washington exaggerating the threat and pursuing its own geopolitical objectives in a strategically important area.   The Truman administration ignored Moscow's legitimate security fears and in the process exacerbated regional instability.

One important lesson to be learned from the Truman Doctrine era is that policymakers should not simplify international realities.   If Professor [Zbigniew] Brzezinski [National Security Adviser in the Jimmy Carter administration] had read the most recent books on the Greek civil war, he would not have attributed the instability in that nation to the Soviet involvement.   John O. Iatrides, Christopher M. Woodhouse, Lawrence S. Wittner, and John R. Oneal have shown that the strife in Greece had indigenous roots, that Greek Communists received little aid from Stalin, and that regional rivalries and ambitions decisively shaped that conflict.   Moreover, both Wittner and Oneal have argued persuasively that the termination of the insurgency inside Greece was more

Melvyn P. Leffler, "From the Truman Doctrine to the Carter Doctrine: Lessons and Dilemmas of the Cold War," *Diplomatic History*, VI (Fall 1983), pp. 247–254.   Copyright © 1983 by Scholarly Resources, Inc.   Reprinted by permission of Scholarly Resources, Inc. "From Cold War to Cold War in the Near East," *Reviews in American History*, 9 (1): 129, pp. 125–129.   Reprinted by permission of The Johns Hopkins University Press.

directly related to the Tito-Stalin split than to the military initiatives undertaken by the United States. In short, we should neither blame the Soviet Union for all regional and local conflicts nor should we think that the United States has the capability to resolve these conflicts.

Likewise, it is important that threats to American interests not be simplified, magnified, and distorted. Dean Acheson acknowledged in his memoirs that, when he, the president, and the secretary of state met with congressional leaders in February 1947, he did not give a measured appraisal of the international situation. He admits rather to portraying the threat in apocalyptic terms, claiming that three continents were vulnerable to Soviet domination. Such hyperbole was necessary because neither the Congress nor the American people seemed eager to undertake the foreign policy initiatives desired by Truman's advisers.

Challenged with the greatest public relations task ever faced by a president, Truman and his advisers could not resist the temptation to simplify Soviet intentions. Throughout 1945 and early 1946 serious efforts had been made to appraise the relative importance of the strategic, economic, political, and ideological factors shaping Soviet policy. After the spring of 1946, however, these efforts ceased. George F. Kennan's assessment in the "long" telegram became the established verity, and a new prominence was given to the ideological and totalitarian character of Soviet foreign policy. This was dramatically evident in James V. Forrestal's fixation with Marxist-Leninist doctrine, in the State Department's March 1946 estimate of Soviet policy which served as a framework for military studies, and in the lengthy memorandum on U.S.-Soviet relations prepared by Clark Clifford and George Elsey for President Truman in the summer of 1946. While detailed and thoughtful assessments of Soviet short-term intentions persisted, almost always emphasizing the Kremlin's desire to avoid war, the notion that the Soviet Union sought world domination became the fundamental postulate of American national security doctrine.

Yet recent studies of Soviet foreign policy underscore the importance of examining the Kremlin's intentions and objectives with rigor, subtlety, and sophistication. The closer historians and political scientists scrutinize Soviet foreign policy in the immediate postwar era, the more difficult it becomes to generalize and simplify. Vojtech Mastny has emphasized Stalin's opportunism; Adam Ulam and William Taubman have portrayed his caution, apprehension, and circumspection; William O. McCagg has imaginatively suggested the host of institutional, economic, personal, and ideological impulses that engulfed Soviet foreign policy; and Werner G. Hahn has argued that the postwar revival of ideology within the Soviet Union had little to do with foreign policy. We now have reason to believe that Stalin was treading warily lest he provoke the West. During 1946 and early 1947 the Soviet leader probably discouraged revolutionary activity abroad. Notwithstanding his determination to dominate the Eastern European periphery, to seek opportunities in Iran and Turkey, and to orient Germany and Austria toward the East, he seemed to prefer an overall policy of détente, to use Taubman's phrase. Only after the proclamation of the Truman Doctrine, the announcement of the Marshall Plan, and the merger of the three western zones in Germany did Stalin accept the reality of the Cold War, encourage revolutionary action in Western Europe, establish the Cominform, and consolidate Soviet domination in the areas occupied at the end of World War II, particularly Hungary, Czechoslovakia, and East Germany.

If it is important to probe more deeply into Soviet intentions, it is equally imperative to develop a correct appreciation of Soviet military strength. At the time of the Truman Doctrine, American analysts recognized two critical features about Soviet military capabilities. First, the Soviet Union, because of prevailing power vacuums, could overrun in a few months all of Western Europe, much of the Middle East, and sizable chunks of Manchuria and North China. Second, the Soviet Union could not inflict serious damage on the American homeland, could not compete with a mobilized American economy, and, therefore, could not wage war successfully against the United States. Because American analysts and policymakers appreciated Soviet military weaknesses vis-à-vis the United States, they remained confident that Soviet leaders would avoid war, back down in a crisis, and succumb to demonstrations of American diplomatic determination. Kennan predicted this in his "long" telegram, and the Soviets behaved, as predicted, when they withdrew from Iran, refrained from intervention in Greece, and avoided military conflict over Berlin. . . .

. . . What is clear is that by 1947 American policymakers no longer wanted to negotiate and compromise. They simplified Soviet intentions, subordinated Soviet strategic and economic concerns, focused on the ideological roots and totalitarian character of the Soviet system, and ignored the possible repercussions of their own policies on Soviet behavior. In the midst of the feverish efforts to build up situations of strength, even those officials like Kennan who sometimes preached the efficacy of nonmilitary and "asymmetrical" containment, gradually lost their influence. Any appraisal of postwar U.S. policy that seeks to establish the Truman Doctrine era as a model of successful policymaking must take note of these developments. . . .

[Bruce R.] Kuniholm's major themes [in his book, *The Origins of the Cold War in the Near East*, (1980)] are simple and straightforward: the postwar clash between the United States and the Soviet Union was just "another episode in the historical struggle for power in the region." As a result of a sequence of minor crises during 1945 and 1946, American policymakers developed "a clear conception of Greece, Turkey, and Iran in their collective historical role of dividing East and West. . . ." With Great Britain financially strained and militarily constrained, American officials assumed the traditional British task of containing Soviet expansionism. The Truman administration did not overreact to events in the region and did not place primacy on economic imperatives. Instead, American officials sought to protect "the broad, complex, and inextricably interwoven strategic and security interests of the United States" by reestablishing the balance of power along the Northern Tier. Correctly assessing Soviet intentions, Truman and his advisors adopted firm and pragmatic policies, including the provision of diplomatic support, economic aid, and military assistance—all of this culminating, of course, in the Truman Doctrine. The Soviets withdrew their forces from Iran, abandoned their demands for Turkish territory, and acquiesced to American support of the Greek government. Successful pursuit of the containment policy in the Near East established the framework for America's global orientation in the Cold War. In short, America's response to the crises in Iran, Greece, and Turkey was realistic; only subsequently did the containment policy become transformed into an inflexible and simplistic approach to world affairs. . . .

Perhaps because Kuniholm has researched so thoroughly in the papers of American officials in NEA he has accepted their view of the world and adopted it as a framework for his overall approach to his subject matter. The postwar situation in the Near East was the result of a complex interaction between the economic, social, and political strife wrought by the war, the collapse of British power, the emergence of new Soviet demands, and the expansion of American economic and strategic interests. Kuniholm is aware of all these factors. But while disclaiming any intention to write a national history he accepts the view of American diplomats and repeatedly claims that the region's crises were initiated by and the responsibility of the Soviet Union. In this respect he has a tendency to project the Iranian example onto Greece and Turkey, to obfuscate the historical record in Turkey, and to appear indifferent to Soviet security considerations.

Kuniholm is correct, of course, in emphasizing the Soviets' violation of an international agreement by not withdrawing their troops from northern Iran in March 1946. Yet once these troops were withdrawn in May there was little subsequent evidence of overtly aggressive and bellicose Soviet behavior in the region (at least during the period under consideration). In fact, Kuniholm acknowledges that American officials did exaggerate Soviet responsibility for the situation in Greece. Yet the Americans' overall approach to the Soviets was justified, in Kuniholm's view, by Stalin's continued aggressive behavior in Turkey and Iran. But what is the evidence for such a claim? The author repeatedly alludes to Soviet demands on Turkey for additional territory and bases, to Soviet troop movements and propaganda barrages, and to Soviet desires to revise the Montreux convention. All of this constituted a continual "war of nerves," to use one of Kuniholm's (and American diplomats') favorite phrases. The record, however, suggests that during 1946 the Soviets dropped their demand for Kars and Ardahan, couched their quest for bases in the Dardanelles in the context of diplomatic notes calling for a new straits convention, and presented these notes without threats or intimidation. Kuniholm continually suggests that Soviet troop movements portended an "impending" attack against Turkey. But while such movements did take place and were noted by American diplomats and Turkish officials, neither Americans nor Turks anticipated an impending Soviet move against Turkey. Despite occasional vitriolic outpourings in the press of both nations, diplomatic relations were conducted in a sober, if not amiable, manner. In short, it is questionable whether there was a crisis in Turkey except in the minds of American officials (who were the subject of manipulation by Turkish diplomats seeking to elicit additional aid from the United States). And, in Iran, in the months between the withdrawal of Russian troops and the declaration of the Truman Doctrine, American officials seem to have had little to complain about regarding Soviet actions, except for Soviet efforts to negotiate an aviation agreement with the government in Teheran.

Meanwhile, Soviet officials continually insisted that Turkey and Iran constituted areas of vital strategic importance to the Soviet Union. Kuniholm pays little attention to these claims. Moreover, he states that [V. M.] Molotov's suspicions of American desires to acquire bases in Iran, Turkey, and Egypt were "absurd." Yet the related questions of

Soviet security apprehensions and American strategic imperatives deserve more careful scrutiny than they receive here. By 1946 American military officials already were assigning a major role to air power in any future conflict with the Soviet Union. And they were considering the utility of bases in Egypt and Turkey, as well as in Great Britain, as particularly desirable. One study by the Joint Chiefs of Staff (JCS) in August 1946 emphasized that from Turkey, Allied air power could operate more effectively against the vital areas of the Soviet Union; Moscow and the areas south of Moscow would fall within range of Allied fighters; and 70 percent of Soviet oil resources would become vulnerable to Allied air raids. American military officials realized that from the Soviet strategic perspective Turkey was of vital importance "because she offers a possible base for Allied air, and eventually for Allied land, sea, and air operations against Russia. . . ."

American military planners could easily understand the strategic imperatives that prompted the Soviets' concern for bases on their southern flank. After all, one major lesson of the war for American strategists had been the importance of defense in depth. Hence, during 1945 and 1946 American strategists and statesmen were together seeking a series of bases that would guarantee American control of the entire Atlantic and Pacific oceans, project American power into North Africa and the Mediterranean, and enlarge the nation's strategic frontier in order to facilitate the application of armed force at a distance from the American homeland and in closer proximity to a prospective enemy. Interestingly, at the same time that the Soviets were violating their agreement to withdraw troops from northern Iran, the JCS called upon the American government to disregard agreements that stipulated the withdrawal of United States troops from foreign bases at an agreed timetable following the conclusion of hostilities. Such a recommendation was not related to events in Iran but to overall United States security considerations.

The above helps to illustrate that Great Power expansionism was endemic in the international environment that existed after World War II. Vacuums of power coupled with almost universal political and social turmoil bred economic uncertainties and reinforced strategic anxieties, already heightened by new technological developments. Soviet actions were a contributing element but were not largely responsible for the postwar crises in the Near East. For the most part Soviet initiatives along the Northern Tier were tentative and circumspect (and perhaps even prompted by many of the same fears and lessons that motivated

United States policy). American officials dwelt upon Soviet actions not because they were so forboding in themselves but because these actions helped to shape a comprehensible, if not always accurate, framework for interpreting an ominous international environment. With this understanding, it was then possible to develop a rationale for reestablishing economic and political stability along lines favorable to the United States and for creating a strategic environment conducive to the protection of American security interests. A major weakness of this volume, then, is that it attributes too much importance to Soviet initiatives, accepts the judgments of State Department officials at face value, and omits any serious discussion of national diplomacy, except for that of the United States. . . .

An analysis of the American impact on the region's economic, political, and social structures might have helped the reader to come to grips with the paradox of American policies, characterized by Kuniholm as pragmatic, realistic, and successful, helping to produce the present incendiary situation in the region. Over the long run American policies of diplomatic support, military assistance, and political alliance did not bring economic vitality, political stability, or strategic security to the region. Will we again consider the Soviets alone to blame for these failures? Or will we realize . . . that Soviet behavior is only one element in a complex environment where all the Great Powers have legitimate strategic and economic interests and where indigenous social and political structures are fragile and volatile, thereby heightening the anxieties of the Great Powers themselves.

Thomas G. Paterson

EXAGGERATIONS OF THE SOVIET THREAT

In an essay from his book *Meeting the Communist Threat: Truman to Reagan* (1988), Thomas G. Paterson calls attention to the Truman administration's persistent inability or unwillingness to gauge accurately either Soviet power or Soviet intentions. Instead, American policymakers consistently

From *Meeting the Communist Threat: Truman to Reagan* by Thomas G. Paterson, pp. 35–36, 42–50, 51–53. Copyright©1988 by Thomas G. Paterson. Reprinted by permission of Oxford University Press, Inc.

exaggerated the danger posed by the Kremlin to American national security—in part because of faulty intelligence, in part because of President Truman's style, in part because of a fixation on communist ideology, and in part because the presence of a formidable adversary helped forge the public, congressional, and bureaucratic support necessary for an expansive foreign policy. Paterson points to a series of unfortunate results that flowed from these exaggerations, many of them counterproductive to American policy objectives. He holds Truman responsible for creating the image of a relentless and powerful Soviet state, driven by ideology—a regime with which negotiations were fruitless.

President Harry S Truman and his Secretary of State Dean Acheson, Henry A. Kissinger once remarked, "ushered in the most creative period in the history of American foreign policy." Presidents from Eisenhower to Reagan have exalted Truman for his decisiveness and success in launching the Truman Doctrine, the Marshall Plan, and NATO, and for staring the Soviets down in Berlin during those hair-trigger days of the blockade and airlift. John F. Kennedy and Lyndon B. Johnson invoked memories of Truman and the containment doctrine again and again to explain American intervention in Vietnam. Jimmy Carter has written in his memoirs that Truman had served as his model—that he studied Truman's career more than that of any other president and came to admire greatly his courage, honesty, and willingness "to be unpopular if he believed his actions were the best for the country." Some historians have gone so far as to claim that Truman saved humankind from World War III. On the other hand, he has drawn a diverse set of critics. The diplomat and analyst George F. Kennan, the journalist Walter Lippmann, the political scientist Hans Morgenthau, politicians of the left and right, like Henry A. Wallace and Robert A. Taft, and many historians have questioned Truman's penchant for his quick, simple answer, blunt, careless rhetoric, and facile analogies, his moralism that obscured the complexity of causation, his militarization of American foreign policy, his impatience with diplomacy itself, and his exaggeration of the Soviet threat. . . .

    . . . Why did President Truman think it necessary to project American power abroad, to pursue an activist, global foreign policy unprecedented in United States history? The answer has several parts. First, Americans drew lessons from their experience in the 1930s. While indulging in their so-called "isolationism," they had watched economic depression spawn political extremism, which in turn, produced aggression and war. Never again, they vowed. No more appeasement with totalitarians, no more Munichs. "Red Fascism" became a popular phrase to express this American idea. The message seemed evident: To prevent a reincarnation of the 1930s, the United States would have to use its vast power to fight economic instability abroad. Americans felt compelled to project their power, second, because they feared, in the peace-and-prosperity thinking of the time, economic doom stemming from an economic sickness abroad that might spread to the United States, and from American dependency on overseas supplies of raw materials. To aid Europeans and other peoples would not only help them, but also sustain a high American standard of living and gain political friends, as in the case of Italy, where American foreign aid and advice influenced national elections and brought defeat to the left. The American fear of postwar shortages of petroleum also encouraged the Truman Administration to penetrate Middle Eastern oil in a major way. In Saudi Arabia, for example, Americans built and operated the strategically important Dhahran Airport and dominated that nation's oil resources.

Another reason why Truman projected American power so boldly derived from new strategic thinking. Because of the advent of the air age, travel across the world was shortened in time. Strategists spoke of the shrinkage of the globe. Places once deemed beyond American curiosity or interest now loomed important. Airplanes could travel great distances to deliver bombs. Powerful as it was, then, the United States also appeared vulnerable, especially to air attack. As General Carl A. Spaatz emphasized: "As top dog, America becomes target No. 1." He went on to argue that fast aircraft left no warning time for the United States. "The Pearl Harbor of a future war might well be Chicago, or Detroit, or even Washington." To prevent such an occurrence, American leaders worked to acquire overseas bases in both the Pacific and Atlantic, thereby denying a potential enemy an attack route to the Western Hemisphere. Forward bases would also permit the United States to conduct offensive operations more effectively. The American strategic frontier had to be pushed outward. Thus the United States took the former Japanese-controlled Pacific islands of the Carolines, Marshalls, and Marianas, maintained garrisons in Germany and Japan, and sent military missions to Iran, Turkey, Greece, Saudi Arabia, China, and to fourteen Latin American states. The Joint Chiefs of Staff and Department of State lists of desired foreign bases, and of sites where air transit rights were sought, included such far-flung spots as Algeria, India, French Indochina, New Zealand, Iceland, and the Azores. When asked where the American navy would float, Navy Secretary James Forrestal replied: "Wherever there is a sea." Today we may take the presumption of a global American presence for granted, but in Truman's day it was new, even radical thinking, especially after the "isolationist" 1930s.

These several explanations for American globalism suggest that the United States would have been an expansionist power whether or not the obstructionist Soviets were lurking about. That is, America's own needs—ideological, political, economic, strategic—encouraged such a projection of power. As the influential National Security Council Paper No. 68(NSC-68) noted in April 1950, the "overall policy" of the United States was "designed to foster a world environment in which the American system can survive and flourish." This policy "we would probably pursue even if there was no Soviet threat."

Americans, of course, did perceive a Soviet threat. Thus we turn to yet another explanation for the United States' dramatic extension of power early in the Cold War: to contain the Soviets. The Soviets unsettled Americans in so many ways. Their harsh Communist dogma and propagandistic slogans were not only monotonous; they also seemed threatening because of their call for world revolution and for the demise of capitalism. In the United Nations the Soviets cast vetoes and even on occasion walked out of the organization. At international conferences their "*nyets*" stung American ears. When they negotiated, the Soviets annoyed their interlocuters by repeating the same point over and over again, delaying meetings, or abruptly shifting positions. Truman labeled them "pigheaded," and Dean Acheson thought them so coarse and insulting that he once allowed that they were not "housebroken."

The Soviet Union, moreover, had territorial ambitions, grabbing parts of Poland, Rumania, and Finland, and demanding parts of Turkey. In Eastern Europe, with their Red Army positioned to intimidate, the Soviets quickly manhandled the Poles and Rumanians. Communists in 1947 and 1948 seized power in Hungary and Czechoslovakia. Some Americans predicted that the Soviet military would roll across Western Europe. In general, Truman officials pictured the Soviet Union as an implacable foe to an open world, an opportunistic nation that would probe for weak spots, exploit economic misery, snuff out individual freedom, and thwart self-determination. Americans thought the worst, some claiming that a Soviet-inspired international conspiracy insured perennial hostility and a creeping aggression aimed at American interests. To Truman and his advisers, the Soviets stood as the world's bully, and the very existence of this menacing bear necessitated an activist American foreign policy and an exertion of American power as a "counterforce."

But Truman officials exaggerated the Soviet threat, imagining an adversary that never measured up to the galloping monster so often depicted by alarmist Americans. Even if the Soviets intended to dominate the world, or just Western Europe, they lacked the capabilities to do so. The Soviets had no foreign aid to dispense; outside Russia Communist parties were minorities; the Soviet economy was seriously crippled by the war; and the Soviet military suffered significant weaknesses. The Soviets lacked a modern navy, a strategic air force, the atomic bomb, and air defenses. Their wrecked economy could not support or supply an army in the field for very long, and their technology was antiquated. Their ground forces lacked motorized transportation, adequate equipment, and troop morale. A Soviet *blitzkrieg* invasion of Western Europe had little chance of success and would have proven suicidal for the Soviets, for even if they managed to gain temporary control of Western Europe by a military thrust, they could not strike the United States. So they would have to assume defensive positions and await crushing American attacks, probably including atomic bombings of Soviet Russia itself—plans for which existed.

Other evidence also suggests that a Soviet military threat to Western Europe was more myth than reality. The Soviet Union demobilized its forces after the war, dropping to about 2.9 million personnel in 1948. Many of its 175 divisions were under-strength, and large numbers of them were engaged in occupation duties, resisting challenges to Soviet authority in Eastern Europe. American intelligence sources reported as well that the Soviets could not count on troops of the occupied countries, which were quite unreliable, if not rebellious. At most, the Soviets had 700,000 to 800,000 troops available for an attack against the West. To resist such an attack, the West had about 800,000 troops, or approximate parity. For these reasons, top American leaders did not expect a Soviet onslaught against Western Europe. They and their intelligence sources emphasized Soviet military and economic weaknesses, not strengths, Soviet hesitancy, not boldness.

Why then did Americans so fear the Soviets? Why did the Central Intelligence Agency, the Joint Chiefs of Staff, and the President exaggerate the Soviet threat? The first explanation is that their intelligence estimates were just that—estimates. The American intelligence community was still in a state of infancy, hardly the well-developed system it would become in the 1950s and 1960s. So Americans lacked complete assurance that their figures on Soviet force deployment or armaments were accurate or close to the mark. When leaders do not know, they tend to assume the worst of an adversary's intentions and capabilities, or to think that the Soviets might miscalculate, sparking a war they did not want. In a chaotic world, the conception of a single, inexorably aggressive adversary also brought a comforting sense of knowing and consistency.

Truman officials also exaggerated the Soviet threat in order "to extricate the United States from commitments and restraints that were no longer considered desirable" [argues Melvyn P. Leffler]. For example, they loudly chastised the Soviets for violating the Yalta agreements; yet Truman and his advisers knew the Yalta provisions were at best vague and open to differing interpretations. But, more, they purposefully misrepresented the Yalta agreement on the vital question of the composition of the Polish government. In so doing, they hoped to decrease the high degree of Communist participation that the Yalta conferees had insured when they stated that the new Polish regime would be formed by reorganizing the provisional Lublin (Communist) government. Through charges of Soviet malfeasance Washington sought to justify its own retreat from Yalta, such as its abandonment of the $20 billion reparations figure for Germany (half of which was supposed to go to the Soviet Union).

Another reason for the exaggeration: Truman liked things in black and white, as his aide Clark Clifford noted. Nuances, ambiguities, and counterevidence were often discounted to satisfy the President's preference for the simpler answer or his pre-conceived notions of Soviet aggressiveness. In mid-1946, for example, the Joint Chiefs of Staff deleted from a report to Truman a section that stressed Soviet weaknesses. American leaders also exaggerated the Soviet threat because it was useful in galvanizing and unifying American public opinion for an abandonment of recent and still lingering "isolationism" and support for an expansive foreign policy. Kennan quoted a colleague as saying that "if it [Soviet threat] had never existed, we would have had to invent it, to create a sense of urgency we need to bring us to the point of decisive action." The military particularly overplayed the Soviet threat in order to persuade Congress to endorse larger defense budgets. This happened in 1948–49 with the creation of the North Atlantic Treaty Organization. NATO was established not to halt a Soviet military attack, because none was anticipated, but to give Europeans a psychological boost—a "will to resist." American officials believed that the European Recovery Program would falter unless there was a "sense of security" to buttress it. They nurtured apprehension, too, that some European nations might lean toward neutralism unless they were brought together under a security umbrella. NATO also seemed essential to help members resist internal subversion. The exaggerated, popular view that NATO was formed to deter a Soviet invasion of Western Europe by conventional forces stems, in part, from Truman's faulty recollection in his published memoirs.

Still another explanation for why Americans exaggerated the Soviet threat is found in their attention since the Bolshevik Revolution of 1917 to the utopian Communist goal of world revolution, confusing goals with actual behavior. Thus Americans believed that the sinister Soviets and their Communist allies would exploit postwar economic, social, and political disorder, not through a direct military thrust, but rather through covert subversion. The recovery of Germany and Japan became necessary, then, to deny the Communists political opportunities to thwart American plans for the integration of these former enemies into an American system of trade and defense. And because economic instability troubled so much of Eurasia, Communist gains through subversion might deny the United States strategic raw materials.

Why dwell on this question of the American exaggeration of the Soviet threat? Because it over-simplified international realities by under-estimating local conditions that might thwart Soviet/Communist successes and by over-estimating the Soviet ability to act. Because it encouraged the Soviets to fear encirclement and to enlarge their military establishment, thereby contributing to a dangerous weapons race. Because it led to indiscriminate globalism. Because it put a damper on diplomacy; American officials were hesitant to negotiate with an opponent variously described as malevolent, deceitful, and inhuman. They especially did not warm to negotiations when some critics were ready to cry that diplomacy, which could produce compromises, was evidence in itself of softness toward Communism.

Exaggeration of the threat also led Americans to misinterpret events and in so doing to prompt the Soviets to make decisions contrary to American wishes. For example, the Soviet presence in Eastern Europe, once considered a simple question of the Soviets' building an iron curtain or bloc after the war, is now seen by historians in more complex terms. The Soviets did not seem to have a master plan for the region and followed different policies in different countries. Poland and Rumania were subjugated right away; Yugoslavia, on the other hand, was an independent Communist state led by Josip Tito, who broke dramatically with Stalin in 1948; Hungary conducted elections in the fall of 1945 (the Communists got only 17 percent of the vote) and did not suffer a Communist coup until 1947; in Czechoslovakia, free elections in May 1946 produced a non-Communist government that functioned until 1948; Finland, although under Soviet scrutiny, affirmed its independence. The Soviets did not have a firm grip on Eastern Europe before 1948—a prime reason why many American leaders believed the Soviets harbored weaknesses.

American policies were designed to roll the Soviets back. The United States reconstruction loan policy, encouragement of dissident groups, and appeal for free elections alarmed Moscow, contributing to a Soviet push to secure the area. The issue of free elections illustrates the point. Such a call was consistent with cherished American principle. But in the context of Eastern Europe and the Cold War, problems arose. First, Americans conspicuously followed a double standard which foreigners noted time and again; that is, if the principle of free elections really mattered, why not hold such elections in the United States' sphere of influence in Latin America, where an unsavory lot of dictators ruled? Second, free elections would have produced victories for anti-Soviet groups. Such results could only unsettle the Soviets and invite them to intervene to protect their interests in neighboring states—just as the United States had intervened in Cuba and Mexico in the twentieth century when hostile groups assumed power. In Hungary, for example, it was the non-Communist leader Ferenc Nagy who delayed elections in late 1946 because he knew the Communist Party would lose badly, thereby possibly triggering a repressive Soviet response. And, third, the United States had so little influence in Eastern Europe that it had no way of insuring free elections—no way of backing up its demands with power.

Walter Lippmann, among others, thought that the United States should tame its meddling in the region and make the best out of a bad arrangement of power. "I do believe," he said in 1947, "we shall have to recognize the principle of boundaries of spheres of influence which either side will not cross and have to proceed on the old principle that a good fence makes good neighbors." Kennan shared this view, as did one State Department official who argued that the United States was incapable of becoming a successful watchdog in Eastern Europe.

American "barkings, growlings, snappings, and occasional bitings," Cloyce K. Huston prophesied, would only irritate the Soviets without reducing their power. Better still, argued some analysts, if the United States tempered its ventures into European affairs, then the Soviets, surely less alarmed, might tolerate more openness. But the United States did not stay out. Americans tried to project their power into a region where they had little chance of succeeding, but had substantial opportunity to irritate and alarm the always suspicious Soviets. In this way, it has been suggested, the United States itself helped pull down the iron curtain. . . .

Truman's alarmist language [in the Truman Doctrine] further fixed the mistaken idea in the American mind that the Soviets were unrelenting aggressors intent upon undermining peace, and that the United States, almost alone, had to meet them everywhere. Truman's exaggerations and his commitment to the containment doctrine did not go unchallenged. Secretary [of State George C.] Marshall himself was startled by the President's muscular anti-Communist rhetoric, and he questioned the wisdom of overstating the case. The Soviet specialist Llewellyn Thompson urged "caution" in swinging too far toward "outright opposition to Russia. . . ." Walter Lippmann, in reacting to both Truman's speech and George F. Kennan's now famous "Mr. 'X'" article in the July 1947 issue of the journal *Foreign Affairs*, labeled containment a "strategic monstrosity," because it made no distinctions between important or vital and not-so-important or peripheral areas. Because American power was not omnipresent, Lippmann further argued, the "policy can be implemented only by recruiting, subsidizing and supporting a heterogeneous array of satellites, clients, dependents and puppets." He also criticized the containment doctrine for placing more emphasis on confrontation than on diplomacy. . . .

Jiang's collapse [in China] joined the Soviet explosion of an atomic bomb, the formation of the German Democratic Republic (East Germany), and the Sino-Soviet Friendship Treaty to arouse American feeling in late 1949 and early 1950 that the Soviet threat had dramatically escalated. Although Kennan told his State Department colleagues that such feeling was "largely of our own making" rather than an accurate accounting of Soviet actions, the composers of NSC-68 preferred to dwell on a more dangerous Soviet menace in extreme rhetoric not usually found in a secret report. But because the April 1950 document was aimed at President Truman, we can certainly understand why its language was hyperbolic. The fanatical and militant Soviets, concluded

NSC-68, were seeking to impose "absolute authority over the rest of the world." America had to frustrate the global "design" of the "evil men" of the Kremlin, who were unrelentingly bent on "piecemeal aggression" against the "free world" through military force, infiltration, and intimidation. The report called for a huge American and allied military build-up and nuclear arms development.

NSC-68, most scholars agree, was a flawed, even amateurish document. It assumed a Communist monolith that did not exist, drew alarmist conclusions based upon vague and inaccurate information about Soviet capabilities, made grand, unsubstantiated claims about Soviet intentions, glossed over the presence of many non-democratic countries in the "free world," and recommended against negotiations with Moscow at the very time the Soviets were advancing toward a policy of "peaceful co-existence." One State Department expert on the Soviet Union, Charles E. Bohlen, although generally happy with the report's conclusions, faulted NSC-68 for assuming a Soviet plot for world conquest—for "oversimplifying the problem." No, he advised, the Soviets sought foremostly to maintain their regime and to extend it abroad "to the degree that is possible without serious risk to the internal regime." In short, there were limits to Soviet behavior. But few were listening to such cautionary voices. NSC-68 became American dogma, especially when the outbreak of the Korean War in June of 1950 sanctified it as a prophetic "we told you so."

The story of Truman's foreign policy is basically an accounting of how the United States, because of its own expansionism and exaggeration of the Soviet threat, became a global power. Truman projected American power after the Second World War to rehabilitate Western Europe, secure new allies, guarantee strategic and economic links, and block Communist or Soviet influence. He firmly implanted the image of the Soviets as relentless, worldwide transgressors with whom it is futile to negotiate. Through his exaggeration of the Soviet threat, Truman made it very likely that the United States would continue to practice global interventionism years after he left the White House.

Michael J. Hogan

THE MARSHALL PLAN AND THE SEARCH FOR ECONOMIC ORDER

Michael J. Hogan disagrees with traditional scholars of the Marshall Plan who view America's commitment to European economic recovery after World War II as a revolutionary break from past policies. Instead, Hogan suggests that the Marshall Plan was yet another step in America's twentieth-century search for a new economic order at home and abroad; he finds sources for the plan especially in the New Era of the 1920s and the New Deal of the 1930s. Throughout these different periods, public and private officials in the United States sought to restructure the world economy along American lines—what Hogan calls corporatism or neocapitalism. Although the urgency that the Truman administration attached to European economic recovery was intensified by the perceived Soviet threat, he argues that the influence of that threat on American Marshall Planners should not obscure continuities with earlier United States efforts to reconstruct Europe. In contrast to some revisionist historians, Hogan offers a largely positive evaluation of the European Recovery Program, calling it a reasonable defense of important economic and strategic interests that was applied in effective collaboration with reliable local elites. In short, the Marshall Plan served American and European interests and stands as one of the most successful diplomatic initiatives launched by the United States in this century.

Author of the prize-winning book *The Marshall Plan: America, Britain, and the Reconstruction of Western Europe, 1947–1952* (1987), from which this selection is drawn, Michael J. Hogan has also written *Informal Entente: The Private Structure of Cooperation in Anglo-American Economic Diplomacy, 1918–1928* (1977). He teaches at Ohio State University and serves as editor of the journal *Diplomatic History*.

Original accounts of the Marshall Plan, or the European Recovery Program as it was known officially, hailed this celebrated enterprise as evidence of America's assumption of world leadership after the Second World War. Together with the North Atlantic Treaty and other instruments of Cold War diplomacy, the Marshall Plan supposedly

Text by Michael J. Hogan, from *The Marshall Plan: America, Britain, and the Reconstruction of Western Europe, 1947–1952*, excerpts from pp. 1–3, 18–24, 26–28, 430–455. Reprinted by permission of Cambridge University Press.

marked the end of the isolationist era and the beginning of what Henry Luce called the "American Century." This interpretation paralleled that found in older works on domestic history. These works viewed the New Deal as a second American revolution, the domestic equivalent of the revolution in American diplomacy engineered by Cold War policymakers in the 1940s. More recent works, to be sure, have begun to overturn the older interpretation. Those on domestic history have portrayed twentieth-century developments as part of a larger historical process by which Americans adjusted their economic and political institutions to the profound transformations brought on by industrialization. In these works, the liberal critique embedded in older scholarship, which separated the New Deal of the 1930s from the New Era of the 1920s, has given way to interpretations that consider both eras related parts of the modern American search for a new economic and political order.

Scholars of American diplomacy have been slow to pursue this theme. Recent works in this field have failed to connect the trends in domestic history to those in the history of foreign relations or to note how institutional adaptations at home influenced the direction of policy abroad. In these works, to put it differently, the Marshall Plan remains essentially cut off from the nation's previous history. . . .

The purpose here is to cast the Marshall Plan in the context of America's twentieth-century search for a new economic order at home and abroad, and to do so by subsuming the three decades after the First World War under an interpretative framework that is new to the study of American diplomacy. This framework is a variant of one that recent historians of the domestic scene have used to understand modern efforts to create what some have called an associative state, others a corporative neo-capitalism. By these I mean an American political economy founded on self-governing economic groups, integrated by institutional coordinators and normal market mechanisms, led by cooperating public and private elites, nourished by limited but positive government power, and geared to an economic growth in which all could share. These efforts married the older traditions associated with the localized and fragmented political economy of the nineteenth century, including individualism, privatism, competition, and antitrust, to the twentieth-century trend toward an organized capitalism characterized by national economies of scale, bureaucratic planning, and administrative regulation. The result as it unfolded after the First World War was something of a hybrid economic order: an American brand of corporative neocapitalism that went beyond the laissez-faire political economy of classical theory but stopped short of a statist syndicalism.

This trend fundamentally altered the shape of American diplomacy, which for all practical purposes sought to restructure the world economy along lines similar to the corporative order that was emerging in the United States. To the open and competitive international system envisioned in classical theory—one founded on the principles of specialization and comparative advantage, and on stable currencies, fixed exchanges, and nondiscriminatory trade—American leaders would add new mechanisms of economic planning, new institutions of coordination and control, and new partnerships between public and private elites in the collective administration of world trade and development. These new elements were to be the bricks and mortar in a multilateral framework, a new system in which multinational arrangements put a limit on competitive nationalisms, market forces and coordinating mechanisms worked to integrate economies, and economic integration cleared a path to stable growth and international harmony. . . .

. . . The New Deal coalition was able to launch initiatives that ushered in a prolonged period of international economic growth, a goal that had not been attained after the First World War. Yet this success should not obscure the important contribution Republican leaders made to a foreign-policy formulation that essentially added new dimensions to the corporative design that Hoover and others had started to draft in the 1920s. Out of this synthesis of New Era designs and New Deal inventions came the Marshall Plan to rebuild Western Europe.

Viewed from this perspective rather than in the context of the Cold War, the Marshall Plan can be seen as a logical extension of domestic- and foreign-policy developments going back to the first American effort to reconstruct war-torn Europe. Indeed, the second generation of American recovery planners confronted problems very similar to those that had confounded the Republicans earlier and devised solutions that elaborated and formalized the stabilization strategies pioneered by their predecessors in the first postwar period. If the Marshall Planners succeeded where the Republicans failed, this success was due in part to policy innovations growing first out of the New Deal and then out of the Cold War. Nevertheless, these innovations must not conceal the lines of continuity that linked the two generations and mark both postwar eras as part of an American effort to remake the Old World in the image of the New.

. . . American Marshall Planners, like the Republicans before them, tried to transform political problems into technical ones that were solvable, they said, when old European ways of conducting business and old habits of class conflict gave way to American methods of scientific management and corporative collaboration. Marshall Planners were far more interested than their predecessors in cutting the web of exchange controls, quotas, and import licenses and the tangled network of over two hundred bilateral trade and payments agreements that stifled intra-European commerce and prevented the most efficient use of local resources. But they echoed the arguments of their predecessors in attacking these and other restrictions as tantamount to the sort of economic autarky that generated conflict and discouraged growth. The Marshall Planners also repeated earlier demands for European self-help and redoubled efforts to reduce reparations, fix exchange rates, and make currencies convertible. They claimed, as the Republicans had claimed earlier, that these measures and those to liberalize trade would permit individual initiative and normal market mechanisms to integrate economies and stimulate growth. And much like the first generation of recovery planners, they sought to reconcile their faith in private enterprise with the institutional imperatives of an integrated order, employing as the agents of reconciliation public-private partnerships and supposedly neutral authorities similar to those Hoover had envisioned in the 1920s.

In the United States, for example, the Marshall Plan carefully delimited the government's role in the stabilization process. This role was perceived as a national-security imperative and as an aid to private enterprise. It was to be performed so far as possible in collaboration with private elites. Policymakers ruled out a government aid corporation to administer the recovery program and established instead an independent agency, staffed it with managerial talent from the private sector, and linked it to private groups through a network of advisory committees. Marshall Planners then urged participating countries to replicate this administrative system. The result was a series of partnerships that blended public and private power, much like the Marshall Planners tried to fuse free-market forces and institutional coordinators to clear the obstacles to a single market in Western Europe. This strategy inspired their plan for a European payments union through which a supervisory board of experts was to use both administrative controls and market incentives to adjust national monetary and fiscal policies in the interest of European stabilization and integration. The same strategy lay behind their efforts to make the Organization for European Economic Cooperation into a corporate body with a competent professional staff and limited authority to coordinate national recovery programs.

As Republicans had in the first postwar period, Marshall Planners attempted to absorb Germany into a wider Western European framework and thus reconcile its recovery with the economic and security needs of its neighbors. The French continued to pose the greatest barrier to change in this direction. Their demands for German disaggregation, for industrial reparations and controls, and for limits on German sovereignty recalled French policy in the 1920s. American recovery planners, as before, resorted to economic leverage and collaboration with the British to overcome French resistance. They traded American aid for concessions on reparations and joined the British in defeating French proposals for international ownership of the Ruhr and permanent limits on German production. These initiatives, together with supranational controls over key resources, security guarantees, and the division of Germany, removed many of the political and financial impediments that had stalled the process of economic recovery and integration after 1929. Out of them also came a series of laboriously constructed compromises that led first to the formation of the Federal Republic and then to its integration into a unified European economic system that Marshall Planners viewed as the key to reconciling Germany's revival with France's economic and security concerns.

Both recovery periods, as the preceding discussion suggests, witnessed the formation of an Anglo-American partnership that subordinated French hopes for economic and political predominance to the reintegration of Germany. Indeed, Anglo-American relations impacted . . . strongly on the history of the Marshall Plan. . . . As in the first postwar period, the partnership between the two countries was inherently unstable and evolved out of initially different British and American strategies for rebuilding the European and world systems. The British again found themselves in a paradoxical position: They depended on American financial support to rebuild their economy and protect their leadership of the Commonwealth and the sterling area, but the terms of this support were often incompatible with their ambitions. For the Americans, trade liberalization and currency convertibility were routes to economic stability and growth. Together with supranational institutions of coordination and control, they would also pave the way to an integrated Europe in which British power balanced that of a revitalized

Germany.   For policymakers in London, however, American plans would increase the drain on British reserves, undermine the value of pound sterling, and wreck Britain's leadersip of the sterling area.

The British, as the records of the Foreign Office, Treasury, and Cabinet make clear, started the Marshall Plan years looking toward an independent bloc of Western European and British Commonwealth countries and then retreated to the vision of a North Atlantic community in which Britain would function as the linchpin between two continents.   A North Atlantic community, one founded on an Anglo-American partnership, appeared to be the key to Commonwealth solidarity and to Britain's resurgence as a great world power.   These were the central goals of British diplomacy, and they ruled out the kind of Anglo-European integration the Americans had in mind.   So did the determination of British policymakers to shield their economy against supranational authorities (which the Americans hoped to build) and natural market forces (which the Americans hoped to unleash).   Anglo-American differences severely tested the leverage that Marshall Planners could bring to bear on behalf of their policy design for Western Europe, leverage that was considerably greater than that in the first postwar period but by no means absolute.

These differences came to a head in the sterling crisis of 1949 when British threats to shelter sterling within a high-cost, soft-currency trading bloc promised to scuttle American hopes for an integrated Europe and a fully multilateral system of world trade.   As we will see, however, British and American leaders finally hammered out an accommodation similar to the informal entente achieved in the 1920s. The British agreed to devalue pound sterling and join in plans to liberalize intra-European trade and payments.   The Americans settled for British cooperation, not integration, with the Continent.   The Anglo-American accommodation grew in part out of overriding strategic considerations, particularly the conviction in Washington that ongoing efforts to push the British into Europe might weaken their position in other areas of the world and actually slow the formation of a Western European unit that could absorb the Germans and contain the Soviets. It shifted the greatest share of the responsibility for integrating Germany to the French, much as the Americans had done in the 1920s, with the outcome in 1950 being the Schuman Plan for a European coal and steel community.

During both postwar periods, then, American recovery planners forged an uneasy partnership with the British, gave Germany's revival parity with France's security, and sought to promote both European integration and German reintegration. In addition, they urged the Europeans to stabilize currencies, fix realistic exchange rates, reduce reparations, and eliminate other barriers to the flow of goods and capital. They said that measures of this sort would permit individual initiative and market incentives to have full play in Europe. But they also tempered their faith in free-market forces by stressing the need for American assistance, for new frameworks of public-private cooperation, and for new institutions of economic coordination and control.

These lines of continuity force us to throw out the notion of a thoroughgoing break in American policy between the first and second postwar eras. But we cannot, of course, deny the influence of intervening developments. In the second postwar period, heightened fears of Soviet expansion led the State Department and the Pentagon to match economic aid with military commitments. These agencies also broke new ground with the North Atlantic Treaty and the related efforts to integrate Western European defense systems, efforts that complemented those of the Marshall Planners to the extent that integration became the conceptual link between strategic and economic goals.

Students of strategic planning have missed this linkage. By focusing on American attempts to build a bipolar equilibrium, they have also slighted parallel efforts to forge a viable balance of power among the Western European states and have failed to note how integration became the key to both objectives. That is, in American thinking, integration was the way to reconcile Germany's recovery with France's security and bring both together in a unit of sufficient scale to contain the Soviets. Integration as a strategic concept forms an important subtheme. . . .

On the economic side, as we will see, Marshall Planners enlarged New Era conceptions to include a number of important policy innovations. They abandoned the earlier reliance on private credits in favor of a major government aid program that enabled the Europeans to rehabilitate their economies and manage their balance of payments without crippling deflation or excessive reparations. They also went beyond earlier notions of an interdependent European economic community of essentially independent states, envisioning now a structural integration that entailed some limitations on the exercise of sovereign power. In addition, Marshall Planners promoted the new strategies of macroeconomic management, broadened the networks of corporative collaboration to include organized agriculture and labor, and sought labor's support by encouraging modest programs of social welfare. These innovations reflected the impact of Keynesian thinking and New Deal experiences on American policy. They added significant increments, as it were, to the rudimentary strategies that Republican leaders had started to develop in the first postwar period.

Out of the blend of old and new came what I call the New Deal synthesis, a policy formulation that guided American efforts to remake Western Europe in the likeness of the United States. Its central component was the principle of federalism as embodied in the American Constitution and subsequently modified by the trend toward an administrative state that had peaked recently in the New Deal. Translated into European terms, federalism meant the fusion of separate economic sovereignties into an integrated market capped by supranational institutions of economic planning and administration. The idea of supranationalism, captured in what [I] call the planners' approach to European recovery, was another component of the American policy synthesis. It coexisted with a third component, which [I] denote as the free-traders' approach and which embodied the older American faith in making currencies convertible, eliminating bilateral barriers, and allowing the normal mechanisms of a free economy to forge a single market. The result was both a strategy of integration that relied on administrative and automatic regulators, and a vision of a mixed capitalist economy in Europe similar to the one that had grown up in the United States. Supplementing the planners' and traders' approaches was a commitment to Keynesian techniques of macroeconomic management, to national and transnational networks of corporative collaboration and public-private power sharing, and to American methods for engineering a productive abundance in which all could share.

Greater productivity, itself a key component of the New Deal synthesis, would adjourn the redistributive struggles that fueled extremist political parties in Western Europe. It would also put participating countries on a self-supporting basis and thus facilitate their entry into the multilateral system of world trade that American leaders considered to be a prerequisite to economic prosperity and democratic freedom in the United States. Virtually all other components of the American synthesis attempted to attain these goals by building a European economic order conducive to recovery and sustained growth. Economic integration would create a framework for enlisting Germany in the cause of recovery while at the same time bringing the gains in resource utilization, specialization, and economies of scale that were needed to balance

Western Europe's accounts with the dollar area. Supranational agencies would guide local elites down the road to integration; transnational networks of corporative collaboration would corral labor, management, and government in common programs for productive abundance; and both would turn the old diplomacy of national rivalry into bureaucratic bargaining, and the old politics of class conflict into the politics of administration.   Similar benefits would come from translating the problem of economic growth into a technical problem soluble by adopting American methods of private production, including American engineering, manufacturing, and marketing techniques and American strategies of labor-management teamwork.

The task was formidable, the opposition strong. As we will see, Marshall Planners had to convince some European governments to reduce public expenditures, others to increase them. They had to defeat Communists in the trade-union movement, win British support for Europe's integration, and get the French to go along with Germany's reintegration. They also had to undercut rivals in the Army Department whose Germany-first orientation threatened efforts to reconcile Franco-German differences within the framework of a comprehensive recovery plan and an integrated Western Europe. This battle had been won by 1950, only to be replaced by another with the Treasury Department, where policymakers were more conservative than the Marshall Planners and less inclined to support a recovery strategy that ran the risk of organizing Western Europe into an economic bloc ringed with restrictions against the dollar.

In addition, Marshall Planners faced challenges from conservatives in Congress who had long been critical of the Truman administration's foreign policies. . . .

Within three years, however, the political balance would begin to shift in both the United States and Western Europe. The outbreak of fighting in Korea, and particularly the Chinese intervention of November 1950, would add to the pressure on American resources and force the Truman administration to reverse its policy of using economic rather than military power to fortify Western Europe. This policy, which initially had relegated rearmament to a secondary strategy and then to a position of parity with recovery, now gave way to one that placed it above reconstruction. Out of this shift came a massive expansion of defense expenditures on both sides of the Atlantic. The economic dislocations that followed, together with greater American pressure to rearm Germany, led to a wave of anti-Americanism in Western

Europe and, in some countries, to a political fragmentation that pitted the forces of the Left against those of the Right. Something similar occurred in the United States. Congressional opponents attacked the administration's military commitments to Western Europe, formulated a conservative critique of the Keynesian policies being used to underwrite the economic aid and rearmament programs, and finally combined forces to bring the Marshall Plan to a premature conclusion. . . .

The Marshall Plan rested squarely on an American conviction that European economic recovery was essential to the long-term interests of the United States. These interests were interdependent and mutually reinforcing, so much so that public officials saw little need to rank them in the order that subsequent historians have tried to establish. They included economic interests. Policymakers in the Truman administration were convinced that a "dynamic economy" at home required American trade and investment abroad, which in turn required the reconstruction of major trading partners in Europe and their reintegration into a multilateral system of world trade. These requirements summed up a world view rooted in political conviction as well as in economic interests. American leaders envisioned an open international economy founded on the principles of liberal capitalism, such as free trade and equal opportunity. But they also equated these principles with democratic forms of government, associated autarkic economic policies with totalitarian political regimes, and assumed that "enemies in the market place" could not be "friends at the council table." "The political line up followed the economic line up," as Cordell Hull once put it.

Strategic interests paralleled those of an economic and political nature. American policymakers viewed European markets, sources of supply, manpower resources, and industrial capacity as strategic assets that must not be controlled by a hostile power or coalition. The recent war had demonstrated the threat to American security inherent in such a development and the concomitant need to preserve American access to Europe's resources while denying them to potential rivals. Postwar developments reinforced wartime lessons. The defeat of Germany and the exhaustion of Britain and France had left a power vacuum in Central and Western Europe into which the Soviet Union might expand unless the United States assembled the components of a viable balance of power. This meant filling the vacuum by rebuilding economic and political systems strong enough to forestall aggression and defeat

Communist parties, whose rise to power seemed the most likely way for the Soviets to extend their influence.

American interests dictated an active role in rebuilding Europe, but enumerating these interests explains neither the full range of American goals nor how American policymakers hoped to achieve them. American ambition subsumed economic, political, and strategic interests in a larger design much like the one that had guided Republican policymakers in the 1920s. The Marshall Planners would replace the old European state system with what they saw as a more viable framework for achieving their policy objectives on the Continent. They would do so by applying the American principle of federalism and using it to create an integrated European economy similar to the one that existed in the United States. The strategic assumptions behind this policy held that an integrated economic order, particularly one headed by supranational institutions, would help to control German nationalism, reconcile Germany's recovery with France's economic and security concerns, and thus create a balance of power in the West sufficient to contain Soviet power in the East. The economic assumptions grew fundamentally out of the American experience at home, where a large internal economy integrated by free-market forces and central institutions of coordination and control seemed to have laid the groundwork for a new era of economic growth and social stability. An economic United States of Europe would bring similar benefits, or so the Americans believed, and in the process would realize all of their goals on the Continent. Besides creating a framework for controlling the Germans and containing the Soviets, it would limit Communist inroads, dissolve class tensions through a shared abundance, and set the continental countries on the path to a multilateral system of world trade.

Although recovery planners would develop other strategies to recreate the American system in Europe, these additional strategies were the beams and buttresses of a grand design that began with the idea of integration. This idea was not new, either in Europe or in the United States. The Europeans had organized a number of unification movements, some of which called for immediate political federation, others for a loose confederation of semiautonomous states, still others for a gradualist approach that would begin with technical cooperation and economic integration in selected lines of industry and agriculture. In the United States, similar visions had inspired a coterie of enthusiasts who championed the cause of economic integration and political federation as two of the keys to peace and prosperity in postwar Europe. . . .

Such proposals at first received only sporadic consideration in Washington, where officials were preoccupied with the war effort or otherwise worried that regional blocs might undercut their plans for a worldwide system of multilateral trade. This situation changed in 1947, however. After initial attempts to stimulate recovery had failed and alternative reconstruction policies had been rejected, American leaders gave the idea of European unification, or at least European economic integration, a prominent place in their policy planning. At that point, economic conditions in Europe had started to deteriorate. The victorious powers had been unable to negotiate a final peace settlement, the wartime alliance was breaking down, and the Soviets were beginning to consolidate their control over Eastern Europe. These developments, which are so familiar to historians of the early Cold War, led American policymakers to see economic integration as the best way to achieve the interrelated economic, political, and strategic goals on their agenda for postwar Europe. . . .

The Marshall Plan was a success if judged simply as a program to control inflation, revive trade, and restore production. By 1950, inflation had been contained in most of the participating countries, France being a notable exception, and both intra-European and extra-European trade had recovered to levels well above those anticipated at the start of the Marshall Plan. The Korean War undercut these gains and also dashed already faint hopes that participating countries might balance accounts with the Western Hemisphere by the end of the ERP period. This is Imanuel Wexler's assessment. But it is also true, as Wexler notes, that these were temporary reversals in an established pattern of recovery that would resume in the early 1950s, continue unabated over the next decade, and lead to the restoration of European currency convertibility and the formation of a "free-world" trading system comparable to the one envisioned in the Bretton Woods agreements of 1944.

Something similar can be said of the recovery of Western European production. During the Marshall Plan period, Western Europe's aggregate gross national product jumped by more than 32 percent, from $120 billion to $159 billion; agricultural production climbed 11 percent above the prewar level, just slightly less than the target set in 1948; and industrial output increased by 40 percent against the same bench mark, greatly exceeding the OEEC's original projection. As a new generation of European revisionists has reminded us, American Marshall Planners cannot take all of the credit for this remarkable record of success. Alan Milward makes this point in his penetrating economic history of postwar reconstruction. Arguing that the crisis of 1947 was not a crisis of production but a payments crisis brought on by the speed at which production had revived, Milward concludes that Marshall aid merely enabled participating countries to cover deficits with the dollar area and thus continue the recovery that had begun earlier. Charles Maier constructs a different version of the same argument. . . . [H]e concludes that local resources accounted for 80-90 percent of capital formation in the major European economies during the first two years of the Marshall Plan. The American contribution was marginal, measured in quantitative terms, and actually declined in the years after 1949.

Although this sort of revisionism is a healthy corrective to earlier American paeans to the Marshall Plan, it succeeds through a feat of analytical legerdemain that denigrates the American contribution and leads to conclusions almost as unbalanced as those it seeks to refute. The payments crisis, after all, portended a serious crisis in production that would come with the collapse of critical dollar imports. Signs of this were apparent early in 1947, and it is impossible to get around them by arguing, as Milward does, that most participating countries might have managed their balance of payments and achieved sustained rates of growth by simply limiting imports to capital goods. This option was not available to the fragile coalitions that presided over many of the participating countries, none of which could retreat from already low levels of consumption and hope to survive. Marshall aid enabled these coalitions to operate within a range of political choice that precluded vigorously deflationary policies, promised higher living standards, and thus closed the door to extremist elements on the Left and the Right. To put it in a way that balances contemporary European revisionism against the encomiums of an earlier day, the Marshall Plan provided what Stephen A. Schuker calls the "crucial margin" that made European self-help possible. It facilitated essential imports, eased production bottlenecks, encouraged higher rates of capital formation, and helped to suppress inflation, all of which led to gains in productivity, to improvements in trade, and to an era of social peace and prosperity more durable than any other in modern European history.

The same judgment, one that weighs American initiative against European self-help, applies to other aspects of the recovery program as well. There is little doubt that the Marshall Plan helped to modernize budgetary systems in Western Europe or that it encouraged the spread of indicative economic planning, the rationalization of production, the developments of corporative patterns of public-private power sharing, and the conviction that economic growth was the way to ameliorate social divisions. These had been American goals from the start. They were parts of the New Deal synthesis and were pursued with particular vigor through the technical-assistance program, the productivity teams, and the national production centers that Marshall aid helped to establish.

Because of the emphasis on self-help, however, and because the ECA's leverage was less than absolute, the new era that dawned in Western Europe was neither solely the result of American initiative nor fully in line with American thinking. During the course of this century, virtually all of the participating countries had begun to move from the liberal economic order of a bygone day toward what some have called a mixed economic system, others an organized capitalism, still others a corporative political economy. Industry had begun to organize and adopt scientific management techniques. Labor had shown a willingness to abandon redistributive political prescriptions for a labor-management partnership that tied wage gains to productivity rates. Government had assumed new responsibilities for coordinating national economic policy, stimulating growth, and performing other tasks once entrusted to private initiative and automatic market regulators. The Second World War accelerated these transformations, as did the nationalizations of the early postwar period, although neither development displaced the private sector, which remained largely intact, nor fully erased all elements of the liberal ideology. The outcome instead was a European synthesis somewhat similar to its New Deal counterpart. . . .

The American drive to liberate market forces, build institutional coordinators, and integrate economies fell short of the mark set at the inception of the Marshall Plan. But if viewed against the pattern of bilateralism that existed in 1947, or from the perspective of the Treaty of Rome concluded a decade later, it seems clear that American recovery policy helped to set the Europeans on a road that led from the economic autarky of the 1930s to the Common Market of the 1960s. Still more might have been accomplished had the Korean War not intervened and had the Europeans been more cooperative. Although Milward exaggerates when he claims that European leaders defeated the integrationist thrust of American diplomacy, they did throw up barriers that forced the ECA to detour down paths different from those originally charted. . . .

The preceding summary puts the conclusions of Joyce and Gabriel Kolko and other New Left historians in proper perspective. Although the Marshall Plan projected American power into Western Europe on a scale far greater than ever before, it did so to protect what policymakers in Washington regarded as important economic and strategic assets and in a way that was far less heavy-handed than the concurrent interventions in Greece or the subsequent interventions in Central America, Southeast Asia, and other parts of the globe. In these interventions, the United States often slighted indigenous economic and political problems, relied primarily on military solutions, and acted more or less unilaterally. By comparison, the Marshall Plan amounted to a reasonable defense of American interests, one in which the means used were largely positive, largely scaled to the interests involved, and largely applied in collaboration with reliable local elites.

Indeed, American interests coincided to a high degree with how the Europeans defined their own interests. Policymakers on both sides saw the need to rehabilitate the European economies, stabilize political systems, and discourage Communist aggression. [Ernest] Bevin [British foreign secretary] and [George] Bidault [French Foreign Minister] took the initiative in responding to Marshall's speech at Harvard University in June 1947. They joined other European leaders to draft a recovery plan, issued what amounted to an invitation to intervention by the United States, and then collaborated with their American and European colleagues in the transnational system of elite management that arose from the Marshall Plan and NATO. Viewed in this light, the outcome came closer to what Geir Lundestad calls "empire by invitation" and what [Charles] Maier terms "consensual American hegemony" than it does to the naked imperialism described by some New Left writers— and not simply because the Europeans invited American aid but also because the Marshall Plan tended to buttress an established pattern of European politics. As European revisionists have argued, for example, it is probably the case that American aid did not fundamentally alter the political fortunes in countries like France and Italy. Communist parties, though large, would have remained minority factions outweighed by "centrist" coalitions at once too conservative for the Communists and too hidebound, statist, or socialist for the Americans.

In addition, the principle of self-help, to which the Americans generally adhered, gave the Europeans a good deal of control over their own destinies and a good deal of leverage over the Americans. So did the fact that American leaders needed their allies as much as their allies needed them. The British capitalized on this mutual dependence, specifically on concerns about the strategic importance of the sterling area, to deflate American pressure for convertible currencies and negotiate a special position for themselves in the ERP. By warning of socialist gains, of a new Rapallo, and of a dangerous neutralism or a resurgent nationalism, the Germans pried support from Washington even while turning their backs on many of the social reforms and Keynesian strategies urged by the ECA. Likewise, the Americans found it difficult to exert too much pressure on the Italian government, pressure for more aggressive industrial development and for housing reform, income redistribution, and social welfare, lest this pressure strengthen the Communists and tilt a precarious political balance in the wrong direction. Much the same was true in France, where local political and economic elites used threats of a Communist resurgence or a Gaullist triumph to deflect American demands for social reform and faster progress on the German front.

By manipulating American dependence and the principle of self-help, participating governments were able to exercise a considerable degree of autonomy within the framework of the ERP. Recovery continued in the years ahead, as did American aid of a largely military nature, so that Western Europe was able to enter the multilateral world envisioned at Bretton Woods. Measured against this and other gains— against the resolution of the German problem, the containment of Soviet expansion, the stabilization of politics, the revival of production, and the progress made toward industrial reorganization and economic integration—the Marshall Plan must be judged as one of the most successful peacetime foreign policies launched by the United States in this century. But participating countries were not clay in the hands of American potters, these impressive gains notwithstanding. They resisted the social-democratic elements in the New Deal synthesis, adapted other elements to their own needs and traditions, and thus retained much of their original form. In the beginning, the Marshall Plan had aimed to remake Europe in an American mode. In the end, America was made the European way.

Melvyn P. Leffler

THE AMERICAN DRIVE FOR SECURITY: MARSHALL PLAN, REVIVAL OF GERMANY, AND NATO

Much of the scholarly work on the Marshall Plan has focused on its political and economic origins. Melvyn P. Leffler finds that that emphasis ignores the geopolitical, strategic, and military dimensions of the European Recovery Program. Acknowledging that revisionist and corporatist scholars have correctly identified economic self-interest in American policy, Leffler argues that they have generally failed to appreciate the more significant strategic elements of policy. He contends that the primary objective of the United States in implementing the Marshall Plan was to thwart any direct or indirect effort by the Kremlin to co-opt the industrial and military potential of Western Europe for Soviet purposes. In this essay, Leffler seeks to explain the Marshall Plan, the revival and integration of western Germany, and the formation of NATO within a strategic or geopolitical framework. The connecting link for these three efforts was the American determination to stabilize Western Europe economically and politically in order to enhance U.S. security and to deny Western European resources, infrastructure, and bases to the Soviet Union. National security, in his view, not economics, drove America's policy toward postwar Europe.

The purpose of this article is to examine the geopolitical, strategic, and military implications and ramifications of the Marshall Plan. Although American officials hoped the Marshall Plan would benefit the American economy, they also wanted to redress the European balance of power and to enhance American national security. By national security, American officials meant the control of raw materials, industrial infrastructure, skilled manpower, and military bases. And from their viewpoint, the most fundamental strategic interest of the United States was to prevent any potential adversary or coalition of adversaries from mobilizing the resources and economic-military potential of Europe for war-making purposes against the United States.

Melvyn P. Leffler "The United States and the Strategic Dimensions of the Marshall Plan," *Diplomatic History*, XII (Summer 1988), pp. 277–285, 305–306. Copyright © 1988 by Scholarly Resources, Inc. Reprinted by permission of Scholarly Resources, Inc.

In this context, American policymakers had two major objectives and one minor one in launching the Marshall Plan in June 1947. First, they wanted to spawn economic recovery in Western and Southern Europe, undermine the appeal of Communist parties, and thereby circumscribe the latent influence and power of the Kremlin. Second, American officials sought to revive the western zones of Germany and to integrate them into a Western economic and political orbit. Third, and much less central than the preceding two goals, American Marshall Planners hoped to drive a wedge into the emerging Soviet bloc of satellite states in Eastern Europe. Only by accomplishing these aims, especially the two major goals enumerated above, could American officials thwart the Soviet Union's capacity to harness Europe's industrial and military potential for its own purposes.

Because the Marshall Plan was such a momentous attempt to mold the balance of power, it triggered reactions in foreign countries that had far-reaching geopolitical and strategic ramifications. Among the most important of these responses were the consummation of a Western Union and the North Atlantic Treaty, the inauguration of a comprehensive American military assistance program, the redesign of American war plans, and the formation of the Federal Republic of Germany and its integration into a transformed North Atlantic Treaty Organization (NATO). In brief, then, the Marshall Plan was the catalyst that brought about the final divisions of Germany and Europe and institutionalized a stable balance of power in the Old World.

From a strategic and geopolitical viewpoint, however, the impact of the Marshall Plan stretched beyond Europe. The framers of the European Recovery Program (ERP) understood at its inception that the productive capabilities of Europe had to be restored so that the Old World could compete successfully in international markets and earn the foreign exchange necessary to purchase raw materials and foodstuffs. In fact, the dollar gap, which had originally prompted the Marshall Plan, defied easy solution. And because this problem was so intractable, American officials focused significant attention on safeguarding European access to Third World markets and natural resources and on preserving triangular patterns of international trade whereby European nations traditionally earned dollars through American purchases of raw materials. Far from limiting American attention to Europe, the Marshall Plan, along with other considerations, accentuated American interest in those areas around the globe that appeared to be of paramount commercial and financial importance to Britain, France, western Germany, and other participants in the ERP.

American policymakers believed that Western Europe was the most critical region in the world in shaping the postwar balance of power between the United States and the Soviet Union. In their testimony before congressional committees, in their public speeches, and in their confidential discussions, Secretary of State George C. Marshall, Secretary of Commerce W. Averell Harriman, and Secretary of Defense James V. Forrestal emphasized the economic importance of Western Europe in terms of the fundamental national security interests of the United States. Before World War II, Marshall told the House Committee on Foreign Affairs, Western Europe (including western Germany) accounted for 50 percent of the world's trade, owned nearly two-thirds of the world's shipping, and produced such basic industrial goods as coal, steel, and chemicals in amounts slightly exceeding those produced in the United States. Marshall's great fear was that "this very vital area of the world—Western Europe, its industrial potential, its skills, and its energy—[would] pass under the same control which is now exercised over the satellite nations of Eastern Europe." According to the Harriman Committee, direct or indirect Soviet control over Western European resources and manpower would enhance Soviet war-making capabilities enormously and would compel "the swift and complete conversion [of the United States] to a military footing which national security would require."

Marshall, Harriman, George Kennan (director of the Policy Planning Staff [PPS]), and their colleagues did not fear imminent Soviet military aggression. In the spring of 1947, even the war planners in the Joint Chiefs of Staff (JCS) explicitly ruled out a Soviet attack. But American officials did fear the prospect of European economic disintegration, social demoralization, and political upheaval. General Lucius Clay, the American military commander in Germany, lamented "the rapid penetration of communism." Robert Murphy, the State Department political adviser to Clay, maintained that since the war he had never seen German morale so low. Along with news of food riots in the Ruhr came alarming reports of Communist victories in Italian municipal elections, drastic cuts in the French bread ration, and an ominous deterioration in the British financial situation. On his return from the Moscow meeting of foreign ministers in late April, Secretary Marshall declared that Europe was "sinking." A month later Undersecretary of State Will Clayton wrote an important memorandum predicting that "there will be revolution" unless the United States offered extensive financial assistance.

The immediate problem was easy to diagnose. In the wake of a modest recovery during late 1945 and much of 1946, bad harvests, winter snows, and frigid temperatures suddenly beset Europe and created shortages of food and fuel. European countries did not have enough dollars to finance these vital imports. Hence, they faced production cutbacks and unemployment, malnutrition and hunger, monetary disorder and inflation, and proliferating exchange controls and quotas. The most essential task in May 1947 was to expedite the shipment of coal and grain to Europe and to provide European governments with the dollars for payment.

If Europe did not receive massive financial assistance and adopt a coherent recovery program, American officials were fearful that the Communist left would triumph, perhaps even through free elections. At the time, American officials regarded all Communist parties as tools of the Kremlin and as instruments through which the Soviet Union could gain control over key resources, skilled manpower, and strategic bases. This was a key theme underlying reports submitted to the administration by the ad hoc subcommittees of the State-War-Navy Coordinating Committee (SWNCC), by the JCS, by the PPS, by American diplomats in Europe, and by European ambassadors in Washington pleading for additional assistance. If the Communists won in France, Ambassador Jefferson Caffery wrote Marshall on 12 May 1947, "Soviet penetration of Western Europe, Africa, the Mediterranean, and the Middle East would be greatly facilitated" and American security imperiled. By granting billions of dollars for the acquisition of foodstuffs and raw materials, by temporarily filling the dollar gap, by overcoming bottlenecks in production, and by encouraging the balancing of budgets, the convertibility of currencies, the reduction of trade barriers, and the integration of economies, American officials hoped to ameliorate the economic conditions upon which Communists capitalized and to circumscribe the long-term growth of Soviet influence and power. If the United States failed in this endeavor, if European and Russian power were joined together even for a few years, Kennan worried that "there would be the possibility of mobilization and employment of such tremendous economic and military strength . . . as to constitute a real threat to the security of the North American continent."

Before dealing with long-term problems, however, American officials believed that European governments had to take short-term risks, agree to mutual self-help, and implement financial, fiscal, and economic programs that Communists were likely to oppose. Although Marshall declared in his famous Harvard speech on 5 June that "our policy is directed not against any country or doctrine but against hunger, poverty, desperation, and chaos," he and his subordinates already had decided that this policy was not likely to be implemented successfully if Communists remained in the governments of Italy and France. In fact, during May the United States invited, and indeed encouraged, centrist and Socialist political leaders to form coalition governments that excluded the Communists. On 1 May, Marshall broached the possibility of offering additional aid to Italy if Premier Alcide De Gasperi excluded the extreme left. A few days later Ambassador Caffery jotted in his notebook: "I told [French Premier Paul] Ramadier no Communists in gov. or else." On 8 May, in his speech to the Delta Council in Cleveland, Mississippi, Undersecretary of State Dean Acheson emphasized that governments fighting to preserve their so-called independence should receive priority in securing aid. On 20 May, Marshall approved an additional package of emergency assistance to Italy on condition that De Gasperi exclude the Communists.

Of course, politicians in France and Italy had their own reasons for ousting the Communists, but it is questionable whether they would have taken such risks without American encouragement and blandishments. Whether such pressure was decisive or not, it is clear that, once having encouraged the expulsion of the Communists from the governing coalitions of France and Italy, American officials were determined to keep them out lest they hamstring the initiatives desired by the United States. In December 1947, Undersecretary of State Robert Lovett acknowledged that American policy called for the suspension of aid to governments that included Communists. In the spring of 1948, Marshall stated this position publicly in order to warn the Italians that if they voted Communists into power they would forfeit American aid. In October 1948, Caffery told French officials in no uncertain terms that aid would be terminated if they readmitted Communists into the government.

In addition to thwarting indigenous Communists in Western and Southern Europe, the Marshall Plan sought to revive and integrate the western zones of Germany into a Western-oriented economic community. In fact, the rehabilitation of German peacetime productive capabilities had been an essential objective of American foreign policy ever since the summer of 1945, when President Harry S Truman designated the production of 25 million tons of coal by April 1946 as a priority of occupation policy. There were two reasons for this. First and foremost, Ruhr coal was viewed as indispensable for the reconstruction of the rest of Western Europe, for the stabilization of Western European politics, and for the containment of indigenous revolution. Second, German reconstruction was essential to thwart Soviet inroads in all of Germany. The Soviets could hold out the lure of Eastern markets, Polish territory, and German national unification; they could bargain for a participatory role in supervising Ruhr industry; they could covertly maneuver to bolster the influence of German Communists. With the Rapallo and Molotov-Ribbentrop pacts resonating in their minds, American officials were not sure that the Germans would opt for a Western orientation once the occupation was over. And because its exorbitant costs and domestic political repercussions meant that the occupation could not be prolonged indefinitely, there lurked the danger of an eventual Soviet-German coalition in which German industrial resources and technological know-how might be linked to Russian manpower. This was the strategic nightmare not of anonymous Pentagon planners but of Marshall, Forrestal, Secretary of War Robert P. Patterson, Army Chief of Staff Dwight D. Eisenhower, and every other high-ranking American policymaker. "We insist," Kennan confidentially told a group of military officers in April 1947, "that either a central German authority be established along lines that will make it impossible for the Soviet Union to dominate Germany and tap its resources, or that we retain complete control over the western zones of Germany." When Marshall instructed Kennan to work on a program for European recovery, the PPS focused its initial attention on boosting German coal production and on designing plans for Germany's participation in the ERP.

Co-opting western Germany and stabilizing Western Europe were the two key geopolitical concerns of the Marshall Plan, but they were not unrelated to a third, albeit less significant, goal: the dilution of Soviet influence in Eastern Europe. To the extent that Eastern Europe shipped foodstuffs and raw materials to Western Europe, that region's inclusion in the Marshall Plan would foster recovery, reduce Europe's need for dollars, and lessen inflationary pressures in the United States. Marshall, Acheson, Clayton, and Kennan made it clear that Eastern European countries would not receive much assistance but would be welcome to participate if they abandoned their Eastern orientation and agreed to provide supplies to Western Europe. Kennan explicitly acknowledged that the aim was to wean Eastern Europe from the Kremlin. British Foreign Secretary Ernest Bevin instantly perceived Marshall's offer as an attempt to break down the Iron Curtain. Revitalized Western markets, the British foreign secretary told Will Clayton, would be irresistibly attractive to Eastern European countries.

American officials tried to avoid responsibility for the division of Europe, however, by inviting Soviet participation. They recognized that a frontal assault on Soviet communism would complicate participation by European countries with large Communist parties. Still, Kennan and Clayton did not envision the Kremlin as a recipient of substantial aid, at least not in the short run, but as a donor of raw materials. "Russia did not need food, fuel, and fiber and would thus have little basis for participating in the short-term phase," Clayton told Bevin. When the British foreign secretary doubted whether the Soviets would go along if they saw no immediate benefits, Clayton was unperturbed. The real fear was that, notwithstanding the unattractiveness of the terms, the Soviets might join the ERP and sabotage it. This consideration led the British and Americans to dismiss the United Nations Economic Commission for Europe, in which the Soviets participated, as a prospective mechanism for working out the details of the Marshall Plan.

The Soviet decision to meet with the British and French in early July to discuss the European response to Marshall's speech engendered much consternation. Bevin did not want to bear responsibility for an open rift, but he was determined to do nothing to accommodate Soviet concerns or to allay Soviet anxieties. The issues [V. M.] Molotov raised during the trilateral talks in Paris were reasonable. Indeed, his insistence that the Europeans total up their requirements and submit them to the United States resembled what the British and French would do the following month. Likewise, Molotov's inquiries about the effect of the Marshall Plan on German economic recovery and reparation payments paralleled subsequent French concerns. But Bevin presupposed Soviet bad faith, and his intransigence was encouraged by American officials in Paris. British financial stringencies and European economic circumstances precluded prolonged negotiation along the lines of the insufferably tedious meetings of the Council of Foreign Ministers. For Bevin, Europe's future was at stake and he pleaded with [Georges] Bidault to make no concessions. When Molotov received instructions from the Kremlin not to budge, the meeting was deadlocked. In truth, Bevin could hardly wait for its conclusion so he could proceed with an Anglo-French invitation to interested European governments.

As the Paris meeting closed, Molotov warned that Western actions might precipitate the division of Europe. When the Czech and Polish governments showed signs of responding to the lure of American dollars, Stalin forbade it. The Kremlin established the Cominform, clamped down on Eastern Europe, encouraged local Communists to denounce American hegemonic intentions, and supported protests, strikes, and demonstrations in France and Italy. Soviet leaders hoped to make the task of governing these countries impossible without the reentry of Communists into the ruling coalitions. These actions did not surprise American Kremlinologists like Kennan and Charles Bohlen. "Under the pressure of events," wrote Kennan, "particularly our own policies, the Communists are finding themselves subject to a squeeze play." From Moscow, Ambassador [Walter Bedell] Smith also noted the "unpalatable" options engendered by the Marshall Plan for the men in the Kremlin. American officials did not relish the prospect of a divided Europe and an unrestrained cold war, but they accepted both as the price they had to pay to achieve recovery and stability in Western Europe, to thwart indigenous Communists, to integrate western Germany, and to gain preponderant strength in the Old World. . . .

Acheson and other influential leaders within the Truman administration looked increasingly to political-military initiatives to shore up the Western alliance and to sustain the progress initially generated by the Marshall Plan. Britain's opposition to additional measures of economic integration served as a powerful inducement to move in this direction. Although official American statements in the spring of 1950 placed European economic recovery and military rearmament on a level of parity, State Department records clearly illustrate that Acheson and his advisers were most preoccupied with Soviet military capabilities and the political shadows cast by the Kremlin's conventional superiority in view of the possible neutralization of America's nuclear arsenal. NSC 68 and the hydrogen bomb were the clearest manifestations of this viewpoint, but the extensive papers prepared for Acheson in April 1950 in anticipation of his meetings in London with [French Foreign Affairs Minister Robert] Schuman and Bevin also underscore this anxiety. For solutions, Acheson's advisers and military planners began to look to a strengthening of NATO, to a closer American association with it, and to an improvement in its decision-making processes. This reorientation was evident at the London tripartite meetings, as was Acheson's readiness to contemplate Germany's eventual association with NATO, his desire to use German industrial production for Europe's immediate military buildup, and his willingness to extend aid beyond 1952. Acheson did not specify the type of aid to which he was referring, but he probably meant military aid and was thinking of Assistant Secretary of the Army Tracy Voorhees's proposal to merge all economic and military assistance into one package. That proposal, which became known as the mutual security idea, was then beginning to circulate in high policy-making circles and would eventually become national policy.

American decisions after the eruption of the Korean War greatly accelerated the pace at which policy was implemented but did not deviate from the direction it had taken prior to June 1950. The North Korean attack confirmed suspicions of Soviet adventurism and engendered the specter of an East German attack on West Germany. Moreover, the initial success of North Korean troops exposed the West's military weakness, highlighted the prospective vulnerability of European defenses, and accentuated neutralist sentiment, especially in Germany. American diplomats in Europe, State Department officials at Foggy Bottom, and military planners at the Pentagon worried about the interlocking psychological and strategic ramifications of the crisis. European self-doubt and German anxiety could imperil the progress made by the Marshall Plan at the same time that European reconstruction made the defense of Europe and the alignment of Germany with the West all the more essential to American national security. The JCS admonished that "the industrial complexes of the Ruhr, one of the world's most important strategic objectives," could not be relinquished in wartime or allowed to be co-opted by the Kremlin in peacetime. "If we are to defend Western Europe," the JCS declared more stridently than ever before, "German manpower and industrial resources must be employed; and the defensive position must be established east of the Rhine River."

Acheson, [John] McCloy, and other State Department officials concurred. But for them the dilemma was to arm Germany without creating "a separate German force under German command [which] would involve serious risk of their playing off east and west and ultimately joining the Soviets." The answer was to create a European army, including armed German contingents, under the auspices of NATO. "At one step," McCloy argued, "it would fully integrate Germany into Western Europe and be the best possible insurance against further German aggression." A European army that included German divisions and that was based on the principle of balanced collective (not national) forces could play a decisive role in defending European resources, integrating Germany and its neighbors, foreclosing a Soviet-German combination, and creating the psychological and strategic framework for sustaining the momentum of European reconstruction. In order to allay prospective French objections and minimize the risks that inhered in any German rearmament, the United States would deploy additional forces on the Continent, extend additional assistance, and permit an American to assume the responsibilities of supreme commander. It would take another five years to work out the details of these strategic arrangements. But once the ERP was under way, American officials could not escape the task of bolstering Europe's defense and Germany's integration with American military commitments, resources, and leadership.

In addition to spinning a web of political-military commitments in Europe, the Marshall Plan also spawned a host of new interests around the globe. From the very inception of the Marshall Plan, key policymakers like Lovett, Kennan, Colonel Charles Bonesteel, Harriman, and [Lewis W.] Douglas emphasized that the economic recovery and financial stabilization of Europe could not take place if Europe did not have access to markets, raw materials, and foodstuffs in Asia and Africa and if Europe could not earn dollars through overseas investments, especially in Asia. Kennan and Bonesteel talked about integrating Africa and Europe; other officials dwelled upon the importance of Middle East oil for European reconstruction; still others emphasized the negative ramifications of the nationalist struggles in the East Indies, Indochina, and Malaya on the foreign exchange earnings of Holland, France, and Britain.

Integration could help make European industry more competitive, but European governments would not solve their balance-of-payments problems if European manufacturers could not undersell American goods in Third World markets and retain access to sources of supply in nondollar areas. The impediments to trade with Eastern Europe accentuated the economic and financial significance of political developments in Asia and Africa. Therefore, despite their rhetorical commitment to self-determination and their desire for "reform" in these areas of the globe, American officials believed that the "orderly guided development of [Third World] peoples toward political maturity" required "time and patience" and had to occur under the aegis of or in a cooperative relationship with the former colonial powers. . . .

Although the core of the Marshall Plan consisted of an economic program, its geostrategic and military ramifications were great. The

Marshall Plan was designed to thwart Europe's indigenous left, co-opt western Germany, and lure Soviet satellites away from the Kremlin. It strategic aim was to prevent the Kremlin from gaining direct or indirect control over European resources, industrial infrastructure, skilled manpower, and military bases. When the Soviet clamped down on Eastern Europe, when unrest intensified in Southern and Western Europe, and when a crisis over Germany appeared unavoidable, American officials recognized that new initiatives were essential to deter the Kremlin, reassure the French, and ensure the success of the Marshall Plan. Therefore, they agreed to retain American occupation troops in Germany indefinitely, to accept strategic commitments, to grant military aid, and to redesign contingency war plans.

But if Western Europe were to be reconstructed, its resources had to be safeguarded. Germany had to be revived, but it also had to be integrated and rearmed, for without German steel, coal, and manpower, Europe could not be defended. Western statesmen, however, would not contemplate German political autonomy and rearmament unless its latent power were balanced and its ties to the West institutionalized through a network of unbreachable financial, economic, and military arrangements. Since the Schuman Plan did not suffice and since Britain rebuffed closer economic and military ties to the Continent, American policymakers decided to utilize NATO as the mechanism for binding the Federal Republic of Germany to the West, containing the Kremlin, and sustaining the progress initiated by the Marshall Plan. Through NATO, the United States would assume military leadership, deploy forces, and institutionalize military aid long after the ERP expired.

These initiatives helped to bolster confidence, stimulate production, and establish a remarkably stable balance of power on the Continent. Initially, however, they appeared to leave Western Europe's payments problems unresolved. During the spring of 1950 consternation was widespread as American officials recognized that, if the dollar gap were not closed, Europe's long-term stability might falter and Germany's integration might unravel. So the imperatives of the Marshall Plan, along with other factors, encouraged American officials to look beyond Europe to safeguard markets, raw materials, and investment earnings in the Third World. Revolutionary nationalism had to be thwarted outside Europe, just as the fight against indigenous communism had to be sustained inside Europe. In this interconnected attempt to grapple with the forces of the left and the potential power of the Kremlin resides much of the international history, strategy, and geopolitics of the Cold War era.   And among the pillars of American policy stands the Marshall Plan.

Thomas J. McCormick

ECONOMIC CRISIS AND AMERICAN MILITARIZATION, 1949–1950

An early proponent of revisionism, Thomas J. McCormick seeks to reformulate that interpretation in his book *America's Half-Century* (1989). Drawing on world-systems theory, he stresses the primacy of economic forces in international relations.   American Cold War policies cannot be understood without reference to the larger structural crisis that plagued postwar capitalism. As the world's leading capitalist power, contends McCormick, the United States sought to create a unitary, integrated world-system—or a system of hegemony. The United States succeeded initially in repairing the structural imbalances caused by world depression and world war, but by 1949–1950 American policy faced a new crisis. The persisting dollar gap, the Soviet detonation of an atomic bomb, and the victory of the Chinese communists, according to McCormick, combined to create one of the most momentous crises of the entire postwar era. The Truman administration responded with what McCormick calls "the militarization option," a policy direction that culminated with the adoption of National Security Council Paper 68 (NSC-68) in early 1950.

Thomas J. McCormick is a professor of history at the University of Wisconsin, Madison.   He has also written *China Market: America's Quest for Informal Empire, 1893–1901* (1967) and coedited *America in Vietnam: A Documentary History* (1985).

On a gloomy, grey, Friday afternoon, February 21, 1947, the British embassy delivered a "blue piece of paper"—an extraordinarily important note—to American Under Secretary of State Dean Acheson.   It announced Britain's intentions to end its military and financial support of the Greek monarchy and the Turkish government within the ensuing thirty days.   The announcement climaxed seven days that had seen

Thomas J. McCormick, *America's Half-Century: United States Foreign Policy in the Cold War*.   The Johns Hopkins University Press, Baltimore/London, 1989, pp. 72–73, 88–98.

Britain end its three-decade control of Palestine and its centuries-old dominion over India. Three days after receiving the "blue note" and following a weekend of frenetic State Department activity, Acheson mused aloud to a journalist friend on their way to lunch at the Metropolitan Club: "There are only two powers left. The British are finished, they are through. And the trouble is that this hits us too soon, before we are ready for it. We are having a lot of trouble getting money out of Congress."

Ready or not, the denouement of British imperium in the eastern Mediterranean would provoke a rapid and decisive American initiative to fill the void. Its most dramatic manifestation would be the Truman Doctrine. Neither British action nor American reaction, however, was as important as the larger context in which both took place. The crisis of British disengagement was but part of a much larger structural crisis in postwar capitalism, exacerbated by a challenge from the Soviet empire. And the Truman Doctrine was but a stop-gap response to that larger crisis, both less important and less enduring than the revolutionary responses embodied in the Marshall Plan of 1948 and the North Atlantic Treaty Organization in 1949. Even those measures, for all their startling innovativeness, would not remedy capitalism's troubles. Renewed structural crisis and renewed Russian challenge in late 1949 and early 1950 would dictate an even more revolutionary turn in American foreign policy. Its ultimate expression would be National Security Council document paper #68, NSC-68. Its consequence would be a new kind of cold war, one both more militaristic and more Third World oriented. . . .

A contemporary television sports program talks about "the thrill of victory and the agony of defeat." From August 1949 until April 1950, American leaders endured the psychic fragmentation of experiencing both feelings at once. On one hand, the United States had weathered the initial structural crisis in world capitalism and responded effectively with the ideological, economic, political, and military innovations of the Truman Doctrine, the Marshall Plan, and NATO. But, like some cosmic dialectic, history repeated and embroidered itself with renewed and deepened crisis in late 1949 and early 1950. The world-system seemed once more threatened from within, this time by the calamitous consequences of the American "reverse course" policy in Japan and by the continued bottlenecks and dollar shortages that plagued the European Recovery Program. (At the same time, this internal crisis was exacerbated from without by Russian acquisition of the atomic bomb and by the triumph of the Chinese communists in the Chinese civil war.)

The near catastrophe of America's Japan policy was more immediately frightening than any other facet of the renewed crisis. Since 1948, the United States had reversed its earlier course of decentralizing and democratizing Japanese economic life. American occupation authorities had ceased efforts to break up large-scale monopoly capital (the *Zeibatsu*) and were exploring strategies of reindustrialization instead. This "reverse course" reflected a number of factors. The U.S. Congress was anxious to make the Japanese occupation self-supporting, able to sustain itself without American subsidies; and the ERP burden of $17 billion only made Congress more eager to put Japan on a pay-as-you-go footing. In addition, American occupation authorities were fearful that earlier attempts at economic decentralization had strengthened the political hand of Japanese communists and socialists. While Japanese radicals preferred nationalization of private industry, they saw competitive capitalism as more acceptable than monopoly capital, because it diminished the power of traditional industrial oligarchs. Finally, the obvious collapse of the Chinese nationalists and the likely triumph of the Chinese communists had killed any notion of China's acting as a regional surrogate for the United States. Only Japan seemed a likely role model to demonstrate to the rest of Asia the advantages of a pro-capitalist, prointegrationist model of economic development. To play the role effectively, however, Japanese industry had to be organized on the same principles as that in North America and the OEEC [Organization for European Economic Cooperation] countries: large-scale, specialized production for the world market that would reap the higher profits of comparative advantage and economies of scale.

Following the blueprint laid out by Joseph Dodge, a prominent banker and consultant, the American government instituted the Dodge Plan in late 1948 and early 1949. It aimed at reviving Japanese industrial productivity, making export goods competitive in world markets, and putting the economy on a self-sustaining basis. While clearly similar to ERP goals for Europe, the Dodge Plan differed in one fundamental way. European reindustrialization was geared as much to the enlargement of an integrated domestic market as it was to giving European nations a greater share of the world market. Japan's reindustrialization was focused more single-mindedly on production for export, and not until 1960 would the Japanese home market receive equivalent stress. This difference had profound implications for Japanese social and economic policy.   Specifically, Japanese workers tended to be viewed largely as cost-factors rather than potential consumers, and this put a greater premium on keeping wage bills as low as possible so Japanese exports could underprice competitors.

Reflecting this difference, the Dodge Plan was even more wedded to austerity measures than was the Marshall Plan.   The latter had financed itself from the pocketbooks of both American taxpayers and European workers.   The former attempted to finance itself almost entirely out of labor's decreased share of national income.   Accordingly, the Dodge Plan called for severe cuts in social services, a sharp reduction of government employees, repression of the more militant labor unions, Draconian measures to outlaw and suppress strikes, reduction of wages to subsistence levels at which three-quarters of income went for food, and a balanced budget to halt inflation and enhance Japan's competitive position in world trade.   Intense resistance by Japanese trade unions did soften American policy somewhat, but by and large the Dodge Plan was enacted as envisioned.

Its consequences, however, were far from anticipated.   Industrial productivity did increase perceptibly, but buyers for those products did not materialize.   The austerity program forcibly repressed domestic demand while various factors continued to inhibit foreign demand. Civil war and revolution severely limited Japan's traditional markets in China, Southeast Asia, and Northeast Asia.   Moreover, protective tariffs still restricted access to North America and Europe, and the Americans retained an insuperable advantage in the high-profit product lines that Japan was determined to enter.   By late 1949 and early 1950, Japan's trade deficit with the United States (its counterpart of Europe's dollar gap) was rising as fast as the strength of the yen was falling.   More than a few Japanese and American observers feared that Japan stood on the precipice of economic catastrophe, in a situation akin to a business teetering on the brink of bankruptcy.   One of earth's four great industrial cores was in danger of becoming a dysfunctional part of the world-system and a drag on the whole.

Compounding that systemic problem were parallel shortcomings in the European core.   The Marshall Plan at midpassage had hardly closed the dollar gap.   Europe still financed a third of its American imports out of grant dollars, while private profits were slow to generate the dollars to take up the slack.   Indeed, dollar scarcity in Britain was so severe that even the United States had to accept the necessity of a sharp devaluation of the pound from $4.03 to $2.80 in September 1949.

Since the ERP was set to expire in 1952 and Congress was unlikely to extend it, there remained real fear that the persistent dollar gap would yet wreak havoc on American exports and European recovery. Secretary of State Acheson summed up the situation in early 1950: "Put in its simplest terms, the problem is this: as ERP is reduced, and after its termination in 1952, how can Europe and other areas of the world obtain the dollars necessary to pay for a high level of U.S. exports, which is essential both to their own basic needs, and to the well-being of the American economy. This is the problem of the 'dollar gap' in world trade."

Part of Europe's continuing difficulties were supply-side problems of nagging bottlenecks in European productivity. Still, these seemed soluble problems and productivity, for both factory and farm, had generally increased. The greater problem seemed on the demand side. As George Kennan put it in August 1949, *"It is one thing to produce; it is another thing to sell."* (Emphasis added.) As in Japan, austerity measures had dampened domestic demand, the Cold War had restricted access to the "socialist" markets, and congressional protectionism and a serious American recession in early 1949 had caused the major capitalist market to contract. Nor did the anticipated alternatives materialize as easily as hoped. European integrationism lagged as the ECA focused on the more immediate problem of production snarls, so inter-European trade and the common market movement were stymied until the European Payments Union helped free the course of commerce in 1950.

To make matters worse, the periphery failed to fill the void. Production of primary commodities in Europe's traditional spheres of influence was static and inadequate. Parts of the periphery, especially in Asia, were beset by wars of national liberation against Western colonialism or by civil wars to see who would rule at home once the imperialists were gone. Even relatively tranquil territories were often more interested in developing domestic manufacturing than in increasing raw material production for their core customers. Because primary commodity production grew so slowly in relation to Europe's demand, Europe paid higher prices for its raw materials than did the United States; and the added costs undercut Europe's ability to compete with America in the world market. It also meant that because Europe's periphery made so little money out of its low-volume exports, it lacked the means to pay for significant amounts of European imports. In short, the revival of European industrial productivity had far less positive impact than expected because it was not accompanied by a parallel and complementary revival of primary commodity productivity in the periphery. The Third World (as it was soon to be called) needed to play its role (assigned it by the core powers) as efficient supplier of low-cost raw materials and as efficient supplemental market for finished products from the core.

This renewed crisis within the world-system was deepened by critical developments in the external world, in both the Russian and the Chinese empire. In two trip-hammer blows that shook the self-confidence of the capitalist world, Russia acquired the atomic bomb and China went communist. The first event broke the half-decade atomic monopoly enjoyed by the United States and provoked a heated debate among American leaders about its implications. Some feared that by 1954, when Russia might have a meaningful weapons stockpile and a delivery system, the USSR would be a serious threat to world peace. Under Secretary of State Robert Lovett, for example, warned, "We are now in a mortal combat. . . . It is not a cold war. It is a hot war." Others disdained that worst-case scenario and were inclined to regard the Russians as inherently cautious and disinclined to take high risks. George Kennan argued that the Soviet A-bomb added "no new fundamental element to the picture," and he saw "little justification for the impression that the 'cold war' . . . has suddenly taken some turn to our disadvantage." Still under his influence, the Policy Planning Staff of the State Department concluded there was little likelihood of a Russian attack on either the United States or its allies, even after 1954.

Both groups, however, agreed that Russian atomic diplomacy might be dangerous even if Russian atomic weaponry was not. However secure some Americans might feel, Europe and Japan were less likely to be sanguine about Russian intentions. Sharing a physical proximity to the USSR, they were apt to be more concerned about the coupling of the Red Army with the atomic bomb. Likewise, both might have been uncertain that America would risk atomic attack on its homeland to defend them against the Russian empire. They might question the credibility of the American military shield to protect the system. Such fears of the Soviets and doubts about the Americans might easily have led other core capitalist powers to waver in their deference to American hegemony and might have tempted them to play the Russian card in ways that would undermine the new world order for which America had fought World War II.

At the same time, the Chinese communists completed their triumph in the civil war as the last substantial nationalist forces fled the mainland to Taiwan. Communist victory heightened the possibility that China would exit the capitalist world-system, and that prospect seemed more certain with the signing of the Sino-Soviet pact of February 1950, creating a bilateral defense commitment, a settlement of historic territorial issues, and a modest Russian economic aid program. This Chinese departure prompted a famous State Department white paper to defend the administration from charges of culpability by "Pacific rim Republicans," but it also stirred an important debate within the executive branch on the nature and importance of the "loss" of China.

Asian specialists among career bureaucrats tended to think that China was not a Russian puppet, notwithstanding the 1950 treaty, and believed that preconditions existed for splitting the two apart and enticing China back into the world-system. Moreover, they dismissed the notion of foreign adventurism by China and assumed that, once Taiwan was captured, China would devote itself to internal affairs and the task of building a new China. Only if provoked would China intervene in Northeast or Southeast Asia. Global thinkers among more highly-placed "ins-and-outers" assumed otherwise: that China already was part of a monolithic external area (international communism) hostile to the American world order and that China would quickly try to export its revolution eastward into Korea and southward into French Indochina.

In one crucial sense, the internal debate was a moot one that made it immaterial which group was right and which was wrong. Whether China was expansionist or not, a Russian lackey or not, the communist revolution had usurped almost all of Northeast Asia from the world-system (North China, Manchuria, North Korea). That area historically had been Japan's most important market and source of raw materials. Given the near bankruptcy of Japan by early 1950, there was real fear among American leaders that beleaguered Japan might be forced to strike a bargain with China. If that occurred, it might spell the beginning of a Japanese drift away from integration with the American-dominated international system and toward an autarkic, regional arrangement with the Asian mainland. Such a direction taken by Japan might well undermine the very goals for which the United States had fought the Pacific war.

From 1947 to early 1950, the American foreign policy elite had persisted in its hegemonic pursuit of a unitary, integrated world-system.

Confronted with Russian opposition, European reluctance, and popular ambivalence at home, American leaders had addressed the structural imbalance in world capitalism that was the chief legacy of world depression and world war. The Truman Doctrine tried to ease Britain's dollar gap while creating the ideological justification for isolating Russia outside of the world-system. It also provided part of the raison d'être for the Marshall Plan and the more ambitious project of European reconstruction and the integration of a reindustrialized Germany into what they hoped would soon be a common market. In turn, NATO provided the political-military-psychic glue to keep Europe together and in the world-system even when the tenure of the Marshall Plan had elapsed. Then, at the height of the American triumph—with NATO secured, West Germany established, and Russian opposition in the Berlin blockade crushed—some hidden hand seemed to pull the plug. The failure of the Dodge Plan in Japan, the shortcomings of the Marshall Plan in Europe, the Russian termination of America's atomic bomb monopoly, and the loss of China to the world-system—all combined to produce yet another crisis, this one of a magnitude that would not be seen again for thirty years. In short, by late 1949 and early 1950, American policymakers faced the awesome task of getting European and Japanese reindustrialization and reconstruction back on track while keeping Europe from playing the Russian card and Japan from playing the China card. Their response would be a staggering reorientation of American foreign policy that would determine its shape and direction for the next twenty-three years.

The Truman administration confronted three alternative ways to respond to this tripartite crisis of the dollar gap, the Russian A-bomb, and the Chinese revolution. One option was to acknowledge the altered equation of world power and to negotiate with the Soviet Union over nuclear arms, German policy, and the status of China. Save for a small group of careerists in the State Department, headed by George Kennan, that was not an option afforded serious consideration by American leaders. *Any* negotiations with Russia, whatever their results, seemed likely to endow that country with a certain legitimacy and co-equal "super-power" status. Such a move seemed tantamount to an end of containment and a readmission of Russia to the world-system, which in turn would mean a diminution of American hegemony.

Such developments could only erode free world deference to American-style internationalism and facilitate separate arrangements by Europe and Japan with the Russian-dominated external world that seemed now to stretch from the Elbe to the Amur. Moreover, any concrete results of Russo-American negotiations could only make such consequences more probable. For example, mutual agreement to forego development of the H-bomb ("the super") could only diminish America's role as nuclear umbrella and military shield for the world-system. Neutralization of a reunified Germany could only impair the American policy of integrationism and raise the specter that any future shift to the left in German politics would also produce a shift to the east in German foreign policy. Recognition of the People's Republic of China would legitimize any Japanese tendency toward accommodation with mainland Asia.

The second American option was to do more of what it had been doing: concentrate on the internal problem central to the world-system, namely the dollar gap crisis, and elaborate upon the tested tools of economic diplomacy epitomized by the ERP. What that meant in the long haul was a lowering of American tariff walls to make it easier for Europe and Japan to earn dollars directly by selling in the American market or indirectly by having their customers in the periphery earn dollars by exporting primary commodities to the United States. In the interim, what that suggested was an extension of the ERP beyond its 1952 cut-off date and a parallel "Marshall Plan for Asia," a temporary plug to the dollar gap until the demand-stimulus of the American market could effect a permanent seal. This option was initially favored by the Policy Planning Staff of the State Department and endorsed by representatives of international business and chief executives of both the AFL and the CIO.

Two factors, however, made the choice impracticable in the early 1950s. Domestically, foreign aid legislation and tariff liberalization faced insurmountable opposition from a hostile Congress influenced by interest groups seeking to protect domestic jobs and markets, by fiscal conservatives trying to balance the budget, by Pacific regionalists persuaded of a European bias in American economic diplomacy, and by middle-class taxpayers unwilling to subsidize foreign consumption at the expense of their own. But even if that domestic opposition could be overcome, an extension of pre-1950 economic diplomacy could not address other considerations raised by the 1949–50 crisis. It could not assuage the fears of those who anticipated a real Russian military threat to the world-system after the mid-1950s. It could not reassure Europe and Japan of the reliability of the American military shield and thus reinforce their acceptance of American hegemony. It could not discipline unstable parts of the periphery to end their revolutions, forego forced industrialization, and accept their subordinate place in the world economic division of labor.

The third alternative was to opt for massive militarization. Concretely, that came to mean the development of the H-bomb; the quadrupling of the military budget, from $14 billion in 1950 to $53 billion in 1952; the expansion of conventional forces, including six permanent divisions in central Europe; the doubling of the air force to ninety-five groups with new strategic bases in Morocco, Libya, Saudia Arabia, and Spain; the transformation of NATO from a political to a military alliance and the addition to NATO of Turkey and Greece; the rebuilding of a German army and its integration into NATO forces; and finally, the substitution of military aid for economic-technical assistance and the merger of both forms in one program in the Mutual Security Act of 1951.

That militarized option was, in economic terms, less ideal than the option of expanded economic diplomacy. There were some well-grounded fears that governmental military purchases might become a substitute for the export of surplus domestic production and thus diminish the demand for multilateral trade and programs that fostered it. Indeed, foreign aid bills did face even tougher sledding and administration efforts to ratify the International Trade Organization (ITO) charter for trade liberalization never made it out of congressional committee. More importantly, massive military spending raised the possibility—again made real over time—that government subsidization of profits would siphon away funds for technical research and capital investment from the civilian goods sector, leaving it less innovative and undercapitalized and thus less competitive in the world economy. Finally, American rearmament would necessitate at least a measure of the same from Europe, a sign to Congress that American taxpayers would not shoulder the whole burden of militarization. While that burden was modest for most European economies, it was heavy for Great Britain, attempting to maintain its military contributions to NATO, the Commonwealth, the Near East, and the Korean War as well. Certainly, that factor helped cause the sterling crisis of 1951–52 and led to a general loss of British foreign markets to German competition.

Countervailing economic advantages, political imperatives, and diplomatic goals combined, however, to outweigh those material shortcomings of the militarization option. Many of the economic calculations were positive. Military spending, in the short term, would salvage the troubled aviation industry and might generate recovery from the American recession of 1949–50. In the medium term, it could maintain full productivity and employment until multilateralism was in place and world trade revived. It might prove more a technological stimulus than a deterrent, especially in electronics and the new sphere of atomic power. Moreover, military aid and military subcontracts to foreign corporations would provide a way to launder foreign aid dollars—that is, to maintain the financial tranfusion to address the dollar gap, but to do it in the name of national security rather than economic internationalism. Not only did those military aid dollars release European and Japanese capital to develop civilian technology and production, they helped make the periphery a better market for their products. In effect, American military spending, with its insatiate demand for raw materials, fueled a world-wide triangular trade in which the periphery exported raw materials to the United States, which in turn exported capital goods and food to Europe and Japan, which exported finished consumer goods to the periphery.

Politically, the militarization choice seemed the only one that could override domestic resistance on the right. Relatively quiescent since 1948, those right-wing elements revived in the congressional election of 1950, which produced a freshman senatorial class headed by Richard Nixon. Tacitly supported and used by mainstream Republicans, the politics of this element took an ominous turn in the McCarthyism and "Red Scare" witch hunts of alleged communists and fellow-travellers in government and in education, the media, and entertainment. However disreputable, McCarthyites and their sympathizers gained credibility from the administration's own internal security programs, from labor union purges of their left-wing opposition, and from business blacklisting of dissidents. That credibility made them a potent source of opposition to administration foreign policy.

Influenced by Pacific regionalists in their midst, many conservatives questioned the "Asia last" policy of the administration (to quote the Republican platform of 1952), echoing General Douglas MacArthur's belief that Europe was "a dying system" and that America's future lay in the western rimlands of the Pacific basin. Not only did the right-wing opposition question policy, it questioned policymakers themselves. Drawing on a constituency of midwestern small businessmen, Sun Belt *nouveau riche* oil men and land developers, and some Americans of Irish, German, and East European backgrounds, that opposition harbored a steady antagonism to the eastern, Yankee, Protestant patricians that they perceived as making policy. ("Fordham's revenge on Harvard" was used as a characterization of McCarthyism.) In that political context, only the alternative of militarization could keep the rightist opposition inside a Cold War consensus. Only an option couched in anticommunism and national security concerns could demonstrate to political critics that the administration's ideology was as pure as Caesar's wife. What had been expedient in selling the Truman Doctrine and the Marshall Plan in 1947 and 1948 now became an ironic imperative in the early 1950s.

Finally, and most importantly, the militarization choice did address three policy considerations not wholly confronted by economic diplomacy: national security, European integrationism, and Third World development. Its stress on American and European rearmament appealed to those, in and out of government, who took a Russian military threat seriously or who simply thought it prudent, in a nuclear age, to operate on the basis of a worst-case scenario. Its reaffirmation of America's role as military protector of the world-system—especially by the building of the H-bomb and an increased conventional presence in Europe—would reassure other core powers of the reliability and efficacy of that protection and keep them oriented to the American goal of integrated production and a common market for Europe itself. Indeed, the American effort to rearm Germany was a powerful incentive to European economic cooperation; it provided the most likely means to subsume German freedom of action—including the freedom to do military mischief—within a matrix of economic interdependence. And the stress on military capabilities might provide an important tool to facilitate the systematic development of Third World extractive economies, so they might function more effectively as markets and raw material providers for European and Japanese recovery. Since much of the periphery, especially the Asian rimlands, was destabilized by war and revolution, military pacification and forced stabilization seemed likely prerequisites to rapid and predictable economic growth. So an updated "big stick" became a potential weapon for coercing parts of the periphery to accept the American rules for the international game.

The National Security Council adopted the militarization option in early 1950, and President Truman examined and approved in principle its position document (NSC-68) in April. One of the most pivotal policy documents in American history, NSC-68 began with an historical preamble that sketched the decline of British paramountcy, the twice-attempted German challenge, the disintegration of European empires, and the Cold War competition for hegemony between the United States and the Soviet Union. Picturing the latter as a revolutionary, fanatical power, driven toward domination of the Eurasian land mass and ultimately the world, the document argued that only superior military force could deter it. Formulated chiefly by Secretary of State Acheson and the new Policy Planning Staff chief, Paul Nitze, this characterization of the Soviet Union evoked sharp protests from within that same department by Russian experts and careerists, notably George Kennan and Charles Bohlen. They counterargued that Russian foreign policy was motivated more by limited geopolitical and geoeconomic goals than by limitless revolutionary zeal. Consequently they urged that NSC-68 either be modified or junked altogether and that ERP-style economic diplomacy be reaffirmed.

While acknowledging possible hyperbole in the policy document, both Nitze and Acheson insisted that the militarization alternative was the only one that could be sold to Congress as well as the Bureau of the Budget and the General Accounting Office. Moreover, it was the only choice that dealt with all the exigencies and long-term concerns generated by the crisis of 1949–50. Whatever the merits of the respective arguments, Kennan and Bohlen were out-gunned. Possessing no power base outside the ranks of State Department bureaucracy, they were no match for their in-and-outer opponents, who not only held positions of greater influence within the government but were plugged into outside sources of power in the Democratic party and the world of corporate business and law.

In its final form, NSC-68 called not only for massive military spending but for significant tax increases to fund it, a reduction of social welfare programs and all services not related to military needs, a civil defense program, tighter loyalty programs for internal security, greater media efforts to build a public opinion consensus for Cold War policies, and psychological warfare and propaganda to encourage popular uprisings in Eastern Europe and Russia itself. The last rested on the possibility that a quantum jump in the arms race might distort the Soviet-bloc economies so badly, and so delay consumer gratification of its subjects, that it might spark internal upheaval.

No precise dollar tag was assigned by NSC-68 to the militarization policy, but guesses by staff people ranged from $37 to $50 billion per year—triple the amount originally requested by the Pentagon for 1950. How to get that kind of money from a fiscally conservative

Congress, even in the name of anticommunism, presented no small task for the administration. What was required was an international emergency, and since November 1949, Secretary Acheson had been predicting that one would occur sometime in 1950 in the Asian rimlands— in Korea, Vietnam, Taiwan, or all three. Two months after the President examined NSC-68, that crisis happened. Acheson was to say later, "Korea came along and saved us."

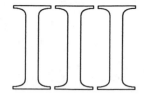

Toward a Global Cold War

John Lewis Gaddis

THE DEFENSIVE PERIMETER STRATEGY IN EAST ASIA

How did United States–Soviet tensions, initially focused on Western Europe
and the eastern Mediterranean, spread to engulf virtually the entire world?
When and why did American diplomats and generals come to see the Soviet
threat in global terms? When and why did they seek to extend containment,
originally a Eurocentric defense strategy, to Asia, the Middle East, Latin
America, and Africa? These questions have stirred intense debate. In this
essay, John Lewis Gaddis explores the defensive perimeter strategy that
United States planners formulated for postwar East Asia. The United States
determined to safeguard its principal interests in that region by defending
offshore islands while avoiding direct commitments on the Asian mainland,
especially in China. This strategy, which Gaddis applauds for its realism,
guided Truman administration policy until the outbreak of the Korean War
on June 25, 1950. The North Korean invasion, and the wider communist
military threat that it seemed to portend, shattered the fragile consensus
undergirding the defensive perimeter strategy and led to direct American
intervention in Korea, Taiwan, and Indochina. Gaddis disparages the accelerating globalist orientation of American foreign policy. He criticizes American officials for failing after the Korean War to distinguish vital from
peripheral interests, for failing to coordinate means with ends, and for
allowing their concerns about America's credibility to shape policy
decisions.

One of the frustrations of being a statesman is that one's speeches are
not always remembered for the reasons one wants them to be. Few
have had better cause to acknowledge this difficulty than Dean Acheson, whose National Press Club speech of January 12, 1950, intended
as the enunciation of a new East Asian strategy in the wake of China's
"fall" to communism, has more often been recalled as having invited the
North Korean attack on South Korea through its exclusion of that latter country from the American "defensive perimeter" in the Pacific.
Acheson always insisted that his speech only reflected established policy

Excerpted from *The Long Peace: Inquiries into the History of the Cold War* by John Lewis
Gaddis, pp. 72–103. Copyright © 1987 by John Lewis Gaddis. Reprinted by permission
of Oxford University Press, Inc.

and could not have had the effect attributed to it; still one wonders whether privately he may not have felt, as General J. Lawton Collins later suggested, "like a batter swinging at a bad ball [who] would have liked to have had that swing back again."

Given presently available evidence, it is impossible to confirm or refute charges that Acheson's speech encouraged the North Koreans to attack. Sufficient evidence does exist, though, to demonstrate that there was nothing casual or inadvertent about his proclaimed strategy of defending offshore islands while avoiding direct commitments on the Asian mainland. By the time Acheson spoke, this "defensive perimeter" concept had received endorsements from the Commander in Chief, Far East, the Joint Chiefs of Staff, the National Security Council, and the President of the United States. The product of no single individual or agency within the government, it had nonetheless come to be accepted, by early 1950, as the most appropriate strategic posture for the United States in East Asia.

But this consensus in support of the "defensive perimeter" proved to be remarkably fragile. Within six months, the Truman administration had reversed its own strategy: it had committed air, naval, and ground forces to the defense of South Korea, it had accelerated military assistance to the French in Indochina, and, by sending the Seventh Fleet to patrol the Taiwan Strait, it had involved the United States directly in the Chinese civil war. This abrupt turnabout reveals much about shifting perceptions of interests and threats in East Asia at the time; it is, as well, an illuminating commentary—as was Acheson's Press Club speech—on the gap between the intentions of statesmen and the consequences of their actions.

"Today, so far as I can learn, we are operating without any overall strategic concept for the entire western Pacific area." This warning, contained in a March, 1948, message from George F. Kennan, Director of the State Department's Policy Planning Staff, to Secretary of State George C. Marshall, did much to stimulate thinking within the government on American priorities in East Asia. With his recipient's background obviously in mind, Kennan apologized "for being so bold, as a civilian, to offer suggestions on matters which are largely military; but it is essential that some over-all pattern including military as well as the political factors be evolved." He then went on to propose the following as "the most desirable political-strategic concept for the western Pacific area":

1. While we would endeavor to influence events on the mainland of Asia in ways favorable to our security, we would not regard any mainland areas as vital to us. Korea would accordingly be evacuated as soon as possible.

2. Okinawa would be made the center of our offensive striking power in the western Pacific area. It would constitute the central and most advanced point of a U-shaped U.S. security zone embracing the Aleutians, the Ryukyus, the former Japanese mandated islands, and of course Guam. We would then rely on Okinawa-based air power, plus our advance naval power, to prevent the assembling and launching [of] any amphibious force from any mainland port in . . . east-central or northeast Asia.

3. Japan and the Philippines would remain outside this security area, and we would not attempt to keep bases or forces on their territory, *provided* that they remained entirely demilitarized and that no other power made any effort to obtain strategic facilities on them. They would thus remain neutralized areas, enjoying complete political independence, situated on the immediate flank of our security zone.

If Washington could accept this approach, then "we would have firm points of orientation for our short-term policies in this area." Without some such concept, "we cannot move at all." Kennan concluded: "I need hardly stress the desirability of an early clarification of our policy in this area in view of the trend of world events and the necessity of having all our hatches battened down for the coming period."

Kennan found few objections to this strategy when he discussed it with General Douglas MacArthur in Tokyo that same month. MacArthur proposed a defensive line including the Aleutians, Midway, the former Japanese mandated islands, Okinawa, the Philippines, Australia, New Zealand, and the British and Dutch islands in the southwest Pacific. Okinawa, he stressed, was the strongpoint: from it he could control each of the ports in northern Asia from which an amphibious operation could be launched. He also agreed with Kennan that it would not be desirable to retain United States troops permanently in Japan, although he did consider it necessary to hold on to Clark Field in the Philippines. For the next year and a half, MacArthur would repeatedly express the idea that as a result of World War II the American strategic frontier had shifted from the West Coast to the Asian offshore island chain, and that the security of the United States depended on keeping those islands out of hostile hands.

By the summer of 1949, the concept of a "defensive perimeter" had also become widely accepted in Washington. A Central Intelligence Agency study in May stressed the importance of the offshore islands in facilitating access to the strategic raw materials of India and Southeast Asia, especially if the Suez route should be closed. The Joint Chiefs of Staff informed the National Security Council in June that "from the military point of view, the ultimate minimum United States position in the Far East vis-à-vis the USSR, one to which we are rapidly being forced, requires at least our present degree of control of the Asian offshore chain." In November, an internal State Department memorandum cited Pentagon authorities in support of the proposition that "our position is not directly jeopardized by the loss of China so long as the security of the islands continues to be maintained." And a draft National Security Council paper concluded the following month that the "minimum position" required to defend Asia "against future Soviet aggression" would consist of "at least our present military position in the Asian offshore island chain, and in the event of war its denial to the Communists."

Acheson was hardly breaking new ground, then, when he told the National Press Club that "this defensive perimeter runs along the Aleutians to Japan and then goes to the Ryukyus . . . [and] from the Ryukyus to the Philippine Islands." As he later recalled, "with the authority of the Joint Chiefs of Staff and General MacArthur behind me, it did not occur to me that I should be charged with innovating policy or political heresy." But an examination of the assumptions that had led the State Department, the Joint Chiefs, and MacArthur to agree on this concept reveals striking disparities; these in turn suggest the unstable nature of the consensus upon which the "defensive perimeter" strategy rested and help to account for the rapidity of its demise.

The State Department based its support of the "defensive perimeter" idea on a strong sense of pessimism regarding the ability of the United States to influence events on the Asian mainland. The frustrating outcome of General Marshall's mission to China just prior to his entering the Department had done much to generate this sense of discouragement; Marshall's own considerable influence as Secretary of State strongly reinforced it. The Department did yield to Congressional pressures for a limited program of economic and military aid to Nationalist China in 1948, but it did so more for the purpose of defusing opposition to the European Recovery Program than from any conviction that aid to China might actually be effective. Acheson, upon becoming Secretary of State, made no effort to conceal his own skepticism. In his August, 1949, letter transmitting the China "White Paper" to the President, he argued bluntly with reference to Chiang Kai-shek's

[Jiang Jiesh's] defeat that "nothing that this country did nor could have done within the reasonable limits of its capabilities could have changed that result; nothing that was left undone by this country has contributed to it." United States assistance could be effective if it was the missing component in the situation, he noted in his National Press Club speech, but "the United States cannot furnish all these components to solve the question. It can not furnish determination, it can not furnish the will, and it can not furnish the loyalty of a people to its government."

Reinforcing the Department's doubts about Washington's ability to shape events on the mainland was the conviction that China was not vital to the security of the United States in any event. This conclusion stemmed from a sharp awareness of the limits of American power, and of the need, as a consequence, to distinguish vital from peripheral interests. It also grew out of a tendency to define interests primarily in terms of industrial war-making capacity: hence, Kennan's conclusion that there were only five vital centers of power in the world—the United States, the Soviet Union, Great Britain, the Rhine valley, and Japan—and that the task of containment was to see to it that the four not then under Soviet control remained free of it. "If this is true," Kennan told an audience at the Naval War College in October,

> you do not need to hold land positions on the Eurasian land mass to protect our national security. If that is true, you can theoretically content yourself with permitting most of these land areas to be in the hands of people who are hostile to ourselves as long as you exercise that power of inhibiting the assembling and launching of amphibious forces from many Asian ports.

Acheson set out the implications of this line of reasoning in executive session testimony before the Senate Foreign Relations Committee in May, 1950: "I think we have to start out with the realization that the main center of our activity at present has got to be in Europe. We cannot scatter our shots equally all over the world. We just haven't got enough shots to do that."

Still another persistent theme in the State Department's thinking had to do with the need to be selective about allies. Progressive nationalism was the wave of the future in Asia, Department East Asian specialists believed; the United States, if it expected to retain influence in that part of the world, would have to accommodate itself to that trend. This obviously meant avoiding commitments to support colonialism , as in the case of the French in Indochina or the Dutch in Indonesia; it also meant putting distance between the United States and what were perceived to be the reactionary nationalist regimes of Chiang Kai-shek in China and Syngman Rhee in South Korea. Departures from this principle ran the risk not only of opposing irreversible forces in Asia but also of associating the United States with unpredictable clients whose interests, however impeccably anti-communist, did not always parallel its own.

Finally, there existed within the State Department the conviction that even if China should become a communist state, the Russians would not necessarily be able to dominate it. In his National Press Club speech and in other public pronouncements early in 1950, Acheson had hinted broadly at the possibility of differences between the Russians and the Chinese Communists. Only with the opening of State Department and other official archives, however, has it become clear to what extent United States policy toward East Asia from 1947 had been based on that expectation. As a Department memorandum put it in November, 1949:

> We anticipate the possibility that great strains will develop between Peiping [Beijing] and Moscow. These strains would not only work to our advantage but would contribute to the desired end of permitting China to develop its own life independently rather than as a Russian satellite.

It was not always clear whether the Chinese people themselves would overthrow the Communists once their ties to the Russians had become apparent, or whether the Communists would follow Tito's example in Yugoslavia and repudiate Moscow's leadership. But since the Russians would control China in neither case, there was general agreement within the Department that the "loss" of that mainland area to communism would constitute no irreparable disaster for American security interests, and hence did not merit remedial action.

The Joint Chiefs of Staff also came to support the "defensive perimeter" strategy, but by a different route. Unlike the State Department, the Chiefs consistently took the position that the United States could influence events on the mainland through a selective and well-coordinated program of military aid. "The latent resources and manpower of China are such," they argued early in 1947, "that even small amounts of United States assistance to the National Government will materially strengthen its morale and at the same time weaken the morale of the Chinese communists." Similar assumptions lay behind Lieutenant General Albert C. Wedemeyer's September, 1947, recommendation that the United States furnish the Nationalists with the material support necessary to prevent Manchuria from becoming a Soviet satellite, and Vice Admiral Oscar C. Badger's subsequent advocacy of limited military aid to anti-Communist regional warlords once it became apparent that Chiang Kai-shek's government was on the verge of collapse.

The Joint Chiefs found it difficult as well to accept the view that significant differences could exist between the Chinese Communists and the Russians. "It is believed," a June, 1947, study pointed out, "that the Chinese communists, as all others, are Moscow inspired and thus motivated by the same basic totalitarian and anti-democratic policies as are the communist parties in other countries of the world. Accordingly, they should be regarded as tools of Soviet policy." A victory for communism in China would, therefore, significantly affect the world balance of power, since it would make that country a satellite of the Soviet Union. The Chiefs concluded:

> The United States must seek to prevent the growth of any single power or coalition to a position of such strength as to constitute threat to the Western Hemisphere. A Soviet position of dominance over Asia, Western Europe, or both, would constitute a major threat to United States security.
>
> United States security interests require that China be kept free from Soviet domination; otherwise all of Asia will in all probability pass into the sphere of the USSR.

But whatever the Chiefs' perception of the interests at stake in China, they shared with the State Department a keen sense of the limits on American resources and of the need to rank interests accordingly. It is significant that in 1947 they placed China thirteenth on a list of countries whose defense they considered vital to the national security of the United States. By mid-1948, China had dropped to seventeenth place on a list of military aid priorities approved by the State-War-Navy-Air Force Coordinating Committee. "[C]urrent United States commitments involving the use or distinctly possible use of armed forces are very greatly in excess of our present ability to fulfill them either promptly or effectively," the Joint Chiefs warned Secretary of Defense James Forrestal in November, 1948. During the MacArthur hearings in 1951, General Marshall recalled that "we would literally have [had] to take over control of the country in order to insure that the [Chinese Nationalist] armies functioned with efficiency. . . . At that time . . . we had one and a third divisions in the entire United States."

Moreover, mainland China did not appear to provide favorable terrain upon which to fight if war with the Soviet Union came. As early as July, 1945, a Joint Chiefs of Staff examination of postwar strategic requirements had defined as among "potentially critical operational zones" the offshore island chain, but no points on the Asian mainland. "[In] the case of warfare with our ideological opponents," another study concluded in April, 1947, "China could be a valuable ally only if we diverted to her great quantities of food and equipment manufactured in this country. It is extremely doubtful that the end result would be any great assistance to our war effort." The Joint War Plans Committee concluded two months later that while it might be desirable to hold certain areas around Qingdao [Tsingtao] for the purpose of aiding Chinese Nationalist forces and conducting strategic air strikes against the Soviet Union, "this course of action would be beyond Allied capabilities during the first phases of the war and . . . any U.S. forces in the area on D-Day should be withdrawn when their positions become untenable." East Asia itself, because of its distance from the centers of Soviet warmaking capability, was not "a feasible avenue of approach to the USSR."

Nor did American strategic planners believe that the Russians would gain much by controlling that part of the world. "Soviet conquest of . . . Asia," the Joint War Plans Committee concluded in August, 1947, "would provide few military advantages and would not substantially increase their over-all military capability." The Joint Staff Planners reiterated this conclusion in September, 1949: "The inability of the USSR to rapidly extend lines of communications, base development operations, and military and political control through the vast areas of Siberia and into Communist-dominated China appears to preclude military exploitation of this area, to our detriment, in the immediate future." A comprehensive National Security Council study of Asian policy determined later that year that the United States possessed neither primary strategic interests nor the means to achieve its objectives in case of war on the Asian mainland. Accordingly, "the current basic concept of strategy in the event of war with the USSR is to conduct a strategic offensive in the 'West' and a strategic defense in the 'East.' " This meant the "minimum expenditure of military manpower and material" in such areas as would show "the most results in return for the United States effort expended."

But the Joint Chiefs of Staff and the State Department were not the only significant shapers of strategy in East Asia. Of almost equal importance was General of the Army Douglas MacArthur, Commander in Chief of U.S. Forces, Far East, and Supreme Commander, Allied Powers, Japan. MacArthur, like the Joint Chiefs, saw possibilities for effective military aid to China, provided the United States concentrated on the issue of security and put aside its concern for internal reform. "Desirable as such reform may be," he wrote in March, 1948, "its importance is but secondary to the issue of civil strife now engulfing the land, and the two issues are as impossible of synchronization as it would be to alter the structural design of a house while the same was being consumed by flame." Chiang Kai-shek might be on his way out, MacArthur commented in August, 1949, "but as long as he will fight I believe in helping him, as I would help anyone else who would fight the Communists."

MacArthur came to this position, though, by a process of reasoning very different from that of the Joint Chiefs of Staff or the Department of State. For him, American strategic interests in the world were undifferentiated: "[I]f we embark upon a general policy to bulwark the frontiers of freedom against the assaults of political despotism, one major frontier is no less important than another, and a decisive breach of any will inevitably threaten to engulf all." Victories of communism in China were those of the Soviet Union; the dangers they posed to United States security were no less than those created by the expansion of communism elsewhere in the world. As Senator H. Alexander Smith noted following a conversation with MacArthur in September, 1949: "He is violently against any form of communism wherever it shows itself and would back any of the anticommunist forces everywhere in the world."

The General's well-known conviction that Asia was being neglected in favor of Europe grew logically out of this perception of undifferentiated interests. "It no longer appears realistic to consider the Far East as a static and secure flank in the military contest with Communism," he cabled General Wedemeyer in November, 1948. By 1949, he was complaining vigorously about a "Europe first" mentality in Washington and a corresponding inclination to "scuttle the Pacific." He attributed these tendencies to the influence of Marshall and the "bright young men" around him, and to the inability of the Joint Chiefs to "understand" East Asia, a failing stemming from their concentration on European affairs during and since World War II. What Washington failed to see, a study prepared by MacArthur's staff argued, was that the Soviet offensive had shifted from the European theater to East Asia, partly as the result of the success of containment in Europe. United States military planning had not shifted accordingly: as a consequence, Soviet utilization of the resources of East Asia, if linked with the industrial machine of Japan, "might prove ultimately decisive."

But MacArthur was much less clear about how the United States should deal with this threat. He was fond of insisting that "anyone in favor of sending American ground troops to fight on Chinese soil should have his head examined," a point of view that would appear to have ruled out direct military assistance to Chiang Kai-shek. Moreover, MacArthur was extraordinarily sensitive to the self-defeating effects of prolonged military occupations (a characteristic he shared with Kennan). One of his chief priorities after 1948 was to end the American occupation of Japan; it seems unlikely that he would have welcomed similar responsibilities elsewhere. Given these circumstances, given the limited resources made available by Washington, it made sense from MacArthur's perspective to endorse the island perimeter concept as the most efficient way to retain a military presence in Asia without getting bogged down either in protracted war or in protracted occupation.

Hence, though the State Department, the Joint Chiefs of Staff, and MacArthur all came to support the "defensive perimeter" strategy, they did so for very different reasons. State saw the offshore island chain as a detached position from which to encourage Asian nationalism as a bulwark against Soviet expansionism. The Chiefs regarded it as a line capable of being held at minimal cost, should war come, while the strategic offensive proceeded elsewhere. MacArthur saw it as the nation's first line of defense and, more distantly, as a series of bases from which to launch offensive operations aimed at regaining the mainland, although he never made clear the nature and precise objectives of those operations. These differences in priorities and expectations became painfully clear as the Truman administration sought to apply the "defensive perimeter" strategy in three areas that did not easily fit it: Taiwan, Indochina, and Korea.

There was never any question, whether in the Pentagon, the State Department, or the Far East Command, as to the strategic importance of Taiwan once it became apparent that Chiang Kai-shek could not retain control of the mainland. The prospect of a Taiwan dominated by "Kremlin-directed Communists," the Joint Chiefs concluded late in 1948, would be "very seriously detrimental to our national security," since it would give the Communists the capability of dominating sea lines of communication between Japan and Malaya, and of threatening the Philippines, the Ryukyus, and ultimately Japan itself. A State Department draft report to the National Security Council early in 1949 argued that "the basic aim of the U.S. should be to deny Formosa and the Pescadores to the Communists." MacArthur was particularly adamant on this point. He told Max W. Bishop, Chief of the State Department's Division of Northeast Asian Affairs, that "if Formosa went to the Chinese Communists our whole defensive position in the Far East [would be] definitely lost; that it could only result eventually in putting our defensive line back to the west coast of the continental United States."

It is interesting to note, however, that neither the State Department, the Joint Chiefs, nor MacArthur initially favored using American forces to deny Taiwan to the new People's Republic of China. The Chiefs, citing "the current disparity between our military strength and our many global obligations," opposed military involvement on the grounds that "this might . . . lead to the necessity for relatively major effort there, thus making it impossible then to meet more important emergencies elsewhere." MacArthur repeatedly made it clear that he did not favor the creation of American military bases on Taiwan; the important thing was to deny the island to potential adversaries, while retaining the use of such other more easily controlled strongpoints as Okinawa and the Philippines. The State Department opposed military action on the grounds that overt attempts to detach Taiwan from China would risk offending Chinese nationalism and might undermine the Department's strategy of attempting to drive a wedge between the People's Republic and the USSR. As Acheson put it: "We are most anxious to avoid raising the spectre of an American-created irredentist issue just at the time we shall be seeking to exploit the genuinely Soviet-created irredentist issue in Manchuria and Sinkiang." . . .

In fact, the administration had not written off Taiwan *in the event of war with the Soviet Union*. Acheson hinted at this in a press conference on January 5, when he was asked the significance of Truman's statement that day that "the United States has no desire to obtain special rights or privileges or to establish military bases on Formosa at this time." The phrase "at this time," Acheson explained, "is a recognition of the fact that, in the unlikely and unhappy event that our forces might be attacked in the Far East, the United States must be completely free to take whatever action in whatever area is necessary for its own security." General Omar Bradley, in off-the-record testimony before the Senate Foreign Relations Committee on January 25, indicated that the

Joint Chiefs were fully aware of the dangers control of Taiwan by a potential enemy would pose to the American position in the Pacific. The next day, the Joint Chiefs concluded that an emergency war plan providing for the denial of Taiwan to the Russians in case of war should remain in effect through the middle of 1951. It is significant also that General MacArthur, after a meeting with the Joint Chiefs in Tokyo early in February, told them "that he had agreed completely with the Joint Chiefs of Staff point of view with respect Formosa." . . .

[There was] an underlying element of consistency in American policy on the Taiwan question: the fact that at no point during 1949 and 1950 was Washington prepared to acquiesce in control of the island by forces hostile to the United States *and* capable of taking military action against other links in the offshore island chain. The problem was to achieve this objective without getting further involved in the Chinese civil war. The United States was willing to install an autonomous regime on the island if that could be done without driving the Chinese Communists and the Russians together. But when it became apparent that autonomy was not feasible, Washington resigned itself to the prospect of control by the People's Republic as long as this did not involve a Soviet military presence as well. That possibility, too, had begun to appear increasingly unlikely by the spring of 1950; as a result, a revision of the administration's "hands-off" policy was well under way at the time the Korean War broke out.

Korea brought about the decision to "neutralize" Taiwan for military reasons, but with the hope that there might still remain some chance for a political *modus vivendi* with the Chinese Communists. Beijing's intervention in the Korean conflict destroyed that prospect; hence, by the end of 1950, the Truman administration had found itself in precisely the position it had sought to avoid: yoked, as it were, for better or for worse, to Chiang Kai-shek.

Just as Taiwan represented an anomaly as an island strongpoint excluded from the original "defensive perimeter," so French Indochina, as a mainland area included within it, constituted another. Certainly there was little promising about the situation there, what with an unpopular colonial government waging an increasingly costly and ineffective war against a guerilla movement that was both communist and nationalist. Nevertheless, the United States had come, by 1950, to regard the defense of Indochina as an interest more vital than denial to the communists of either Taiwan or South Korea. As early as March, 1949, a Policy Planning Staff study had recommended that "we should

. . . view the SEA [Southeast Asian] region as an integral part of that great crescent formed by the Indian Peninsula, Australia, and Japan." NSC 48/1, a comprehensive review of East Asian policy submitted to the National Security Council in December, 1949, concluded that if Southeast Asia were to be swept by communism, "we shall have suffered a major political rout the repercussions of which will be felt throughout the rest of the world." And in April, 1950, the Joint Chiefs of Staff proclaimed that "the mainland states of Southeast Asia . . . are . . . of critical strategic importance to the United States."

None of this meant, of course, that the United States was willing to endorse everything the French were doing in Indochina. "We will get nowhere by supporting the French as a colonial power against the Indochinese," Acheson told the Senate Foreign Relations Committee; "that is something which has very little future in it." Nor did Washington's policy extend to the point of being willing to promise American troops if Indochina was subjected to external attack. But it did mean support for, and, by February, 1950, recognition of the Bao Dai government established by the French in an effort to encourage an anticommunist variety of nationalism in Indochina. And it also meant approval by the President, on April 24, 1950, of a directive instructing the State and Defense Departments to "prepare as a matter of priority a program of all practicable measures designed to protect United States security interests in Indochina."

American officials appear to have made an exception to their general rule of not regarding mainland areas as vital, in the case of Indochina, for several reasons: (1) the conviction that Ho Chi Minh was a more reliable instrument of the Kremlin than Mao Zedong; (2) the belief that the Soviet Union had designated Southeast Asia as a special target of opportunity; (3) concern over the importance of Southeast Asia as a source of food and raw materials; and (4) in an early version of what would come to be known as the "domino theory," fear of the strategic and psychological consequences for the rest of non-communist Asia if Indochina should fall to communism. . . .

By the end of 1950, then, the United States faced an apparently insoluble problem in Indochina. Administration officials were unanimous in their estimates of the region's strategic importance; nevertheless, the burdens of military commitment in Korea, a country once thought less vital than Indochina, meant that the United States had to continue to rely for the defense of the territory on the French, whose very ineptitude had made their colony vulnerable in the first place. It took longer than expected to validate it, but the reluctant conclusion of a 1951 National Security Council staff study proved, in the end, to be correct: "The United States cannot guarantee the denial of Southeast Asia to communism."

Korea, of course, represented the most striking departure from the original "defensive perimeter" concept. In contrast to Taiwan and Indochina, here was an area in which United States troops had been stationed. After deliberations in Washington lasting almost two years, these troops had been withdrawn in the spring of 1949, on the grounds that the defense of South Korea was not a vital strategic interest for the United States. Throughout this period, American officials harbored serious reservations about both the intentions and capabilities of the South Korean government. And yet, when that country was attacked on June 25, 1950, the Truman administration, with a rapidity that surprised itself as well as its adversaries, committed air, naval, and ground forces to repel the invasion. Five months later, Washington found itself in an undeclared war there with the People's Republic of China as well.

The initial decision to withdraw troops from southern Korea had been made in the fall of 1947, primarily for strategic reasons: it appeared unwise to retain some 45,000 men in that area at a time of increasingly severe manpower shortages and proliferating commitments in Europe. The United States had occupied the southern half of Korea at the end of World War II to forestall a Soviet takeover, but it had never expected to have to keep troops there indefinitely, nor did it consider it strategically sound to do so. As the Joint War Plans Committee of the Joint Chiefs of Staff noted in June, 1947, existing forces in southern Korea would not be capable of repelling a Soviet attack if one should come; reinforcements from Japan would only weaken the security of that more vital and more defensible position, while in no way matching force levels the Russians had the capability to send in. "A withdrawal from Korea immediately after the outbreak of hostilities is indicated." By September, the Joint Chiefs had concluded that "in the light of the present severe shortage of military manpower, the corps of two divisions . . . now maintained in south Korea, could well be used elsewhere."

It is important to note, though, that Washington planners made a distinction between strategic interests in Korea, which they considered negligible, and the very different problem of interests in terms of credibility. "This is the one country within which we alone have for almost two years carried on ideological warfare in direct contact with our ideological opponents," the Joint Strategic Survey Committee noted in April, 1947, "so that to lose this battle would be gravely detrimental to United States prestige, and therefore security, throughout the world." An analysis by the State-War-Navy Coordinating Committee concluded in August that "the U.S. cannot at this time withdraw from Korea under circumstances which would inevitably lead to Communist domination of the entire country." General Wedemeyer, in his report to the President in September, argued that the withdrawal of American forces from southern Korea and the consequent occupation of the country by Soviet or northern Korean troops "would cost the United States an immense loss in moral prestige among the peoples of Asia."

The compromise eventually reached was succinctly stated in the minutes of a meeting of State Department East Asian advisers held in Secretary Marshall's office on September 29, 1947:

> It was agreed that (a) ultimately the US position in Korea is untenable even with expenditure of considerable US money and effort; (b) the US, however, cannot "scuttle" and run from Korea without considerable loss of prestige and political standing in the Far East and in the world at large; (c) that it should be the effort of the Government through all proper means to effect a settlement of the Korean problem which would enable the US to withdraw from Korea as soon as possible with the minimum of bad effects.

An agreement with the Russians looking toward unification of the country having proven impossible to achieve, the United States fell back on a policy of providing military and economic assistance to the anticommunist government of Syngman Rhee, established under United Nations auspices in 1948, while gradually withdrawing American troops. This policy did not mean the abandonment of South Korea to Soviet domination, though, as two National Security Council papers on the subject made clear: "The overthrow by Soviet-dominated forces of a regime established in south Korea under the aegis of the UN would . . . constitute a severe blow to the prestige and influence of the UN; in this respect the interests of the U.S. are parallel to, if not identical with, those of the UN."

Just what the United States would do to defend South Korea in case of attack, however, remained unclear. . . .

The decision to come to the aid of South Korea following the June 25 attack was by no means a foregone conclusion. MacArthur's initial impression was that the invasion was not an all-out effort, that the Russians were probably not behind it, and that the South Koreans would win. Secretary of the Army Frank Pace and Secretary of Defense Johnson initially opposed the commitment of ground combat forces, and the Joint Chiefs expressed concern about the impact such a decision would have in weakening the defenses of Japan and reducing the number of troops available for deployment to Western Europe. Dulles supported the use of air and naval forces in Korea but warned that the Russians and the Chinese could indefinitely supply the North Koreans and that "it was hazardous for us to challenge communist power on the mainland." Secretary Pace replied that "the Defense Department's disposition to send divisions into Korea was not because of *their* desire to do so, but because they thought it necessary to support the political policies of the government."

This was a perceptive comment, for in the end it was political and not strategic considerations that brought about American intervention in Korea. The blatant nature of the North Korean attack made resistance necessary, in the eyes of administration officials, not because South Korea was important in and of itself, but because any demonstration of aggression left unopposed would only encourage further aggressions elsewhere. "You may be sure," Charles Bohlen wrote to Kennan on June 26, "that all Europeans to say nothing of the Asiatics are watching to see what the United States will do." Kennan himself believed that if the United States did not act, "there will scarcely be any theater of the east-west conflict which will not be adversely affected thereby, from our standpoint." The fact that in attacking South Korea the North Koreans had directly challenged the United Nations made the argument even more compelling. Philip Jessup recalls Truman, at the Blair House meeting of June 25, repeating half to himself: "We can't let the UN down! We can't let the UN down! . . .

Ideally, a "defensive perimeter" strategy should seek to contain the expansive tendencies of potential adversaries without unnecessarily dispersing resources. Such an approach assumes that because capabilities are finite, interests must be also; ends must be framed in such a way as to be consistent with means. Implicit also is the notion of selectivity, whether in the choice of terrain to be defended, instruments with which to carry out that defense, or allies to be enlisted in the effort. The overall objective is, or should be, to counter the other side's initiatives without unduly restricting one's own.

At first glance, American strategy in East Asia after World War II would appear to have met that standard. The primary interest involved was to ensure that that part of the world did not come under the domination of a single hostile power. But because United States capabilities lay more in the realm of technology than manpower, and because of competing obligations in Europe, it made sense to confine the American presence in Asia to islands capable of being defended by air and naval forces, thus avoiding operations against high-manpower but low-technology adversaries on the mainland. This was a realistic recognition both of global priorities and of regional asymmetries of power.

As with most general concepts, though, application proved more difficult than articulation. It was all very well to relinquish commitments in mainland China, which was thought "lost" to the West for the foreseeable future, but the problems of Taiwan, Indochina, and Korea defied such easy solution. Taiwan had been excluded from the perimeter for reasons of international politics: Acheson's desire to avoid further involvement in the Chinese civil war and to exploit potential Sino-Soviet tensions. But domestic political pressures, together with concern over strategic implications should the island fall under Soviet control, quickly forced a reconsideration of that approach. Despite its mainland position, indigenous insurgency, and decaying colonial administration, Indochina was always included within the perimeter. South Korea was quite deliberately left out, only to be included abruptly as a consequence of the North Korean attack. Indecision regarding the new perimeter on the Korean peninsula in turn provoked intervention by the People's Republic of China, with the result that the "defensive perimeter" by the end of 1950 looked very different from the way it had at the beginning of that year.

These anomalies suggest that while both the immediate *strategy* of maintaining a "defensive perimeter" and the long-term *objective* of preserving a non-hostile Asia were capable of eliciting agreement in Washington, no such consensus existed as to how to get from one to the other. What, for example, was the threat to the balance of power: Soviet expansionism or international communism? Could the threat best be contained by encouraging resistance to it wherever it appeared, or by opposing it selectively with a view to promoting fragmentation? What allies might appropriately be enlisted in these efforts? And what priorities should be assigned to them, given responsibilities in other parts of the world? Nor was there always sufficient coordination of political, economic, and military planning, with the consequence that actions taken in one field were not always thought out in terms of their implications for others.

There was also a tendency to exaggerate the psychological dimensions of strategy: decisions to defend Taiwan, Indochina, and South Korea were based as much on considerations of "prestige" and "credibility" as on the importance of these territories in and of themselves. Finally, the Truman administration may have erred in delineating its strategy too precisely. Governments should never be ambiguous with themselves in defining vital interests, but a certain amount of public ambiguity in such matters can, at times, contribute toward the deterrence of adversaries, both foreign and domestic.

By 1951, the "defensive perimeter" concept was, to all intents and purposes, dead. Instead the Truman administration had backed into a strategy of resisting aggression wherever it occurred, but only at a corresponding level of violence. Almost immediately, frustrations over the costs of this approach led the administration to seek ways of achieving its objectives less expensively, but it never succeeded in implementing them. It would be left to Eisenhower and his advisers to devise a strategy that capitalized upon the advantages of ambiguity to achieve both deterrence and economy. Two decades later, in reaction to an even more costly flirtation with "flexible response" in Asia, the Nixon administration would embark upon a strategy of encouraging Asian self-reliance while taking advantage of Sino-Soviet tensions to move toward a rapprochement with the People's Republic of China. It was an approach not too far removed from the original "defensive perimeter" concept as Acheson and his colleagues in the State Department had understood it. It was also—in a backhanded way—their ultimate vindication, for the long-delayed but now virtually complete withdrawal of American military power from the Asian mainland has produced, not a loss of American political and economic influence there, but on the whole a more successful reassertion of it than at any point since the end of World War II. Sometimes nations can, by losing, win.

Asia and the Middle East After the Second World War

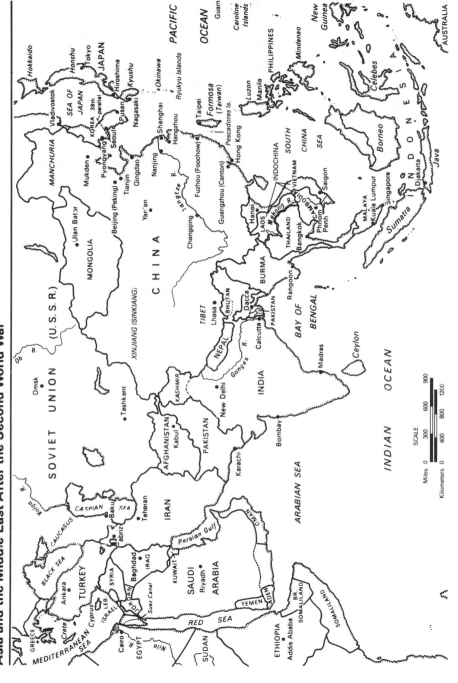

Michael Schaller

AMERICA'S ECONOMIC AND STRATEGIC INTERESTS IN ASIA

Michael Schaller dates the origins of the Cold War much earlier than John Lewis Gaddis. Unlike Gaddis, who sees the Korean War as the seminal event leading the United States significantly to extend its Asian commitments, Schaller emphasizes the importance of the year 1947. Schaller especially stresses the regional economic crisis that peaked in 1947, precipitated by Japan's continuing economic stagnation. Fearful that Japan might collapse completely, opening the door to chaos and communism, the Truman administration moved quickly to stimulate full Japanese economic recovery. The "reverse course" in occupation policy, Schaller suggests, deepened America's concern with and commitment to Southeast Asia as well; most senior United States officials became convinced that Japan's economic revival, given its need for external markets, necessitated a politically stable and economically revitalized Southeast Asia. America's strategic interests intersected with its economic interests in this regard: an economically vital Japan would stimulate regional and world economic recovery while also serving as a barrier to possible communist expansion in Asia.

Michael Schaller teaches American history at the University of Arizona. He has written The U.S. Crusade in China, 1938–1945 (1979), The United States and China in the Twentieth Century (1989), The American Occupation of Japan: The Origins of the Cold War in Asia (1985), and Douglas MacArthur: The Far Eastern General (1990).

The links between policy toward Occupied Japan and the origins of containment in Southeast Asia are both intriguing and elusive. While a few historians suggest that these policies sprang from similar roots, most studies contrast the constructive American record in Japan to the military and ideological crusades pursued in China, Korea, and Indochina.

However, planners and policy makers in the late 1940s did not compartmentalize Japan and Southeast Asia, but saw them as linked sectors on a "great crescent" that stretched in an arc from the Kurile

Michael Schaller, "Securing the Great Crescent: Occupied Japan and the Origins of Containment in Southeast Asia," *Journal of American History*, 69 (Sept. 1982), pp. 392–96, 400–07, 413–14. Reprinted by permission of The Journal of American History.

Islands to the borders of Iran and Afghanistan. Those most concerned with Japan in the State and Defense Departments, Economic Cooperation Administration, and in Douglas MacArthur's Occupation Headquarters not only accepted the necessity of Japan reassuming a major regional role but eventually supported the joint assumption by Washington and Tokyo of the mantle of empire Americans had wrested from the Japanese at the close of World War II.

Once the Occupation had proclaimed, or pressed the Japanese government to enact, a variety of basic economic and political reforms, American planners faced the problem of how to integrate Japan into the Asian community. By 1948 they envisioned Japan as an industrial hub, sustained by trade with less developed states along an Asian economic defense perimeter. A secure Japan would help support Southeast Asia against Chinese communism, and vice versa. Above all else, the relationship required that Japan have access to secure, affordable raw materials and markets in Southeast Asia, while minimizing trade with China. Although never as formal or explicit as parallel programs in Europe—Truman Doctrine, Marshall Plan, North Atlantic Treaty Organization (NATO)—this idea shaped both policy toward Japan and the growing commitment to Southeast Asia.

A regional approach toward the Far East began incrementally among several groups in Washington. But by the spring of 1947, the rough outline of a policy emerged. Speaking in Cleveland, Mississippi, on May 8, 1947, in a speech foreshadowing the Marshall Plan, Under Secretary of State Dean Acheson called for pushing forward "with the reconstruction of those two great workshops of Europe and Asia—Germany and Japan—upon which the ultimate recovery of the two continents so largely depends." Acheson's public disclosure followed many interagency discussions and private warnings regarding the internal economic situation in Japan. While the American public heard General MacArthur boast of his successful "spiritual revolution" and Japan's readiness, in March 1947, for a quick peace treaty, few policy makers shared his optimism.

The former enemy might now enjoy a democratic constitution and a greatly liberalized political structure, but its 1947 production had declined to barely one-third of pre-war levels. Japan had lost its merchant fleet, an empire, much productivity capacity and a predominant economic position in East Asia. Synthetic fibers had virtually wiped out its profitable silk exports to the United States while the chaos of post-war Asia, occupation restrictions, and anti-Japanese sentiment prevented the revival of intraregional trade. Only relief aid by the United States Army—"Government and Relief in Occupied Areas" (GARIOA)—at a cost of almost $400 million per year, prevented a total economic collapse.

Aware of this situation and fearful of the "complete collapse of Japan" followed by chaos and communism, leading figures in the State, War, and Navy Departments as well as influential private citizens mobilized against MacArthur's effort to terminate the Occupation. They favored a radically different approach, stressing the fastest possible economic recovery to precede a peace settlement. This required abandonment of most punitive economic controls and guidance by American civilian economic experts.

As early as February 1947, the State Department's Division of Japanese and Korean Affairs, led by Edwin F. Martin, outlined a comprehensive recovery program for Japan. Previous assumptions that a politically reformed Japan would quickly become self-supporting with only minimal American direction were outdated, Martin wrote, by the radical changes that had overtaken the world economy. In its postwar condition, inefficient and outdated, Japanese industry would never be able to sell enough to the United States or Europe to finance food and commodity imports. Since United States relief must eventually terminate, the resulting economic stagnation would quickly undermine democratic reforms and hurt the rest of Asia by depriving it of "markets for their raw materials and sources for cheap manufactured goods." Martin proposed a two-tiered recovery program designed both to stimulate Japanese industry and redirect its long-term sources of trade. His plan entailed temporarily increasing United States financed raw material imports for processing in Japan and export to nondollar Asian markets. Simultaneously, the previous punitive approach to reparations payments, decartelization, and levels-of-industry limits would be altered to promote rapid recovery. The temporary infusion of dollars and raw materials would prime Japanese production as it promoted intraregional trade. Eventually, as exchanges based on trading Japanese manufactured goods for Asian raw materials expanded, American aid would no longer be required. This "economic crank-up" would solve the chronic dollar-gap problem, reduce occupation costs, and establish a long-term basis for an integrated Asian economy.

By July, Martin's proposal grew into a sixty-page paper submitted by the department to the State-War-Navy Coordinating Committee (SWNCC). SWNCC 381, "The Revival of the Japanese Economy," proposed a crash $500-million program to revive the "great workshop" of Asia to a state of "self-sufficiency" by about 1950. After pro forma consultation with other Far Eastern Commission members, the United States would eliminate or drastically reduce all economic constraints on Japanese industry. American aid would finance a large volume of raw material imports for production and export. The program would encourage Japanese sales to nondollar Asian markets with payments in raw materials. This process would reverse the current trend of Japanese dependence on dollar imports, while stimulating a major revival of intraregional trade.

The proposal contained a strongly revisionist and favorable description of Japanese economic expansion in Asia before 1941. Overall, it described Japan as a catalyst for Asian development, much like Britain in relation to the industrialization of Western Europe and North America. Specifically, the proposal endorsed Japanese economic expansion into the "natural frontier" of Southeast Asia. The draft looked toward a time when Japan would enjoy a large trade surplus with Southeast Asia. At that point, American dollar aid to both areas could be reduced. The Southeast Asian currency surplus held by Tokyo could be taken by Washington as debt repayment for GARIOA and then recycled in Southeast Asia in some form of aid program.

Although this call for an "economic crank-up" received informal approval on October 20, the army and State Department still debated the language of the document. The army wanted to use the phrase "shift in emphasis" to describe the program and, more seriously, favored enacting the program unilaterally, with virtually no consulting of foreign governments. Army Under Secretary William Draper, an investment banker who played a key role in economic planning for both Germany and Japan, promoted this approach in the army's policy document, SWNCC 384. In any case, both agencies shared a general goal for Japan, and their specific actions over the next year and a half led to basic reversals of policies regarding the purge program, decartelization, reparations of equipment, limits on industry, and promotion of the rights of organized labor.

Strategic concerns mirrored economic considerations, as demonstrated in August 1947, when Under Secretary of State Robert Lovett requested that George Kennan's Policy Planning Staff (PPS) reevaluate a preliminary draft peace treaty for Japan. In a scathing critique, PPS staff member John Davies dismissed the draft as ignorant of the need for a "stable Japan, integrated into the Pacific, friendly to the U.S., and, in case of need, a ready and dependable ally." Instead of concern with liberal reforms and social experiments, MacArthur's headquarters and Washington treaty drafters ought to stress economic recovery and the development of central military forces to resist a Soviet-inspired coup.

Lovett promptly ordered the existing treaty draft to be scrapped while the PPS prepared a new version. During August and September, the PPS worked with army and navy representatives to set an agenda for a post-Occupation Japan, amenable to American leadership and a powerful economic force in Asia. This new Japan would not "possess an identity of its own" but would "function as" an "American satellite."

The PPS draft asserted what became a major theme of later policy documents: that Japanese recovery could be gravely impaired by communist control of most of Northeast Asia. While communist authorities might encourage trade, this would inevitably be used by the communists "as a lever for Soviet political pressure, unless Japan is able to obtain these raw materials and markets elsewhere—particularly in South Asia and the Western Hemisphere." During the next one or two years, the PPS draft concluded, Washington must compel MacArthur to hasten recovery by accepting expert civilian advice, working with the Japanese government and business community, and ceasing to push a program of economic-social reform.

During the remainder of 1947 and 1948 Kennan and Draper ceaselessly promoted Japanese economic recovery, often over the protest of MacArthur. Through their fact-finding trips to Japan, frequent testimony before Congress, briefings of the press, and recruitment of American businessmen to oversee Supreme Commander for the Allied Powers (SCAP) economic policy, these pivotal State Department and army officials effected a tremendous change in almost all Occupation policies. By the end of 1948, the "shift in emphasis" and "economic crank-up" redefined the direction of economic and social reform in Occupied Japan. Although civilian and military planners continued to disagree violently on questions regarding posttreaty base rights and the development of military forces within Japan, as early as October 1947 they shared an outlook on the pace and direction of economic orientation. . . .

A report on the "Strategic Importance of Japan," prepared by the CIA in May 1948 for circulation in the State Department and armed forces, echoed the theme that whoever controlled Japan held the key to the Far East. Considering Japan's location and industrial potential—especially if integrated with the Soviet Far East and Manchuria—its possession by the Kremlin might actually tip the balance in the Cold War. Communist possession of Northeast Asia, the report warned, would make Japanese recovery slow and difficult. Were access to Southeast Asia also lost, "the ensuing economic distress, with its attendant political instability, might force Japan to align itself with the U.S.S.R." Under the right conditions, Japan could become a powerful, pro-American, "stabilizing force in Asia." But if left a hostage to Soviet control of its trading zones, "the probability that Japan would eventually succumb to Communist domination would become almost a certainty."

Circumscribing both the hopes and fears for Japan's future, of course, lurked the specter of China's civil war. The terms of its outcome, the policy of the Communists, the attitude of the United States—all bore directly on proposed recovery programs. Throughout 1948 and early 1949, intense debates raged between the State Department, which favored a relatively moderate approach to China, and those in the Defense Department and the Congressional "China bloc" who demanded increased militancy against the communists, including a virtual economic blockade.

In a series of decisions reached by the NSC in March 1949, the State Department's moderate position prevailed. Rather than attempting to reverse the verdict of China's revolution through outside intervention, the United States would neither intervene on the mainland nor use force to defend Taiwan. While trade would not be encouraged, no barriers would be imposed on United States or Japanese nonstrategic trade with China. Finally, in hopes of inducing, or at least not delaying, a Sino-Soviet split, Washington would try to avoid provoking the communist regime.

At the same time, these successful moves by the State Department required that it demonstrate to its many critics a commitment to containment beyond China. The need to show resolve in a threatened area, combined with an awareness that any Asian strategy must promote Japanese recovery, focused attention on Southeast Asia. The region abutted China, was itself in the throes of political upheaval, and held the promise of providing Japan with an economic alternative to Northeast Asia. In a strong parallel to Tokyo's actions of 1940–1941, American policy makers hoped to resolve or escape their dilemmas in China by adopting a "southern strategy" that would contain China even as it opened a new economic zone for Japan.

Until 1949 the United States had not been directly committed to a defense of Indochina. While some military and economic aid to France filtered down to its forces fighting Ho Chi Minh's Viet Minh guerrillas, the State Department remained reluctant to actively support the colonial war. By June 1948, both the State and Defense Departments felt concerned enough by the growing instability throughout the region to convene a "Southeast Asia Regional Conference" in Bangkok. The conference brought together diplomatic officers and military attachés from throughout Asia to discuss the regional impact of nationalism and communism. They quickly concluded that while nationalism had deep local roots, the Kremlin had placed a top priority on capturing control of the movement. Consequently, the United States must forge a counterstrategy to secure the loyalty or Western orientation of Asian nationalism.

Extensive conference reports sent to Washington stressed the often-overlooked economic importance of the region to the world economy. Malaya's tin and rubber exports, for example, formed the mainstay of the British economy's "dollar arsenal." To varying degrees, France and the Netherlands also depended on dollar earnings from colonial investments and the sales of Asian commodities to balance their chronic deficit in trans-Atlantic trade. The dollar gap, the report noted, was one of the main problems which had required the creation of the ERP [European Recovery Program]. To make matters worse, the desperate colonial wars of France and the Netherlands and their refusal to deal with moderate nationalists played into Moscow's hands. Communists who attacked the colonial regimes posed as "Bolivars," while "each additional day of fighting works for Moscow."

Early in 1949, even as the NSC decisions of March 3 confirmed the relatively moderate policy towards China advocated by the State Department, the PPS prepared an outline for a more assertive program in Southeast Asia. Presented for the department's consideration on March 29, PPS 51 called for a comprehensive "U.S. policy toward Southeast Asia." It described a region remarkable for its undeveloped natural wealth, convulsed by nationalism and the "target of a coordinated offensive plainly directed by the Kremlin."

The long report examined the important role Southeast Asia played as a producer of raw materials and arena for investment by European colonial powers. Since 1941, however, military and political disruptions had blocked the region from producing the surplus needed by Europe or for "Indian and Japanese economic self-support." The atavistic colonial policies of the Europeans not only radicalized the region but also enhanced the Kremlin's efforts to gain a foothold.

The report suggested two reasons behind the Soviet offensive. Although Moscow had no direct need for the region's resources, it saw great value in denying the West and Japan access to the area's raw materials and transportation routes. Moreover, a communist victory there, in the wake of the China debacle, would have a tremendous destabilizing impact "throughout the rest of the world, especially in the Middle East and in a then critically exposed Australia." The PPS paper described Southeast Asia as a "vital segment" in a "great crescent" of containment that ran from Japan through island and mainland Southeast Asia, India, and Australia. Each sector of the crescent, in Southeast Asia or Japan, was vital to "the development of an interdependent and integrated counter-force to Stalinism in this quarter of the world."

The United States must compel its European allies to "rationalize" their policies by devolving power onto moderate nationalist regimes, the paper declared. Then genuine nationalists would flock to the western banner. Thereafter, the confrontation throughout the region would pit nationalist against communist, rather than against the West. In Indochina, the strategic key to the region, Kennan's staff predicted a prolonged campaign of "working through a screen of anti-communist Asiatics, to ensure, however long it takes, the triumph of Indochinese nationalism over Red Imperialism."

The long-range goal of this program, the report concluded, lay in fully integrating Southeast Asia (SEA) with the other major units of the great crescent—India, Australia, and Japan. Washington should "develop the economic interdependence between SEA as a supplier of raw materials, and Japan, Western Europe and India as suppliers of finished goods, with due recognition, however, of the legitimate aspirations of SEA countries for some diversification of their economies." When the PPS paper went before the secretary and under secretaries for consideration, the recorded minutes summarized its message in a concise sentence. The political problems of the area must be solved so "the region could begin to fulfill its major function as a source of raw materials and a market for Japan and Western Europe."

During the summer of 1949, despite the absence of an Asian Marshall Plan, two new programs promoted the connection between Japan and Southeast Asia policy. The Mutual Defense Assistance Act of 1949 established a Mutual Assistance Program (MAP) with funds for a wide range of military purposes. At the same time, Secretary of Defense

Louis Johnson initiated a major study of Asian policy (NSC-48), which, he hoped, would commit the administration to a more aggressive stance against communism. By early 1950, the NSC 48 guidelines, combined with MAP, forged new links in American policy between Japan and Southeast Asia.

Originating as SWNCC 360 in April 1947, MAP proposed to give the administration a massive $1.5 billion fund for military aid. The program remained in legislative limbo until the autumn of 1949. While most of the proposed aid would go to Western Europe, both the administration and Congress discussed the need for some additional aid to Asia. During congressional testimony, Acheson specifically described MAP as a way to fight communism in Asia outside the bounds of China. The secretary of state and Gen. Omar Bradley urged that Congress give up any illusion that further aid to Chiang Kai-shek would save either China or Asia from conquest. Acheson, especially, pleaded that Americans not "concentrate every thought we have on China." He urged that more attention be paid to how "we can prevent the spread of this Communist menace throughout Southeast Asia." As an example of this new concern, Acheson described the appointment of Ambassador Philip Jessup to head a group of outside experts, the Far Eastern Consultants, who would study regional security.

The secretary followed the lead of PPS 51 in its description of the "vast area that extends from Pakistan to Japan." The United States must encourage moderate nationalism in this zone even as it induced the European allies to abandon colonial power. Rather than appropriating any more money for Chiang or for a guerrilla war in China, Acheson said, Congress ought to "give the administration some money—not very much—that could be used in Asia on a confidential basis. . . ."

While a few diehard Kuomintang supporters in the House and Senate continued to badger the administration, most representatives supported Acheson's suggestion that a special unvouchered fund be created and used for various programs in Southeast Asia and other areas that the Jessup group might recommend. As signed by the president on October 6, 1949, the MAP program contained "Section 303," a unique provision for an unvouchered $75-million fund to promote containment in the "General Area of China," at the president's discretion.

The promise of an initial $75-million MAP for Asia, with the likelihood of subsequent unvouchered funds, generated a scramble for control of the money and for a program to expend it upon. The "303" funds could be applied toward anything—military aid or the formation of a centralized Asia-aid agency so widely discussed. With these considerations in mind, Defense Secretary Johnson requested the NSC to review overall United States policy in Asia. His June 10, 1949, letter to the NSC complained that while America pursued "day to day, country to country" containment, "global" communism gobbled up Asia. The United States, he argued, must institute a "comprehensive plan" of containment in Asia based on more effective coordination of current and future political, economic, and military programs. During the next six months, Defense Department aides worked with the small NSC staff to prepare an aggressive, anticommunist program under military control.

The background drafts of NSC 48, only recently declassified, reveal the Defense Department's concern over the relationship between economic and strategic security. Their analysis of American policy in Asia focused as much on that area's long-term economic relationships to Russia and the West as on its current political and military balance. American security depended in large part on keeping Asian resources available to the West and Japan while preventing Soviet control over those resources. More specifically, the United States must deny the Soviets "the richest economic prize in the Far East," Japan. Defense planners were certain that Moscow intended to integrate Japan with Siberia, Manchuria, and Korea into a "Communist Co-Prosperity Sphere" that would be a "self-sufficient war-making complex" designed to supplement the European Soviet base.

Japan's advanced industrial base, unique in Asia, would add at least 25 percent to Soviet industrial power, the reports estimated. Yet to acquire this prize, the Kremlin need risk no invasion nor even stress subversion. Simply by holding Northeast Asia, Southeast Asia, and Formosa, it could ensure that Japan would soon slip into the Communist orbit. Only by adopting a program of harassing the Chinese communists and, in Formosa and Southeast Asia, organizing a "properly guided anti-communist effort" might a "bulwark" be erected to preserve a vital zone for Japan.

Since any rollback of Chinese communism remained a long-term proposition and since Formosa and Korea could not fill all Japan's raw material requirements, Southeast Asia appeared the most important potential economic partner for Japan. Using a European analogy, a September draft of NSC 48 compared Manchuria to Central Europe and Japan to England.

The powder keg Southeast Asia (Balkans, Middle East) occupies a similar position, with the more or less secondary, but not to be overlooked India (Iberian Peninsula) in the offing. Therefore, to carry the analogy further, it must be concluded, (tempered only by the broad concept of defense in the East and offense in the West) that a strong Western oriented Japan, with access to the raw materials of as much of the rest of Asia as possible, is essential to the U.S.

A comprehensive economic analysis of Japan's role, prepared by the CIA, compared Japan's dependence on Southeast Asia to the area's prewar importance to the European empires. Promoting the future economic integration of the two regions would embrace "at once a number of economic interests of the U.S." Japan would benefit greatly from access to cheap and secure raw materials, while Japanese exports and technological guidance to Southeast Asia would promote stability in the wake of retreating European influence. Noting the "comparative advantages" of the Japanese economy, the CIA analysis urged that the United States lift Occupation limits on Japanese monopoly and, instead, assist the formation of "a number of rather large financial and trading concerns." Japanese exporters and developers should be encouraged and helped in returning to Southeast Asia where they could "make full use of their special knowledge and experience in these matters." The CIA even favored American funding of Japanese trading companies, which would then loan development funds to increase commodity production in Southeast Asia.

The drafts officially circulated by the Defense Department in mid-October portrayed Asia under coordinated Soviet attack. Utilizing its Chinese puppets, the Kremlin planned to acquire Japan through economic strangulation via its control of Northeast and Southeast Asia. In response, the defense planners urged that the United States create a "Pacific Association" to serve as a vehicle for rolling back communism in China, seizing control of Formosa, and coordinating economic affairs in Asia. This formidable program would be supervised by a high-ranking American specifically charged with revitalizing the struggle against communism in Asia.

Not surprisingly, State Department experts expressed shock at this immense undertaking. The commitments to Formosa, the idea of a Pacific Association, and a program for fighting China ran counter to almost everything Acheson and his advisors advocated. In contrast, Acheson, his Far Eastern Consultants, and area specialists like Davies and Butterworth hoped to temper the Chinese Revolution through gradual accommodation. They had no faith in Chiang, saw no Asian support for a Pacific Association, and believed that the Chinese communists would themselves move away from Moscow if only Washington steered clear of any provocations. The danger to Southeast Asia, in turn, came as much from European intransigence toward moderate nationalists as from Moscow's subversion. As for Japan, State Department experts ridiculed the Defense Department for its refusal to acknowledge that the lack of a peace treaty (blocked by Defense Department objections) undercut Japan's faith in America almost as much as did economic insecurity.

During an arduous redrafting process, which continued from October through late-December 1949, State Department Asia specialists pulled the teeth from most of the NSC 48 proposals. Much of the bellicose rhetoric remained, partly as a sop to Secretary Johnson's enthusiasm. The redraft, NSC 48/1, did call for containing and reducing Soviet and Chinese communist power in Asia, but avoided specifics. The paper did not preclude informal trade and discussions with the Chinese Communists, nor did it call for defending Taiwan or for covert warfare in Manchuria. Regarding Japan, the paper now endorsed a prompt peace settlement, permitting limited trade with China, and a general program to encourage trade with Southeast Asia.

The final State-Defense compromise over the Asia paper came in NSC 48/2, approved on December 30. While Acheson succeeded in barring any new aggressive programs toward China, he did agree to the Defense Department's demand that the $75-million MAP fund be "programmed as a matter of urgency." In effect, the scramble of Defense and State Department planners to promote a new Asian policy had been transferred from NSC 48 to the MAP program. Almost at once, a variety of policy-making groups in Washington seized upon the idea of using the MAP funds and authority as a way to create an integrated containment program in Asia.

During the six months that preceded the outbreak of the Korean War, the State Department, the Defense Department, the Joint Chiefs of Staff (JCS), SCAP, and the Department of the Army continued to disagree about most aspects of Asian policy. No consensus could be reached on the timing and nature of a Japanese peace settlement, nor was there agreement on whether the United States ought to "roll back" or merely "contain" Chinese communism. In contrast, almost all the competing policy-making bureaucrats accepted the argument that linked Japan's fate to Southeast Asia.

Testifying in executive session before the Senate Foreign Relations Committee on January 10, 1950, Acheson drew together the diverse strands of policy in Asia. After denouncing Soviet efforts to tie Eastern Europe to its own economy, the secretary boasted of American plans to promote economic and military integration in Western Europe and Asia. As before, Acheson dismissed arguments that the United States ought to move against China or defend Formosa. While it let the dust settle on the Chinese Revolution, Washington would forge a new bulwark based on Japan, Southeast Asia, and India. Japan, the anchor of this bulwark, must be permitted flexible trade with China to meet immediate economic needs while Southeast Asian resources were developed. Economic aid to the region, rather than an exclusive military program, Acheson argued, would serve to isolate China and expand interdependence.

Acheson repeatedly attacked the pleading of Senators Arthur Vandenberg and William Knowland who insisted on linking American security to the defense of Chiang on Formosa. Similarly, when Ambassador-at-Large Jessup testified in March regarding his tour of the region, he admonished the senators that strong economic links between Japan and Southeast Asia would provide the best barrier to Soviet and Chinese expansion. Any program based on defending Chiang, he warned, was doomed.

The JCS, in a report of January 17, described how the MAP program could achieve the goals described by Acheson. The report described Japan as central to the integrated offshore island chain on which United States security in Asia relied. Japan itself depended on access to strategic raw materials—food, fuel, ores, and fibers. Its security required both trade with Pacific islands and a "buffer on the mainland." In "simpler terms," the JCS report declared,

> the security interest of the United States in the Far East, short of military action, hinges upon finding and securing an area to complement Japan as did Manchuria and Korea prior to World War II. Accepting Communist control of China for the foreseeable future and realizing that a Japanese economy depending largely on resources from China and Korea could draw Japan into the communist orbit; or that a Japanese economy depending for the foreseeable future upon financial assistance and resources from the U.S. is unacceptable; the urgency strategically, of an arrangement with Southeast Asia stands out strongly. . . .

Inevitably, the American attitude of linking Japan and Southeast Asia together as an economic unit carried over into the military sphere. The outbreak of fighting in Korea in June swept away most of the factional and tactical disputes concerning the proper balance of economic and military aid, defense of Formosa, and dealing with the Chinese communists. Dulles's October reference to Japan as the real target in Korea voiced the conclusions of most policy makers. General Bradley, Chairman of the JCS, put the issue directly before President Truman in a June 26 memorandum urging that the United States respond to the Korean crisis by defending not only Korea but also Formosa and the rest of Asia. Bradley told Truman of his firm conviction that "Korea, Japan, Okinawa, Formosa, the Philippines and Southeast Asia are all part of the same problem. Since these positions are interdependent, there is an urgent need for a coordinated overall policy in the Far East."

Ultimately, of course, the financial rewards that the Korean War brought to Japan helped spur the economic miracle of the post-Occupation era. As the United States moved to defend all the regions that Bradley named, Japan's industrial exports reentered those American and European markets in which they supposedly could not compete. Two decades later, in the wake of the American disaster in Vietnam, both a bruised United States and an immensely prosperous Japan would turn back toward political and economic links with the long-shunned communist regime in China.

The very scale of these ironies hampers our understanding of how contemporary policy makers viewed the postwar crises of Japan, China, and Southeast Asia. Nevertheless, among those many planners and agencies concerned with charting the future of Japan after 1945, the fate of Southeast Asia stands out as a central issue around which they constructed a regional policy.

Thomas G. Paterson

CONTAINING COMMUNISM IN CHINA

Critics of the Truman administration's China policy at the time, and some scholars since, have chided the administration for committing itself to the containment of communist expansion in Europe while not preventing the communist triumph in China. Thomas G. Paterson contends that American officials actually did seek to prevent communist victory in the Chinese civil war because they believed that the Soviets would exploit that victory; for example, Washington extended more than $3 billion in aid to the nationalist regime of Jiang Jieshi (Chiang Kai-shek) between 1945 and 1949. But United States officials recognized that available American resources were limited, that Europe ranked as a higher priority than China, that China's vast size precluded significant intervention, and that Jiang was a weak, corrupt leader whose prospects for success were exceedingly dim. Paterson concludes that the Truman administration practiced containment in China less successfully than in Europe because of peculiar local conditions, not because it considered containment inapplicable in the Asian context. And, he argues, the United States exaggerated the Soviet presence in China and rejected opportunities to negotiate with the Chinese communists.

"In Europe we were playing with good stuff," Dean Acheson remembered two years after leaving his secretaryship. "When you went ahead, you helped people who were willing, who had the will to be helped. The great trouble in China was that there wasn't that will." Like Harry S Truman, he guessed that one million American soldiers would have been needed to "save" China from the Communists. Once in, "how to let go of the thing?" For years, Washington would have to impose reforms on China's government and spend a colossal amount of money. "I don't know if the American people would have taken on a task like that." And, "would we have ended up being enemy foreigners? There would have been Communist propaganda all over the place. No one wants to be governed." Acheson concluded in defense of Truman Administration policy that "there are too many people in China and too little arable land, while the damned Americans ride around in Cadillacs—Oh, you would have one hell of a time."

From *Meeting the Communist Threat: Truman to Reagan* by Thomas G. Paterson, pp. 35–36, 42–50, 51–53. Copyright © 1988 by Thomas G. Paterson. Reprinted by permission of Oxford University Press, Inc.

On March 18, 1947, when he was Acting Secretary of State, Acheson spoke less forthrightly. The initial question addressed to him in the State Department's first formal press conference after President Truman announced his doctrine was blunt: "What difference is there between the situation in China and Greece which leads us to help one put down Communism and help the other to bring them into government?" Acheson shot back: "Is that a question which is asked to try to lure me into trouble, or are you really looking for information?" No doubt grumbles rippled through the assembled journalists; they had seldom enjoyed comfortable relations with the often stiff and overbearing Acheson. Although the correspondent assured Acheson that he was seeking information, not trouble, the diplomat dodged this query. He strangely said that he would "talk about that with you privately," then began to tell a second-hand story, which hardly clarified the issue. Once upon a time, Acheson remarked, his old friend and law associate Judge Covington was feasting at an oyster roast on the Eastern Shore. When the oysters were brought in, an elderly politician immediately grabbed a piping hot one, put it in his mouth, and quickly spat it out on the carpet, exclaiming: "A damn fool would have swallowed that."

Acheson's reluctance to handle the delicate question was typical of the Truman administration's hesitancy before 1949 to speak frankly when comparing American policies and aid programs for civil-war–wracked China on the one hand with those for an economically hobbled Europe on the other. In public, the administration did not adequately explain, after the announcement of the Truman Doctrine and the publication of George F. Kennan's "X" article in *Foreign Affairs*, both counseling containment on a global scale, why the United States did not commit itself to major activity in China to match that undertaken for Europe. Compared to the energetic American programs in Europe, which promised billions of dollars in aid to Greece and Turkey, post-UNRRA assistance, Interim Aid, the Marshall Plan, and NATO, and around which the United States built a protective economic and military shield, United States military and economic projects for China, while expensive, seemed hesitant and uncoordinated, given the perceived threat of a Communist victory. And until 1947, through mediation efforts like those of the Marshall Mission, the United States seemed to be inviting the Chinese Communists into a coalition government, whereas in Europe it was seeking to isolate them politically. The administration thus left itself vulnerable to the charge of inconsistency in implementing containment, the central principle of American Cold War diplomacy. "If Europe, why not China?" demanded the critics.

Criticism of America's China policy actually began before Truman enunciated his doctrine in March 1947. Ambassador to China Patrick Hurley resigned his post in November 1945 amid a storm of protest against "professional diplomats" who, he charged, "sided with the Chinese Communist armed party." Early in 1946 the administration released the secret text of the Yalta agreements on the Far East. A flurry of accusations bombarded officials in Washington, with the "Manchurian Manifesto" of May 1946 signed by Congressman Walter Judd, Mrs. Clare Booth Luce, and Henry Luce, among others, complaining that the agreements reached at Yalta, granting territory in Asia to the Soviet Union, were "made behind China's back. . . ." The notion gained vague currency that the United States had sold out Nationalist Jiang Jieshi (Chiang Kai-shek) to the Communists of Mao Zedong (Mao Tse-tung), and that the Truman Administration was simply not paying enough attention to China. Senator Arthur H. Vandenberg mused in January 1947, "we might just as well begin to face the Communist challenge on every front"—not just in Europe or Iran but also in China. There were complaints, too, about the Marshall Mission of 1945–47. General George C. Marshall had attempted to create a unified government of Jiang Nationalists and Mao Communists, but he had failed. Critics were uneasy about Marshall's design to bring the Communists into a new Chinese government because, as Vandenberg asserted: "I never knew a Communist to enter a coalition government for any other purpose than to destroy it."

The unveiling of the Truman Doctrine helped focus American concern about Communism in China directly on methods the United States could use to contain the danger. At a White House meeting two days before his speech, the President briefed leading congressmen on his forthcoming request for aid to Greece and Turkey. Vandenberg told him then that China was as important as Greece. Three months later the Michigan senator informed Marshall, now Secretary of State, that Congress wanted to see the total balance sheet for the distribution of American aid. Where, in short, would the containment line be drawn? In the fall 1947 hearings for interim aid to Europe, Vandenberg again reminded Marshall that an assistance package that excluded China would be considered by some congressmen as "just a one-legged program."

A stalwart of the so-called China Lobby also hammered on the issue of implementing containment in both Europe and China. Walter Judd, Republican congressman from Minnesota and self-professed expert on China affairs, wanted to make sure that "the Russians do not eliminate one front and become able to concentrate all their attention on the other—Europe." He complained that the United States was spending billions on the European flank, but little or nothing on the other flank, Asia. Judd liked to use a familiar analogy: Communism had to be stopped at first base, China, or it would get to second base, Asia (including Japan), then to third base, Africa, and finally across home plate in Western Europe and the United States itself. Governor Thomas E. Dewey of New York, in a November 1947 speech prepared in part by Republican congressmen, sketched another picture: The world was a patient with gangrene in both legs, Europe and Asia. The patient could not survive, the soon-to-be Republican candidate for President warned, by saving only one leg. General Douglas MacArthur took time from administrative duties in Japan to inform the House Foreign Affairs Committee that the "Chinese problem is part of a global situation. . . . Fragmentary decisions in disconnected sectors of the world will not bring an integrated solution." Republican Senator William Knowland added that "it did not make sense to try to keep 240,000,000 Europeans from being taken behind the iron curtain while we are complacent and unconcerned about 450,000,000 Chinese going the same way. . . ."

Did the United States, as the critics charged, neglect the Chinese "front," "leg," or "flank" while concentrating on Europe? The criticism voiced by the Judds and Knowlands did not accord with the realities of American Cold War diplomacy. In postwar Asia the United States assumed new obligations, made influential decisions, and operated programs which belied the critics' charge that the Truman Administration slighted that region. Unabashedly the United States took control of former Japanese islands in the Pacific to use them as military bases, and American officials administered the Ryukyu Islands. American troops were stationed in South Korea until 1949. The Philippines gained independence in 1946 but remained an American bastion and economic satellite with the help of the Philippines Rehabilitation Act of 1946, which provided for $520 million in aid and the transfer of $100 million worth of American surplus property to the new government. In Southeast Asia, American acquiescence in the re-establishment of French colonial rule in Indochina helped determine the history of that area. In the Dutch East Indies, American pressure and advice were pivotal in mediating between the Dutch and Indonesians, leading to independence for the Republic of Indonesia in 1949 and creation of a non-Communist nationalist government. And under the tutelage of General MacArthur, Japan was rebuilt as an ally, especially after 1948 when it became evident that China was going Communist.

As for China itself, American assistance in the period 1945 to 1949 was substantial—over three billion dollars, continuing the aid programs that had begun in World War II. Indeed, the United States became involved in the Chinese civil war overwhelmingly on the side of Jiang's Nationalist regime. President Truman was exuberant, if premature, when he remarked at a cabinet meeting in August 1946: "For the first time we now have a voice in China and for the first time we will be in a position to carry out the policy of 1898." Once begun, American assistance to Jiang built up a momentum that was difficult to reverse. Marshall told a State-War-Navy Coordinating Committee meeting in mid-1947, for example, during a discussion about supplying the Nationalist army with more ammunition, that "it appears that we have a moral obligation to provide it inasmuch as we aided in equipping it with American arms."

During the war, China received $846 million in Lend-Lease supplies; in 1942 Jiang obtained a $500 million stabilization credit; from 1944 to 1947 the United Nations Relief and Rehabilitation Administration spent $670 million in China, about three-quarters of the amount being American in origin. At the end of the war, Americans equipped and helped train thirty-nine Chinese divisions and United States planes transported one-half million Nationalist troops to North China and Manchuria. American Marines occupied North China until mid-1947 (peak strength 55,000), and the U.S Army Advisory Group and Naval Advisory Group, numbering over fourteen hundred in mid-1948, were assigned to aid Jiang's forces. In the postwar period, China received a total of $769 million in Lend-Lease aid; in June 1946 Washington granted China a $50 million loan for "pipeline" goods. In 1946 and 1947, some 131 American naval vessels valued at $140 million were transferred to China; excess Army stocks in West China went to Jiang's regime in 1945 under an American loan of $20 million; in 1945 and 1946, United States Navy ordnance supplies worth $17.7 million also became Nationalist property. In the summer of 1947, when United States Marines retired from North China, 6,500 tons of American ammunition were left for Jiang's forces. In sum, American surplus property with a value of more than one billion dollars had been shifted to Jiang by early 1949. China also received approximately $44 million in post-United Nations Relief and Rehabilitation Administration assistance. In 1945 and 1946 the Export–Import Bank authorized six credits totaling another $69 million for exports to China of American cotton, ships, railway, power plant, and coal mining equipment. Early in 1946, the Bank also designated $500 million as additional credits for China, but the earmarked amount expired in mid-1947. In the China Aid Act of April 1948, Congress authorized $338 million in economic assistance ($275 million was appropriated) and another $125 million primarily for military purposes. And the Mutual Defense Assistance Act of 1949 provided $75 million for China.

Secretary Acheson claimed in early 1949 before a congressional committee that the United States had done more for China than for any other country in the postwar period. He insisted, drawing upon the reports of General David G. Barr, head of the military advisory group, that not one engagement in China had been lost through the lack of equipment or military supplies. Mao had angrily complained that the United States, active in the civil war, "supplies the money and guns and Chiang Kai-shek the men to fight for the United States and slaughter the Chinese people. . . ." The Communist leader would have been more accurate had he noted, as did the Foreign Service Officer O. Edmund Clubb, that the "American arms supply had sufficed for *both* sides," because large caches of American military equipment fell into the hands of Communist forces.

In the period 1945 to 1949, the United States became Jiang's major ally and chief quartermaster in the civil war. At the same time, the Truman Administration urged the Nationalist government to undertake political and economic reforms. From August 1946 to May 1947, Washington actually curtailed exports of munitions to China, although items already contracted were shipped. Washington seldom met Jiang's requests for aid in full, deciding instead on conditional support. American officials constantly pressed the Guomindang (Kuomintang) leader to form a more representative regime and to ferret out corruption from his government. "There are few harder stunts of statesmanship," Herbert Feis has written, "than at one and the same time to sustain a foreign government and to alter it against its fears and inclinations." Failing in its reform thrusts, the United States still clung to the faltering Nationalist regime, feeding and fueling its armies and politicians. The perception of a Soviet-Communist threat against China and the postwar United States commitment to the containment of such a threat help explain why the United States, however reluctantly, backed and sustained Jiang—and ultimately went down to defeat with him.

After World War II American leaders perceived a Soviet-Communist danger in Asia, particularly in China. Although they recognized that the civil war in China had indigenous roots, they believed its consequences carried global implications. They came to interpret Chinese events through a Cold War lens; they foresaw an ultimate Soviet-American contest for influence in China. American policy was designed to deny the Soviets that influence and to preserve the traditional Open Door policy, which insured some American influence. Continued political and economic instability or Communist victory in the civil war might permit the Soviets into China. If this occurred, it was feared, Russia could use China as a springboard to Communize, through infiltration, the rest of Asia; threaten America's ally, Japan; close trade routes and commercial opportunities; block Western access to such raw materials as tin and rubber; and in the event of Soviet-American war, launch military operations from the vast Chinese mainland.

In the immediate postwar period, the Soviet threat against China was often explained as indirect, quiescent, and long-term, but ever present. In the American mind, the threat became more ominous as the Chinese Communists unrelentingly threw defeat at Jiang. The United States had to make a strong stand in China, declared Truman in 1945, or Russia would take the place of Japan in the Far East. General Marshall reported from China early in 1946 that he had pressed the Nationalists to build a unified government "at the fastest possible pace so as to eliminate her present vulnerability to Soviet undercover attack, which exists so long as there remains a separate Communist government and a separate Communist army in China." In his influential "long telegram" of February 22, 1946, George F. Kennan included the Chinese Communists as a group willing to lend itself to "Soviet purposes." Acheson spoke of Russia's "predatory aims in Asia" and argued at an August 1946 cabinet meeting that United States Marines should remain in China, for "we will prevent by our very presence and by the presence of our Marines some other country from interfering in China to our regret." The other country was, of course, Russia.

Soviet behavior in Manchuria throughout 1945 and 1946 confirmed fears of a Soviet thrust. Despite American protests, the Soviets thwarted Nationalist authority over the province, seized war booty in the form of food and industrial equipment, and, when they departed

Manchuria in April, turned over large stocks of weapons to Mao's Communist forces. The American ambassador to China, John Leighton Stuart, expressed a popular assumption when he reported that Soviet favoritism toward the Chinese Communists "fits customary Soviet predilection for indirect activity wherever possible." American officials reported after 1946 that they could not detect direct Soviet involvement in the civil war. Still, they saw Russia hovering like a menacing giant over the Chinese tumult, waiting to take advantage of chaos and American weakness. An American withdrawal from China, the Asian expert John Carter Vincent said, would open the door to Soviet influence. Thus there was no intention to abandon or "wash our hands" of the China problem, he assured the Chinese Ambassador to the United States in August 1946.

The Joint Chiefs of Staff (JCS) were more emphatic than most officials in 1947 that the Soviets were plotting to master China. Taking the prevalent global perspective as expressed in the Truman Doctrine, they concluded that "in China, as in Europe and in the Middle East and Far East, it is clearly Soviet policy to expand control and influence wherever possible." Vincent dissented from their call for increased military aid to Jiang and questioned not so much the Soviet threat, but its schedule: "A USSR-dominated China is not a danger of sufficient immediacy or probability" to justify large-scale intervention. Still, Vincent seems to have been in the minority in minimizing the Soviet danger, and he was removed from the debate in July 1947 when he was sent off to Switzerland to be the American minister there. By November 1947 Secretary Marshall summarized American policy as preventing the "Soviet domination of China."

American officials increasingly saw the Chinese Communists as tools, instruments, or vehicles for exercising Soviet influence. Throughout 1948 and 1949, as the Cold War intensified in Europe, American officials expanded upon their earlier feelings about the Soviet threat, with growing emphasis on the linkage between Mao and Moscow. Stuart beat the theme constantly in his cables to Washington. He bemoaned Mao's parroting of Soviet theories, Chinese Communist ideological subservience to Moscow, the Chinese Communist Party's aping of the Soviet model in dealing with foreign correspondents, and, in general, Mao's commitment to international Communism. Mao, concluded the Ambassador, was a "brilliant disciplined if somewhat junior ally in [the] 'world anti-imperialist front.' . . ." In September of 1948 the Policy Planning Staff prepared a report, ultimately circulated as National Security Council Paper No. 34, which reflected the thinking of the Truman Administration. The report identified the USSR's covetous designs on Manchuria and North China and asserted: "It is the political situation in China which must arouse the aggressive interest of the Kremlin." The Policy Planning Staff warned that from China, Russia could mount a political offensive against the rest of East Asia. In short, Russia's objective was to control all of the territory comprising China.

Thus, by July 1949, when the Truman Administration published the justification for its post-1945 policies in a White Paper, it was not surprising to read that the Chinese "Communist leaders have foresworn their Chinese heritage and have publicly announced their subservience to a foreign power, Russia . . ." or that the Chinese Communist government served the interests of Soviet Russia. By March of the following year Acheson was speaking about Soviet-Communist imperialism in Asia as part of the Kremlin's attempt to extend its absolute domination over the widest possible areas of the world.

Throughout these years, there was lingering speculation that the Chinese Communists would resist Soviet intrusion upon Chinese sovereignty. Americans hoped that Mao would become an Asian Tito, practicing a brand of independent Communism like that of Yugoslavia. Some American officials commented upon Titoist tendencies, but were uncertain whether the immediate examples of Sino-Soviet tension portended a long-term split. The Central Intelligence Agency suggested in November 1948 that "Chinese nationalism might well prove stronger than international communism" and that "their potential independence of the Kremlin is greater than that of Tito and, except for him, unique." The Consul General in Shanghai, John M. Cabot, was more convinced than most Americans that China would go the way of Yugoslavia and that Russia would fail to control the independent-minded Chinese. He pointed out to the Secretary of State that the Chinese Communists were even less beholden than Tito to the Soviets for their assumption of power; that the Chinese were not committed to the Soviet economic bloc; that the Chinese had traditional links with the West; that Russia was historically an imperialist threat to China; and that Chinese Communism hardly resembled Soviet Communism.

In the White Paper Acheson noted the possibility that in the future Sino-Soviet relations might sour. After boldly declaring China subservient to Russia, he remarked that "ultimately the profound civilization and the democratic individualism of China will reassert themselves and she will throw off the foreign yoke." National Security Council Paper No. 48, prepared in December 1949, after Jiang's fall, provided extensive discussion of this possibility. Like so many other American analyses, it identified Russia's aggressive intentions in Asia and its domination of the Chinese Communist Party. But it suggested that serious friction might develop if Russia tried to establish control over China similar to that of the subjugated Eastern European states, and concluded that American policy should exploit rifts between Communist China and Soviet Russia. Acheson told the Joint Chiefs of Staff, a few days after the paper circulated, that he perceived inevitable conflict between Beijing (Peking) and Moscow: "Mao is not a true satellite in that he came to power by his own efforts and was not installed in office by the Soviet Army." American leaders thus seemed aware of a possible means of implementing containment—encourage a Sino–Soviet split. The United States goal remained what it had been since the end of the Second World War—to contain Soviet influence in China. Although remarking on a potential Stalin-Mao split, Truman Administration officials nonetheless took no steps to encourage a schism. Instead, they repeatedly pointed to the Soviet menace in the guise of Chinese Communists and assisted Jiang to the moment of his defeat. The President's comment to a January 1949 Cabinet meeting that "we can't be in a position of making any deal with a Communist regime" represented the core of American policy, even in the late fall 1949 through early spring 1950, after Jiang's collapse on the mainland, when American officials may have been warming to the idea of some degree of accommodation with Mao's government.

China Lobbyists like Congressman Judd and Senator Styles Bridges asked, if the Truman Administration admitted that Communism directed by Russia threatened China, why did not the United States, as in Europe, initiate a new assistance program, comparable to the Marshall Plan, to contain the threat? Truman officials, they charged, were failing to fulfill the logic of their own containment doctrine. The administration replied accurately that it *was* devoted to containment, but it had sufficient reasons for treating Europe and China differently. Some of these explanations were stated publicly, some not. Never were they pulled together in a comprehensive statement, a failing that brought upon the administration a continued hail of criticism.

Shortly after the launching of the Truman Doctrine and the Marshall Plan, American officials said that the China problem had not reached emergency status; China was not approaching collapse as

Greece was. In the spring of 1947 that assessment seemed correct because Nationalist troops were enjoying some success. But after the Communists unleashed their summer offensive and began to drive Jiang's forces back, this argument had to be abandoned. Several other explanations followed. At one time or another from 1947 to 1949 administration spokesmen explained the uniqueness of China by stating that there were far more rebels and Communist sympathizers in China than in Greece; that the Chinese Communists showed some willingness to negotiate (witness the Marshall Mission), unlike the National Liberation Front in Greece; that equipment and goods shipped to China might very likely fall into Communist hands, as was happening; and that a military route to a stable, non-Communist government and peace in Greece seemed feasible, whereas in China it had already proven impossible after two decades of internecine warfare.

Four other reasons were accorded more emphasis. The administration adhered to a Europe-first priority in the Cold War; China was too large, too unmanageable, and had too uncertain a terrain for large-scale American intervention; Jiang Jieshi's regime was resistant to American advice and so corrupt that it squandered American aid; and China did not satisfy an important criterion for receiving a major aid program before the Korean War: A recipient government must have the support of a large percentage of the indigenous population and must be committed to the principle of self-help. . . .

For these reasons, then, the Truman Administration distinguished between China and Europe in applying containment and refused to undertake a massive new aid program for China or to dispatch American troops there to halt a Communist victory. By the fall of 1947 it was evident to American officials that Jiang was slipping badly, that a reconciliation of Nationalists and Communists was impossible, and that infusions of aid would be unlikely to reverse the tide. American hesitancy to invest further in Jiang's deteriorating regime surfaced about the same time that Washington was preparing the European Recovery Program. Some members of the Republican Eightieth Congress of 1947–48, always alert for opportunities to besmirch the record of the President and unable to exploit the well-received Truman Doctrine and Marshall Plan programs, found the China question a useful stick for beating the administration. Bipartisanship, Vandenberg asserted, did not apply to China. Truman's suppression of the secret Wedemeyer Report of September 1947 further fed criticism that something was amiss in China policy. General Albert C. Wedemeyer had urged extensive American military assistance for China, and Truman's refusal to make his report public aroused suspicion of a cover-up of information damaging to the White House. And the administration introduced in February 1948, with tempered enthusiasm, a China aid bill perhaps intended to quiet critics who might delay action on the Marshall Plan until more assistance was extended to China. Marshall's statement that the new request for $570 million for China was designed to give China only a breathing space did not comfort those who wanted to "save" China. Nor did the sluggish administration of the new assistance. Dewey's defeat in the 1948 presidential election, which seemed to destroy Republican hopes for a change in China policy, further emboldened Truman's political foes to attack the seeming neglect of China. . . .

Why was the administration unable to explain in a frank, persuasive manner that it had poured millions of dollars into Jiang's treasury, had armed Jiang's legions to halt the feared Communist victory, had done everything possible to apply containment in China—in short, that the critics were distorting the record? When the administration finally put together its case for not standing in the last Chinese ditch with Jiang, the explanations came too late in the bulky White Paper read by few Americans. It also smacked too much of an apology for failure rather than an explanation for treating Europe and China differently.

Until 1949 Truman officials suffered under the self-imposed restraint that they would not publicly highlight Jiang's ineptitude. Thus, they chose not to explain one of the primary reasons for the difference in applying containment in Europe and Asia. They believed that such a public statement might weaken the beleaguered Jiang regime even further and insure its early collapse. Marshall starkly identified the problem for the Cabinet in November 1948:

> The Nationalist Government of China is on its way out and there is nothing we can do to save it. We are faced with the question of clarifying [this for] the American people and by so doing deliver the knock out blow to the National Government in China—or we can play along with the existing government and keep facts from the American people and thereby be accused later of playing into the hands of the Communists.

Acheson further noted that "you cannot explain why you cannot do anymore, because if you do, you complete the destruction of the very fellows you are trying to help." When Truman released the White Paper, he admitted publicly that certain facts had not been revealed earlier because they "might have served to hasten the events in China which have now occurred." "Our case," regretted the Director of the Policy Planning Staff, "has never been adequately and forcefully presented to the public, largely out of deference to the generalissimo." American leaders believed they had to risk political wounds at home to avoid inflicting them on their collapsing, unregenerate ally Jiang. In so doing, the administration invited charges that it was Washington's fault that the Communists were winning in China and that containment had not been applied vigorously enough. The administration thus had to suffer "misrepresentation, distortion, and misunderstanding," complained the President.

Truman himself might have made public before 1949, the facts damaging to Jiang, but he chose not to. Why? In the final analysis he could not abandon Jiang—could not deliver the knockout blow—because Jiang was America's only real instrument for containing Chinese Communism. The debate between Truman and his critics was not, after all, over whether to abandon Jiang; few advocated that. The question was conditional aid or full-scale support. The administration itself decided by fall 1947 that something had to be done to arrest China's economic deterioration and came to view the China Aid Act of 1948, however futile it might prove in the long run, as a chance to remedy some economic ills and thereby keep Jiang in power longer. . . .

What is striking is that the United States backed the wrong horse almost to the very end of the Nationalist regime on mainland China, and, after the outbreak of the Korean War a few months later, continued its backing for Jiang on Formosa. Although some American officials hoped that Titoist tendencies would erode a Sino-Soviet alignment, they did "not think it is safe to bank on it," as Philip Jessup indicated. The Truman Administration never withdrew recognition from the Nationalist government or attempted to reach a *modus vivendi* with Mao; it never approached the People's Republic of China (proclaimed October 1, 1949) to establish trade relations or to discuss reconstruction aid; and it never recognized the new Communist government, although Britain, Norway, India, and other nations soon did, and still others, like Australia, Canada, and France, preferred recognition but bowed to American policy.

Washington also spurned two Chinese Communist overtures to improve relations. One demarche came in May 1949 from Zhou Enlai, a pragmatic, high-ranking official. He urged closer ties, suggested some disaffection with the Soviet Union, and requested American foreign aid.

Truman killed the opportunity by directing the State Department "to be careful not to indicate any softening toward the Communists. . . ." Then, in June, Mao invited Ambassador Stuart to visit him in Beijing; Washington instructed him to avoid such high level contact, and he did not go. Truman did not reject accommodation or recognition just because he feared the China Lobby or negative public opinion. The President for years had successfully defied the Lobby, and he would do so again in 1951 when he fired General MacArthur from his Asian command. As for public opinion, as some members of a State Department roundtable on China commented in October 1949, it "can either be ignored or educated to a new view of the China scene." Truman and Acheson never undertook such a re-education of the American people, because neither man himself held a "new view" of China.

In September of 1949 the United States informed Britain that it would not recognize Mao's government, even though it hoped to play for a split between China and the USSR. The British not only recognized the People's Republic of China but also, at odds with the United States, worked for its admission to the United Nations. London wondered how Washington could drive a wedge between Beijing and Moscow without an American presence in China itself. Indeed, the British sensibly reasoned, American hostility to the People's Republic of China would very likely drive the two Communist states closer to one another. After the failure of the Marshall Mission and years of support for Jiang, about the only way the United States might have contained the Soviet Union was to have come to terms with the Chinese Communist Party, kindling the Titoist inclinations some American officials themselves detected. They rejected that option in favor of non-recognition as a tool of containment. President Truman, by the fall of 1950, seemed to have abandoned all thought of Sino-Soviet differences. British Prime Minister Clement Attlee told Truman in a private conversation that "opinions differ on the extent to which [the] Chinese Communists are satellites." He wondered "when is it that you scratch a communist and find a nationalist." The President would have none of such thinking: "They are satellites of Russia and will be satellites so long as the present Peiping [Beijing] regime is in power." Moreover, they were "complete satellites." And, "the only way to meet communism is to eliminate it."

The Truman Administration practiced containment in China less successfully than in Europe because of peculiar local conditions created by the unreliable Jiang, not because it thought containment was inapplicable to Asia. Truman officials did attempt to use Jiang, through extensive aid, to thwart Mao's ascendency, for in his success they perceived a Soviet threat to China that had global implications. Truman and his advisers invited much of the heavy criticism they received by choosing to sustain Jiang while suppressing official American criticism of him. In their reading of the strategic-economic setback handed the United States by Mao's triumph and by the Sino-Soviet Treaty struck in early 1950, Truman officials opted for a policy of isolation rather than intercourse. After American and Chinese soldiers shed each other's blood in the Korean War, that policy became fixed. America's Asian diplomacy then devoted itself to salvaging Indochina for the French, constructing a regional alliance (Southeast Asia Treaty Organization), reconstructing Japan, and defending Jiang on Formosa. Not until the Nixon presidency, at a time when the Sino-Soviet schism had become cavernous, did the United States act upon a "new view" of China. In 1972 the United States and China began a diplomatic process that culminated in 1979 in a formal exchange of ambassadors. Beijing and Washington took the momentous step toward one another for the same reason: to counter the Soviet threat.

Robert J. McMahon

DECOLONIZATION AND COLD WAR IN ASIA

Areas long viewed as peripheral to core United States interests suddenly became critical as postwar American policymakers redefined national security imperatives in the face of what appeared to be an ominous, global Soviet threat. American interests in and commitments to southern Asia, for example, increased dramatically during the early Cold War years. Robert J. McMahon discusses the evolution of United States policy toward South and Southeast Asia during the Truman administration. He shows how the desire to contain communist power led to very different policies toward the

Text by Robert J. McMahon, from *The Truman Presidency* edited by Michael J. Lacey, pp. 339–340, 343, 344–358, 359–365. Copyright ©1989. Reprinted by permission of Cambridge University Press.

colonial struggles in Indochina and Indonesia and toward the newly independent governments in India and Pakistan. He concludes that the Truman
administration's approach to an Asia just emerging from colonialism was
ultimately as ineffective as it was short-sighted. Instead of adjusting American policy to the powerful dynamic of Asian nationalism, the Truman
administration filtered all developments through an East-West lens. That
the Cold War ultimately proved a distorting lens for viewing Asian events is
one of the central contentions of this essay.

Robert J. McMahon teaches history at the University of Florida. He is the
author of *Colonialism and Cold War: The United States and the Struggle for
Indonesian Independence, 1945–49* (1981) and the editor of *Major Problems in the History of the Vietnam War* (1990). In 1988 he won the Society
for Historians of American Foreign Relations' Stuart L. Bernath Article Prize.

When Harry S Truman suddenly entered the White House in April
1945, he faced a staggering array of problems, many of which
demanded immediate attention. Certainly the future of colonial rule in
South Asia and Southeast Asia did not rank very high among them.
Indeed, the administration of Franklin D. Roosevelt had already agreed
not to challenge the reassertion of European colonial authority in
Southeast Asia and not to pressure the British on the sensitive subject of
Indian independence. The untested chief executive from Independence,
Missouri, had no reason to question those decisions. Nor did he have
cause to question the conventional wisdom that both areas were periph-
eral to core U.S. interests. To be sure, during World War II the United
States evinced a growing interest in the colonial territories of southern
Asia; not only did those regions possess a wealth of valuable natural
resources—as the events leading up to Pearl Harbor amply attest—but
American strategic planners called for an enhanced U.S. military presence in the postwar Pacific. Still, as the new president prepared for the
daunting tasks ahead of him, most knowledgeable observers inside and
outside the government anticipated that the U.S. stake in colonial Asia
would remain circumscribed indefinitely.

They could not have been more mistaken. For Truman's presidency dramatically—and probably irrevocably—transformed America's
approach to the world. When Truman left office in January 1953, it
was difficult indeed to distinguish vital U.S. interests from secondary
ones; given the administration's expansive definition of the Soviet
threat, all interests appeared suddenly critical. By then the United
States had embraced what one historian has called the doctrine of
national security: a concept that "postulates the interrelatedness of so

many different political, economic, and military factors that developments halfway around the globe are seen to have automatic and direct
impact on America's core interests." A study of the Truman administration's record in South and Southeast Asia provides an instructive micro-
cosm of the "globalization" of U.S. foreign policy during the postwar
era. Areas that had traditionally been of distinctly minor interest to
Washington were transformed during the Truman years into critical
cold-war battlegrounds, as the United States redefined its national security interests in the face of what it considered an unprecedented threat
from the Soviet Union. . . .

. . . U.S. policy makers were almost completely unprepared for the
depth and intensity of the nationalist rebellions that erupted in Southeast Asia in the wake of the Japanese surrender. Within days after the
Pacific War reached its final denouement, nationalists in the East Indies
boldly proclaimed an independent Republic of Indonesia. Two weeks
later, Vietminh guerilla fighters in Indochina followed suit, declaring
independence for a Democratic Republic of Vietnam. Although some
of the more astute Asian experts in the U.S. government had warned
that the war would lead to intensified nationalist sentiment in these
areas, none anticipated the rapid establishment of popular and broad-
based local governments. Most top U.S. policy makers, preoccupied
with more pressing matters, expected the reassertion of European
authority to be relatively smooth and orderly. Poor intelligence on
actual conditions in Southeast Asia reinforced that complacency. At
least one official report even predicted that the Indonesians would greet
their returning Dutch rulers as liberators.

When it quickly became apparent during the fall of 1945 that the
return to imperial rule in Southeast Asia would be neither smooth nor
orderly, the Truman administration adjusted its policy to meet the new
realities. Intent on maintaining warm relations with its European allies
and yet unwilling to alienate colonial nationalists, the administration
adopted a position of strict neutrality and noninvolvement. "Hands-
off" would remain the keynote of U.S. policy toward the colonial
upheavals in Southeast Asia until 1947. Thus, while conceding the
legal right of France and Holland as "territorial sovereigns" to restore
their prewar rule, the United States periodically indicated that it would
favor any steps toward eventual self-government in both Indochina and
the Indies. . . .

To U.S. policy makers, studied noninvolvement appeared the only
workable response to the nationalist revolts in Indochina and the East

Indies. Those revolts, which constituted the first major challenge to the Truman administration's plans for postwar Asia, posed an insuperable dilemma for Washington. According to the administration's first policy paper on the subject, U.S. interests would best be served by "a Far East progressively developing into a group of self-governing states—independent or with Dominion status—which would cooperate with each other and with the Western powers on a basis of mutual self-respect and friendship." European efforts to restore the old colonial order would clearly undermine that long-term goal. Would the United States, then, press its allies to make commitments to eventual native self-rule even if they proved reluctant? Anticipating this problem, the paper acknowledged that "a problem for the United States is to harmonize, so far as possible and without prejudice to its traditional position, its policies in regard to two objectives: increased political freedom for the Far East and the maintenance of the unity of the leading United Nations."

Left unexplored was the potentially contradictory nature of these policy objectives. Given the extreme sensitivity of the decolonization question in France and Holland—two countries, after all, that were just recovering from the shattering psychological and economic effects of prolonged German occupation—how could the United States realistically expect to pressure them in Southeast Asia and still maintain their staunch support in Europe? Yet if the colonial powers refused to make concessions to legitimate nationalist demands, the United States would soon have to choose between these conflicting policy objectives. The "hands-off" posture reflected U.S. reluctance to make that choice.

At that time, the manifest tilt toward the colonial nations reflected the sober calculation at the upper reaches of the Truman administration that European interests rated a distinctly higher priority than Asian ones. The steady deterioration of U.S.-Soviet relations during this period underscored the critical importance of cultivating reliable partners in Western Europe. Pressing European priorities—political, economic, and strategic—were inextricably linked to the emerging U.S. global foreign policy, formulated in response to perceived Soviet ambitions. In comparison, Southeast Asia seemed an annoying, and potentially divisive, sideshow. Besides, U.S. policy makers had reason to believe that enlightened self-interest would eventually compel the British, French, and Dutch to adopt colonial policies that would be consonant with U.S. interests.

The Truman administration hoped that the U.S. record in the Philippines might serve as a model in that regard. Moving quickly to honor Roosevelt's wartime pledge, the United States, with great fanfare, granted independence to its Asian colony on 4 July 1946. The enormous influence that the United States maintained in the Philippines after independence—best symbolized by the massive U.S. military bases at Clark Field and Subic Bay and the dependent economic relationship enshrined in the Bell Trade Act—certainly suggests that the United States neither expected nor desired a precipitous removal of European influence from the colonial areas. Rather, U.S. policy makers sought the gradual transfer of political authority to responsible, West-leaning native elites. In the view of U.S. planners, such elites would best ensure long-term political stability while protecting legitimate Western strategic and economic interests.

That objective appeared near realization in the Indies when the Dutch and Indonesians initialed the so-called Linggadjati agreement in November 1946. The United States quickly extended congratulations to both parties for their statesmanship. By providing for the peaceful evolution toward native self-rule, while maintaining intact Dutch political, military, and economic influence in the islands, the agreement appeared to conform perfectly with U.S. policy objectives for colonial Asia. In contrast with the rapidly deteriorating situation in Indochina, where the brutal French bombing of Haiphong harbor that same month signaled the beginning of outright warfare, Linggadjati indeed seemed to represent a hopeful and rational precedent for other colonial powers to follow. It was, in the words of former Under Secretary of State Sumner Welles, "the most encouraging development of recent months."

Equally encouraging to the United States was the evolution of a more liberal British colonial policy under the leadership of Prime Minister Clement Attlee. No colonial issue had proved more divisive during the war than that of India's future; at times it threatened to embitter Anglo-American relations. FDR persistently urged Winston Churchill during the early years of the war to make an explicit commitment to postwar independence, much to the prime minister's discomfiture. Despite Roosevelt's various efforts, including the dispatch of two presidential representatives on much publicized fact-finding missions, Churchill remained intransigent on this highly emotional subject. Recognizing the depth of his ally's feelings about the British empire and being unwilling to jeopardize wartime harmony for an issue that was of distinctly secondary interest to Washington, Roosevelt relaxed his pressure by 1943. Ironically, by then critics were accusing the president, with considerable justification, of turning his back on India and acquiescing in the ill-conceived British efforts to suppress the Indian independence movement.

The Truman administration accordingly welcomed the dramatic transformation in Britain's colonial policy that followed the accession of Attlee in July 1945. Committing itself almost immediately to early independence for India and other Asian possessions, Attlee's Labour government moved toward that goal, albeit haltingly, throughout 1945 and 1946. Pleased with what it viewed as a progressive and realistic policy, the Truman administration only occasionally prodded London during this period, suggesting politely that it might move more speedily and boldly. Such friendly advice, however, was invariably offered in a low-key manner; U.S. officials carefully shied away from the confrontations of the war years.

Much to the delight of U.S. officials, in December 1946 Britain announced its intention to grant independence to Burma and two months later publicly committed itself to full independence for India. Those decisions conformed perfectly with the U.S. vision of a peaceful and gradual evolution of southern Asia from colonialism to self-rule. Accordingly, Secretary of State George C. Marshall promptly congratulated the British for their statesmanship. In the hope that a gracious and orderly end to nearly two centuries of the British raj might have a catalytic effect on the French and Dutch, Washington suggested several times that the British accelerate their timetable for Indian independence. Although the rapid ascent of Mohammed Ali Jinnah's Muslim League and the sheer complexity of the subcontinent's communal problems perplexed U.S. observers, the Truman administration supported Britain's controversial decision to create the independent Muslim state of Pakistan. American diplomats rejoiced at London's decision to grant independence to India and Pakistan on 14 August 1947. Finally, it appeared, a European power had recognized its own enlightened self-interest.

Developments in Southeast Asia at this juncture evoked considerably less optimism. In Indochina, full-scale guerrilla warfare raged throughout 1947. In Indonesia, the promising Linggadjati settlement, ratified by both parties in March 1947, collapsed shortly thereafter. Unwilling to acquiesce to nationalist demands for true independence, the Dutch, like the French, inexorably gravitated toward a military solution. Ignoring U.S. entreaties, on 20 July 1947 they suddenly launched a full-scale offensive against the Republic of Indonesia, quickly capturing substantial portions of the republic's territory and presenting the United States—and the world—with a fait accompli.

The United States viewed the colonial conflicts in Southeast Asia with alarm. To be sure, neither the French-Vietminh nor the Dutch-Indonesian struggle for power preoccupied the president or his senior advisers during the early cold-war years. With tension mounting between Washington and the Kremlin over such divisive areas as Eastern Europe, Germany, Iran, and Greece, top U.S. policy makers could hardly be expected to devote much attention to hostilities in far-off Southeast Asia. But Indochina and Indonesia were inseparably linked to other, more central, concerns. The political and economic stabilization of Western Europe (one of the leading postwar priorities for the United States) was intimately connected to the tumultuous developments in that region. A report prepared for President Truman in 1947 by the newly created Central Intelligence Agency emphasized this interrelationship. "Of important concern in relation to Western European recovery," it noted, "is the existing instability in colonial (or former colonial) areas upon the resources of which several European powers (the United Kingdom, France, and the Netherlands) have hitherto been customed to depend. . . . The continuance of unsettled conditions hinders economic recovery and causes a diversion of European strength into efforts to maintain or reimpose control by force."

Given those interlocking concerns, it should not be surprising that, in the wake of the Dutch military action, the United States abandoned its hands-off policy by offering its services as a mediator to the two parties. After failing to prevent the Dutch "police action" with its last-minute representations, the Truman administration reasoned that U.S. mediation might at least limit the damage of that ill-conceived assault and perhaps bring both sides back to the negotiating table. Still, the United States proffered its good offices only after the governments of India and Australia had called formally for action by the United Nations Security Council. Fearing that international debate on the Dutch offensive would prove contentious, and might compromise as well its cherished neutrality stance, the United States sought to preempt United Nations intervention by its unilateral mediation offer. But Indonesian leaders, wary of Washington's decidedly pro-Dutch orientation, opted instead for United Nations consideration, in effect rejecting the U.S. overture. Its initiative rebuffed, the Truman administration quickly shifted gears; if international involvement was unavoidable, then it would try both to limit and control the nature of that involvement. The subsequent action of the Security Council in forming a Good Offices Committee whose counsel would be strictly noncompulsory, with the United States in the strategic middle position on the three-nation grouping, well accommodated that new strategy.

From the formation of the Good Offices Committee in October 1947 to the establishment of a sovereign nationalist government on 27 December 1949, the United States played a major, and ultimately decisive, role in the resolution of the Dutch-Indonesian conflict. The U.S.-sponsored Renville settlement of January 1948, signed on board a U.S. naval vessel after perceptible U.S. pressure on both sides, established a framework for a settlement. Much to the dismay of U.S. diplomats, the unilateral Dutch abrogation of that internationally sanctioned agreement in late 1948 culminated in their preemptive military offensive in December of that year. In response, the United States threatened to withhold its substantial economic and military assistance to the Netherlands unless the Dutch committed themselves clearly and irrevocably to Indonesian independence. Recognizing the necessity of U.S. support, the Dutch relented. In April 1949 they agreed to transfer sovereignty within months to an independent nationalist government. Before the close of the year they proved true to their word, although persistent U.S. pressure during the final negotiating stages was necessary to remove some lingering obstacles.

That U.S. policy smoothed the path toward Indonesian independence is indisputable. Probably more than any other factor, the application of direct U.S. economic pressure early in 1949 compelled the Dutch to relinquish their prized colony.

It must be emphasized, however, that U.S. support for the Indonesian Republic came only very slowly and with the greatest reluctance. Before the second Dutch military offensive, the actions of the Truman administration consistently bolstered the position of the Netherlands. The statements of U.S. spokesmen at the United Nations as well as the actions of U.S. representatives on the Good Offices Committee reflected that bias. Marshall Plan aid to the Netherlands, which began to flow in the spring of 1948, hopelessly compromised any remaining pretense to neutrality. "The practical effect of ECA [Economic Cooperation Administration] aid on the political conflict," noted a State Department intelligence report in April 1948, "is to strengthen the economic, political, and military position of the Netherlands in Indonesia. . . . Reactions to ECA grants by the Dutch and by the Indonesians show that this effect is clearly understood by both sides."

The reason for this marked U.S. tilt toward the Netherlands lies in the European orientation of Truman's foreign policy during this period. No initiatives during the early cold-war years were more important to the administration's overall foreign policy objectives than the Marshall Plan and the North Atlantic Treaty Organization. Those programs, designed to rehabilitate and strengthen Western Europe in the face of a perceived global Soviet threat, were indispensable to the administration's developing strategy of containment. As Dutch support was important, if not crucial, to the success of both programs, the Truman administration carefully avoided any rupture with its ally over the sensitive issue of colonial relations. The United States was not uncritical of Dutch policy, of course; it repeatedly urged the negotiation of an equitable settlement with the republic, pressured the Dutch to sign the Renville agreement, and warned against resorting to force before both police actions. Still, the administration operated within certain clearly defined parameters. As the State Department instructed its representatives in Indonesia prior to the signing of the Renville agreement: The "Netherlands is [a] strong proponent [of] US policy in Europe. Dept believes that [the] stability [of the] present Dutch government would be seriously undermined if Netherlands fails to retain very considerable stake in NEI and the political consequences of failure [of] present Dutch Govt would in all likelihood be prejudicial to US position in Western Europe."

The sharp reversal in U.S. policy following the second Dutch police action occurred when it became clear to the administration that the new offensive jeopardized those European priorities. Appalled by the unilateral Dutch violation of an agreement backed by the United States, a vocal minority in Congress threatened to cut off funds to the European Recovery Program and block passage of the Atlantic pact in retaliation. The very cornerstone of the administration's foreign policy thus appeared likely to unravel as a result of what many U.S. policy makers considered a foolishly anachronistic resort to military muscle. Consequently, Secretary of State Dean Acheson bluntly informed his Dutch counterpart in a climactic meeting that an immediate change of policy would be essential for a continuance of U.S. economic support. "Money talked," as one U.S. diplomat later recalled wryly.

Asian considerations joined with these European ones to hasten the abrupt change in U.S. policy. Most important in this regard was the abject failure of the Dutch to accomplish their military objectives. Months after the offensive began, guerrilla warfare in Java and Sumatra was intensifying, with Dutch forces actually on the retreat in some areas. A report by the National Security Council (NSC) predicted that the Dutch would prove unable to pacify the archipelago and in the process would likely strengthen the appeal of radical elements within the nationalist movement. Given the demonstrably moderate character of the Republic of Indonesia government, the NSC paper recommended that the administration support Indonesian independence as "the only channel lying between polarization and Stalinization." Recognizing that support for native self-rule would be "a difficult course," the NSC nonetheless judged it necessary in order to develop "an effective counterforce to communism in the Far East leading eventually to the emergence of [Southeast Asia] as an integral part of the free world."

Ironically, a similar blend of European and Asian concerns, shaped, as in Indonesia, by the administration's global strategy for containing the Soviet Union, prompted a sharply differentiated response to the Vietnamese struggle for independence. Until mid-1947 U.S. officials tended to view both of Southeast Asia's colonial conflicts in broadly comparable terms. With the advent of the first Dutch police action, however, U.S. policy toward the two struggles began to diverge markedly. The Truman administration inserted itself actively into the Indonesian imbroglio at that juncture while clinging to its hands-off posture in Indochina. Cautious optimism toward the prospects for a settlement in the Indies helps explain the adoption of an active U.S. policy toward that dispute; senior officials were far less sanguine about the possibility of a breakthrough in the French-Vietminh war. As Secretary of State Marshall conceded in a cable to the U.S. embassy in Paris early in 1947, the United States simply had "no solution of [the] problem to suggest." In addition, United Nations consideration of the Indonesian question added a significant new dimension to that conflict. With the issue suddenly thrust before the world community, continuing American noninvolvement became increasingly untenable. By exercising its veto in the Security Council, France could, of course, easily circumvent any proposed international mediation of its colonial difficulties.

The fact that Ho Chi Minh and many of his key advisers were avowed communists greatly exacerbated the U.S. policy dilemma in

Indochina.   Although U.S. diplomats privately acknowledged on numerous occasions that the French, like the Dutch, were guilty of "a dangerously outmoded colonial outlook and method," support for a communist-led nationalist movement was virtually unthinkable. To be sure, some Asian specialists in the State Department bravely advanced the thesis that Ho might emerge as an "Asian Tito." But such speculation, however prescient it might appear in retrospect, never was seriously considered by top administration planners. "It should be obvious," Marshall emphasized in a review of U.S. policy options, "that we are not interested in seeing colonial empire administrations supplanted by [a] philosophy and political organization directed from and controlled by [the] Kremlin." Implicitly, he and other leading officials assumed that all local communists were allied with, and served the interests of, the Soviet Union.

With the intensification of the cold war in the late 1940s, the Truman administration desperately explored alternatives in Indochina. Its dilemma proved daunting. The "Asian Tito" option never attracted high-level support; at the same time, official approval of France's misguided efforts to return to the days of imperial glory appealed to only the most hopelessly uncritical Francophiles in the State Department. Yet most administration planners viewed some settlement as essential. The colonial war in Indochina was draining France's economy, thereby significantly curtailing its contribution to European recovery. U.S. officials often acknowledged with embarrassment, moreover, that Marshall Plan support was indirectly underwriting France's attempted suppression of Vietnamese nationalism.

In the absence of any other clear alternatives, by early 1949 the Truman administration gradually acquiesced in France's so-called Bao Dai solution. That effort to create a non-communist nationalist alternative under the aegis of Bao Dai, emperor of Annam under the former French and Japanese colonial regimes, raised modest hopes in Washington. Those hopes were tempered, of course, by the realization that the much-maligned playboy emperor was a weak reed upon which to base a policy. Nonetheless, his emergence seemed to presage a softening in France's hard-line colonial policy, and by this time Washington was convinced that a French military victory was unattainable.

As a result, the Truman administration swallowed its misgivings and publicly backed the Elysée Agreement of June 1949, which called, albeit vaguely, for the transfer of authority to a nationalist government in Vietnam under Bao Dai's leadership. On 7 February 1950, the

United States formally recognized the puppet Bao Dai government, along with the Kingdoms of Laos and Cambodia, as independent states within the French Union. The State Department, perhaps in an act of wishful thinking, called U.S. recognition "consistent with our fundamental policy of giving support to the peaceful and democratic evolution of dependent peoples toward self-government and independence." On 8 May, the United States quietly announced the extension of military assistance to Bao Dai—and the French—beginning an ultimately tragic involvement in Indochina. The next month, after the outbreak of war in Korea, the Truman administration deepened that commitment.

The evolution of the Truman administration's policy toward Indochina from strict noninvolvement to unconditional support for the French can be understood only within the context of a deepening cold war. As relations with the Soviet Union deteriorated steadily during the early postwar years, Truman and his advisers groped for an explanation of Soviet behavior. By late 1946, they became convinced that the ambitions of America's former partner in the Grand Alliance were limitless and that the threat posed to U.S. security by that inherently expansionistic state and its revolutionary ideology was unprecedented. In response, for the first time in its history the United States sought to formulate and execute an integrated global foreign policy. The intensification of the cold war in Europe during 1948 and 1949—with the Soviet coup in Czechoslovakia, the Berlin crisis, and the formation of NATO and the Warsaw Pact—heightened fears of outright military confrontation between the two superpowers. The successful detonation of a Soviet atomic bomb in mid-1949, followed quickly by the decisive victory of Mao Tse-tung's [Mao Zedong's] communists in China, underscored for Truman administration planners the gravity of the international situation.

Viewed against that backdrop, the continuing hostilities in Indochina took on new significance. Leading U.S. policy makers increasingly saw the French effort there as part of the West's worldwide struggle to contain communist expansion. That Ho Chi Minh's forces had indigenous roots was incontestable but also largely irrelevant. What was important was the communist character of the nationalist movement—and the firm resolve of U.S. officials in the wake of Mao's shattering successes to prevent yet another triumph for the forces of international communism. "If Southeast Asia is also swept by communism," an NSC paper of December 1949 warned, "we shall have suffered a major political rout, the repercussions of which will be felt throughout the world. . . . It is now clear that Southeast Asia is the target for a coordinated offensive directed by the Kremlin."

The tendency to view all local disorder through the prism of East-West conflict was reinforced by the outbreak of war on the Korean peninsula in June 1950. Although historians still debate the amazingly complex origins of that conflict, the Truman administration determined with remarkable alacrity that it represented a new stage in the aggressive designs of a Soviet-directed world communist movement. Consequently, only three days after the fighting broke out in Korea, Truman publicly announced four major decisions: U.S. forces would be sent to Korea; the U.S. Seventh Fleet would be dispatched to the Taiwan Strait; and increased aid would be provided to help the French combat the Vietminh and to help the Philippine government suppress the Huk insurgency. The implication of Truman's decisions is unmistakable. The enemy in Korea, Taiwan, Indochina, and the Philippines, in the administration's view, was the same: a unified, Kremlin-directed communist movement. Subtleties and shadings were lost in the rush to adopt a more active policy. The cold war in Asia had been joined.

The inclination to view Asian affairs within an East-West context, a tendency greatly accentuated by the victory of the Chinese communists and the onset of the Korean War, also exerted a profound influence on U.S. relations with South Asia. Initially, the Truman administration accorded a low priority to the new nations of India and Pakistan. More pressing international flash points left Truman and his advisers little time to spend on those struggling young countries. The subcontinent, after all, had long been within the British sphere of influence, and, in the view of many U.S. experts, would probably remain there indefinitely. Even during the immediate postpartition period, however, American officials invariably measured the two new nations in terms of their potential contribution to larger cold-war priorities.

Judged by that critical litmus test, India attracted far more attention than Pakistan. U.S. officials routinely speculated that India, with its vigorous leadership, rich natural resources, and vast size and population, was destined to play a major role on the world stage. They viewed Pakistan, in sharp contrast, as an anomalous creation whose ultimate survival was much in doubt. The U.S. chargé in Karachi reported in October 1947 that Pakistan's problems were so overwhelming they had already "assumed such proportions as to threaten the very existence of the new State." Some American specialists considered Pakistan's eventual absorption into India to be a strong possibility.

At the same time, other officials speculated that Pakistan might have considerable strategic value. That view, which found resonance especially in the military and intelligence communities, was based on two principal considerations: Pakistan's contiguous border with the Soviet Union, and hence the desirability of establishing air bases and intelligence-gathering facilities there, and Pakistan's proximity to the Persian Gulf, and hence its potential role in the defense of Middle East oil fields.

The predominant view within the administration during the late 1940s, however, held that India was by far the larger and more valuable diplomatic prize in South Asia. The deepening cold war and the imminent success of the communist revolution in China tended to reinforce such thinking. "India," the CIA concluded in July 1949, was "a major Asiatic power" and was "alone in a position to compete with Chinese Communism for hegemony in Southeast Asia." Leading administration planners indeed hoped that India would soon emerge not only as the principal ideological rival to China but as a bulwark against further communist expansion on the Asian mainland.

With the steady collapse of the Chinese Nationalists providing a dramatic backdrop, Indian Prime Minister Jawaharlal Nehru made his first official visit to the United States in October 1949. "There is no personality more important for the United States today than Pandit Nehru," wrote influential columnist Dorothy Thompson. "Every American word and gesture during Mr. Nehru's visit," she predicted, "will have repercussions from the Middle East to East and South Asia and Southern Africa. It is a diplomatic event of the most far reaching consequences." Many U.S. policy makers agreed; the establishment of the People's Republic of China earlier that month, they reasoned, rendered India crucial to the containment of communism in Asia. "Mr. Nehru," emphasized Secretary of State Acheson in a memorandum for the president, "is today and will probably continue to be for some time the dominant political figure in Asia." Philip Jessup, Acheson's close adviser, called Nehru "outstandingly the most vital and influential person for the accomplishment of U.S. objectives in Asia." Although some policy makers sought to temper official expectations with the caveat that Nehru's trip was primarily intended as an educational one, the deceptively attractive notion that India now was the "cornerstone" or "fulcrum" of U.S. policy in Asia was difficult to suppress.

Given such unrealistically lofty expectations, it is difficult to judge the Nehru visit as anything less than a serious setback for U.S. plans.

Although Nehru's meetings with Truman, Acheson, and other leading American officials were unfailingly courteous, they yielded little of substance. Instead, they revealed quite starkly that on numerous critical international issues Nehru's views diverged fundamentally from those of the Americans. Nehru refused to budge from his policy of nonalignment, disagreed with his hosts on the nature of the Soviet threat, revealed his intention to recognize the new communist government in China at the earliest possible opportunity, and insisted that colonialism, not communism, was the gravest danger to world peace.

On these and other issues U.S.-Iranian relations foundered in the aftermath of Nehru's American tour. Reporting from New Delhi in April 1950, Ambassador Loy Henderson decried the "steadily increasing" Indian "feelings of unfriendliness" toward the United States. Not only were there major philosophical differences about foreign policy, but also he noted India's deep resentment about Washington's unwillingness to provide it with sufficient levels of economic assistance. India's friendly relations with China, its muted criticism of the Soviet Union, its lack of support for the United States during the United Nations debates on the Korean War, its uncooperative policies toward Indochina and Japan, and the tangled financial aid question all managed to heighten tensions between the two democracies. The same U.S. officials who had expressed so much hope for India on the eve of the Nehru visit could express little more than dismay in the months following the outbreak of war in Korea. The steady deterioration in relations between Washington and New Delhi so alarmed the British Foreign Office that in September 1950 a senior British diplomat remarked to his American counterparts that U.S.-Indian differences "constituted a running sore."

Pakistan, in marked contrast, largely supported U.S. positions on world affairs during this period. . . . By early 1951, with a hot war raging in Korea and crises brewing in Iran and Egypt, the defense of the Middle East was rapidly emerging as a high-level priority for the Truman administration, and Pakistan's possible role in such a defense was assuming singular importance. On 2 April 1951, during a meeting in London with British Foreign Office representatives, Assistant Secretary of State for Near Eastern, South Asian, and African Affairs George C. McGhee noted that Pakistan's contribution "would probably be the decisive factor in ensuring defense of the area." The British agreed, indicating their belief that the defense of the Near East was "probably not possible without the effective support of Pakistan." Both American and British officials applauded Pakistan's well-trained army, martial tradition, strategic location, and eagerness to cooperate with the West. On 2 May, McGhee underscored these points during a meeting at the Pentagon. "With Pakistan, the Middle East could be defended," he stated flatly. "Without Pakistan, I don't see any way to defend the Middle East."

Accordingly, throughout 1951 and 1952 the Truman administration wrestled with various plans for ensuring the defense of the Middle East, almost all of which included some form of Pakistani participation. After the proposed Middle East Command met determined resistance in late 1951 from Egypt and certain other Arab states, U.S.-sponsored regional defense efforts shifted to the so-called Middle East Defense Organization (MEDO). Well aware that the price of Pakistani cooperation would likely be U.S. military assistance, in March 1952 the Defense Department entered into preliminary negotiations with Pakistani representatives regarding the feasibility of such an arms deal. The Truman administration came to an end, however, before plans for a MEDO were completed and before plans for a military assistance pact with Pakistan had advanced beyond the talking stage. Once again, fears of an adverse Indian reaction gave the administration pause in consummating the controversial arms deal.

The Truman administration's failed efforts to enlist India in the containment umbrella and its flirtation with a Pakistani arms pact were mirrored in its search for reliable partners in Southeast Asia. In Indonesia, as in India, that search proved counterproductive. Following independence, relations between Washington and Djakarta appeared to be based on a firm foundation; certainly U.S. support for Indonesian independence, although belated, created an immense reservoir of goodwill. The rapid U.S. provision of much-needed economic, technical, and military assistance to the new government seemed to foreshadow an era of deepening ties between the United States and Southeast Asia's largest country. The Truman administration's interest in Indonesia was quite explicit, as Acheson informed Truman in January 1950: "The loss of Indonesia to the Communists would deprive the United States of an area of the highest political, economic and strategic importance."

Those cold-war considerations were of course accentuated after the onset of the Korean War. Consequently, the United States sought on various occasions to enlist Indonesia within a contemplated U.S. alliance system in Asia. When the administration began discussing the prospects for a Pacific defense pact in 1950, Indonesia was regularly touted as a possible participant. Unfortunately for U.S. planners, Indonesia's determination to pursue a self-styled "active and independent" foreign policy clashed with any plans for aligning it with the West. Thus in October 1950 Indonesian officials informed the United States that they were unwilling to accept military assistance under the Mutual Defense Assistance Program, because such aid would clearly imply taking sides in the cold war. In a particularly ill-conceived initiative, the United States tried nonetheless to conclude just such a pact with Indonesia in December 1951 only to have a preliminary agreement rejected as a violation of fundamental nationalist values. As a result of this incident, the West-leaning government of Prime Minister Sukiman, the most pro-American of Indonesia's early leaders, was toppled from power and nationalist resentment of U.S. machinations rose sharply. Coupled with the Truman administration's deference to the Netherlands on the supercharged issue of West New Guinea's ultimate disposition, the fall of the Sukiman cabinet increasingly strained the relations between Washington and Djakarta.

The continuing quagmire in Indochina, meanwhile, proved even more disheartening to the Truman administration. It faced an usually cruel predicament there. Without U.S. assistance the French position was likely to collapse; as a result, the communists would gain a foothold in Southeast Asia. Nearly all senior U.S. policy makers viewed this prospect as constituting a decisive cold-war defeat. Consequently, the administration inexorably deepened its commitment to the French. Following the initial aid decision of May 1950, Truman announced stepped-up deliveries, and he increased aid after the Korean War began. By late 1950 the United States had committed $133 million in aid to the French. Military reverses led the Truman administration in June 1952 to advance an additional $150 million in military assistance. Yet, despite this substantial U.S. commitment, the administration remained pessimistic about ultimate French prospects for concluding the war successfully. Only promises of increased autonomy for Vietnamese nationalists could reverse the unfavorable trend, U.S. officials believed, but the French proved absolutely intransigent on that point. Acheson conceded that the United States might ultimately "lose out" if it supported France's "old-fashioned colonial attitudes," but he was unwilling to exert pressure on a key European ally. Not only did the French often threaten to withdraw from Indochina entirely when subjected to what they viewed as unwarranted U.S. meddling, but their support was critical to the high-priority European Defense Community initiative, demonstrating once again how European interests could override Asian interests. Thus Truman left office with the United States deeply embroiled in a colonial conflict, supporting approximately 40 percent of the French effort, with the military prospects poor, the political prospects worse, and the chances of a complete collapse growing daily.

On the most basic level, Truman left to his successors a legacy of deepening American involvement in the affairs of South and Southeast Asia. The growing American stake in those regions was, by the time the Korean War had ended, inseparably linked to America's global effort to contain Soviet communist expansion. Given the veritable explosion in U.S. economic power and perceived strategic needs during World War II, some wider concern with developments in colonial Asia was probably inevitable. Political unrest and economic instability in those areas, moreover, had a direct and immediate bearing on the economic rehabilitation of Western Europe, a policy goal of commanding significance to the United States. It was the cold war, however, that lent force and urgency to U.S. diplomatic objectives in South and Southeast Asia. And it was the cold war that hopelessly distorted U.S. perceptions of the revolutionary forces that were rapidly transforming those regions.

Viewed on its own terms, the Truman administration's record in South and Southeast Asia is a mixed one. Despite its high hopes and vigorous efforts, the administration clearly proved unable to construct bastions of anticommunism in those regions. Nor with a widening conflict raging in Indochina can it be said that the administration achieved the order and stability that it so desperately sought. Yet Truman and his advisers could boast that none of the newly emerging nations of South and Southeast Asia—Vietnam excluded—had embraced communism, and none of those nations was gravitating toward the Soviet bloc. The neutralist inclinations of India and Indonesia deeply disturbed U.S. policy makers, to be sure; it can be argued, however, that both nations remained on friendlier terms with Washington than with Moscow and Peking [Beijing]. As Truman's tenure in office came to a close, the prestige and influence of the United States were substantially higher than those of the Soviet Union or China in nearly all the newly independent nations of southern Asia. Using the barometer of cold-war loyalties, then, the administration's record can perhaps be called moderately successful.

A broader perspective, however, is in order here. The eruption of nationalist movements in South and Southeast Asia following World War II was a historical development of truly epic proportions. The process of decolonization, in which the peoples of southern Asia took such a leading role, must rank among the most profound and far-reaching developments in modern world history.   Certainly, Asian nationalist stirrings created numerous new problems and opportunities for U.S. policy makers.   Consequently, one critical element in any over-all assessment of the Truman administration's policies in southern Asia must be its response to the nationalist challenge.

Viewed from that perspective, those policies appear both ineffective and short-sighted.   Certainly, one can argue that the administration deserves credit for helping to bring about the relatively peaceful transition from colonialism to independence.   That so many nations could achieve independence within so short a period of time and with so little bloodshed is at least in part a tribute to the constructive role played by the United States.   U.S. support for Indonesia's independence is perhaps its most striking accomplishment in this regard, although the Truman administration's quiet role in helping to speed independence for India, Pakistan, Burma, and Ceylon should not be overlooked.

The subordination of all other diplomatic goals by 1949–50 to a global geopolitical strategy for containing the Soviet Union, however, largely negated those positive accomplishments.   Thus by the early 1950s, efforts to align India and Indonesia with the West led to strained relations with both new countries.   The administration's consideration of a military assistance pact with Pakistan promised to cement relations with the world's largest Muslim nation but only at an enormous cost. And in Indochina the administration had committed itself to a cause that increasingly appeared doomed.

These policy failures stemmed from a common cause: a tendency to overlook the historical roots of local and regional developments in the rush to strengthen America's global defense posture vis-à-vis the Soviet Union.   The revolutionary changes in southern Asia were thus seen through the invariably distorting lens of East-West conflict.   Perhaps the supreme irony of the Truman administration's efforts to "contain" southern Asia is that they ultimately contributed to the region's instability, thus unwittingly undermining the very diplomatic goal that they were designed to achieve.

Aaron David Miller

COLD WAR, PALESTINE, AND OIL IN THE MIDDLE EAST

Aaron David Miller discusses the varied ways in which the Cold War transformed the American relationship with the Middle East. He explores the interconnection between America's growing economic and strategic stake in the region's fabled oil riches, United States efforts to prevent any extension of Soviet influence into the area, and Truman's controversial but unequivocal support for the new state of Israel. Those factors combined in the early Cold War years to catapult the Middle East into a critical national security question for the United States. Yet Miller insists that one of the three was paramount: the fear of Soviet expansion especially shaped the Truman administration's Middle Eastern policy.

Aaron David Miller serves as a policy analyst for the United States Department of State in Washington, D. C. He has written Search for Security: Saudi Arabian Oil and American Foreign Policy, 1939–1949 **(1980),** The PLO and the Politics of Survival **(1983), and** The Arab States and the Palestine Question **(1986).**

Throughout 1946, as tensions between the United States and the Soviet Union continued to increase, officials began to attach new importance to the security of American and British interests in the Near and Middle East. Although the Americans continued to view Western Europe as the area of primary importance in any potential struggle with the Soviets, the Middle East was rapidly emerging as a crucial factor in postwar strategic planning. Not only did the area contain almost one-third of the world's known petroleum reserves, but it possessed supply lines, communications facilities, and air bases vital for defense of much of the British Empire. In view of the United States' reluctance to assume a stronger military role in the area, the maintenance of the British position in the eastern Mediterranean and Persian Gulf was considered essential to the preservation of American interests. Writing to Clark Clifford, special counsel to the president, Robert Patterson, secretary of war, observed that Soviet activities directed toward weakening the British in the Middle East "threaten to create a vacuum into which Soviet political and military influence may move."

From *Search for Security: Saudi Arabian Oil and American Foreign Policy, 1939–1949*, by Aaron David Miller, pp. 166–169, 171–174, 176–179, 184–190, 201–203. ©1980 The University of North Carolina Press. Reprinted by permission.

Soviet maneuvering in Turkey and Iran only seemed to confirm official suspicions of Russian intentions. To the Americans, Russian policy appeared unchanged since the time of Peter the Great. Not only did the Soviets seem eager to gain control over the Bosporus and Dardanelles, but they appeared determined to push their quest for warm water from the Mediterranean to the Persian Gulf. Although many military planners believed that the Soviets primarily sought to construct a defensive perimeter in Iran in order to keep the Allies at bay, they were disturbed by the new aggressiveness of Soviet policy. The Soviet delay in removing its troops from northern Iran only increased Washington's fear of Russian plans to dominate the entire area. "Present Soviet maneuvers to control North Iran," a navy intelligence source noted in January 1946, were designed to push the "front" farther away from the Soviet oil areas of Baku, Batum, and Grozny and closer to the "enemy's" oil in Mosul and the Persian Gulf. Permanent Soviet control of the Iranian province of Azerbaijan, the Joint Chiefs informed SWNCC [State-War-Navy Coordinating Committee], would constitute "a permanent penetration" into Iran and allow movement of Soviet forces near the oil fields of Iraq.

By July, the Joint Chiefs of Staff had concluded that the Soviets sought nothing less than to bring Greece, Turkey, and Iran within their orbit. Toward that end, the JCS noted, the Russians had attempted diplomatically to gain control of the Dardanelles, the Dodecanese, and Tripolitania, and to undermine the British position in Greece, Egypt, and the Middle East. In October, the State Department added its own caveat. In a memorandum prepared in the Office of Near Eastern and African Affairs and approved by Byrnes, Acheson, and Henderson, NEA concluded: "A Russian-dominated Turkey would open the floodgates for a Soviet advance into Syria, Lebanon, Iraq, Palestine, Transjordan, Egypt and the Arabian Peninsula, all of which are at present still relatively free from Russian activities and direct Russian pressure. . . . It would also dangerously, perhaps fatally, expose Greece and Iran."

One of the State Department's most vocal opponents of Soviet expansion in the Near and Middle East was Loy W. Henderson, the Arkansas-born diplomat who would shape many of NEA's attitudes and policies in the postwar years. Henderson, whose career had carried him from chargé in Moscow to assistant chief of the Division of European Affairs, had earned quite a reputation for baiting the Russian bear. In fact, during the 1943 State Department "purge," Henderson was "exiled" to Baghdad as minister to Iraq, presumably for the intensity of his anti-Soviet views. Nevertheless, by March 1945, he had returned from the field to head the Office of Near Eastern and African Affairs. There is little doubt that Henderson was picked for the job because of his experience in dealing with the Russians—qualifications which his superiors believed would put him in good stead for dealing with the Soviets in Turkey, Greece, and Iran.

Henderson brought new commitment and dedication to NEA. He not only continued the anti-Soviet orientation of his predecessor Wallace Murray (who had since become ambassador to Iran) but carried it to new heights. For Henderson, Soviet expansionism was an inescapable and harsh reality of the postwar world. There was no point in babying the Soviets nor even maintaining the fiction of international cooperation as long as Moscow pursued its expansionist designs. This was particularly true, Henderson believed, in areas where the Russians had long-standing objectives—like the Near East. "The Soviet Union seems to be determined," Henderson wrote to Acheson, "to break down the structure which Great Britain has maintained so that Russian power and influence can sweep unimpeded across Turkey and through the Dardanelles into the Mediterranean, and across Iran and through the Persian Gulf into the Indian Ocean."

Recognizing the Soviet threat, however, was only part of the challenge. It was imperative, Henderson believed, that the United States begin to pursue a policy in the entire Middle East area more attuned to its own strategic and economic interests—and those of its allies. Although Henderson hoped to strengthen the United Nations he also looked with contempt upon naive concepts of international cooperation. Here he and his NEA colleagues had waged a running battle with [Assistant Secretary of State Will] Clayton's economists over the importance of using Export-Import Bank loans to further American political objectives throughout the Middle East. Similarly, Henderson urged that the United States work to maintain its prestige and influence in the Arab world. Fundamental in this regard was his unfailing opposition to United States' support for political Zionism—a support Henderson passionately believed would not only destroy American influence and interests and throw the Arabs into the arms of the Soviets, but also ultimately endanger the peace of the postwar world.

The threat of Soviet penetration into the eastern Mediterranean and Middle East inevitably focused the attention of the diplomats and generals on the security of American and British petroleum interests throughout the area. Although military planners were the first to concede that access to Middle Eastern oil might be restricted in the event of war, they believed it imperative to secure and develop Persian Gulf petroleum as a potential source of supply for counteroffensive action and to deny it to the enemy. The JCS had already estimated that the Soviet Union did not produce enough oil within its own borders to fight a major war. With proven reserves perhaps equal to those of the United States, Middle Eastern oil fields were certain to become a primary Soviet objective in any future conflict. The plan of the Soviet Union, an army intelligence report noted in May 1946, was to "choke off" American and British oil reserves in Iran, Iraq, and Saudi Arabia and ultimately to establish joint companies designed to control the area's wells and refineries. Writing to SWNCC regarding the strategic importance of Iran, the JCS concentrated heavily on oil:

> Loss of the Iraq and Saudi Arabia sources to the United States and her allies would mean that in case of war they would fight an oil-starved war. Conversely, denial of these sources to the USSR would force her to fight an oil-starved war. However, due to Russia's geographic position, great land mass, and superior manpower potential, any lack of oil limiting air action by the United States and her allies or hampering their transportation ability or their war production would be of great advantage to the USSR. It is therefore to the strategic interest of the United States to keep Soviet influence and Soviet armed forces removed as far as possible from oil resources in Iran, Iraq, and the Near and Middle East.

By the fall of 1946, however, increasing American involvement in the Palestine question seemed to present a potential threat to the security of American interests and influence throughout the Middle East. Troubled by Truman's support for increased immigration to Palestine and his official endorsement of a Jewish homeland, State Department and military officials continued to point out the dangers of American support for any plan to partition Palestine. Not only would the creation of an independent Jewish homeland lead to chronic instability in the area, they argued, but also it would directly strengthen Soviet influence among the Arabs. In May 1946, [Walter] Bedell Smith, ambassador in Moscow, informed the department that once the United States adopted an official pro-Zionist policy the Soviets would exploit the Palestine issue fully—particularly to capitalize on Arab dissatisfaction and to "seize every opportunity to expand Soviet influence in the Near East." Writing to SWNCC regarding the Anglo-American Committee of Inquiry's recent report on Palestine, the JCS reached similar conclusions. Any attempt to implement the report by force might prejudice British and American interests throughout the Middle East. The Soviet Union might replace Allied influence and power in an area in which the United States has a "vital security interest." Finally, in a memorandum to Acheson in October, Henderson warned of the consequences of American support for the establishment of a Jewish state in Palestine: "Vigorous advocacy of this extreme program will cause a serious deterioration in our over-all relations with the British and with the Arab and Moslem World. . . . Already the almost childlike confidence which these people have hitherto displayed toward the United States," Henderson concluded, "is giving way to suspicion and dislike, a development which may lead the Arab and Moslem World to look elsewhere than toward the West for support." . . .

By early 1947, government officials were becoming increasingly concerned about the security of American and British interests in the eastern Mediterranean and Middle East. Many of the strategic concerns of the war years, which had temporarily subsided after the defeat of Germany and Japan, had now reemerged in the cold war atmosphere of the postwar period. The increasing preoccupation with national security, perhaps the most fundamental theme of American foreign policy in the postwar period, was reflected in the State Department's attitude toward the oil companies' new joint ventures and toward the problem of Palestine. In both cases State Department and military planners continued to emphasize the importance of strengthening American oil interests in the area and maintaining American prestige within the Arab world. Implicit in each situation and indeed in the entire issue of national security was the now vital importance of the Middle Eastern area and its place in a hot or cold war with the Soviets. "As to the importance of a stable Middle East, friendly to the Western Powers," the JCS observed, "it is obvious that this area is the buffer between Russia and the British Mediterranean life line. If the peoples of the Middle East turn to Russia, this would have the same impact in many respects as would military conquest on this area by the Soviets."

The strategic importance of the Middle East inevitably focused attention on the area's petroleum. Certainly, Middle Eastern oil was not the only American concern in the area. In the event the Soviet Union penetrated into the Persian Gulf or succeeded in establishing its influence in Iran or Iraq, the security of American-controlled oil reserves would become entirely academic. Continued access to Middle Eastern oil, particularly Saudi oil, was the most visible and tangible

American interest. With known reserves at least equal to those of the United States, and unproven estimates of several hundred billion barrels, the oil constituted a prize of enormous strategic and political potential. Determined to redefine the American postwar strategic interest in the Middle East and to highlight the importance of the area, officials at all levels began to use Arabian oil as a common reference point in their presentations. In short, Saudi Arabian oil—the all-American enterprise—offered both a convenient and impressive foundation on which officials could begin to build a more active American role in Middle Eastern affairs. Although the postwar advantages of Middle Eastern crude were yet unproven, State Department and military officials continued to urge the administration to protect a potentially valuable interest. Warning of the possible dangers of American involvement in the Palestine question, a JCS memorandum reflected the renewed interest in Middle Eastern petroleum: "For very serious consideration from a military point of view is control of the oil of the Middle East. This is probably the one large undeveloped reserve in a world which may come to the limits of its oil resources within this generation without having developed any substitute. A great part of our military strength, as well as our standard of living, is based on oil."

During the immediate postwar years, the Americans continued their efforts to secure their interest in the oil of Saudi Arabia and the Persian Gulf. There was little need, however, to pursue the stopgap aid programs which had characterized the war years. The two problems which had dogged officials during the war—[Saudi King] Ibn Saud's lack of money and Britain's influence with the king—now seemed to have dissipated or become less pressing. By 1946, Saudi crude production, while still undeveloped, exceeded 164,000 b.p.d. [barrels per day], reportedly adding $20,000,000 in royalties to the king's coffers. Similarly, greater Anglo-American cooperation throughout the Middle East had quieted any lingering concerns about British intentions toward the ARAMCO [Arabian-American Oil Company] concession. "In the economic field, British oil interests are so extensive and the possibilities for the free development of U.S. oil interests are so extensive," a State Department memorandum noted in 1947, "that there is little logical basis for political conflict with the British in the development of oil in these Arab lands." In fact by November 1947, after a series of talks at the Pentagon, British and American representatives had even pledged to support their mutual interests in Saudi Arabia. For the most part, postwar petroleum policy focused on the development of facilities to market Saudi Arabian crude and on the maintenance of American influence and prestige with Ibn Saud.

The postwar years, as mentioned earlier, soon revealed new and more dangerous challenges. The emergence of the Soviet Union as a world power raised new fears of Russian expansion into the eastern Mediterranean and Middle East. Similarly, the United States' increasing involvement in the Palestine question aroused concern about the security of American petroleum interests throughout the area. Although neither Soviet activities nor the Palestine problem presented any immediate threat to American petroleum reserves, officials were clearly uneasy about the future. Writing to Loy Henderson in February 1947, [Dean] Acheson predicted that the coming year was likely to be "a bad year in Palestine and the Middle East, with increasing violence and grave danger to our interests in that area." . . .

Although containment soon emerged as the cornerstone of American policy in the eastern Mediterranean and Middle East, policymakers were becoming increasingly aware of the importance of maintaining Western influence in areas not immediately threatened by "Soviet-Communist infiltration." Countries like Iraq and Saudi Arabia possessed vast petroleum reserves and refining facilities, and contained air and communications links vital to Allied planning in the event of conflict with the Soviets. Moreover, much of the Near and Middle East, the Joint Chiefs noted, offered possibilities for "direct contact with our ideological enemies." In view of the increasing strategic importance of the entire area, the JCS repeatedly cautioned against "orienting" the peoples of the Middle East away from the Western powers.

Increasing American involvement in the Palestine question, however, seemed to undermine American influence throughout the area. To those State Department and military planners who were determined to shape a new consensus regarding the strategic importance of the Middle East, American support for a Jewish homeland was an error of catastrophic proportion. Washington's identification with Zionist objectives, the Arab hands argued, would arouse the undying opposition of the Arab and Muslim world. Equally dangerous, instability in Palestine might make the area more vulnerable to Soviet influence. By 1947, the Palestine problem was becoming increasingly more complex. In February, unable to find a compromise plan acceptable to both Jews and Arabs, Great Britain announced its intention to return the mandate to the United Nations. The situation seemed particularly troublesome to the United States. With the focus of the Palestine question shifting to the UN it was more than likely that the Americans would be called upon to play a major role in the resolution of the problem. In short, the United States might soon be forced to make or support a decision which could adversely affect its influence and interests throughout the Middle East.

The increasing importance of the Middle East and its new role in cold war strategy inevitably aroused official interest in the oil of Saudi Arabia and the Persian Gulf. In view of the indispensability of petroleum to national security and the vast size of Persian Gulf reserves, Middle Eastern oil quickly emerged as one of the more visible elements in strategic planning. One of the six "specific objectives" which might "enhance" the national security of the United States, a JCS committee concluded, was the continued availability of Middle Eastern oil. "In general, the War Department feels," Kenneth C. Royall, secretary of war, noted, "that . . . the use of mid-east oil to reduce exports from the U.S. and to augment our domestic supply should be encouraged within the limits necessary to prevent an undue strain upon our domestic production."

Military planners were well aware of the risks of utilizing Middle Eastern oil. "Petroleum from the Middle East," the ANPB [Army-Navy Petroleum Board] noted, "could make a major contribution toward fulfilling the U.S. requirements in event of a war emergency if that oil were available." In view of the Soviet Union's proximity to the oil fields of Iran and Iraq and the uncertainties of tanker and pipeline transport, unrestricted access to the oil was problematic. To some, Persian Gulf oil was even a liability. In the event of conflict with the Soviets, the army's *Intelligence Review* noted, "Middle East oil would be of negligible if not negative strategic value to the United States." From a strictly strategic point of view, the problem confronting military planners was clear. Although the value of Middle Eastern oil might prove critical in a wartime situation, it simply could not be guaranteed as a source of oil for campaign operations or resupply.

Although the military advantages of Middle Eastern oil were yet undetermined, its economic potential emerged as an important element in postwar planning. Nowhere was this fact more apparent than in plans for the reconstruction of the European economy. With Europe facing the prospect of severe coal shortages, postwar planners sought to encourage the conversion from coal to oil. Coal was expected to remain the mainstay of Europe's energy base for some time, yet petroleum offered a vital source of fuel which might prove "essential" to the complete recovery of European industrial and transportation sectors. By 1951, planners estimated that total petroleum requirements for participating Marshall Plan countries would exceed 76,760,000 metric tons—consumption in 1938 had totaled 36,224,000 tons. Writing to Clifford in September 1947, C. H. Bonesteel, special assistant to the under secretary of state, observed: "This, together with the increasing demands for petroleum products resulting from the mechanization of agriculture, the expansion of industry and the growth of road transport presents a formidable problem to all participating countries, for this whole area has no natural resources of oil."

The petroleum resources of the Middle East seemed to offer a natural source of supply for the European Recovery Program (ERP). Caribbean crude, to be sure, might be the main source for European requirements during the early years of the ERP. Still, the importance of conserving Western Hemisphere reserves and the costs of shipping Venezuelan crude indicated that exports to the Middle East from the Caribbean area would decrease rapidly. Moreover, rising oil consumption in the United States seemed to suggest that there would be little surplus crude available for export. "The European Recovery Program," Oscar Chapman, acting secretary of the interior, observed, "was most carefully designed to relieve the present drain on American petroleum supplies and to result in most of Europe's requirements being met from the Middle East."

Postwar trends were dramatically clear. In 1946, the Western Hemisphere had supplied 77 percent of Europe's petroleum needs, with the Middle East accounting for the balance. By 1951, Middle Eastern sources were expected to supply over 80 percent of European needs. Although Europe's refining capacity would have to be increased to handle the anticipated flow of crude, the relationship between Middle Eastern oil and European markets was already unmistakable. "Should Middle East oil not be available on the basis as now estimated," Robert Eakens concluded, "a full review of the energy requirements under the program would be required."

Despite its potential importance for European recovery, Arabian oil was not the overriding American concern in the Middle East. For the most part, oil interests were shadowed by Washington's preoccupation with containment. In the event the Soviet Union succeeded in weakening the British position in the eastern Mediterranean, penetrating the northern tier, or establishing its own influence in the Persian Gulf, access to Middle Eastern oil reserves would become entirely academic.

Similarly, the security of American oil interests, particularly in Saudi Arabia, seemed inextricably linked to maintaining the United States' prestige and influence in the Arab world—a task which was becoming increasingly more difficult in view of American policy on Palestine. Still, the oil of Saudi Arabia and the Middle East had emerged as a prominent American interest in its own right. With proved reserves of at least 27,000,000,000 barrels and unproven estimates of billions more, Middle Eastern oil represented a tangible interest of enormous potential.

Even more important, at a time when American officials were nervously weighing the prospects and pitfalls of a more active role in Middle Eastern affairs, the American stake in Arabian oil offered both continuity with past policy and direction for the future. Faced with the uncertainty of Soviet intentions, the possibility of British withdrawal from Palestine, and the unpredictability of a president who seemed committed to supporting Zionist objectives, State Department and military officials sought to define an American policy more attuned to what they believed to be the strategic realities of the postwar world. Convinced of the importance of the Middle East, these officials searched for a way to highlight their concerns. By 1947 Arabian oil seemed to provide just such an opportunity—offering both the means and motivation to reshape American attitudes and policies toward the Middle East. . . .

By the fall of 1947, the Palestine question was rapidly emerging as a crucial consideration in the development of American policy toward the Middle East. The United States had no legal or historical responsibility for the disposition of the Palestine mandate, yet both the Roosevelt and Truman administrations had become intimately involved in the fate of the "much too Promised Land." Responding to a curious mixture of humanitarian concern and domestic political considerations, the Truman White House had taken up the issues of Jewish immigration and homeland. Despite the opposition of State Department and British officials, between 1945 and 1947 Truman had expressed support for increased Jewish immigration to Palestine and for the idea of a Jewish homeland. The president's policy, to be sure, was not entirely his own. Previous congressional resolutions and party platforms together with current public opinion seemed to commit policymakers to support the idea of a Jewish homeland. Although Truman was personally moved by the horrors of the Nazi genocide and eager to alleviate the suffering of the survivors, he had no illusions about the constraints and pitfalls of the Palestine problem. In a memorandum to David Niles in

May 1947, the president, already annoyed by Zionist lobbying, such as that by Rabbi Abba Hillel Silver, observed: "We could have settled this Palestine thing if U.S. politics had been kept out of it. Terror and Silver are the controlling causes of some, if not all, of our troubles. I surely wish God almighty would give the Children of Israel an Isaiah, the Christians a St. Paul and the sons of Ishmael a peep at the Golden Rule. Maybe He will decide to do that."

Truman's homespun advice, however, provided little comfort to State Department officials committed to protecting the national interest in the Middle East. To the Arab hands and cold warriors, the "official" association with political Zionism seemed nothing short of a "major blunder in statesmanship." Not only would the creation of a Jewish state in Palestine jeopardize the stability of the Middle East, William Yale of NE [Office of Near Eastern Affairs, Department of State] noted, it "might even threaten world security." Similarly, William Eddy, passionately anti-Zionist, concluded that implementation of the UNSCOP [United Nations Special Committee on Palestine] plan for partition is an endorsement of a "theocratic sovereign state characteristic of the Dark Ages."

American support for the partition plan also seemed damaging to the United States' position in the Arab World. Although the State Department was uneasy over the security of American petroleum interests in the area, officials were far more concerned about increasing Soviet interest in the Palestine question. Moscow's preferred solution, Ambassador Bedell Smith informed the department in August, was a binational state which would be predominantly Arab. Such a state, the Soviets believed, would lead to weakness, internal conflict, and eventual communist penetration and party control. Bill Eddy could not have agreed more. American support for partition, he warned, might force the Arab League, "for the sake of survival," to align itself with the Russians.

Fear of partition and its relation to cold war strategy was not confined to the department's Arab experts. Speaking to the United States Delegation to the United Nations in September, Secretary of State [George C.] Marshall noted that: "Adoption of the majority report . . . would mean very violent Arab reaction. To be consistent with the integrity of its position, the United States should avoid actively arousing the Arabs and precipitating their 'rapprochement' with the Soviet Union in the first week or ten days of the General Assembly." During a luncheon meeting of the Cabinet in late September, [James] Forrestal also lobbied for a more realistic handling of the Palestine issue. It was important, the secretary of defense informed Truman, to "lift the Jewish-Palestine question out of politics and to be more aware of the security needs of the United States."

Despite the State Department's objections to partition and the diplomats' determination to avoid committing the United States to its defense, officials had little choice but to support UNSCOP's majority report. Already publicly committed to the support of a Jewish homeland and aware that failure to endorse the recommendations of an established United Nations committee might damage the credibility of the organization, Truman overrode the objections of his State Department. On 11 October, Herschel V. Johnson, United States deputy representative on the UN Security Council, announced that the United States supported the "basic principles" of the majority report.

Although the State Department had no alternative but to support partition publicly, officials were quick to register their opposition in private. In late September, Loy Henderson submitted a memorandum to Marshall which signaled the opening round in the State Department's campaign to force revision of the partition plan. Henderson was not alone in his opposition. The views expressed in this memorandum, Henderson began, "are also those of nearly every member of the Foreign Service or of the Department who has worked to any appreciable extent on Near Eastern problems." Henderson's presentation rested squarely on the importance of maintaining stability in the Middle East and its relation to American strategic interests. The attitude which the United States assumed toward the Palestine problem, Henderson continued, "may greatly influence the extent of success or of failure of some of our efforts to promote world stability and to prevent further Soviet penetration into important areas free as yet from Soviet domination." Specifically, advocacy of partition, "would be certain to undermine our relations with the Arab, and to a lesser extent with the Moslem world." The United States not only needed "Arab cooperation" in maintaining the British presence as a "stabilizing power" in the eastern Mediterranean, Henderson concluded, but also in preventing "violent Arab nationalist uprisings" against the French in North Africa.

Middle Eastern oil was also a part though not the focus of Henderson's presentation. During the next few years, he noted, the United States would rely "heavily" on the "resources" of the area not only for its own use but for the reconstruction of Europe. In a draft of the memorandum forwarded to Dean Rusk, director of the Office of Special Political Affairs, Henderson emphasized the importance of safeguarding the American stake in Persian Gulf oil:

> We shall need Arab friendship if we are to retain our petroleum position in the Arab world. During the next few years we are planning to obtain huge quantities of oil from Iraq, Bahrein, Kuwait and Saudi Arabia, not only for our use but for the reconstruction of Europe. Furthermore we are intending to transport oil from Persia, Iraq, and Saudi Arabia across a number of Arab countries by pipelines to Mediterranean ports. Already, partly as a result of our policies regarding Palestine the attitude of Saudi Arabia towards the United States has changed sharply and its demands on the oil companies are becoming more and more truculent and extravagant.

Finally, Henderson noted that, although the Arabs "have in general no use for communism," the establishment of a Jewish State in Palestine might force them "to consider the United States as their foremost enemy and enter into at least temporary cooperation with the Soviet Union against us just as we cooperated with the Russians during the war years against common enemies."

The State Department was not the only agency concerned about the danger of the proposed partition plan. Military planners had also repeatedly cautioned against jeopardizing American influence in the Middle East. If, as a result of American support for partition, the peoples of the area turned to the Soviet Union, the Joint Chiefs informed the secretary of defense in October, it would have the "same impact in many respects" as military conquest of the Middle East by the Russians. It was Middle Eastern petroleum, however, which provided the central focus of JCS concern. "The most serious of all possible consequences, from a military point of view," the JCS noted, "is that implementation of a decision to partition Palestine would gravely prejudice access by the United States to the oil of Iran, Iraq and Saudi Arabia." In the event of war, the JCS continued, the loss of Iraqi and Saudi sources would force the United States to fight "an oil-starved war." "Conversely, denial of these sources to our most probable opponent, . . . the USSR, would force her to fight an oil-starved war." It is therefore of "great strategic importance," the Joint Chiefs concluded, that the United States maintain the "goodwill" of the Arab and Moslem states. . . .

The General Assembly's endorsement of partition in November deepened official concern about the security of American interests throughout the Middle East. Immediate reaction in the Arab world seemed to confirm the department's worst fears. . . .

Official reaction to partition if not to the entire Palestine question reflected the Americans' increasing awareness of their strategic interests in the Middle East. In this sense, the Palestine problem serves as a kind of barometer to measure State and Defense Department sensitivity on a broad range of strategic concerns—not the least of which was the importance of Saudi Arabian oil. The Americans overestimated the threat of Soviet expansion into Iraq and the Persian Gulf and overreacted to Arab threats against United States' interests. Reports from Jidda indicated that Ibn Saud would not take direct action against the oil concession. In fact, it was clear even after the November vote on partition, that the king would go to great lengths to protect ARAMCO's interests—a fact which the Arab experts conveniently omitted in communications to their superiors. Nonetheless, with rare exception, State Department officials sincerely believed that American endorsement of partition would ultimately jeopardize the United States' interests throughout the Middle East. Cancellation of oil concessions was not likely, yet all-out war in Palestine (a condition the department argued which would inevitably follow attempts to partition the country) would disrupt petroleum development, hinder TAPLINE, [ARAMCO's trans-Arabian pipeline], and thus interfere with European recovery. Similarly, a United States–supported UN decision to implement partition by force might open up the area to Soviet penetration and even push the reluctant Saudis into more aggressive action.

To the State Department's Arab hands and cold warriors, American policy was an error of catastrophic proportion. At best, officials conceded, endorsement of Zionist objectives was a result of misguided humanitarianism; at worst, it was a product of narrow-minded political concerns. Neither motivation, Henderson and Forrestal argued, should interfere with the protection of the nation's interest in Middle Eastern oil.

Arabian oil was not the dominant element in strategic planning. The importance of securing Saudi oil was encompassed by an even greater strategic priority—containing Soviet influence in the eastern Mediterranean and Middle East. So, too, access to Middle East reserves was far too unpredictable a factor to be relied upon in an emergency situation, let alone in a full-scale war with the Soviets. Still, the advantages of preserving access to the rich wells of al Hasa and the Persian Gulf highlighted the value of maintaining a stable Middle East and a friendly Arab world. By 1948 the State Department frantically searched for allies and arguments in its fight against partition. Arabian oil seemed to provide officials with just such opportunities—a means to demonstrate the risks of supporting the UN decision and a motivation for adopting a policy more attuned to what they believed to be the new strategic realities of the postwar world. . . .

Despite its increasing importance, the oil of Saudi Arabia and the Middle East played little, if any, role in Truman's final consideration of the Palestine problem. It is possible that without State and Defense Department lobbying for the importance of Saudi oil Truman might have gone further in his support of Israel, yet this seems unlikely given the president's desire to minimize U.S. involvement in the Palestine question. White House support for partition and eventual recognition of Israel was rooted in a curious mixture of moral, political, and cold war considerations. Truman was certainly aware of the strategic concerns of his State Department and defense establishment. He was apparently not impressed, however, by the "arguments of the diplomats," and seemed to believe that he could still support a Jewish homeland, protect his own political future, and safeguard American national interests in the Middle East. In fact, in view of the reality of a Jewish state and Moscow's plans to recognize it, Truman apparently believed that prompt U.S. recognition was quite compatible with American national interests. Truman's personal advisers, David Niles and Clark Clifford, supported this argument and provided an effective counter to State and Defense Department concerns about oil. In fact, Niles had informed Truman that he should not be prevented from supporting Jewish claims because of the fear of alienating Ibn Saud. "You know that President Roosevelt said to some of us privately he could do anything that needed to be done with Ibn Saud with a few million dollars."

The view that Washington could buy off the Saudis also found its way into Clark Clifford's arguments. Writing to Truman in support of partition in March, Clifford noted, "there are those who say that such a course of action will not get us oil if we back up the United Nations partition plan. The fact of the matter is the Arab States must have oil royalties or go broke." Ninety percent of Saudi Arabia's revenue, he continued, comes from American oil royalties. Moreover, Ibn Saud "has publicly and repeatedly" refused even to threaten the United States with cancellation of the concession. In short, "military necessity, political and economic self-preservation," Clifford concluded, "will compel the Arabs to sell their oil to the United States. Their need of the United States is greater than our need of them."

Truman no doubt appreciated his advisers' straightforward "common sense" approach to the problem. If the president had not succumbed to the pressure of his own State Department, it was unlikely that he would be intimidated by the Saudis. Truman must also have realized the difficulties of maintaining assured access to Saudi oil even under the best of circumstances. Although Persian Gulf sources offered a valuable supply of petroleum for European recovery, the area's resources might simply not be available in times of instability, let alone in the event of a determined enemy attack. From the standpoint of our national security, Senator Owen Brewster of Maine noted, "the oil reserves of the Middle East are not worth a tinker's dam. This is the testimony of every competent and responsible military authority. . . . [s]acrificing our honor in Palestine for the unattainable oil of Arabia is not only dishonourable—it is stupid." More important, Middle Eastern oil played a relatively small role in supplying the nation's own energy requirements. By March 1948, the United States was importing approximately 450,000 b.p.d. [barrels per day] of foreign crude—about 8 percent of its total domestic production. Imports of crude oil from Saudi Arabia in 1948 averaged a mere 29,300 b.p.d.

Finally, Saudi Arabia's moderate reaction to American Palestine policy further downplayed the importance of the oil factor. From partition to recognition, Ibn Saud continued to exercise extreme caution in his relations with Washington. Exchanges between the king and the president, with rare exception, remained exceptionally cordial and even Amir Faisal kept his diatribes to a minimum. Moreover, both in private conversation and in Arab League councils, the king continued to draw a distinction between official American policy and that of the companies. In fact, in late May, Duce informed Henderson that Ibn Saud considered ARAMCO personnel to be members of his own household. . . .

If Saudi Arabian oil had little, if any, effect on White House consideration of the Palestine issue, by 1948 it had emerged to shape State Department and military views of the Middle East. Impressed by the size and potential of the area's petroleum reserves, officials continued to emphasize the importance of maintaining Western access to this rich resource. Eager to secure the American interest in the king's oil, NEA's Arab hands urged their superiors to maintain and increase American influence and prestige with Ibn Saud. Saudi-American relations suddenly assumed new importance and generated new challenges. The days of lend-leasing trucks and silver riyals had yielded to Ibn Saud's requests for large-scale military assistance and diplomatic support. So too, the Palestine problem and attendant arms embargo hindered American efforts to meet the king's requests and to strengthen Saudi-American ties. Still, by the end of 1948, there was little doubt that relations between the two countries would steadily improve. If ties between Washington and Riyadh were not broken over Palestine, Childs informed the department in December, "one can only imagine the extent of relations in a normal period."

It was the emerging cold war atmosphere of the postwar years, however, that stimulated official interest in Saudi oil and strengthened American ties with Ibn Saud's desert kingdom. "The oil resources lying within the Saudi Arabian peninsula," JCS planners concluded in May, "are of major importance to the United States and her Allies both in peace and in the prosecution of war against the USSR." Although strategic planners were fully aware of the logistical problems involved in securing Arabian oil, these reserves assumed an important role in contingency planning. Both the "emergency" and the 1952 war plans, the Joint Logistics Plans Committee informed the JCS, "envisage a major effort to regain or retain the Persian Gulf oil by the second year of warfare." In the event the Allies could not immediately secure Saudi or Persian Gulf oil, military planners were determined to deny them to the Soviet Union.

Officials also began to attach new importance to continuing American control of the Dhahran airfield. For the State Department, the question of the airfield was of immediate concern. The agreement covering United States' rights at Dhahran was due to expire on 15 March 1949, and officials were anxious to renew the accord in order to maintain American influence with the king. Military planners also had a stake in the air base. Although the air force did not consider Dhahran "vital" to American interests, the JCS informed Marshall in November that "our world-wide strategic position would be greatly improved if, in the event of war, the means could be developed to defend successfully and to conduct sustained air operations from Dhahran Air Base." In short, Dhahran provided further evidence of the increasing strategic value of the entire area. "Saudi Arabia is strategically the most important nation in the Arabian Peninsula," the Joint Strategic Survey Committee wrote to the JCS, "and the Arabian Peninsula is the most important area in the Middle East–Mediterranean region."

Finally, there were the economic advantages of securing Saudi reserves. Concerned by the projected patterns of domestic consumption, government officials urged the development of sources in the

Middle East. Although this oil supplied only a fraction of total world requirements in 1948, loss or impairment of Arabian oil, the State Department's petroleum experts argued, might "create extremely serious consequences," particularly for the European Recovery Program. Moreover, if the United States were forced to "underwrite" Europe's petroleum needs, in addition to meeting its own requirements, widespread rationing of gasoline and fuel oil might have to be considered. To the department's petroleum and trade analysts and experts on Middle Eastern affairs, the importance of Arabian oil was undeniable. Writing to the Office of United Nations Affairs in may 1948, the assistant chief of PED [Petroleum Division of the Department of State] cautioned against adopting a policy which might jeopardize "what is probably the richest economic prize in the world in the field of foreign investment, i.e., Saudi Arabian oil."

Latin America and the United States After the Second World War

San Francisco

Los Angeles

UNITED STATES

Mississippi River

Chicago

New York

Washington, D.C.

ATLANTIC OCEAN

PACIFIC OCEAN

Rio Grande

New Orleans

San Antonio

Miami

MEXICO

GULF OF MEXICO

Havana

CUBA

HAITI

DOM. REP.

PUERTO RICO

Mexico City

BR. HONDURAS

Belize

HONDURAS

JAMAICA

VIRGIN ISLANDS

GUATEMALA

Guatemala

Tegucigalpa

CARIBBEAN SEA

Caracas

Georgetown

SURINAM

Paramaribo

Cayenne

San Salvador

EL SALVADOR

NICARAGUA

Managua

Panama Canal

Maracaibo

Orinoco River

VENEZUELA

BR. GUIANA

FR. GUIANA

San José

COSTA RICA

Panamá

PANAMA

Medellín

Bogotá

COLOMBIA

Quito

ECUADOR

Amazon River

Belém

PERU

BRAZIL

Lima

BOLIVIA

La Paz

Sucre

Brasília

Salvador

SCALE

Miles 0 200 400 600 800

Kilometers 0 400 800

PARAGUAY

Asunción

São Paulo

Rio de Janeiro

CHILE

ARGENTINA

URUGUAY

Pôrto Alegre

Valparaíso

Santiago

Buenos Aires

Montevideo

Stephen G. Rabe

UNITED STATES ANTI-COMMUNISM IN LATIN AMERICA

United States policy toward Latin America during the early postwar years
has received far less scholarly attention than has policy toward either Asia
or the Middle East. Yet North America's relations with its southern neighbors, as Stephen G. Rabe explains, were also shaped to a great extent by
Cold War considerations. Anti-communism, he argues, became the overriding issue in inter-American relations, much to the detriment of the economic vitality and democratic institutions of the region. By 1947–1948,
heightened administration fears of a communist threat to the hemisphere
led to the inauguration of military-assistance programs and an expanded
interpretation of the Monroe Doctrine. Rabe argues that United States policies ultimately destabilized Latin America economically and politically while
promoting Washington's own hegemonic position throughout the region.

Stephen G. Rabe is the author of *The Road to OPEC: United States Relations with Venezuela, 1919–1976* (1982) and *Eisenhower and Latin America:
The Foreign Policy of Anticommunism* (1988). The second work, from which
this essay is drawn, received the Stuart L. Bernath Memorial Book Prize
from the Society for Historians of American Foreign Relations. Rabe teaches
at the University of Texas, Dallas.

During the presidential campaign of 1952, Dwight Eisenhower
deplored the state of inter-American relations. In a speech in New
Orleans on 13 October 1952, he charged that Latin Americans had lost
confidence in the United States. He recalled that during World War II
"we frantically wooed Latin America"—but after the war the Truman
administration "proceeded to forget these countries just as fast," and
"terrible disillusionment set in throughout Latin America." The United
States reneged on promises to cooperate economically with its neighbors. The result was economic distress, "followed by popular unrest,
skillfully exploited by Communist agents there." "Through drift and
neglect," the Truman administration had turned a good neighbor policy
into "a poor neighbor policy." Eisenhower promised change.

In his New Orleans address, Eisenhower expressed sentiments that

From *Eisenhower and Latin America: The Foreign Policy of Anticommunism* by Stephen G.
Rabe, pp. 6–8, 12–25. © 1988 The University of North Carolina Press. Reprinted by
permission.

were popularly held in both the United States and Latin America. Inter-American relations were strong and cordial between 1933 and 1945 because of Franklin Roosevelt's "Good Neighbor Policy." But, since 1945, relations had deteriorated, because President Harry S Truman and his advisors neglected Latin America. In making these charges, Eisenhower did not explain why the Good Neighbor policy worked or why the Truman administration would foolishly abandon such a popular and productive approach. Moreover, Eisenhower did not propose any new policies for Latin America. He implied, however, that he would return to the principles of Roosevelt's Good Neighbor and discard the practices of the Truman administration. Indeed, the course and conduct of inter-American relations during the Roosevelt and Truman administrations would profoundly influence Eisenhower's policies toward Latin America.

When Franklin D. Roosevelt assumed office in March 1933, he found inter-American relations dangerously strained. The most explosive issue was the question of intervention. Under the aegis of the "Roosevelt Corollary" to the Monroe Doctrine, the United States, during the first three decades of the twentieth century, had repeatedly intervened in the internal affairs of Caribbean and Central American nations. As the dominant power in the Western Hemisphere, the United States claimed the right to exercise, in Theodore Roosevelt's words, "international police power" to ensure that Latin Americans paid their international debts and respected foreign lives and property. Military interventions, by forestalling European influence in Latin American affairs, also upheld the Monroe Doctrine and barred any threat to the Panama Canal. . . .

Franklin D. Roosevelt and his advisors quickly repaired inter-American relations. They withdrew U.S. troops and financial advisors from the Caribbean. The administration also relinquished treaty rights, such as the Platt Amendment of 1903, that the United States had imposed on Cuba (the Platt Amendment, although nominally guaranteeing the independence of Cuba, served as a pretext for intervention). And, beginning with the Seventh International Conference of American States held in Montevideo, Uruguay, in late 1933, the U.S. delegation consistently voted with Latin Americans on resolutions outlawing military intervention. This process culminated in 1948, during the Truman administration, when the United States accepted the charter of the Organization of American States, which prohibited any state from intervening "directly or indirectly, for any reason whatever, in the internal or external affairs of any other state."

The Roosevelt administration also revived inter-American trade. Armed with the Reciprocal Trade Agreements Act of 1934, which gave the president the power to reduce tariffs by up to 50 percent in exchange for equivalent concessions, the administration negotiated, by the end of 1939, trade agreements with eleven Latin American countries. By 1939 the value of U.S.–Latin American trade had nearly doubled from its 1933 low, although it was still significantly below its 1929 peak. In addition, the administration responded to economic nationalism in Latin America. It tacitly conceded that Latin Americans needed to diversify their economies when, in 1940, it granted Brazil a $45 million credit to construct a steel mill. It grudgingly accepted Mexico's expropriation of the holdings of U.S. oil companies, and it helped Venezuela write its oil law of 1943, a bill that required foreign oil companies in Venezuela to share at least 50 percent of their profits with Venezuela.

These Good Neighbor policies not only resolved key differences with Latin America but also helped forge a strong wartime alliance. . . .

Latin Americans would have been disappointed with the postwar policies of the United States, even if President Roosevelt had been able to complete his fourth term. The people in the State Department most closely linked with the policy of assigning priority to inter-American relations—Undersecretary Sumner Welles and Laurence Duggan, chief of the Latin American division—had left government. But the new direction in postwar U.S. foreign policy transcended personalities. The United States emerged from World War II as the world's dominant power with global ambitions and responsibilities; regional concerns would be subordinated to the large task of rebuilding Europe and Japan and containing the Soviet Union.

During President Harry Truman's first term, the Latin American policy of the United States seemed confused and inconsistent. In form, the Truman administration continued to focus U.S. foreign policy on Latin America. At the United Nations Conference on International Organization in San Francisco in 1945, the U.S. delegation, at the urging of the new assistant secretary of state for Latin American affairs, Nelson Rockefeller, agreed with Latin Americans that the United Nations should sanction regional security organizations. This agreement was transformed into Article 51 of the U.N. charter. Thereafter, in 1947, the administration signed a mutual defense pact with Latin

America at Rio de Janeiro, and a year later, at Bogotá, Colombia, it joined with Latin Americans in incorporating Pan-Americanism into the charter of the Organization of American States (OAS). These treaties served as models for other regional pacts, such as the North Atlantic Treaty Organization.

The Rio Treaty and the OAS reflected the spirit of the Good Neighbor policy. But they also revealed vastly different perspectives on inter-American relations. With Article 51 the United States was able, in Secretary of War Henry L. Stimson's view, to preserve "the unilateral character of the Monroe Doctrine"; if the United States needed to enforce peace in Latin America, it would not be "at the mercy of getting the assent of the Security Council." In accepting Article 51 President Truman was affirming the views of President Roosevelt, who, during the war, assured Latin Americans that the inter-American system would not be supplanted by a new international organization. But, while pursuing U.S. foreign policy objectives, both Truman and Roosevelt were also acceding to Latin American wishes. Indeed, Latin Americans, led by Mexico and Colombia, vigorously lobbied at the San Francisco conference for the inclusion of regional alliances into the U.N. Charter. Latin Americans believed that Article 51 would help "contain" the United States. With the OAS, Latin Americans would have a forum to influence the United States, a treaty that guaranteed the nonintervention principle, and a vehicle for transferring economic aid.

Although Latin Americans achieved their organizational goals, they were alarmed by the substance of inter-American relations. In the first postwar years the question of intervention again dominated inter-American affairs. After Secretary of State Hull resigned because of poor health in late 1944, the United States reassessed its Argentine policy. The new secretary of state, Edward Stettinius, accepted the arguments of Assistant Secretary Rockefeller and of Latin Americans that Argentina should be admitted to the United Nations in order to maintain regional solidarity. But by the end of 1945, the department had once again changed U.S. policy. The new ambassador to Argentina, Spruille Braden, interfered in Argentine politics: Braden, who had established a reputation as a tough foe of fascism during his wartime ambassadorships in Colombia and Cuba, denounced the military rulers of Argentina as erstwhile sympathizers of Nazi Germany. For his efforts, he reaped the disdain of Argentine military men, popular support in the United States, and a promotion in December 1945 to assistant secretary from the new secretary of state, James F. Byrnes. From

Washington, Braden continued his noisy campaign, particularly against the leading presidential candidate, Colonel Juan Perón. Two weeks before the Argentine election, the department published the "Blue Book," a study that purported to document the Fascist proclivities of leading Argentinians. Perón cleverly seized upon Braden's impolitic behavior and turned the election into a campaign against Yankee imperialism; he won a landslide victory on 24 February 1946.

In Braden's view, intervention was a false issue. The United States dominated the hemisphere; "whatever we refrain from saying and whatever we refrain from doing may constitute intervention, no less than what we do or say." Braden therefore feuded with Perón, denounced Rafael Trujillo, and warmly praised fledgling democracies in Peru and Venezuela. He also embraced the Larreta Doctrine: in October 1945 Eduardo Rodríguez Larreta, the foreign minister of Uruguay—one of Latin America's few staunch democracies—had proposed that the Pan-American nations consider multilateral action against any member state violating elementary human rights. The proposal received an indifferent reception from all the Latin American countries except Uruguay and Venezuela; this response was predictable, for repressive, authoritarian governments wielded power in many of these lands, and the Larreta Doctrine raised the specter of intervention.

However, by mid-1947 both Byrnes and Braden had left Washington, and the State Department once again altered its Argentine policy. In January 1947, in a dispute over European questions, President Truman asked Byrnes to resign and appointed General George C. Marshall to be secretary of state. In June 1947 Marshall fired Braden, for he found that his Argentine policy had not weakened Perón and that it endangered hemispheric solidarity by delaying the scheduled defense conference: the Rio Conference had been scheduled to meet in 1945, but Braden had twice postponed it because of the dispute with Argentina. In late 1948, the department officially buried Braden's policies. After extended debate and review, it decided to issue a statement deploring "the use of force as an instrument of political change," even as it recognized the military dictators who overthrew popularly elected governments in Peru and Venezuela.

In part, these oscillations in policy can be attributed to bureaucratic disorder and clashes among strong personalities. In three years, Truman had three secretaries of state and three assistant secretaries for Latin America. But U.S. policy on Argentina and intervention also changed because the imperatives of the cold war had triumphed over the democratic idealism engendered by World War II. Secretary Marshall decided to form a military alliance that would include Argentina, because of the ongoing confrontations with the Soviet Union over Europe and the Middle East: the goal of a united hemisphere outweighed misgivings about Perón's past associations and beliefs. The military rulers in Peru and Venezuela coupled their requests for diplomatic recognition with promises to oppose communism and support the United States at the United Nations. And Rafael Trujillo assured Washington that he had undergone metamorphosis from an anti-Fascist into the hemisphere's most vigorous anti-Communist.

Although the cold war had intruded into inter-American affairs, the Truman administration was not prepared by 1948 to battle communism with every means. At the Bogotá Conference, the delegates denounced international communism and resolved to exchange information on international Communist activities. But the United States opposed "a multilateral inter-American anti-Communist agreement." In what became the first National Security Council (NSC) document devoted exclusively to Latin America, NSC 16, the Truman administration decided that "communism in the Americas is a potential danger, but that, with a few possible exceptions, it is not seriously dangerous at the present time." It feared "that there would be many cases in which such anti-Communist agreements would be directed against all political opposition, Communist or otherwise, by dictatorial governments, with the inevitable result of driving leftist elements into the hands of the Communist organization." It was an apt prediction. Between 1947 and 1952, five Latin American countries, with U.S. approval, severed relations with the Soviet Union. They also simultaneously outlawed Communist activities, a category that often was broadly defined.

The Truman administration's position on intervention and communism, thus, was in evolution between 1945 and 1948. What remained constant was the policy toward economic cooperation with Latin America. Latin Americans expected economic aid from the United States. During the war, Undersecretary Summer Welles had consistently pledged that the United States would cooperate with Latin America, once the enemy was defeated. Whether the Roosevelt administration would have redeemed those promises is uncertain, but it seems doubtful. In 1944 Cordell Hull twice postponed a hemispheric economic conference because of the imbroglio with Argentina. When the American republics met in Chapultepec, near Mexico City, in early 1945 to discuss "problems of war and peace," Latin Americans were interested in economic questions. They spoke of international commodity agreements, controls on foreign investment, linking the prices of raw materials to finished goods, and economic aid. The U.S. delegation responded indifferently to these overtures, but, in order to avoid a wartime clash, it agreed to explore economic issues at a special conference scheduled for 15 June 1945.

The Truman administration refused to attend an inter-American economic conference. Between 1945 and 1947, the administration argued that economic cooperation could not be discussed until the Argentine issue was resolved. But the State Department feared that an economic conference would be a fiasco, with the United States resisting demands for economic aid and commodity agreements—in early 1946, for example, Brazil requested a five-year $1-billion loan. Latin America would prosper if it implemented free trade and investment principles and prepared for the massive orders of raw materials that would surely come from a rebuilding Europe. By 1946, department officials wanted "to kill" the conference idea but, fearing a stormy reaction from Latin Americans, chose only to postpone it. The United States had reneged on the promises of Sumner Welles, perhaps because, as department officer Louis Halle bluntly put it, with the war over, "the United States no longer desperately needs Latin America."

Latin Americans were dismayed not only by the U.S. position on economic aid but also by its handling of wartime contracts. During the war, Latin America sold its strategic commodities in a controlled market, with prices fixed. Latin Americans accumulated credits of $3.4 billion, because the capital goods they wanted to purchase were scarce in the United States. This influx of money contributed to inflationary pressures, with the cost of living rising over 80 percent in Latin America during the war. In 1945 at Chapultepec, the United States promised not to terminate wartime contracts suddenly and to allocate capital goods fairly. But after the war, the United States abruptly lifted price controls and prices rose rapidly; Latin America quickly exhausted its wartime credits. Chile, for example, by selling its copper and nitrates at artificially low prices and buying goods it wanted for industrial development in a free market, may have lost more than $500 million. In effect, Latin America made a $3-billion non-interest-bearing loan to the United States and could not collect on the principal. The United States answered, however, that it had sacrificed men and matériel in protecting the hemisphere from totalitarianism.

Latin American hopes for economic aid revived in 1947, after Secretary Marshall announced his plan to reconstruct Europe. If the United States was ready to help its former enemies, then a "Marshall Plan for Latin America" might follow. At the Rio Conference, Latin American delegates wanted to focus on economic cooperation, but Marshall persuaded them to wait until the meeting in Bogotá. There, he quashed all hopes of economic aid. In a speech that was greeted by stony silence, Marshall promised only to increase the lending authority of the Export-Import Bank by $500 million. The European Recovery Program would aid Latin America by restoring markets for raw materials and tropical foods. Once Europe rebuilt its industrial plant, Latin America would also have another source of supply for capital goods. Such arguments meant to Latin Americans that their region would be confined to its traditional role of supplying the industrial world with raw materials. In any case, between 1945 and 1952 the twenty Latin American nations together received less economic aid from the United States than did Belgium and tiny Luxembourg.

In lieu of economic assistance, the U.S. prescription for Latin America's economic health included self-help, technical cooperation, liberal trade practices, and, in particular, private enterprise and investment. The State Department repeatedly told Latin Americans that they could have the capital they so desperately needed by creating a "suitable climate" for foreign investors and by not imposing unreasonable barriers to transferring capital and earnings. The Truman administration backed these pronouncements by vigorously opposing economic nationalism. It refused to approve loans to state companies such as PEMEX and the new Brazilian national oil company, PETROBRÁS. The Export-Import Bank would make loans only if they supplemented domestic and foreign private investment. The administration also threatened to reduce Cuba's sugar quota and to cancel Bolivian tin purchases in an attempt to " 'put across' U.S. corporation practices and safeguards" to those countries. And it scrutinized Latin American laws and constitutions, such as the Venezuelan constitution of 1947, and forcefully objected if they violated free trade and investment principles.

Latin Americans reacted angrily to these policies, charging that the United States had misled them during the war and now "neglected" them. But although Latin America was the one non-Communist area of the world not under a direct aid program, the Truman administration was not uninterested in the good neighbors. The area remained strategically significant and economically vital. In the early postwar years,

U.S. businessmen counted on Latin America for approximately 30 percent of their international trade and nearly 40 percent of their global direct investments. The Truman administration did not develop a Marshall Plan for Latin America because it believed in the efficacy of international capitalism and because it grounded its analyses of inter-American relations of the cold war. Unlike Europe, Latin America did not seem threatened by the Soviet Union. As Ambassador Herschel Johnson explained to the Brazilian press, "the situation might be graphically represented as a case of smallpox in Europe competing with a common cold in Latin America."

By the end of 1948, the Truman administration had decided on its hemispheric policies: it would work with non-Communist governments in Latin America and defend the foreign economic policy of free trade and investment. During Truman's second term the State Department, led by Secretary of State Dean Acheson and Assistant Secretary Edward G. Miller, Jr., continued to apply those policies. What changed was that, under the continuing impact of the cold war, the Truman administration expanded its concept of national security in regard to Latin America. It also began to criticize sharply the attitudes and policies of Latin Americans.

Secretary Acheson set the tone for inter-American relations during Truman's second term when, in September 1949, he addressed the Pan American Society. The speech, which the State Department called "the most complete restatement of Latin American policy in many years," covered familiar ground. Acheson conceded there had been "occasional disappointments," with the overthrow of freely elected governments; yet, he rejected the Larreta Doctrine and reaffirmed a de facto recognition policy. He argued that "our long-range objectives in the promotion of democracy" would be better served by maintaining communication with unelected governments. As for a Marshall Plan for Latin America, Acheson could not have been more unequivocal. The United States "has been built by private initiative, and it remains a land of private initiative." The State Department would not approve loans for development projects, when private capital was available. In any case, he did not "believe that rapid industrialization is good per se." Instead, Latin Americans should increase agricultural productivity and negotiate treaties that attracted and protected international investors. Acheson concluded: "I cannot stress too strongly that progress will come most rapidly in countries that help themselves vigorously."

The State Department was true to Secretary Acheson's words. It continued to postpone indefinitely an inter-American economic conference, and it repeatedly informed Latin Americans that "the greatest single obstacle to economic development in Latin America is the slow rate of private foreign investment." It also unsuccessfully tried to persuade Latin Americans to abolish the Economic Commission for Latin America, a U.N. agency. The commission irritated U.S. officials by issuing reports demonstrating that the prices of raw material and food exports were declining relative to the prices of imported manufacturers, and by suggesting that the solution to these declining terms of trade was to attract development capital, presumably from the U.S. government, for industrialization and economic diversification. Ignoring this unsolicited advice, the United States confined its aid to Export-Import Bank loans and technical cooperation. The Export-Import Bank loans were primarily short-term credits to finance the purchase of imports from the United States. Technical cooperation, the "Point Four" initiative of President Truman, amounted to about $25 million a year in grants for agricultural modernization. So limited were U.S. economic efforts in Latin America that the interest the U.S. Treasury collected on Export-Import Bank loans actually exceeded the amount of aid granted to the region. Assistant Secretary Miller dutifully upheld these foreign economic policies, although he was not oblivious to the irony in them. As he wondered in a confidential memorandum: "How is it possible to justify on either moral or logical grounds the extension of U.S. grants to a heavy dollar and gold earner such as Saudi Arabia, when similar assistance is not available to such poverty-stricken, dollar-short countries as Paraguay and Ecuador?"

Miller also, as instructed by Acheson, maintained "channels of communication" with unsavory governments. In particular, he worked hard for a rapprochement with President Perón of Argentina. With the approval of President Truman, Miller went to Buenos Aires in February 1950 to meet with the Argentine strongman. Perón had said that he was anti-Communist and that he would support the United States in a war with the Soviet Union, and he implied that he would send the Rio Treaty of 1947 to the Argentine legislature for ratification. Accordingly, it did not seem "wise to jeopardize this cooperation by making what would probably be an unfruitful effort to inject into the Perón government a respect for civil liberties." The visit appeared successful: Perón agreed to back the Rio Treaty, and a few months later he voted with the United States at the United Nations in condemning North

Korea's invasion of South Korea. In return, Argentina received a $125-million credit from the Export-Import Bank. Argentina's return to the fold was, however, short-lived. By the end of 1950 Perón, perhaps responding to domestic pressure, was reasserting Argentina's traditional independence, denouncing both communism and capitalism and upholding the "third ideological position," *justicialismo*.

The Truman administration's position on economic aid and its special efforts toward Argentina, the only neutral nation during World War II, engendered a new wave of complaints and criticisms from Latin Americans. But the problem, as Secretary Miller saw it, was that Latin America wanted to ignore the cold war and return to the 1930s when "the Good Neighbor Policy was virtually our sole foreign policy"; that experience, combined with a consequential high-level attention devoted to Latin America, "had fostered an exaggerated and extreme sense of self-importance on the part of individuals connected with Latin American governments." Miller, whose father owned sugar plantations and mills in Cuba, also told the House Foreign Affairs Committee in executive session that, during the 1930s, "we went too far in the direction of not protecting American interests." Miller kept such views confidential, but he authorized Louis Halle, under the pseudonym "Y," to reveal in the influential journal *Foreign Affairs* the State Department's "impatience with Latin America." In that article, Halle argued that the United States would have to follow the dictates of "noblesse oblige" toward Latin American countries, for they were like children, not yet ready to exercise, for themselves, the responsibility of adult nations. Dean Acheson would later ascribe problems in Latin America to "Hispano-Indian culture—or lack of it."

Although, during its second term, the Truman administration spoke frankly to Latin America, it had not restructured the policies it had developed by 1947–48 on recognition, nondemocratic governments, and economic aid. What was new was a heightened fear and perception of communism in the hemisphere. These anxieties were not based on developments within Latin America. In his speech to the Pan American Society in 1949, Secretary Acheson noted there was not a "direct threat against our independence." In 1950, in a comprehensive review of Latin America, the State Department concluded that the Communists had "lost ground." As late as 1951, Assistant Secretary Miller assured Congress that the Soviet Union's role in Latin America "at this time will not be great." Miller criticized the social and economic policies of Guatemala, but he concluded they could be blamed on

President Juan José Arévalo, a "wooly-head." U.S. officials also knew that by 1952 the Soviet Union had diplomatic relations with only three Latin American countries—Argentina, Mexico, and Uruguay—and a minuscule amount of trade in the hemisphere.

Yet, despite its own evidence and its continuing belief that an inter-American, anti-Communist agreement might be used by some governments to "suppress all types of liberal opposition," the Truman administration decided to redefine the Monroe Doctrine and the OAS charter. In a speech in April 1950, two months before the outbreak of the Korean War, Miller reviewed the history of intervention. He condoned the decisions of presidents like Theodore Roosevelt, Woodrow Wilson, and Calvin Coolidge, arguing that they had ordered troops into Caribbean nations to forestall European interference and perhaps colonialism—these decisions had been "necessary evils," or "protective interventions." Miller accepted the Good Neighbor policy, the juridical equality of states, but he warned that "if the circumstances that led to the protective interventions by the United States should arise again today, the organized community of American states would be faced with the responsibility that the United States had once to assume alone." The doctrine of nonintervention incorporated in the OAS charter of 1948 was not absolute; if a member state was threatened by Communist political aggression, the OAS would have to act for the common welfare. This action would be "the alternative to intervention," the "corollary of non-intervention." What Miller left unanalyzed was the policy the United States would adopt, if it could not convince Latin American nations to sanction an intervention against another American republic.

The Truman administration coupled the "Miller Doctrine" on intervention with a decision in 1950 to arm Latin America against communism. Since the middle of World War II, defense planners had wanted Latin America to be militarily dependent upon the United States. Prior to the war, South Americans had purchased their arms and accepted military training missions from Europe, including the Axis nations of Germany and Italy. In order to exclude foreign influence from the hemisphere and to "promote with respect to the American continent, the United States policy regarding the organization of peace and security," defense officials proposed an arms standardization policy for the hemisphere. The United States would provide arms, if Latin America would cooperate in postwar hemispheric defense, make available its military bases to U.S. air and naval forces, and agree not to purchase equipment and training from foreign sources.

Although the Truman administration submitted to Congress in both 1946 and 1947 a military aid package for Latin America, it did not secure funding. Congressional critics managed to delay legislation, arguing that military aid was wasteful, would bolster authoritarian regimes, and would trigger a hemispheric arms race. Officials in the Latin American section of the State Department did not lament the postponement, for they also feared the political effects of military aid. In any case, the United States lacked arms to transfer, because programs such as Greek-Turkish aid, NATO, and support for Chinese nationalist forces took priority over inter-American military cooperation.

But on 19 May 1950 President Truman authorized military aid for Latin America when he approved NSC 56/2, "United States Policy Toward Inter-American Military Collaboration": Defense officials would design with Latin Americans a plan for hemispheric defense; the United States would then provide "such mutual assistance among the American republics as may be necessary to assure adequate implementation of the Hemisphere Defense Scheme." The preparation of NSC 56/2 was done while the Truman administration was conducting the broad review of national security policy that would be tagged NSC 68. Like NSC 68, the new policy on inter-American military collaboration assumed that the United States was locked in a momentous global struggle with the Soviet Union and that "the cold war is in fact a real war in which the survival of the free world is at stake." Yet, neither NSC 68 nor NSC 56/2 explained precisely how the Soviet Union threatened Latin America. And, whereas NSC 56/2 recognized, for example, that Latin Americans might use U.S. weapons against one another, it did not resolve the political and diplomatic issues raised by transferring arms to poor, weak, undemocratic nations. These problems seemed inconsequential, however, after the outbreak of the Korean conflict. As it did with NSC 68, the war helped "sell" NSC 56/2. In 1951 Congress voted $38,150,000 for direct military assistance for Latin America, and in 1952 it added $51,685,750 to that sum.

In expanding its interpretation of the Monroe Doctrine and arming Latin America, the Truman administration was working "to strengthen the free world and frustrate the Kremlin design." As the administration concluded in late 1950, "U.S. security is the objective of our world-wide foreign policy today," and "U.S. security is synonymous with hemisphere security." What the United States wanted from Latin

America was for the other American states to "identify with our policy." The Truman administration failed, however, to achieve that "identification." After President Truman declared a national emergency following attacks on U.S. troops in Korea by Chinese forces, Secretary Acheson hastily called an inter-American conference of foreign ministers, which met in Washington between March and April 1951. But, for this war, Latin Americans were willing to give only "rhetorical" support to their northern neighbor. The conference's key resolution, calling for increased production of strategic materials, was tied to a statement citing Latin America's need for economic development. Moreover, only Colombia responded to requests for troops, and with only a token battalion of volunteers.

Latin America did not rally behind the United States in Korea because of the Truman administration's policy on economic aid. Secretary Miller found "apathy and sullenness resulting from the feeling that the United States has abandoned Latin America in the post-war era and is giving priority to new friends in other parts of the world." When he journeyed to Rio de Janeiro in February 1951 to request a division of Brazilian troops for Korea, Miller received a frosty reception. As the Brazilian Foreign Minister João Neves da Fontura observed to Miller, "Brazil's present situation would be different and our cooperation in the present emergency could probably be greater," if Washington "had elaborated a recovery plan for Latin America similar to the Marshall Plan for Europe." Alarmed at the course of inter-American relations, Miller began to argue that the United States would have to grant Latin America at least a small amount of assistance. But the administration was too harried and the economy too strained by the Korean conflict for the United States to consider another economic aid program. Miller's only significant success was to obtain in late 1952 an emergency $300 million loan for Brazil to relieve balance-of-payment and currency difficulties.

In lambasting the Truman administration's Latin American policy, Dwight Eisenhower accurately depicted the disillusionment that Latin Americans felt over inter-American relations. He also correctly charged that the United States was not devoting the same amount of energy and imagination to relations with Latin America that it had in the 1930s. But the presidential candidate exaggerated when he implied that the Truman government did not have a policy for Latin America. President Truman and his advisors wanted to wage cold war, and their policies toward Latin America reflected that overriding objective. The administration's stance on the issues of recognition, military aid, and intervention was designed to build a dependable and secure hemisphere, a region the United States could rely on while confronting the Soviet Union. Whereas its approach toward Latin America was perhaps less conciliatory and sympathetic than that of President Roosevelt, Sumner Welles, and Laurence Duggan, the Truman administration retained the central feature of the Good Neighbor policy. The United States would maintain its hegemony in the Western Hemisphere.

To be sure, the Truman administration would leave President Eisenhower with dilemmas and unresolved issues in inter-American relations. Latin Americans placed a higher priority on economic development and diversification than on winning the cold war. They were being swept up in the nationalist fervor and the "revolution of rising expectations" that characterized nations in Asia, Africa, and the Middle East, as they emerged from colonialism in the postwar world. Latin Americans might begin to identify more with the "Third World" than with Pan-Americanism. Moreover, the Truman administration, in choosing to subordinate human rights issues to security concerns and in deciding to work with and arm dictators, was frustrating, demoralizing, even radicalizing Latin American progressives and reformers who might be natural allies of the United States; the security that a Trujillo could provide in the short term might jeopardize the long-term interests of the United States in Latin America. Finally, in espousing, as it did in NSC 68, the doctrine that every manifestation of communism on the globe was a gain for the Soviet Union and a direct threat to the United States, the administration was ensuring that the issue of unilateral intervention would again arise in inter-American relations. Remembering past violations of their sovereignty, Latin Americans were unlikely to accept Secretary Miller's judgment that collective intervention against communism was an "imperative" of the Monroe Doctrine and the OAS charter. These issues of economic nationalism, human rights, communism, and intervention would be the ones that the Eisenhower administration would encounter in formulating policies for Latin America.

SUGGESTIONS FOR FURTHER READING

For an extensive annotated bibliography, including articles and books on all aspects of Soviet-American relations, see Richard Dean Burns, ed., *Guide to American Foreign Relations since 1700* (1983). A handy reference, with brief essays on major events, concepts, and leaders, is Richard S. Kirkendall, ed., *The Harry S. Truman Encyclopedia* (1989).

General works on the Soviet-American relationship include John Lewis Gaddis, *Russia, the Soviet Union, and the United States* (1990) and N. V. Sivachev and N. N. Yakovlev, *Russia and the United States* (1979), a pre-*glasnost* Soviet account. For America's response to the Bolshevik Revolution, including military intervention, see Betty Miller Unterberger, *The United States, Revolutionary Russia, and the Rise of Czechoslovakia* (1989); Lloyd C. Gardner, *Safe for Democracy* (1984); N. Gordon Levin, *Woodrow Wilson and World Politics* (1968); George F. Kennan, *Russia Leaves the War* (1956) and *The Decision to Intervene* (1958); and Benjamin D. Rhodes, *The Anglo-American Winter War with Russia, 1918–1919* (1988). Books on early relations are Joan Hoff Wilson, *Ideology and Foreign Policy: U.S. Relations with the Soviet Union, 1918–1933* (1974); Peter Filene, *Americans and the Soviet Experiment, 1917–1933* (1967); George F. Kennan, *Russia and the West under Lenin and Stalin* (1969); and B. Ponomaryov et. al., eds., *History of Soviet Foreign Policy, 1917–1945* (1974). An important topic is discussed in Anthony Sutton, *Western Technology and Soviet Economic Development, 1917–1930* (1977).

For the 1933 United States decision to open diplomatic relations, see Edward Bennett, *Recognition of Russia* (1970), and Donald G. Bishop, *The Roosevelt-Litvinov Agreements* (1965). The 1930s are treated in Edward Bennett, *Franklin D. Roosevelt and the Search for Security* (1985); Beatrice Farnsworth, *William C. Bullitt and the Soviet Union* (1967); Thomas R. Maddux, *Years of Estrangement* (1980); and Keith D. Eagles, *Ambassador Joseph E. Davies and American-Soviet Relations, 1937–1941* (1985).

For the Second World War, see Herbert Feis, *Churchill, Roosevelt, and Stalin* (1957) and *Between War and Peace: The Potsdam Conference* (1960); James MacGregor Burns, *Roosevelt: The Soldier of Freedom* (1970); Gabriel Kolko, *The Politics of War* (1968); Gary Hess, *The United States at War, 1941–1945* (1986); William H. McNeill, *America, Britain, and Russia* (1953); Steven M. Miner, *Between Churchill and Stalin* (1988); Gaddis Smith, *American Diplomacy during the Second World War* (1985); Robert Dallek, *Franklin D. Roosevelt and American Foreign Policy, 1933–1945* (1979); Robert A. Divine, *Roosevelt and World War II* (1969); Ralph B. Levering, *American Opinion and the Russian Alliance* (1976); George C. Herring, *Aid to Russia, 1941–1945* (1973); Vojtech Mastny, *Russia's Road to the Cold War* (1979); and Mark A. Stoler, *The Politics of the Second Front* (1977). A key wartime conference that produced Cold War consequences is the subject of Diane Clemens, *Yalta* (1970), a sympathetic account, whereas Russell D. Buhite, in *Decision at Yalta* (1986), is critical of Roosevelt's diplomacy.

General analyses of the origins of the Cold War that for the most part reflect the traditionalist perspective include John Lewis Gaddis, *The United States and the Origins of the Cold War, 1941–1947* (1972), *The Long Peace* (1987), and *Strategies of Containment* (1982); Herbert Feis, *From Trust to Terror* (1970); Paul Y. Hammond, *Cold War and Detente* (1975); Walt Rostow, *The Diffusion of Power* (1971); John Spanier, *American Foreign Policy Since World War II* (1988); William Taubman, *Stalin's American Policy* (1982); Hugh Thomas, *Armed Truce* (1987); Kenneth W. Thompson, *Cold War Theories* (1981); Adam Ulam, *The Rivals* (1971) and *Expansion and Coexistence: The History of Soviet Foreign Policy, 1917–1973* (1974).

For works largely revisionist in perspective, see Thomas G. Paterson, *On Every Front: The Making of the Cold War* (1979), *Meeting the Communist Threat* (1988), and *Soviet-American Confrontation* (1973); Stephen Ambrose, *Rise to Globalism* (1988); Richard J. Barnet, *The Giants* (1977); Barton J. Bernstein, ed., *Politics and Policies of the Truman Administration* (1970); Lloyd C. Gardner, *Architects of Illusion* (1970); Gabriel Kolko and Joyce Kolko, *The Limits of Power* (1972); Athan Theoharis, *The Yalta Myths* (1970); Thomas J. McCormick, *America's Half-Century* (1989); Daniel Yergin, *Shattered Peace* (1977); and Walter LeFeber, *America, Russia, and the Cold War* (1985).

Other works that discuss early Cold War questions, with a variety of perspectives, are James L. Gormly, *The Collapse of the Grand Alliance, 1945–1948* (1987); Linda Killen, *The Soviet Union and the United States* (1989); Hugh DeSantis, *The Diplomacy of Silence* (1980); Mark R. Elliot, *Pawns of Yalta: Soviet Refugees and America's Role in Their Repatriation* (1982); Charles Gati, ed., *Caging the Bear: Containment and the Cold War* (1974); Michael Sherry, *Preparing for the Next War* (1977); Deborah Larson, *The Origins of Containment: A Psy-*

chological Explanation (1985); Philip J. Funigello, *American-Soviet Trade in the Cold War* (1988); Robert L. Messer, *The End of an Alliance* (1982); Frank Ninkovich, *The Diplomacy of Ideas* (1981); William O. McCagg, *Stalin Embattled, 1943–1948* (1978); Ronald Radosh, *American Labor and U.S. Foreign Policy* (1969); Göran Rystad, *Prisoners of the Past: The Munich Syndrome and Makers of American Foreign Policy in the Cold War Era* (1982); Hannes Adomeit, *Soviet Risk-Taking and Crisis Behavior* (1982); Marshall D. Shulman, *Stalin's Foreign Policy Reappraised* (1963); Wesley T. Wooley, *Alternatives to Anarchy: American Supranationalism since World War II* (1988); and Patricia Dawson Ward, *The Threat of Peace* (1979).

Analyses of scholars' interpretive differences, especially the traditionalist-revisionist debate, can be found in Robert W. Tucker, *The Radical Left and American Foreign Policy* (1971); Richard Kirkendall, ed., *The Truman Period as a Research Field* (1974); Warren F. Kimball, "The Cold War Warmed Over," *American Historical Review*, LXXIX (October 1974), 1119–1136; J. Samuel Walker, "Historians and Cold War Origins," in Gerald K. Haines and J. Samuel Walker, eds., *American Foreign Relations: A Historiographical Review* (1981); Edward Crapol, "Some Reflections on the Historiography of the Cold War," *The History Teacher*, XX (1986/87), 251–262; William Welch, *American Images of Soviet Foreign Policy* (1970); Peter Novick, *That Noble Dream: The "Objectivity Question" and the American Historical Profession* (1988); John Lewis Gaddis, "The Emerging Post-Revisionist Synthesis on the Origins of the Cold War," *Diplomatic History*, VII (Summer 1983), 171–190; Richard A. Melanson, *Writing History and Making Policy* (1983); and Geir Lundestad, "Moralism, Presentism, Exceptionalism, Provincialism, and Other Extravagances in American Writings on the Early Cold War Years," *Diplomatic History*, XIII (Fall 1989), 527–545.

Two works which place the early Cold War period and the two major adversaries in broad, comparative perspective are Paul Kennedy, *The Rise and Fall of the Great Powers: Economic Change and Military Conflict from 1500 to 2000* (1987), and Michael Mandelbaum, *The Fate of Nations: The Search for National Security in the Nineteenth and Twentieth Centuries* (1988).

General studies of Harry S Truman and his presidency abound. They include Alonzo L. Hamby, *Beyond the New Deal* (1973); Donald R. McCoy, *The Presidency of Harry S. Truman* (1984); William E. Pemberton, *Harry S. Truman: Fair Dealer and Cold Warrior* (1989);

Gary W. Reichard, *Politics as Usual* (1988); Robert J. Donovan, *Conflict and Crisis* (1977) and *Tumultuous Years* (1982); John P. Diggins, *The Proud Decades* (1988); and Michael J. Lacey, ed., *The Truman Presidency* (1989). The election of 1948 is discussed in Robert A. Divine, *Foreign Policy and U.S. Presidential Elections, 1940–1960* (1974).

Other American political and diplomatic leaders in the early Cold War era can be found in Michael T. Ruddy, *The Cautious Diplomat: Charles E. Bohlen and the Soviet Union* (1986); Ronald Pruessen, *John Foster Dulles* (1982); Gaddis Smith, *Dean Acheson* (1972); Stephen E. Ambrose, *Nixon* (1987); Herbert Parmet, *Jack: The Struggles of John F. Kennedy* (1983); David McLellan, *Dean Acheson* (1976); Forrest C. Pogue, *George C. Marshall: Statesman, 1945–1950* (1987); Mark A. Stoler, *George C. Marshall: Soldier-Statesman of the American Century* (1989); Frank Merli and Theodore Wilson, eds., *Makers of American Diplomacy* (1974); Kendrick A. Clements, ed., *James F. Byrnes and the Origins of the Cold War* (1982); and Walter Isaacson and Evan Thomas, *The Wise Men* (1986). George F. Kennan has received intensive analysis in Barton Gellmann, *Contending with Kennan* (1984); Walter L. Hixson, *George F. Kennan: Cold War Iconoclast* (1990); David Mayers, *George Kennan and the Dilemma of U.S. Foreign Policy* (1988); and Anders Stephenson, *Kennan and the Art of Foreign Policy* (1989).

American dissenters from Truman policies can be explored in J. Samuel Walker, *Henry A. Wallace and American Foreign Policy* (1976); Lawrence S. Wittner, *Rebels Against War: The American Peace Movement, 1941–1960* (1974); Justus Doenecke, *Not to the Swift: The Old Isolationists in the Cold War Era* (1979); and Thomas G. Paterson, ed., *Cold War Critics* (1971).

For anti-communism at home, including Truman's role in fostering McCarthyism, see Michael R. Belknap, *Cold War Political Justice* (1977); David Caute, *The Great Fear* (1978); Richard M. Fried, *Men Against McCarthy* (1976) and *Nightmare in Red* (1990); Robert Griffith, *The Politics of Fear* (1970); Robert Griffith and Athan Theoharis, eds., *The Specter* (1974); William W. Keller, *The Liberals and J. Edgar Hoover* (1989); Stanley I. Kutler, *The American Inquisition* (1982); Mary S. McAuliffe, *Crisis on the Left: Cold War Politics and American Liberals, 1947–1954* (1978); William L. O'Neill, *A Better World: Stalinism and the American Intellectuals* (1983); Richard G. Powers, *Secrecy and Power: The Life of J. Edgar Hoover* (1987); Ronald Radosh and

Joyce Milton, *The Rosenberg File* (1983); Thomas C. Reeves, *The Life and Times of Joe McCarthy* (1982); Ellen W. Schrecker, *No Ivory Tower: McCarthyism in the Universities* (1986); Athan Theoharis, *Seeds of Repression: Harry S. Truman and the Origins of McCarthyism* (1971); Athan Theoharis and John S. Cox, *The Boss: J. Edgar Hoover and the Great American Inquisition* (1988); and Allen Weinstein, *Perjury: The Hiss-Chambers Case* (1978).

The impact of the atomic bomb on American thinking, Soviet-American relations, and international relations is the topic of several works: Gar Alporovitz, *Atomic Diplomacy* (1985); Paul Boyer, *By the Bomb's Early Light* (1986); Herbert Feis, *The Atomic Bomb and the End of World War II* (1966); Gregg Herken, *The Winning Weapon* (1981); Richard Hewlett and Oscar Anderson, *The New World* (1962); Michael Mandelbaum, *The Nuclear Question* (1979); Charles R. Morris, *Iron Destinies, Lost Opportunities* (1988); Daniel Holloway, *The Soviet Union and the Arms Race* (1984); Ronald E. Powaski, *March to Armageddon* (1987); Richard Rhodes, *The Making of the Atomic Bomb* (1987); Martin Sherwin, *A World Destroyed* (1975); J. Samuel Walker, "The Decision to Use the Bomb: A Historiographical Update," *Diplomatic History*, XIV (Winter 1990), 97–114; John Newhouse, *War and Peace in the Nuclear Age* (1989); and Barton J. Bernstein, ed., *The Atomic Bomb* (1975), which provides surveys of the literature and issues.

The creation of the United Nations and disputes over and in it are explored in James Barros, *Trygvie Lie and the Cold War: The UN Secretary-General Pursues Peace, 1946–1953* (1989); Thomas Campbell, *Masquerade Peace: America's UN Policy* (1973); Robert A. Divine, *Second Chance: The Triumph of Internationalism in American Foreign Policy During World War II* (1967); Max Harrelson, *Fires All Around the Horizon* (1989); Evan Luard, *A History of the United Nations* (1982); and George T. Mazuzan, *Warren T. Austin at the U.N., 1946–1953* (1977).

For events in Eastern Europe, over which the Soviets and Americans frequently clashed, see Phyliss Auty, *Tito* (1970); Michael M. Boll, *Cold War in the Balkans* (1984); Richard Lukas, *Bitter Legacy: Polish-American Relations in the Wake of World War II* (1982); Thomas Hammond, ed., *Witnesses to the Origins of the Cold War* (1987); Geir Lundestad, *The American Non-Policy Towards Eastern Europe, 1943–1947* (1975); Stanley M. Max, *The United States, Great Britain, and the Sovietization of Hungary, 1945–1948* (1985); Walter Ullmann,

The United States and Prague, 1945–1948 (1978), and Pjotr Wandycz, *The United States and Poland* (1980).

Anglo-American relations in the early Cold War and the growing partnership on many issues and competition over others have received active attention as British records have been opened to scholars. Among the many studies are Terry H. Anderson, *The United States, Great Britain, and the Cold War, 1944–1947* (1981); Elisabeth Barker, *The British Between the Superpowers, 1945–1950* (1983); Richard A. Best, Jr., *"Co-operation with Like-Minded Peoples"* (1986); Timothy J. Botti, *The Long Wait: The Forging of the Anglo-American Nuclear Alliance, 1945–1958* (1987); Allan Bullock, *Ernest Bevin* (1984); Robin Edmonds, *Setting the Mould* (1987); Fraser J. Harbutt, *The Iron Curtain* (1986); Robert M. Hathaway, *Ambiguous Partnership* (1981) and *Great Britain and the United States* (1990); W. Roger Louis and Hedley Bull, eds., *The Special Relationship* (1986); Richard Ovendale, *The English-Speaking Alliance* (1985); Henry B. Ryan, *The Vision of Anglo-America* (1988); and Kenneth W. Thompson, *Winston Churchill's World View* (1983).

For Canada's relationship with the emerging Cold War, see Denis Smith, *Diplomacy of Fear* (1988); Joseph T. Jockel, *No Boundaries Upstairs: Canada, the United States and the Origins of the North American Air Defence, 1945–1958* (1989); Robert Bothwell et al., *Canada Since 1945* (1981); and Lawrence Aronsen and Martin Kitchen, *The Origins of the Cold War in Comparative Perspective* (1988).

Postwar wrangling over the status of Germany, including the Berlin Blockade, is explained in John H. Backer, *Winds of History: The German Years of Lucius DuBignon Clay* (1984); Avi Shlaim, *The United States and the Berlin Blockade, 1948–1949* (1983); Daniel F. Harrington, "The Berlin Blockade Revisited," *International History Review*, VI (February 1984), 88–112; Frank Ninkovich, *Germany and the United States* (1988); John Gimbel, *The American Occupation of Germany* (1968), *The Origins of the Marshall Plan* (1976), and *Science, Technology, and Reparations: Exploitation and the Plunder in Postwar Germany* (1990); Robert Wolfe, ed., *Americans as Proconsuls* (1984); Bruce Kuklick, *American Reparations Policy and the Division of Germany* (1972); and Edward N. Peterson, *The American Occupation of Germany* (1976).

For the American response to developments in Greece and Turkey, including the Truman Doctrine and its aftermath, consult Bruce R. Kuniholm, *The Origins of the Cold War in the Near East*

(1980); Christopher M. Woodhouse, *The Struggle for Greece, 1941–1949* (1976); John Oneal, *Foreign Policy Making in Times of Crisis* (1982); John O. Iatrides, *Revolt in Athens* (1972); John O. Iatrides, ed., *Greece in the 1940s* (1981); Lawrence S. Wittner, *American Intervention in Greece, 1943–1949* (1982); Howard Jones, *"A New Kind of War": America's Global Strategy and the Truman Doctrine in Greece* (1989); David J. Alvarez, *Bureaucracy and Cold War Ideology* (1980) (on Turkey); Harry N. Howard, *Turkey, the Straits, and U.S. Policy* (1974); Melvyn P. Leffler, "Strategy, Diplomacy, and the Cold War: The United States, Turkey, and NATO, 1945–1952," *Journal of American History*, LXXI (March 1985), 807–825; Richard Barnet, *Intervention and Revolution* (1972); Richard Freeland, *The Truman Doctrine and the Origins of McCarthyism* (1971); and Jon V. Kofas, *Intervention and Underdevelopment: Greece During the Cold War* (1989).

Relations with various European nations and European issues can be studied in Josef Becker and Franz Knipping, *Power in Europe: Great Britain, France, Italy and Germany in a Postwar World, 1945–1950* (1986); A. W. DePorte, *De Gaulle's Foreign Policy, 1944–1946* (1968); Geir Lundestad, *America, Scandinavia, and the Cold War* (1980); James Edward Miller, *The United States and Italy, 1940–1950* (1986); John L. Harper, *The United States and the Reconstruction of Italy* (1986); Audrey K. Cronin, *Great Power Politics and the Struggle over Austria, 1945–1955* (1986); Donald Whiting and Edgar L. Erickson, *The American Occupation of Austria* (1985); John W. Young, *Britain, France, and the Unity of Europe, 1945–1951* (1984); Roberto G. Rabel, *Between East and West* (1986) (on Trieste); and Frank Costigliola, *The Cold Alliance* (1990) (on France).

For the Marshall Plan, European reconstruction, and economic issues, see Harry Price, *The Marshall Plan and Its Meaning* (1955); Richard Gardner, *Sterling-Dollar Diplomacy* (1969); Fred L. Block, *The Origins of International Economic Disorder* (1977); Alfred E. Eckes, Jr., *A Search for Solvency* (1975); Richard Mayne, *Recovery of Europe* (1973); George C. Herring, *Aid to Russia, 1941–1946* (1973); Thomas G. Paterson, *Soviet-American Confrontation* (1973); Robert A. Pollard, *Economic Security and the Origins of the Cold War* (1985); John Gimbel, *The Origins of the Marshall Plan* (1976); Fred L. Block, *The Origins of International Economic Disorder* (1977); Hadley Arkes, *Bureaucracy, the Marshall Plan, and the National Interest* (1972); Charles S. Maier, "The Politics of Productivity: Foundations of American International Economic Policy after World War II," *International Organization*, XXXI

(Autumn 1977), 607–633; Immanuel Wexler, *The Marshall Plan Revisited* (1983); Alan S. Milward, *The Reconstruction of Western Europe, 1945–51* (1984); Armand Clesse and Archie C. Epps, eds., *Present at the Creation: The Fortieth Anniversary of the Marshall Plan* (1990); and Michael J. Hogan, *The Marshall Plan* (1987).

Joseph Stalin is the subject of Isaac Deutscher, *Stalin* (1967); Adam Ulam, *Stalin* (1973); Ian Grey, *Stalin, Man of History* (1979); and Robert H. McNeal, *Stalin: Man and Ruler* (1988).

The origins of the North Atlantic Treaty Organization are explored in Lawrence Kaplan, *NATO and The United States* (1988) and *The United States and NATO: The Formative Years* (1984); Olav Riste, ed., *Western Security* (1985); and Timothy P. Ireland, *Creating the Entangling Alliance* (1981). Two articles that discuss postwar Soviet military capabilities and American assumptions about the Soviet threat are Matthew A. Evangelista, "Stalin's Postwar Army Reappraised," *International Security*, VII (Winter 1982/1983), 110–138, and Samuel F. Wells, Jr., "Sounding the Tocsin: NSC 68 and the Soviet Threat," *International Security*, IV (Fall 1979), 116–158.

General works on Asian-American relations include Akira Iriye, *The Cold War in Asia* (1974); Yōnosuke Nagai and Akira Iriye, eds., *The Origins of the Cold War in Asia* (1977); Russell Buhite, *Soviet-American Relations in Asia, 1945–1954* (1982); Edward Friedman and Mark Selden, eds., *America's Asia* (1971); Mark Selden, ed., *Remaking Asia* (1974); Mark S. Gallicchio, *The Cold War Begins in Asia* (1988); Lisle A. Rose, *Roots of Tragedy: The United States and the Struggle for Asia, 1945–1953* (1976); William W. Stueck, Jr., *The Road to Confrontation* (1981); Robert Blum, *Drawing the Line* (1982); and Warren I. Cohen, ed., *New Frontiers in American–East Asian Relations* (1983).

For relations with China, see Herbert Feis, *China Tangle* (1953); Tang Tsou, *America's Failure in China* (1963); John Paton Davies, Jr., *Dragon By the Tail* (1972); Ross Koen, *The China Lobby in American Politics* (1974); Russell Buhite, *Patrick J. Hurley and American Foreign Policy* (1973); Louis M. Purifoy, *Harry Truman's China Policy* (1979); Warren I. Cohen, *America's Response to China* (1989); Dorothy Borg and Waldo Heinrichs, eds., *Uncertain Years: Chinese-American Relations, 1947–1950* (1980); Harry Harding and Yuan Ming, eds., *Sino-American Relations, 1945–1955* (1989); Michael Schaller, *The U.S. Crusade in China* (1979) and *The United States and China in the Twentieth Century* (1989); Nancy B. Tucker, *Patterns in the Dust* (1983);

Gary May, *China Scapegoat: The Diplomatic Ordeal of John Carter Vincent* (1979); Ronald C. Keith, *The Diplomacy of Zhou Enlai* (1989); James Reardon-Anderson, *Yenan and the Great Powers* (1980); William W. Stueck, *The Wedemeyer Mission* (1984); Edward W. Martin, *Divided Counsel: The Anglo-American Response to Communist Victory in China* (1986); David Allan Mayers, *Cracking the Monolith: U.S. Policy Against the Sino-Soviet Alliance* (1986); Gordon H. Chang, *Friends and Enemies: The United States, China, and the Soviet Union* (1990); and David McLean, "American Nationalism, the China Myth, and the Truman Doctrine," *Diplomatic History*, X (Winter 1986), 25–42.

For the American occupation of Japan and Japanese-American relations, see William Neumann, *America Encounters Japan* (1963); William S. Borden, *The Pacific Alliance* (1984); Roger Buckley, *Occupation Diplomacy* (1982); Lawrence H. Redford, ed., *The Occupation of Japan* (1984); Michael Schaller, *The American Occupation of Japan* (1985) and *Douglas MacArthur: The Far Eastern General* (1989); Michael M. Yoshitsu, *Japan and the San Francisco Peace Settlement* (1983); D. Clayton James, *The Years of MacArthur*, vol. 3 (1985); Howard B. Schonberger, *Aftermath of War: Americans and the Remaking of Japan, 1945–1952* (1989); John W. Dower, *Empire and Aftermath* (1979); and Toshio Nishi, *Unconditional Democracy* (1982).

For United States policy toward Southeast Asia, see Russell H. Fifield, *Americans in Southeast Asia* (1973); Evelyn Colbert, *International Politics in Southeast Asia, 1941–1956* (1977); Gary R. Hess, *The United States' Emergence as a Southeast Asian Power* (1987); George R. Taylor, *The Philippines and the United States* (1964); Stephen R. Shalom, *The United States and the Philippines* (1981); and Robert J. McMahon, *Colonialism and Cold War: The United States and the Struggle for Indonesian Independence* (1981).

The historical literature on United States policy toward Indochina during the early Cold War is voluminous. See especially Andrew J. Rotter, *The Path to Vietnam* (1987); Lloyd C. Gardner, *Approaching Vietnam* (1988); George C. Herring, *America's Longest War* (1986); Gary R. Hess, *Vietnam and the United States* (1990); Gabriel Kolko, *Anatomy of a War* (1985); Ronald H. Spector, *Advice and Support: The Early Years of the U.S. Army in Vietnam* (1983); Stanley Karnow, *Vietnam: A History* (1983); Anthony Short, *The Origins of the Vietnam War* (1989); and George McT. Kahin, *Intervention* (1986).

United States–South Asian relations can be studied in Gary R. Hess, *America Encounters India, 1941–1947* (1970); William J. Barnds,

India, Pakistan, and the Great Powers (1972); M. S. Venkataramani, *The American Role in Pakistan* (1982); H. W. Brands, Jr., *India and the United States* (1990); Dennis Merrill, "Indo-American Relations, 1947–1950: A Missed Opportunity in Asia," *Diplomatic History*, XI (Summer 1987), 203–226; and Robert J. McMahon, "United States Cold War Strategy in South Asia: Making a Military Commitment to Pakistan, 1947–1954," *Journal of American History*, LXXV (December 1988), 812–840.

For developments in the Middle East, see Robert W. Stookey, *America and the Arab States* (1975); William R. Polk, *The United States and the Arab World* (1975); Nadav Safran, *Israel: Embattled Ally* (1978); Gail E. Meyer, *Egypt and the United States* (1980); Kenneth R. Bain, *The March to Zion* (1979); George Lenczowski, *American Presidents and the Middle East* (1989); Michael J. Cohen, *Palestine and the Great Powers, 1945–1948* (1979); Evan M. Wilson, *Decision on Palestine* (1979); John Snetsinger, *Truman, the Jewish Vote and the Creation of Israel* (1974); Leonard Dinnerstein, *America and the Survivors of the Holocaust* (1982); Michael Cohen, *Truman and Israel* (1990); W. Roger Louis, *The British Empire in the Middle East, 1945–1951* (1984); W. Roger Louis and Robert W. Stookey, eds., *The End of the Palestine Mandate* (1986); Barry Rubin, *Paved with Good Intentions: The American Experience and Iran* (1980); Mark H. Lytle, *The Origins of the Iranian-American Alliance, 1941–1953* (1987); James A. Bill, *The Eagle and the Lion: The Tragedy of American-Iranian Relations* (1988); Steven L. Speigel, *The Other Arab-Israeli Conflict* (1985); Michael B. Stoff, *Oil, War, and American Security* (1980); Aaron D. Miller, *Search for Security* (1980); and David S. Painter, *Oil and the American Century* (1986).

United States relations with Latin America during the Truman years can be followed in Samuel Baily, *The United States and the Development of South America, 1945–1975* (1976); John Child, *Unequal Alliance: The Inter-American Military System* (1980); Cole Blasier, *The Hovering Giant* (1976); Gordon Connell-Smith, *The United States and Latin America* (1975); Chester J. Pach, Jr., "The Containment of U.S. Military Aid to Latin America, 1944–1949," *Diplomatic History*, VI (Summer 1982), 225–243; Stephen G. Rabe, "The Elusive Conference: United States Economic Relations with Latin America, 1945–1952, *Diplomatic History*, II (Summer 1978), 279–294; Gerald K. Haines, *The Americanization of Brazil* (1990); David Green, "The Cold War Comes to Latin America," in Barton J. Bernstein, ed., *Politics and Policies of the Truman Administration* (1970); Richard H. Immerman, *The CIA in Guatemala* (1982); and Walter LaFeber, *Inevitable Revolutions* (1983).